METEOR
Gloster's First Jet Fighter

METEOR

Gloster's First Jet Fighter

Steven J. Bond

Edited and first published in 1985 by
Midland Counties Publications (Aerophile) Ltd,
24 The Hollow, Earl Shilton, Leicester
LE9 7NA, England.

ISBN 0 904597 55 5

Printed in the United Kingdom by
David Green Printers Ltd, Newman Street,
Kettering, Northants.

Bound by WBC Bookbinders Ltd,
Forge Industrial Estate, Maesteg, Mid-Glamorgan

Contents

Foreword

by

Air Commodore

D. B. FITZPATRICK

CB, OBE, AFC, MRAeS, FRMETS
FBIM, RAF, Ret'd.

I was delighted to be asked to contribute something towards the history of this famous and very versatile aircraft, which must surely compete with the famous Bristol Fighter F2B of World War I vintage for long service with the Royal Air Force.

I first flew an early mark of Meteor in February 1949 and continued my long association with it, in numerous roles, until I made my last flight in the Royal Air Force in a Mark 7 at Woomera in 1972.

I am sure this excellent book will revive many memories for a great number of ex-Meteor pilots and I wish it all success.

D.B. Fitzpatrick

Introduction and Acknowledgements

The Gloster Meteor served with the Royal Air Force for thirty-eight years, during which time it was used by virtually every fighter squadron in the service in one form or another, as well as by a great many second-line units, in a variety of tasks. It secured a place in the history books as the Allies' only operational jet aircraft of the Second World War and although outdated, it found further action in the skies over North Korea and later still in the Middle East.

Yet despite all this, the Meteor has almost become Britain's forgotten milestone in aviation; for although it was our first jet fighter, chronologically it is sandwiched between the seemingly more glamorous Spitfire and Hunter, both of which are extremely well documented and are familiar to the man in the street. This history is an attempt to redress the balance and show the Meteor for what it was - a great spur and export success for the British aircraft industry and a very fine and versatile aeroplane.

My own interest in the aircraft was sparked by the regular sight of them overflying my home in Buckinghamshire and later, by several visits to the sad Meteor graveyard at RNAS Brawdy in the early 'sixties. From that time, I slowly accumulated information until in 1980, I decided to try to bring it all together in this book which will be the first to examine the Meteor in detail in well over twenty years. My aims have been fairly straightforward; not only to present the facts surrounding the design, development and production of the aeroplane, but more especially to try and capture in text and photographs its character, and particularly to present a broad picture of the aircraft 'in service'.

Nevertheless, there still remains much more which could be said, especially concerning the use of the Meteor in some overseas countries, several of which are remarkably reluctant to answer enquiries about it even today. However, I am sure nothing of great significance has been overlooked, and this must be due in great measure to the enormous help I have had from organisations and individuals from many countries, in particular the following: *Aeroplane Monthly*, Air-Britain, *Aviation News*, Flt Lt F. N. Bate RAFVR, Roy Bonser, Michael J. F. Bowyer, Ron Clarke, G. J. F. Cruikshank, Ray Deacon, Flt Lt W. J. Dobson RAF (Ret'd), Air Commodore D. B. Fitzpatrick CB, OBE, AFC, FBIM, MRAeS, RAF (Ret'd), Information and Public Relations Service of French Defence Ministry, Pete Gosden of A&AEE Boscombe Down, Reg Griffiths, D. Hornsby, Imperial War Museum, Derek N. James, Len Lovell of the Fleet Air Arm Museum, Roy Montgomery, Major J. M. Monteiro of the Brazil Aerospace Museum, Sqn Ldr Philip Murton RAF (Ret'd), H. Orme, Arthur Pearcy Jr, Flt Sgt L. M. Perry of the RAAF Museum, Royal Air Force Museum, Rolls-Royce (in particular R. A. Forrester), David Sargent, E. T. N. Short of RAE Llanbedr, Wg Cdr D. J. Simmons RAF, Col Y. Simon of the Israeli Embassy in London, Malcolm Spaven, R. F. Symes, Flt Lt Reg Thackeray RAFVR (Ret'd), Den C. Todd, Sqn Ldr D. A. Wood RAF and especially Michael A. Fopp who has been of enormous help with the final text and tracking down the last few elusive illustrations.

The photographs have been carefully chosen from many thousands which have kindly been made available by contributors, to show the most varied and interesting, sometimes rare colours and markings. This may lead to some of the illustrations included being less than elegant pieces of photographic art - but I am sure that they will be well appreciated by all those who know and love the 'Meatbox'. I have done my best to trace the origins of all the photographs and to acknowledge their source in the captions but in case some have still eluded me, or become confused over the years of collecting, I apologise for it now.

Finally, the drawings which enhance the finished book have been carefully prepared by Keith Woodcock, whose work is a model of its kind.

Holyhead, Gwynedd
January 1985

Steve Bond

1

Origins and Testing

Advances in research, both in Great Britain and elsewhere, notably Germany, and the urgencies of conflict, made it inevitable that a jet fighter would appear fairly early in the Second World War. Frank Whittle had at last got the Air Ministry to sit up and take notice of his jet engine, and in 1938 they began looking around for an airframe manufacturer with the necessary spare design and production capacity to tackle the task of getting Whittle's brain-child into the air. Fortuitously for the Gloster Aircraft Company, it was around this time that Frank Whittle was invited to their factory at Hucclecote, near Gloucester, to see George Carter, who at that time was the company's chief designer.

It transpired that design capacity was immediately available at Hucclecote and coupled with the undoubted good relationship that grew up between Carter and Whittle, this strongly influenced the Air Ministry decision in 1939 to award a contract for Britain's first jet aeroplane to the company. Thus was born the Gloster E.28/39, which was also known as the Pioneer.

The Pioneer was basically a very simple airframe, made as small and light as possible to enable the low-powered early engine to get into the air. This was successfully achieved for the first time on 15 May 1941 from RAF Cranwell in Lincolnshire, which had been chosen for its remoteness. Successful as this aeroplane was in proving that Whittle's theories really did work in practice, the Air Ministry decided that an operational jet fighter should be a logical and rapid follow-on to this early first step. George Carter too had been following this line of thought and it very soon became apparent to him that the limited power available would not permit a single engined aircraft to carry a worthwhile warload. It thus became inevitable that the operational aeroplane should be twin engined, especially so when the Ministry decreed that they expected the aircraft to carry a heavy armament of no less than six 20mm cannon (although this was subsequently reduced to four). It was in August 1940 that Glosters submitted their initial design, and in November specification F.9/40 was written around it. Thus what was to become the Meteor was born, with an order for twelve prototypes, with serials DG202/G to DG213/G, although this was later reduced to six and then back up to eight. The /G indicated aircraft of a secret nature, which were to be guarded at all times.

The choice of the name Meteor was a very lengthy process, during which the Ministry suggested a large number of others, including Thunderbolt, Cyclone, Wildfire, Scourge, Terrific, Terrifier and Tempest, and after a rethink, a further long list which included Avenger, for which Glosters showed a marked preference. The company also responded with a list of their own, which included Ace, Annihilator and Reaper, which they also liked and would later revive for their private venture ground attack version. It was not until February 1942 that the Ministry of Aircraft Production chose, and insisted on, Meteor, after having to change from Thunderbolt, a name which had by then been taken by the Republic P-47.

Shortly after this, with construction of the first aircraft well under way, the first Rover W.2B engines arrived at Glosters, but these were not to flight standard, the problem being the continual break-up of the turbine blades, which was only fully resolved when Rolls-Royce took over their manufacture. As the months went by with no sign of flight standards becoming available, the Ministry came very close to abandoning the entire project. Fortunately however, the first flight-standard Halford H.1 engines were delivered in November 1942 and the project was saved at the eleventh hour.

There were in fact, several different engine options open to the Gloster team. The original Whittle engine was now being produced by the company he set up, Power Jets Ltd, although it was in the process of being sub-contracted out to Rover Motors for large scale production under the designation W.2B or W.2/500. A basically similar engine was also being produced by Rolls-Royce as the W.2B/23, which was later named the Welland and went on to be developed into the famous Derwent, which was to power the vast majority of all the Meteors built. The other competitor for space in the F.9/40s, was the de Havilland/Halford H.1 designed by Major Frank Halford. Fitted to two of the Meteor prototypes, this went on to become the Goblin engine, which was ordered in large numbers for the de Havilland Vampire fighter being developed at Hatfield on a slightly later time-scale than the Meteor.

Despite the differences in manufacturer, all these engines were basically very similar and were all of the centrifugal compressor type, in which the air drawn into the engine is accelerated and compressed by a one-piece impeller. Although this results in a very simple and strong engine, it has the disadvantage of a large frontal area, necessitating large nacelles on the aeroplane, and a consequent high degree of drag. The Metropolitan Vickers company on the other hand, had decided to pursue the alternative type of engine, and their F.2 was fitted with an axial-flow compressor, wherein a series of compressor blade rings progressively speed-up the air through the engine, whilst keeping the flow in a straight line. This considerably reduces the frontal area of the engine, and thus the performance penalties incurred by the other large nacelles. The F.2 was fitted to one of the prototypes (DG204/G) but was not a success and since the aircraft was destroyed in a crash after only just over three hours flying time, no further effort was devoted to fitting these engines to the Meteor.

In the meantime, the flight standard Halford H.1s having been installed in DG206/G in January 1943, ground runs began, and very quickly highlighted in a most dramatic fashion a major problem with jet engines which remains to this day. On 27 January Michael Daunt, the Gloster chief test pilot, was standing in front of the port engine during a run, and as it was opened up to high rpm he was sucked off his feet head first into the nacelle. Despite the efforts of four of the ground-crew, he could not be pulled free until the engine was stopped, but he was fortunately uninjured, although considerably shaken and bruised. After this, intake guards were fitted for ground runs, and these became known to the Gloster men as 'anti-Daunts'! Nevertheless, incidents still occurred, and in fact one of the Metropolitan Vickers engines on DG204/G was later destroyed when an overcoat was sucked into it; a graphic demonstration of the vulnerability of the axial-flow compressor to foreign object damage, when compared to the more durable centrifugal compressors.

With the engines proved on the ground, DG206/G was taken by road to Cranwell in preparation for its first flight. The original idea had been to fly from the grass airfield at Newmarket Heath, near Cambridge, and during the previous summer, DG202/G had been taken there for taxying trials, but it was thought that the undulating surface would not be suitable for flight trials. On 5 March 1943, DG206/G was flown for the first time, with Michael Daunt at the controls. The flight lasted for only some twelve minutes and a problem which was to plague the Meteor for some time became immediately apparent, the aircraft began to yaw violently from side to side as soon as speed passed 230mph. This resulted in the flight being rapidly curtailed, although Michael Daunt did have the opportunity on his final approach, by opening up the throttles, to prove that the directional instability was due to airspeed and not jet effect. The rather long landing run also showed a need for an improvement in the brakes,

Above: **Prototype DG202 restored to its former glory, on public view at RAF Gaydon 'Battle of Britain' Day in the mid-'sixties.** *(Air-Britain)*

Opposite: **DG202, the very first Gloster F.9/40, photographed guarding the main gate at RAF Yatesbury in Wiltshire, before its historical importance was realised. Stripped of its original green and brown camouflage with yellow undersides, it had been allocated the ground instructional airframe serial number 5758M.** *(MAP)*

Below: **Still on the gate at RAF Yatesbury in August 1958, the prototype marking has been added and the maintenance serial had been replaced by 'DG202'. At the time of going to press this aircraft is in the safe keeping of the Cosford Aerospace Museum.** *(C.J.Salter)*

but otherwise, the aeroplane was felt to be generally satisfactory.

The Royal Aircraft Establishment suggested fitting trimmer cords to the trailing edge of the rudder in an attempt to cure the yawing problem, but before this could be tested, the arrival at Cranwell of a group of Turkish Air Force officers necessitated a halt to test flying. It was decided to try using Newmarket Heath again, until a more suitable site could be found, and the aeroplane was taken there by road, re-assembled, and flown again on 17 April, when it was found that the trimmer cord appeared to have the desired effect on the directional stability.

Two more flights were made from Newmarket, but the bad surface on the airfield, combined with the great distance from the factory in Gloucestershire, were causing many problems

for the test team, so a plan was put into effect to upgrade the company's airfield at Moreton Valence for Meteor operations by laying down a hard runway. As an interim measure, the airfield at Barford St John near Banbury, in Oxfordshire, was brought into use. and for several months from May 1943, all the test-flying was transferred there, the first aircraft to arrive being DG202/G, which came by road from the Bentham factory on 22 May, although it did not fly until 24 July. It was followed on 23 May by DG205/G again by road, then by DG206/G on 28 May, on its first cross country flight. Finally, during June, DG204/G joined the fleet, accompanied by Pioneer W4041/G.

At Barford St John, which was again a Royal Air Force station, Glosters were given the use of their own hangar on the far side of the airfield, which was at that time occupied by the Wellingtons of 16 Operational Training Unit. The Gloster pilots would often fly over from the company aerodrome at Hucclecote by Gladiator each day - quite a contrast - and when they were ready to fly, all Wellington flying would be brought to a halt by the firing of a red Verey cartridge, and all the public roads in the vicinity were closed off by the RAF police. Flights usually took place when there was cloud cover, in order to conceal the activities from prying eyes on the ground and were mostly of only about twenty minutes duration, the Verey light procedure again being used as the aircraft returned to land.

The other occupants of the airfield naturally heard nothing officially about the aircraft, which were referred to by them as 'The Squirt' or 'The Hoover' and many seem to have been convinced that the engine nacelles simply housed some form of high speed ducted propeller. By October 1943, the new runway at Moreton Valence was ready and Barford St John returned to normal.

The apparently random order in which the F.9/40 prototypes flew is explained by the erratic availability of the various power-plants. Since the aircraft were all built to accept only one make of engine, it was not possible to interchange them. The original proposal by Glosters was to produce a mix of production aircraft, powered either by the W.2 or the H.1 and the latter aircraft eventually came to be designated the F.2, with DG207/G being the fully representative prototype and ultimately, the only example, since the Ministry had decided to press ahead with the use of this engine in the Vampire and obviously did not wish to overstretch the resources of the H.1 builders. By this time, flight testing was proceeding fairly smoothly, although the yawing problem was not yet completely under control and both Glosters and the Ministry felt confident enough in the aircraft's potential to go ahead with production of the Meteor F.1 operational aircraft, powered by the W.2B/23C Welland engine from Rolls-Royce. However, even at this early stage engine development was gaining momentum rapidly and it had already been decided to produce only twenty F.1s for use as operational trainers, and that the initial full service model would be the F.3, fitted with the new Derwent engine.

Below:
DG207/G was the one and only Meteor F.2 It was the sixth F.9/40 and was completed to F.2 standard by being fitted with Halford H.1 engines. The photograph was taken in 1948, when the aircraft was on the strength of the de Havilland Engine Company at Hatfield. *(MAP)*

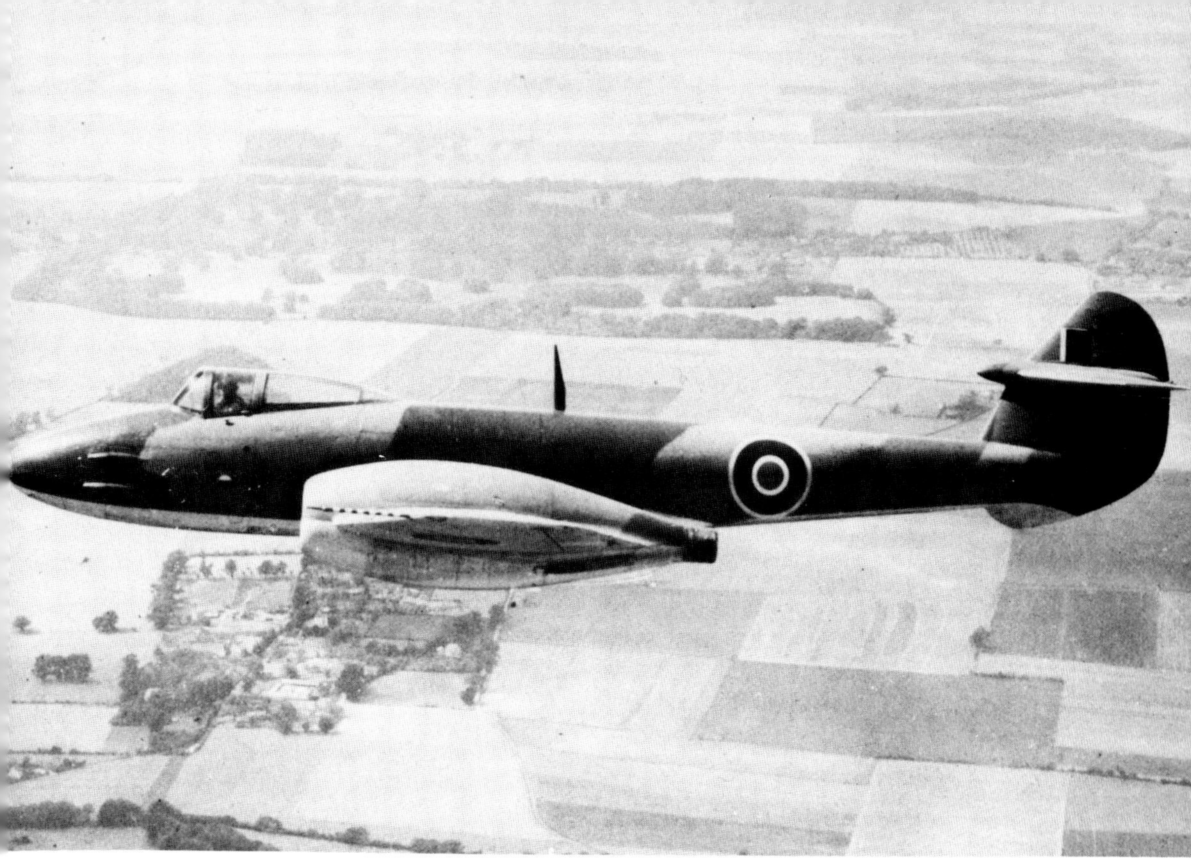

Above: **EE214/G - the fifth production Meteor F.1 had a fixed steel ventral tank containing 100 gallons of fuel installed. After use by RAE Farnborough and CRD Defford it passed to 11 School of Technical Training as 5790M.** *(Imperial War Museum CL2955)*

The team of Gloster test-pilots had done a magnificent job coping with what was virtually an unknown quantity, and between them they discovered and came to terms with such new problems as compressor surge and stall, flame-out of the engine, etc, and it is a great tribute to them that during the company's F.9/40 testing, not a single aircraft was lost. Michael Daunt was joined early in the programme by John Grierson, John Crosby-Warren who was later killed in a Meteor, and Eric Greenwood; among the many trials they carried out were a modified fin and rudder on DG208/G, which was yet another way of tackling the yawing difficulty, which in the event would not be successfully countered until the introduction of the 'long fuselage' F.4.

Of the other prototypes, DG209/G went to Rolls-Royce for engine development, and the original aircraft, DG202/G was used for deck-handling trials on HMS *Pretoria Castle,* although no flights were made from or to it. This aircraft was later retired for use as a ground instructional airframe, and by good fortune survives to this day in the Cosford Aerospace Museum.

At the height of this work, the first F.1 EE210/G, made a successful maiden flight from Moreton Valence on 12 January 1944 in the hands of Michael Daunt. In the next few months, with the ever increasing pace of production, several more aircraft flew including EE212/G, which was the aerodynamic prototype for the improved F.3 and service trials were commenced with delivery of examples to the Royal Aircraft Establishment at Farnborough and the Aeroplane and Armament Experimental Establishment at Boscombe Down.

Boscombe Down were none too highly impressed with these early Meteors; they praised the ease of ground handling with the still fairly novel tricycle undercarriage, but seem to have liked little else. The view from the heavily framed cockpit was criticised, and this was later corrected in the F.4, and many of the cockpit controls were found to be poorly placed. In the air, the old handling problems were again highlighted, but the Boscombe pilots found the slow response to throttle movements from the engine most disconcerting and also considered the performance in terms of speed and altitude to be only marginally superior to most of the existing piston-engined fighters, and inferior to several.

Above: **A 616 Squadron F.3 taken in early 1945. At that time, the aircraft were painted white overall to provide effective camouflage on the ground during that very severe winter.**
(via M.Fopp)

At best, they considered the aircraft to be suitable only as an operational trainer, but the Ministry was keen to get the type into service at the earliest possible date, and pressed ahead with plans to get the type to the RAF squadrons. The handling reports are reproduced in 'Most Secret Place' (Janes 1983).

The F.1 differed very little from the F.9/40s apart from having the four cannon armament installed; it also featured a clear-view rear canopy, which had been tried on several of the prototypes, and which went part of the way towards meeting the Boscombe Down criticism in that direction. Thus it was that, although the first true F.3 EE230 flew in September 1944, the RAF were also eager to try out the new type at the earliest opportunity and the F.1 was passed as fit for service use.

In May 1944, 616 Squadron, Auxiliary Air Force, moved from Fairwood Common in South Wales, to Culmhead in Somerset. Equipped with Spitfire VIIs, its main task was to fly armed reconnaissance missions over occupied France in preparation for the imminent Normandy invasion, but rumours were rife in the squadron that it was shortly to re-equip, the most popular one quoting the Spitfire XIV as the new type. However, the squadron commander, Sqn Ldr Andrew McDowall, together with five other pilots, were doubtless surprised to be sent to the RAE at Farnborough to convert to the Meteor, using EE213 and EE214 and shortly after this, the squadron's first aircraft, EE219, was delivered to Culmhead on 12 July. The unit almost immediately moved to Manston in Kent, and for another month tried to fly operations with the Spitfires and convert to Meteors at the same time - a ludicrous situation which was soon brought to a halt with the departure of the last piston machines at the end of August.

The squadron pilots apparently found the task of converting to the jets surprisingly easy, the main problem being associated with getting used to the tricycle undercarriage, and at the end of their first week at Manston, 616 had converted thirty-two of their pilots. Ultimately, the squadron would receive fourteen of the twenty F.1s built, and on 27 July 1944, they flew their first patrol with the type; a so-called 'diver' patrol looking for V1 flying bombs. These weapons had long been considered as potential 'easy meat' for the Meteor, since its respectable turn of speed outweighed the V1's previous advantage over the Spitfires previously predominant in the campaign to shoot them down.

Flying in pairs, the Meteor's first combat success came on 4 August, when Flying Officer Dean spotted a target some way ahead of and below him. Going into a shallow dive, and increasing his speed to 450mph, Dean saw that his target was indeed a V1, but after a brief burst with his guns, they jammed - a frequent occurence with the early Meteors - so he eased alongside the flying-bomb and pulling hard over, tipped it up with his wingtip, causing it to spin out of control and crash in woodland near Tonbridge. In fact, he had only just succeeded in beating another 616 pilot for the distinction of the first 'kill', for Flying Officer Roger had also downed a V1 at about the same time, though this time using his guns.

At this stage of the war, both the RAF and USAAF were becoming increasingly concerned over the appearance of the Me 163 rocket and Me 262 jet fighters over Germany, which, with their considerable speed advantage over existing allied fighters, were beginning to cause considerable problems amongst the heavy bomber formations. Therefore, in October 1944, 616 Squadron moved temporarily to Debden in Essex then the home of the 8th Air Force's 4th Fighter Group, for trials with the USAAF's heavy bombers. The intention was to give the B-17 and B-24 gunners experience against high-speed jets. It was found that, even when the bombers were escorted by P-47s and P-51s, arguably the best fighters the Americans had, if the Meteors adopted hit-and-run tactics against the bombers, they could expect to conflict considerable damage on them and escape long before the escorts had time to retaliate. The only defence turned out to be to station the escorts 5,000 ft above the bombers, and then half-roll and dive at high speed when the jets attacked.

By December, the trials were completed, and 616 returned to Manston and the arrival of the first 'definitive' F.3s, which Glosters felt would prove to be a totally combat-worthy aeroplane. Even so, there were still delays with the Derwent engines, and the first fifteen aircraft produced were still fitted with Wellands. Ultimately, 210 F.3s were built.

Shortly after they started to arrive at Manston, 616 moved again, this time to Colerne in Wiltshire, which had been chosen as the RAF's first permanent Meteor station. Nevertheless, it was felt that the time was ripe for the Meteor to prove itself in jet versus jet combat, and so a flight of F.3s was sent across the Channel to airfield B.58 at Melsbroek in Belgium, with the deliberate intention of drawing the Me 262 into combat and thus gaining the opportunity to compare the two types. The aircraft were attached to the 2nd Tactical Air Force and were painted white overall for better camouflage on the ground in that very severe winter.

The aircrew were forbidden to fly over enemy territory in order to prevent a Meteor falling into German hands, but at the end of March 1945, the whole squadron came together again at B.77 Gilze-Rijen in Holland, the Colerne detachment having staged out via a short deployment to the 8th Air Force station at Andrewsfield in Essex. Re-united, caution was thrown to the wind in a last-ditch attempt to find the Me 262s before the war ended, and the squadron went on the offensive, flying armed reconnaissance missions, and made its first attack on 17 April on mechanised transport near Ijmuiden.

Although these operations continued until the end of the war, no German jets were ever encountered, which must have been a bitter disappointment to 616's crews, although it is arguable that the Meteor may have been at a disadvantage against the faster German aircraft, whose main fault was desperately unreliable engines. At the war's end, the squadron made several more moves, from airfield B.109 to Luneberg and finally to Lubeck in May, where it remained as part of the Allied occupying forces until surprisingly disbanded on 29 August 1945. This was no means the end of 616 Squadron's association with the Meteor, whose service career was about to mushroom dramatically.

Below:
A fine in-flight study of the fifth F.1, EE214/G. This machine spent all its time on trials work, before being scrapped in 1949. *(via M. Fopp)*

Gloster Meteor IV
Rolls Royce
Derwent
Engines

2

Development and Improvement

With the Meteor F.3 well established in service, Glosters' thoughts turned towards improving the Meteor's rather marginal high speed and high altitude performance. At the RAE at Farnborough, tests had revealed that the airflow around the engine nacelles tended to break down at around Mach 0·75, resulting in greatly increased drag and severe buffeting. It was found that this situation could be greatly improved by increasing the length of the nacelles both ahead of and behind the wing and consequently, the second production F.3, EE211, was fitted with long chord nacelles and commenced trials in March 1945.

The new shape was highly successful and improved maximum speed by up to 60 mph and Flt Lt Philip Stanbury, who carried out the test programme, reported that the aircraft now handled well up to Mach 0·84. Glosters were naturally delighted with these results and introduced the modification on the final fifteen production F.3s. But already greater things were on the horizon; Glosters had long expressed a desire to install Rolls-Royce's more powerful Nene engine into their fighter, but it was considerably larger than the Derwent, necessitating a major re-design effort. Rolls-Royce were therefore encouraged to produce an up-rated Derwent, and obliged with the 3,000 lb thrust Derwent 5, which ran succesfully for the first time in the late summer of 1945 and was test flown in F.3 EE360 by Eric Greenwood, who reported a dramatic increase in the aircraft's performance.

Opposite page, top: **Meteor F.4 EE454 of the RAF's High Speed Flight, named 'Britannia' and flown by Group Captain H.J.Wilson set a world air speed record of 606 mph at Herne Bay on the 7 November 1945.** *(IWM CH16623)*

Opposite page, bottom: **Meteor F.4 EE455 also flew the record attempt over the Herne Bay course achieving 603 mph on 7 November 1945.** *(Royal Air Force Museum, P100288)*

The service version of this re-engined aeroplane also incorporated a much strengthened airframe to cope with the extra power and performance and in addition featured cabin pressurization for the first time: it was known as the F.4. It appeared at about the same time that Glosters became keen to make an attempt on the world air speed record and two aircraft, EE454 and EE455, both built as F.3s, were brought up to F.4 standard, had their armament removed and were given a special high speed paint finish. They were issued to the re-formed RAF High Speed Flight based at Tangmere in Sussex, and on 7 November 1945, Grp Capt H J Wilson, flying EE454, which was named *Britannia,* established a new record of 606 mph along a course at Herne Bay in Kent. On the same day, Eric Greenwood had a go in the all yellow EE455, but could only manage 603 mph.

However, word reached the Gloster team that the Americans were preparing a Lockheed P-80 to snatch the record back, so it was decided to try to push the speed still higher. Thus, two further F.4s were prepared, EE549 and EE550, and on 7 September 1946, Grp Capt Donaldson took the first aircraft over the south coast course at a new record speed of 616 mph, a most appropriate figure, 616 having been the first Meteor squadron. Despite this success, all was not quite right with the service F.4, however, and in the autumn of 1946, after some 100 aircraft had been produced, it became evident that the aircraft was not structurally strong enough to cope with the stresses imposed by the higher performance. What was needed was a major redesign, but this would have meant delaying further deliveries to the RAF for some time and was rejected as being unacceptable. The Gloster team came up with the idea of clipping 2 ft 10 ins off each wing tip, which partially solved the problem, since most of the increased stress was being taken by the wing structure. It also had the effect of improving the aircraft's rate of roll, although at the expense of a higher landing speed and reduced rate of climb and ceiling.

With orders for the F.4 totalling almost 500,

it could be seen that Gloster's production facilities were almost at full stretch and consequently, Armstrong Whitworth Aircraft, who were already building Meteor components, started to produce complete aircraft at their Baginton factory near Coventry in 1946, eventually completing a total of forty-four F.4s. They then moved on to building many other marks and finally took over responsibility entirely for the Meteor night-fighters.

A further modification introduced on the F.4 (from RA382 onwards), was a 30 inch fuselage stretch. As a result of the re-design going on to produce a two-seat Meteor, it was felt that the longer fuselage necessary, might improve the old problem of poor directional stability, which had manifested itself on the very first flight of the F.9/40. The idea proved successful and was subsequently employed on all further single-seat Meteors.

Many F.4s were used for experimental purposes, especially by Rolls-Royce, and Glosters had their own demonstration aircraft, G-AIDC, which was produced in an attempt to encourage overseas sales and which left Moreton Valence in April 1947 for a European tour. All went well until May, when during a flight by a Belgian pilot at Melsbroek, one of the mainwheels became partially extended at over 500 mph and as a result, the weakened oleo collapsed on landing, bringing the tour to an abrupt end, although the pilot was uninjured, and the aircraft was later rebuilt in a different guise. Nevertheless, compensation for Glosters came with the widespread adoption of the F.4 by European air forces.

1947 had also seen a further resurgence of record attempts by Glosters, when the world record machine, EE549, took the London to Paris honours on 16 January, by covering the 208 miles in twenty minutes eleven seconds, flown by Sqn Ldr Waterton. Then, on 6 February 1948, another F.4 VT103, took the 100 km closed-circuit record at a speed of 542.9 mph, flying from Moreton Valence then to Evesham, Defford, a point on the Gloucester to Ross-on-Wye railway line and back to Moreton Valence.

Other versions of the F.4 which were put forward by the company but which never progressed beyond the design stage, included the Project 203, a high altitude version with extended wings put forward in January 1946, and the P.209 of June the same year, which would have been fitted with the Rolls-Royce AJ.65 axial-flow turbojet.

Numerically, the next version to appear was the FR.5 fighter-reconnaissance variant. Gloster had already tried a camera nose on F.3 EE338, but this was not entirely successful, because of a tendency for the cameras to ice up at altitude. The FR.5 was fitted with vertical cameras in the rear fuselage and oblique cameras in the nose, but otherwise was identical to the F.4. Regrettably, the sole example built, VT347, was written-off on its first flight at Moreton Valence on 15 June 1949, killing the pilot, Rodney Dryland, and the FR.5 was abandoned in favour of the much improved FR.9.

The F.6 was another still-born version version which in fact closely resembled the later F.8 and was abandoned in favour of it, although it had often been confused in the past with the P.262 of the same period, which was a Meteor development featuring an almost delta shaped wing, but which again was not proceeded with.

By far the most important model to be brought into production at this time, and one which was ultimately destined to outlive all the others in British military service, was the tandem two-seat T.7. Although in 1947 there was no official requirement for a trainer version of the Meteor, Glosters were quick to realise that the old practice of putting only experienced fighter pilots into the Meteor would have to come to a close as more and more squadrons re-equipped and this, coupled with a sudden spate of export orders for the F.4, provided the spur that was needed for R A Walker and his team to embark on a two-seater as a private venture. The urgency of the situation as far as Glosters were concerned, was amply emphasised by the plight of the Argentine Air Force pilots who had come to England for conversion onto the F.4. The only

Top: **EE338 was a Meteor F.3 modified to FR.3 standard by the addition of a camera nose, and issued for trials to the PRDU at Benson. This sole example was written off in a flying accident on 10 October 1946.** *(Royal Air Force Museum, P5562)*

Middle: **An historic aeroplane. Meteor F.4 EE549, used so successfully for record-breaking with the High Speed Flight, later passed to the Fighter Command Communications Squadron at Bovingdon, where it was coded JMR for the use of AVM J.M.Robb. It is seen here at Gloster's airfield at Moreton Valence, with the personal code being removed before the aircraft was sent to the CFE. It now resides at the St Athan museum.** *(MAP)*

Bottom: **The carmine-coloured private-venture Meteor two-seater G-AKPK attracted great interest from the RAF, leading to them buying huge numbers of T.7s. G-AKPK later went to the Royal Netherlands Air Force and survives today in their museum at Soesterberg.** *(MAP)*

way they could be converted to type, was by removing the canopies from the single-seaters, which the Argentines then taxied round the aerodrome getting used to the controls, while Gloster test pilots sat astride the fuselage just behind the cockpit, yelling instructions at them before sending them aloft on their first solos!

In order to produce the prototype T.7, the experimental department took the stored remains of the ill-fated F.4 G-AIDC and built a new front fuselage onto it. Bearing the new registration G-AKPK, the aircraft first flew on 19 March 1948, piloted by Bill Waterton. The Air Ministry was suitably impressed with its performance and issued specification T.1/47 to cover its purchase for the RAF. The original aircraft was at one time expected to go to Rolls-Royce, but was eventually sold to the Royal Netherlands Air Force, although not before it had helped in establishing a London to Paris city centre to city centre speed record of forty-eight and three quarter minutes in September 1948.

The T.7 had all armament deleted and despite provision for both ventral and drop-tanks, had a higher rate of climb than the F.4. At first, it was fitted with the Derwent 5, but later production aircraft had the higher-powered Derwent 8, which necessitated the fitting of larger diameter air intakes. In all, 640 aircraft were produced for the RAF and Royal Navy, with many more going to overseas customers and four were still flying in the UK in the autumn of 1984. In addition, some F.4s were converted to T.7 standard and many of the type were used for experimental purposes, especially by Martin-Baker at Chalgrove in Oxfordshire, for the testing of ejection seats.

The next model was destined to be the one produced in greater numbers by far than any other. Well over 1,000 F.8s were built by Glosters and Armstrong Whitworth, with further production taking place in Holland and Belgium under license. The basis of the design was the realisation in 1947, that the F.4, although much improved on the original F.9/40, was already beginning to be seriously outclassed by more modern aircraft. In addition, the stability problem, although much improved, was still there and control from the F.4's vertical tail was very difficult. The answers came when Farnborough was asked to test a newly designed fin and rudder which Glosters proposed for their experimental E.1/44 single engined research aircraft. Tests in the RAE wind tunnel soon proved that the more square-cut and greatly enlarged tail would provide the answer to the Meteor's problems and on 12 October 1948, Jan Zurakowski took a modified F.4, VT150, aloft for its first flight as the prototype F.8.

Further refinements included the provision for the first time in an operational RAF aeroplane of an ejection seat and an improved canopy which greatly increased the pilot's field of vision to the sides and rear, and handling tests at the A & AEE at Boscombe Down were immediately highly favourable. Thus, the first 100 F.8s, which had already been ordered with F.4 type tail units, were all built with the new one and all standardised on the improved Derwent 8 engine. The F.8 was to be the RAF's standard day fighter for several years until the advent of the North American Sabre and the Hawker Hunter in the early fifties and although it was never used in anger in Europe, the coming of the Korean war brought about what was arguably the Meteor's finest hour, in the hands of the Royal Australian Air Force. Production of this model ended in 1954.

The Australians found the F.8 to be a superb ground-attack aircraft, echoing a private venture development of the model by Glosters in 1950. The GAF (Ground Attack Flighter) or Reaper, G-AMCJ later G-7-1, was fitted with strengthened wings of increased span to accommodate hard-points for rockets and bombs and was flown for the first time by Jim Cooksey on 4 September, later appearing at the SBAC show at Farnborough both that month and in the following year. However, with the ground-attack market being cornered by the American Republic F-84 Thunderjet, no orders were forthcoming and the only aircraft was converted to T.7 standard in 1954 as G-ANSO. However, experience gained with the GAF lead directly to the Meteor purchase by the Israeli Air Force, who specified this capability.

Top: **In 1950, Gloster produced their Ground Attack Fighter, a version of the F.8 also referred to as the 'Reaper'. Sole example, G-AMCJ, is shown here at the 1950 SBAC display at Farnborough with a representative selection of underwing stores and gunpacks.** *(via M.Fopp)*

Middle: **The 'Reaper' featured strengthened wings for extra hard points, and tip tanks, as clearly seen here on the sole prototype, now serialled G-7-1 at Farnborough.** *(via M.Fopp)*

Bottom: **The former Ground Attack Fighter, now modified to two-seat configuration, and re-registered G-ANSO, at Farnborough during September 1954. Gloster eventually sold this aircraft to Swedair in 1959 as SE-DCC, following conversion to standard T.7 format. Today this aircraft resides in a museum at Ugglarp.** *(Military Aircraft Photographs)*

G-AMCJ
ROYCE 'DERWENT ENGINES
G-7-1
GLOSTER
G-ANSO

A more successful variant of the F.8 was the FR.9, of which 126 were built, all by Glosters. The model was produced in response to a request by the RAF for a replacement for its obsolete Spitfire and Mosquito reconnaissance aircraft and the prototype was flown by Jan Zurakowski on 23 March 1950. The airframe was identical to the F.8 apart from the extreme nose, which featured an updated version of the camera equipment fitted to the ill-fated FR.5, and retained the full four cannon armament. The type was used almost exclusively overseas, in Germany and the Middle East and ex-RAF aircraft refurbished and sold to Ecuador were destined to be amongst the last Meteors of any mark in front-line service anywhere in the world.

Developed in parallel with the FR.9 was the PR.10, intended for high-altitude unarmed reconnaissance. Still retaining the basic F.8 fuselage, it reverted to the long-span wings and smaller tail unit of the early F.4s. Also flying for the first time in March 1950, only fifty-nine of the model were built before production ceased in 1952 and served exclusively with the RAF, in Germany, the Middle East and finally in the Far East.

The most radical re-design ever attempted of the Meteor, was that which produced the two-seat night fighter variants, produced in response to an Air Ministry requirement in 1947 for an interim type to replace the Mosquitos which then formed the backbone of the force. Glosters' original proposal was the P.300, which featured re-heated Derwent 5s and a modified wing with slight sweep-back on the outboard sections. This was not proceeded with and by 1949, the Gloster team was so heavily involved with work on the F.8 and the Javelin night and day all-weather fighter, that it was decided to hand over total responsibility for the Meteor night-fighter to Armstrong-Whitworth at Coventry, who finalised drawings and specification for the first model, the NF.11 and flew a modified T.7 VW413, as the aerodynamic prototype in October 1949. The first NF.11 built from scratch, WA546, was flown from Baginton on 31 May 1950 by Eric Franklin, and the first production aircraft, WD585 followed on 13 November.

The NF.11 had the centre-section and rear fuselage of the F.8, to which was added a T.7 style cockpit, PR.10 wings and a new elongated nose housing Mk.10 AI radar; the Derwent 8 was retained, although uprated to 3,700 lbs thrust. In all, 341 aircraft were built, with Armstrong-Whitworth producing 32 aircraft per month at its peak, and a great many were used for experimental purposes as well as becoming the RAF's standard night-fighter of the day, albeit supplemented by the de Havilland Venom NF.2 and NF.3. The NF.11 also proved popular in Europe, going to the air forces of Belgium, Denmark and France: the latter country still flying several of the model in 1984 on trials and chase duties. In Britain, many aircraft were converted to target-towing configuration as the T.T.20 for service with both the RAF and Royal Navy and a few survived in use until the early seventies. For this purpose, all the armament was removed, a wind-driven winch fitted to the upper surface of the starboard inner wing for operation by the rear seat occupent and a special target housing provided in the rear fuselage.

The next variant, in the numbering sequence, although not in fact flying until 21 April 1953, was the NF.12, which had an even longer nose to incorporate an American APS.21 radar, the extra length being balanced by a slight increase in fin area to maintain stability. This model also had the more powerful Derwent 9, which again meant further strengthening of the wings; 100 examples were built.

The NF.13, which came before the NF.12, was simply an NF.11 with modifications to suit it for use in a tropical environment, and flew for the first time (WM308) on 21 December 1952. The changes included cold-air intakes on the fuselage, new equipment in the form of DME (distance measuring equipment), a radio compass and on some aircraft, increased flap area to compensate for the extra 450 lbs weight over the NF.11. Only forty aircraft were built, and they were used by just two RAF squadrons, although one aircraft survived in use at Boscombe Down until as late as 1968, and several aircraft were re-sold to Middle East countries when their RAF days were over.

Top: **Carrying the distinctive red trim of the Odiham Station Flight, Meteor F.8 WK654 also has, unusually, its serial repeated on the under-wing tanks.** *(MAP via David Sargent)*

Middle: **A trio of 208 Squadron FR.9s, showing the early natural metal finish, and the unit's blue and yellow markings on the rear fuselage. The nearest aircraft is WX962/Q, which spent all its time with 208 Squadron, before being struck off charge for scrap in 1958.** *(via M.Fopp)*

Bottom: **A delightful photograph of a 231 OCU PR.10 at its Bassingbourn base in 1952, with some of the same unit's Canberras in the background. The Meteor element moved out to Merryfield in July 1955, taking WB160 with it.** *(Crown Copyright, PRB 4537)*

X
WK654
WK654
WB160

WA547
WS615
F
T
WS783
R
WS789

Opposite page photographs, top to bottom:

WA547 was the second true prototype of the NF.11, and is seen here at Farnborough for the SBAC display in 1950. It spent the remainder of its career with the A & AEE at Boscombe Down. *(via M.Fopp)*

NF.12 WS615 from 238 OCU at Colerne, on the visiting aircraft pan at Bovingdon in 1956, shortly before the unit moved to North Luffenham. The only identifying marking carried by this unit was the black painted lower portion of the fin. *(MAP)*

One of two Meteors displayed at the RAF's Golden Jubilee Anniversary Exhibition and Flying Display at Abingdon in June 1968 was a rare beast indeed. Boscombe Down's NF.13 WM367, was at that time, the only example of its mark in the country, and was retired from use shortly after the show. It is believed to be still extant, and possibly undergoing restoration. *(Author)*

152 Squadron from Stradishall indulges in a little formation practice with NF.14s WS783/T, WS789/R, WS735/X and probably WS786/F. When the unit disbanded in July 1958 these were put into storage at 33 MU, Lyneham, and were eventually pushed out in the open and gradually dismembered from 1963 onwards. *(Royal Air Force Museum, 6603-11)*

Above: **A photograph which has appeared in print before, but which is none the less interesting for showing a Meteor U.15 in unmanned flight. VW280/T was caught during a sortie from RAE Llanbedr during the late '50s.** *(Flight Refuelling Ltd, 5198)*

Below: **Crewed up and ready to go at Luqa, is this TT.20, WM292, out from the Airwork Fleet Requirements Unit at Hurn. One of the same unit's all-black Sea Hawks can be seen in the background. The FRU provided a variety of target facilities for ships at sea and for naval shore installations.** *(Dennis Robinson)*

Last of the night-fighters, and indeed the last of all the newly-built Meteors, was the NF.14, which had an even longer fuselage still, but which was basically an NF.12 fitted with a one-piece blown canopy, giving much improved vision over the old multi-framed T.7 type. One hundred were built from 1953 onwards and the last one (WS848) made its maiden flight on 18th May 1954, just a month after the last Gloster-built Meteor F.8 had flown.

All the other variants of the Meteor were modifications of existing airframes, starting with the U.15, U.16 and U.21 target-drones (the last two later being re-designated D.16 and D.21; the designations U and D indicating Unmanned and Drone respectively). In the early fifties it became

Above: **WH460 was originally built as an F.8 and served with 64 and 65 Squadrons before going to Flight Refuelling Ltd for conversion to a U.21 in September 1960. It was subsequently sent to Edinburgh Field in Australia, where this photo was taken in 1965.** *(MAP)*

apparent, that with the increasing use of the guided missile, there was a distinct need for a high-speed manouverable target for test purposes, the existing drone conversions of the Fairey Firefly being somewhat lacking in performance. By coincidence, at about this time, Meteor F.4s were being retired by the RAF in large numbers and put into storage at Maintenance units, and these seemed to present an ideal opportunity.

In September 1954, a T.7 was tested at Farnborough with a remotely controlled throttle unit, and this aircraft made an automatically controlled take-off on 17 January 1955 with a monitoring pilot aboard. Once again however, Glosters' heavy work-load precluded their involvement in the programme for a Meteor drone, which was passed to Flight Refuelling Ltd of Tarrant Rushton in Dorset, who were already familiar with the type from their air-to-air refuelling work on F.4s and F.8s. Thus, on 11 March 1955, the first F.4 to be converted to U.15 standard, RA421, made its first automatic take-off controlled from the ground. The modifications necessary to produce the drones included removing all armament, and fitting radio link equipment, an automatic pilot (despite which, all drones could still be flown in the normal way by a human pilot), infra-red homing flares and jettisonable wing-tip camera pods. The aircraft were all painted in a high-visibility red and orange colour scheme. A total of ninety-two U.15s was produced for use at both the Woomera range in Australia, flying out of Edinburgh Field, and the Cardigan Bay range off the coast of Wales, using the RAE airfield at Llanbedr.

Performance limitations with the U.15 soon led to the U.16, which was a similar conversion of the F.8, and well over 100 were produced. This version featured an elongated nose for the drone equipment, and in addition to Woomera and Llanbedr, also saw service with the Royal Navy in Malta, alongside a few U.15s. Two aircraft were still flying from Llanbedr in 1984.

The aircraft that went to Australia were mostly brought up to U.21 standard, reflecting local requirements and differences in operating techniques, and Fairey Aviation Pty went on to convert many ex-RAAF F.8s to the same standard, some of these aircraft remaining in use well into the 'seventies. In fact, many of the Meteor drones flew in this form for some considerable time, in some cases for years. They were not always the target on missile sorties, frequently towing targets themselves, or releasing flares for the missiles to home onto and thus return for use another day. It is only fairly recently that the need for a much faster target, coupled with the rapidly diminishing stock of Meteor airframes, led to a programme to utilise the de Havilland Sea Vixen as a replacement drone, again under the control of Flight Refuelling Ltd, though this type has been found unsuitable for the role, and alternatives are being considered. At one time it was proposed to produce target versions of the Meteor nightfighters, but this did not proceed beyond the design stage, although it is thought that the designations U.17, U.18 and U.19 were reserved for conversions of the NF.11/TT.20, NF.12 and NF.14 respectively.

These then, are all the major Meteor variants; the many modified and experimental models will be covered in later chapters.

3

The Meteor on the Line

Despite the strange disbandment of the pioneer Meteor squadron, 616, at Lubeck in the late summer of 1945, the aircraft had been proved in service and was starting to leave the factory in ever increasing numbers. Colerne in Wiltshire had already been picked as the first major Meteor base, and by the autumn of 1945 was home to 74 and 504 Squadrons, both equipped with the F.3, although 504 was almost immediately re-numbered as 245 Squadron. Also briefly at Colerne at this time was 1335 Conversion Unit, destined to be the forerunner of a vast Meteor training establishment in later years.

Throughout 1946 and 1947, the pace of the build-up of the Meteor force continued to accelerate, with bases at Bentwaters, Boxted, Duxford and Acklington coming into use. Duxford had three Meteor squadrons, 56, 66 and 92, all flying the F.3 still and typically, despite the lack of a two-seat trainer at this time, converting piston-engine experienced pilots to the jet seems to have caused few problems, as Sqn Ldr P G Murton, who was serving on 92 at the time, recalls:

'Whilst attending the Day Fighter Leaders course at West Raynham' - (the home of the Central Fighter Establishment) - 'flying Spitfires,

Below: **Meteor F.3 EE354 of 1335 Conversion Unit, taxies round the perimeter track at Molesworth, followed by others of the same unit.** *(Imperial War Museum, 16363)*

Top left: **Flying Officer Philip Murton in the cockpit of his personal Meteor F.3, 'Letitia III', while the squadron was detached to Lubeck from its Duxford base in 1947. Unfortunately, the serial number of this aircraft is not known. Note 92 Squadron's cobra and maple leaf badge.** *(Philip Murton)*

Below left: **Groundcrew busy preparing 92 Squadron's Meteor F.3s for the day's flying from Lubeck in 1947. The squadron code letters DL, were later changed to 8L, before being dropped altogether in 1951.** *(Philip Murton)*

Opposite page: **Horsham St Faith on 30 June 1947, with work in progress on several Meteor F.3s. The aircraft just outside the hangar doors bears the codes HR-F of 263 Squadron, while the one inside has the AF code of the Air Fighting Development Unit.** *(Crown Copyright, MoD, R783)*

I was privileged as one of the few course pilots to fly a Meteor 3. This was basically because I had just finished a tour as a Flight Commander on the first Vampire squadron' - (247 at Odiham) - ' and was *au fait* with jets. It was a marvellous experience to fly a twin-jet and I much enjoyed the F.3'.

In fact, the F.3 was destined to have a very short life in the front-line squadrons, for in 1948, the much improved F.4 came along. 92 Squadron received theirs in May and immediately took them to Germany for their annual armament practice camp at Lubeck. Philip Murton has good reason to remember what was a rather eventful return to Duxford in June:

'On the day we were all due to fly back to Duxford, one aircraft went unserviceable needing an engine change. As I was due to get married on the 19th, the CO detailed me to stay behind to supervise, do the air test and then fly back on my own. He knew full well, of course, that I would do everything in my power to gee up the groundcrew and, regardless of weather, press on back on the Friday so that I could go up to Hull for the ceremony on the Saturday. All went well at Lubeck and I even managed to stow three straw-wrapped bottles of champagne in the false front of my long-range belly tank' - (the F.4 being the first model so equipped) - ' and got through customs at Manston without a hitch'.

'However, at Manston the weather-man advised no further trips that day, at least to Duxford, as a front was moving south very rapidly giving low cloud and rain. But, intrepid birdman Murton did not want to miss his wedding and pressed on regardless, duly running into very low cloud and pouring rain as predicted. Eventually, flying at about 300 feet with everything out, down and open, I managed to pick up the Whittlesford railway line east of the airfield and, knowing the exact location of the local farms, villages, churches and other landmarks, was able to make a pretty blind circuit and land on the correct runway. I taxied in towards the hangar, where I was waved in with my engines still running and before I could shut them down, the doors were closed behind me. Needless to say I was not only soaked with sweat, but also with rain, as I had flown the last half hour or so with the hood open; but at least I had got there safely and the groundcrew very carefully removed my bottles of champagne!'.

The large numbers of new Meteors by now necessitated the setting up of maintenance units for the type, not only to carry out major servicings and modifications, but also to receive aircraft from the manufacturers, and despatch them to the squadrons as required. Likewise,

earlier models were sent to the MUs as the squadrons re-equipped, and were later passed on to second-line units for training purposes. One of the first such units to handle the Meteor was 6 MU at Brize Norton in Oxfordshire, which began receiving new F.4s in January 1948 and went on to handle all the marks up to the PR.10. Other major units to deal with the Meteor were the MUs at Aston Down (No.20), High Ercall (29), Kirkbride (12), Llandow (38), Lyneham (33) and Kemble (5) which was destined to be the last, not finally disposing of its Meteors until the mid-seventies. Overseas, this work was carried out chiefly by 390 MU at Seletar.

With the coming of the F.4, re-equipment moved into top gear, and eventually over twenty squadrons would have this model alone, one of the first being 74 Squadron at Horsham St Faith near Norwich, which received its first examples in January 1948, and disposed of its last F.3 in March. This unit was chosen to take its aircraft to Denmark on a flag-waving visit in September 1948 and eight Meteors accompanied by two Halifaxes carrying the groundcrew and equipment left England on the 16th on the first leg of the journey, to Eindhoven in Holland, subsequently staging through Lubeck. The eventful flight to Kastrup in Denmark the next day is described by Den Todd, one of the pilots:

'The event that was to make our arrival at Kastrup memorable, was the fact that shortly after take-off from Lubeck, both Sqn Ldr Wootten and myself reported that our belly-tanks were not feeding fuel. This would not have been a problem if we had been flying at high altitude, but at 6,000 feet our fuel consumption was, to say the least, a bit gluttonous'.

'Our call sign 'British Meteor Squadron' also led to some confusion, as air traffic at Kastrup began calling us 'British Catalina', 'British Airliner' and later a few other less complimentary things! To add to this confusion, we were also an hour early, due to the time difference; however, when we were in sight of our destination, Wg Cdr Lapsley, who was leading the flight, informed air traffic that he had two aircraft requiring emergency landing clearance'.

'Unfortunately, this proved to be difficult as, apart from language problems, Kastrup was a joint-user airfield with frequent airliner movements. At this point, Sqn Ldr Wootten said that according to his fuel gauges, he was flying on borrowed time and was therefore going to make a straight-in approach and landing. I also left the formation intending to follow him, but at 1,500 feet over the water while making my approach, I heard control say, 'Military aircraft landing at Kastrup, you are landing downwind".

HE
245

WH307

A
VZ417

Opposite page, top: A line up of F.4s from the Horsham St Faith wing in 1948 with aircraft present from 74, 245 and 263 Squadrons. This shot was taken at the time of the arrival of the F.4s, which explains why there has not yet been time to finish applying the front aircraft's code (it became HE-J). *(D.C.Todd)*

Opposite, middle: Wymeswold in Leicestershire in 1955, and local 504 (County of Nottingham) Squadron, Royal Auxiliary Air Force, has its Meteor F.8s lined-up ready to fly. Markings are green outlined in red . *(Neville Franklin)*

Opposite, bottom: Meteor F.4 VZ417, with its first service user, 63 Squadron. Note miniaturised squadron badge, flanked by checks, on the engine nacelle. '417 was eventually modified to U.15 standard during 1956/57. *(via D.Sargent)*

Above: On a fine summer's day in the early fifties, North Weald's two resident auxiliary squadrons, 601 and 604, line up their shiny Meteors for the camera. Each line includes the respective squadron commander's aircraft, which have the multi-coloured fins.
(Royal Air Force Museum, P100310)

Below: Ready to scramble. Basking in the sun at RAF Leuchars in the early 'fifties, with the 'trolley-acc' plugged in ready for starting, is F.8 WA794 of the resident 43 Squadron. The early-style canopy, as seen here on '794, attracted much criticism for its poor rearward vision and was eventually replaced by a completely clear version. This particular aircraft went on to serve with 72 Squadron and 5 CAACU before being written-off in October 1957. *(MAP)*

'This of course was Sqn Ldr Wootten, in fact making a dead-stick landing with dry tanks, and I was now forced to make a very tight circuit onto the runway in use, only to find a DC-6 on final approach ahead of me! I had no alternative however, and landed to the right of the runway, overtaking the DC-6 on his landing run. I imagine the passengers on the starboard side will never forget that arrival at Kastrup, and neither will I!'.

That same month, September 1948, saw large numbers of Meteors being displayed to the British public at the annual Battle of Britain open days on the 18th, when eighty-two RAF stations had displays. Meteors (and Vampires) appeared at most of them, and at Thorney Island in Hampshire, which was by then the home of 56, 63 and 222 Squadrons, the Secretary of State for Air, Mr Arthur Henderson was witness to a scramble by all three squadrons, which must have been quite a sight.

Above: **Meteor F.8s of 63 Squadron (front row) and 56 Squadron (back row), lined up at Waterbeach in June 1953, ready for the Coronation flypast over London.** *(H.Orme)*

Opposite page, top: **Meteor WA893 heads a line of 263 Squadron aircraft at Wattisham. '893 spent its entire life with this unit before being scrapped in 1958.** *(MAP)*

Below: **Outside the squadron hangar at Biggin Hill in 1955, 41 Squadron's F.8 WE949/E is refuelled through the 325 gallon main tank just behind the cockpit. At this time, the unit was eagerly awaiting the arrival of its Hunter F.5s, and the Meteors were beginning to look somewhat tatty.** *(Military Aircraft Photographs)*

In 1950, the coming into service of the ultimate day fighter Meteor, the F.8, heralded a further expansion of the RAF's jet fighter force and the final passing of the piston-engine in combat aeroplanes. Once again, the redundant Meteors, F.4s this time, found further lengthy periods of service in training roles and as target drones and they had all left the squadrons by the end of 1951.

With the widespread introduction of the F.8, RAF Fighter Command, (and the Royal Auxiliary Air Force, which also received a large number of Meteors), entered what was arguably its most colourful period ever, surpassing even the period in the early thirties when it seemed that, in terms of aircraft markings, anything went. Not long after the end of the war, camouflage was dropped from fighter aircraft as being unnecessary, although the wartime system of two-letter squadron codes was retained on the unpainted aircraft. However, towards the end of the F.4s front-line service, and in the following years, fighter aircraft, and Meteor in particular, adopted a dazzling variety of squadron markings.

Each unit had its own colour combination, usually presented in horizontal bars on either side of the fuselage roundel, and the squadron commander's aircraft would usually have additional decoration in the form of a multi-coloured fin and rudder. Many senior pilots contrived to have their initials presented on the aircraft, and this was particularly prevalent amongst wing, station and group commanders, who frequently had Meteors allocated to them as their private taxis.

This form of bravado was at its height at the time of the Coronation of Queen Elizabeth II in June 1953, when the RAF was tasked with both a flypast over London on Coronation Day, and a large scale review by the new monarch at Odiham. Not since the war had so many aeroplanes been seen in formation, and the events of Coronation Day were later recalled by M J F Bowyer:

'It rained and rained. For much of the day a flypast seemed unlikely. Yet, by 17.00 hours, the weather had slightly improved - it was on. At 17.25, the Meteors of the Waterbeach wing were away, shortly after eight of the RCAF Sabres from North Luffenham had roared overhead. The squadrons formed up in wings off Bexhill, in the bad weather plan, flying in line astern thirty seconds apart in very bumpy weather with a 1,000 feet cloudbase. The order of procession was, Duxford Wing (64 and 65 Squadrons), Tangmere (54 and 247 Squadrons, normally at Odiham), Biggin Hill (1 and 41), North Luffenham (RCAF Sabres), Wattisham (257 and 263), Waterbeach (56 and 63) and Horsham St. Faith (74 and 245). All the Meteor wings sent twenty-four aircraft, of which several were T.7s, and they crossed the Mall at 17.45 at 320 mph'.

The review of the Royal Air Force at Odiham, later in July, would make even this event pale by comparison. The static display comprised no fewer than 318 aircraft, with a further 639 in the flypast, and of these, a very large percentage were Meteors. Mike Bowyer remembers the final rehearsal from a vantage point at Duxford:

'Duxford reverberated to the sound of twenty-six Meteors and twenty-five Sabres. The Meteors took off in pairs, with 64 Squadron leading. Very low and fast, smoking furiously and in pairs, came the Sabres, with twenty-four Venoms from Wattisham overhead. By now the sky was full of Meteors, and I noticed the colours of 56, 63, 74, 245, 257 and 263 Squadrons'.

Aircraft positioned for display on the ground at Odiham included aircraft from most of the Auxiliary squadrons and the Advanced Flying

Schools, while the flypast consisted of the following: eleven F.4s and one T.7 from 206 AFS at Oakington, twenty-four F.8s from 1 and 54 Squadrons, twenty-four from 64 and 65 Squadrons, twenty-four from 74 and 245 Squadrons, twenty-four from 56 and 63 Squadrons, twenty-four from 66 and 92 Squadrons, twenty-four from 257 and 263 Squadrons, twenty-four from 43 and 222 Squadrons at Leuchars (the latter being the first jet aircraft to be based in Scotland), twenty-four from 19 and 247 Squadrons, together with eighteen NF.11s from each of 29, 85, 141, 151 and 264 Squadrons.

The NF.11 had entered service in 1951 as the first of the Armstrong Whitworth designed Meteor variants. At that time, our night fighter strength consisted almost entirely of the Mosquito NF.36, which was already considerably outdated, and with the threat of war with the Soviet bloc enhanced by the Korean war, extra emphasis was given to getting the Meteor NF.11 into service at the earliest possible date, with 29 Squadron at Tangmere being the first to get it. Some idea of the flavour of squadron life in those days comes from Reg Griffiths, who was a radar mechanic on 29 at that time.

'I arrived at Tangmere in April 1952 and soon learnt about the aircraft in general as I was detailed to assist in start-ups, along with giving a hand with refuelling. One thing that sticks in my mind is the need to connect a venting hosepipe to the ventral tank, otherwise it burst! At times the squadron sent up its T.7 to do target towing, and on these occasions the groundcrew used to go up for a trip. We had to maintain a steady course with the drogue target to enable the rest of the squadron to do air to air firing practice. After the target was dropped over the runway, we went for a little sightseeing along the coastline - all very nice'.

'As a radar man I also had to work in the radar bay. Once on night duty, whilst I was running up the Meteor's AI radar in the bay, I noticed a soldier walking past the window carrying a neon valve. I beamed the radar scanner towards him and the valve lit up in his hands; he was so surprised that he dropped it!'.

The NF.11 was quite a big aeroplane, weighing 3,000 lbs more than the F.8, but it was quite agile and many pilots claimed that it was capable of out-turning the F.8 at low altitude. The radar had a range of about ten miles in most conditions, and with the GEE Mk.3 and radar altimeter, the NF.11 was quite advanced for its time. One problem encountered early on in its career, was a tendency for the 100 gallon underwing drop-tanks to collapse when the aircraft was travelling at high speed. This was cured by fitting them with strengthened nose-caps.

The night-fighters were also the first Meteors to serve in large numbers overseas, especially with 2 TAF in Germany, where initially at Geilenkirchen, Ahlhorn and Wahn and later at Bruggen and Laarbruch, they survived for some time after the UK based squadrons had re-equipped with the Javelin or disbanded. The normal strength of the night-fighter squadrons was sixteen in the UK and fourteen in Germany, although in September 1957, 29 Squadron had no fewer than twenty-four NF.11s, plus the usual two T.7s.

Two other Meteor variants which were destined to see more service overseas than in the UK, were the FR.9 and PR.10, which were confined mainly to 2 TAF in Germany and the RAF's Middle East and Far East Air Forces. The PR.10s in particular were moved around a great deal, since there were so few aircraft, and 13 and 81 Squadrons had frequent detachments to such places as Luqa, Idris, Habbaniya, El

Opposite page:
151 Squadron Meteor NF.11 WM246/B is seen here on a visit to Kinloss, sometime in 1954. It was based at Leuchars at the time. WM246 later served in Germany and after conversion to TT.20, in Singapore. *(J. Gascoine via D.Sargent)*

This page, top:
Meteor NF.11 WD663/C had just been retired from service with 5 Squadron in Germany when photographed at Hullavington on 15 July 1961. Six months later it had been consigned to the scrap-heap. *(Robin Forbes)*

Above:
Meteor FR.9 WB116/G from Wahn in Germany visits an air display in 1956, wearing the black and white markings of 2 Squadron, including a small unit badge on the engine cowling. *(MAP)*

Adem, Muharraq and to Eastleigh in Kenya, where on 16 March 1954, WB168, piloted by Flt Lt W J Dobson, became the first jet aircraft ever seen in that country.

13 Squadron shared its airfield at Kabrit in the Canal Zone, with 39 and 219 Squadrons, which were the only units ever to fly the tropicalised NF.13. After 219 had been disbanded in 1954, its aircraft were absorbed by 39, which later moved to Cyprus and became involved in *Operation Musketeer* - the Suez crisis - in November 1956. The squadron flew many defensive patrols, and although both Egypt and Israel were also flying Meteors NF.13s by this time, there is no record of any Meteor versus Meteor combat taking place.

As far as the regular air force is concerned, the Meteor started to fade from the front-line units with the advent of the Hunter in July 1954

Top: 219 Squadron flew Meteor NF.13s from Kabrit for just over three years before disbanding and WM321 was captured on film in April 1954. Although the squadron adopted the standard style of markings, red and black in this case, it was unusual in that it does not appear to have given its aircraft individual code letters and with a small squadron badge on the nose. *(Crown Copyright MoD 7921)*

Above: 13 Squadron Meteor PR.10s, headed by WB176/J, at Fayid in Egypt. *(M.Dobson)*

Below: One can almost feel the heat in this atmospheric shot of FR.9, WX978/Z of 8 Sqn, being refuelled at Khormaksar in Aden in the late 'fifties. *(Ron Clarke)*

Above: **The shock disbandment of the Royal Auxiliary Air Force was responsible for some sad sights at a number of MUs in the following months. This scene at 12 MU Kirkbride in 1958 was typically depressing, but yet interesting in the variety of markings to be seen. The nearest F.8 is WL167, the former squadron leader's aircraft from 601 at North Weald, with a red and black striped fin. Next to it are WH255 of 504 Sqn, WF649 of 610 Sqn and an unidentified aircraft from 500 Sqn.** *(David Gray)*

and the Javelin in February 1957. The contest for the last operational Meteor flight was eventually narrowed down to two Far East Air Force units: 60 Squadron with NF.14s and 81 Squadron with PR.10s - both based in Singapore. In the event, 81 were the losers, making their last flights with the type in July 1961, while 60 managed to soldier on until the September, even though their first Javelins had arrived some six months before that.

With the Royal Auxiliary Air Force, the Meteor began large-scale use in 1951 and 1952, supplanting both Spitfires and some Vampires with the week-end flyers. In fact, during the initial war emergency state declared on the onset of the Korean War in June 1950, all the auxiliary squadrons were mobilised for three months continuous regular service. Thus, despite their apparent amateur status, these units formed a valuable part of the UK air defence system, and in addition to their annual armament camps, which usually took place overseas, they were involved in every major exercise held in the UK until their mass disbandment in 1957. In fact there was not, as might have been expected, a gradual run-down of the R.Aux.AF flying units. Flying continued normally until the issue of an Air Ministry signal on 6 January 1957, which recalled and grounded them all, in many cases while the squadrons were actually involved in exercises. Interestingly, several former 610 and 611 Squadron pilots were still flying Meteors from Llanbedr in the early 'eighties.

As a combat aeroplane, the Meteor's handling characteristics, especially in the later versions, were quite pleasant. The F.8 for example, was stressed to plus 6.0g and minus 3.0g and could be aerobatted and spun provided no drop tanks were fitted, and the belly tank empty. Due to the widely-spaced engines positions however, considerable problems could arise with an engine failure. In particular, the night-fighters, which would take-off at between 120 and 125 knots, would not reach safety speed until 160 knots. In the event of an engine failure below 140 knots, the aircraft would yaw violently and roll rapidly towards the dead engine, control only being regained by closing both throttles and making liberal use of both rudder and ailerons. The pilots notes recommended that in such cases the drop tanks should be jettisoned, and the aircraft landed straight ahead.

Above 140 knots, such a failure would still result in yawing, but once the aircraft had been levelled out, it could be climbed away on the good engine. The main problem with an engine failure during flight would arise if it was the starboard engine which failed, since it carried the only hydraulic pump, and should the failed engine seize, or the pump pack-up of its own accord, there would probably be insufficient reserve of pressure to get the wheels and flaps down, despite the fact that it was recommended to attempt forced landings only with a lowered undercarriage!

Abandoning those marks not fitted with ejection seats was also interesting, the method being to reduce speed as much as possible, jettison the hood and abandon the aircraft by diving over the inboard trailing edge of the wing; never by inverting the aircraft and falling out!

This would have been even more interesting in the case of the night-fighters, in which intentional spinning was forbidden, due to the aircraft developing extremely unpleasant behaviour in such a manoeuvre, with severe oscillation in both yaw and pitch and very heavy stick forces. In the event of the pilot being unable to recover from this, his prospects of successfully diving out must have been slim indeed.

Above:
603 Squadron, Royal Auxiliary Air Force, was a Vampire unit at Turnhouse during the 'fifties, and in common with many such units, acquired one or two Meteor T.7s for communications duties. Shown here is their WG949, resplendent in light and dark blue checks, bordered in black. The photograph was taken on 13 April 1958, just a year after the squadron had disbanded, at the infamous Meteor graveyard at Kirkbride, home of 12 MU. *(David Gray)*

Nevertheless, the Meteor soon became a popular mount for aerobatic displays and a large proportion of the squadrons had their own teams at one time or another. One of the first was 245 at Horsham St Faith, which put together a four man team of F.4s in 1948 for display not only in this country, but also overseas. In fact, Glosters were asked to modify six aircraft to take wing tanks, to enable the team to go to the Middle East for *Exercise Gestic* in November 1948, after which they gave displays at Fayid and Deversoir.

The following year, 245's place was taken by 263 Squadron at Wattisham as Fighter Command's premier aerobatic team, and they were chosen to perform at the RAF display at Farnborough in July 1950. Other squadrons which came to the fore in Meteor aerobatics included 19 at Church Fenton in Yorkshire, 74 from Horsham St Faith, which sent a four aircraft team around the continent in 1951 and the famous 111 Squadron at North Weald, which started with again, four aircraft in 1954 under the guidance of Sqn Ldr Pears, and went on the following years to Hunters and international fame as the Black Arrows.

Although 245 Squadron's moment of glory in the field of aerobatics had passed, it was later to achieve considerable acclaim as the first RAF unit to experiment with air to air refuelling. As far back as 1944, it had been realised that the much higher fuel consumption of a jet engine when compared with the piston variety, would severely limit the range of the Meteor. Underwing auxiliary tanks were part of the answer, but they had the negative effect of reducing the aircraft's performance and manoeuvrability due to drag, and although the F.4, with a longer fuselage, had room for an extra internal tank behind the cockpit, it was still only a partial answer.

Thus in 1949, F.3 EE397 was fitted with a refuelling probe and became the first of the type to refuel in mid-air on 24 April, when it made contact with a Lancaster tanker operated by Flight Refuelling from Tarrant Rushton in Dorset. Six further flights were made that day before the refuelling probe, which was installed in the extreme nose, began to work loose, but on 7 August the same year, the Meteor set an endurance record for jet aircraft by staying up for twelve hours and three minutes. Subsequently, two F.4s were similarly modified, and one of these, VZ389, demonstrated the system with a Lincoln tanker at the 1950 SBAC Show at Farnborough, as a result of which, on 15 November, Flight Refuelling received a sub-contract from Glosters to install and test their equipment in sixteen F.8s, all from 245 Squadron.

The first acceptance flights of the modified aircraft began in February 1951 and over the next few months, the squadron carried out many contacts, mostly using USAF KB-29 Superfortress tankers and occasionally, the Lancaster and Lincoln already mentioned. Although the trials were a complete success and thoroughly proved the worth of the system, almost all the aircraft were de-modified at the end of the year (although at least one aircraft retained its probe until the mid-fifties while serving with Horsham's Station Flight), and 245 reverted to normal operations. In fact, four further F.8s and one T.7 were later modified by Flight Refuelling for trials with the Lancaster and a Canberra tanker, but after this the idea of the probe Meteor was quietly forgotten.

An interesting aside to this part of the story concerns the actual type of fuel used by the Meteor. Naturally, the Derwents were normally run on AVTAG or AVTUR jet fuel, but they would happily run on AVGAS piston engine fuel in an emergency, get-you-home situation, although the fuel consumption increased by some 11%.

During the revolution in Argentina in 1955, rebel forces captured three undamaged Meteor F.4s, and flew them against the Government forces, fuelled entirely with ordinary petrol. Rolls-Royce laid down strict rules for running the Derwent this way in an emergency, stipulating that lubricating oil should be mixed with the petrol and altitude limited to 15,000 feet. Needless to say, the Argentine rebels had no time for such niceties, and inevitably, one of the aircraft was lost when an engine overheated and exploded.

From the groundcrew point of view, the Meteor was a nice aeroplane to handle, being fairly simple with good accessibility to all major components including the engines, which were quite easy to change. The Derwent was a very strong and reliable engine, one of the few in-service problems encountered being during the period of 208 Squadron's operations in the Middle East, when their habit of flying reconnaissance missions 'on the deck' over the desert, had the effect of sand-blasting the engines!

On the flightline, the Meteor required little in the way of ground-support equipment beyond the usual gas bottles for the pneumatic and oxygen systems, and the engine starts were accomplished using the venerable battery trolley or trolley-acc as it was (and still is) universally known. All the same, problems could still occur, as was vividly illustrated very early on in the aircraft's career. Most Meteors had a safety system for the guns, whereby either the undercarriage locking down, or the aircraft's weight coming onto the wheels, would render them incapable of being fired; for the necessary test-firing into the butts from time to time, this system could be overidden by operating a FIRE/SAFE switch in the starboard undercarriage bay. However, the F.1 was not fitted with this safety device, and on 20 September 1944 at Manston, a ground-crewman on 616 Squadron inadvertantly fired the guns while sitting in the cockpit of EE225, and destroyed EE224 which was parked in front of it!

Below:
On 18 December 1947, 245 Squadron's Meteor F.3 EE297 ran out of fuel when trying to get in at its Horsham St Faith base, in bad weather. and crashed at nearby Horsford. *(D. C. Todd)*

4

Training and Other Roles

With the introduction of the Meteor in increasing numbers during 1945, a training scheme for pilots was established with the formation of 1335 Conversion Unit, which after short periods at Colerne and Molesworth, settled at Bentwaters in Suffolk, where it was re-designated 226 Operational Conversion Unit. The unit was equipped with a variety of types in addition to the Meteors, such as Vampires and Hornets, with Oxfords and Ansons for communication duties, and together with 203 Advanced Flying School at Stradishall, which flew Harvards and Spitfires, comprised the entire training organisation for fighter pilots in the immediate post-war period.

By the middle of 1949 it became obvious that these two units would not be able to cope with the growing demand for trainee pilots for jet fighter squadrons and it was decided to form a jet training school within Flying Training Command for converting pilots to Meteors and Vampires as soon as they had completed their basic flying training on the Harvard. A small nucleus of jet Qualified Flying Instructors, under the command of Sqn Ldr D B Fitzpatrick, transferred the Meteor squadron within the Bentwaters organisation, to Driffield in Yorkshire, which had been selected as the first jet training station. This was accomplished in August 1949, and the unit took over the 203 AFS title from the Stradishall unit and was equipped with both Meteors and Vampires.

By this time, the long-awaited Meteor T.7 was available, and it soon became obvious to the more experienced instructors that it was a sturdy and very efficient training aircraft. However, it was apparent that in instrument flying conditions the very short endurance of the Meteor could be a problem. Similarly, approach and landing aids were unsophisticated and could easily become saturated if several aircraft required a talk-down in a short space of time. In 1949, Driffield was equipped with VHF/DF, which was an approach aid only.

With the average training sortie lasting for forty minutes, or just over an hour if the belly-tank was fitted, the need for a satellite airfield became paramount to relieve the circuit pressure at the home base and the wartime emergency strip at nearby Carnaby was brought into use. In addition, new techniques for high-level let-down, to try to alleviate the overcrowded circuit problem, were pioneered with the help of the Examining Wing of the Central Flying School and in a short time, most QFIs were operating quite happily with the Meteor in cloudbases down to 1,000 feet and lower around Driffield. If a low fuel state precluded the instructor from going round again in the circuit, this often produced some very hairy moments if the aircraft had made a rapid descent from high-speed runs at 35,000 feet or more. The Meteor T.7 was unpressurised, and it was quite common for the canopy to mist-up or ice-up and cause a serious restriction in the pilot's vision on approach. There was a clear view panel which could be opened in flight, but this did not help much, and QFIs soon started carrying a plastic scraper with them to try to cure the problem!

Opposite page, top:
Stradishall, Suffolk, on a fine summer's day in June 1950 and flying is in full swing with 226 OCU busy training fledgling fighter pilots. Meteor F.4 RA492/HX-W taxies past VW312/KR-J, VT325/KR-N, VT293/KR-K, VW283/KR-L and RA415(?)/KR-R: only KR-K carries the newer post-war style roundels with enlarged white portion. Note the grass scorched by the jet-blast. *(Crown copyright, PRB 368)*

Opposite page, bottom:
A 'four-ship' formation of Meteor T.7s from 203 AFS at Driffield on 8 October 1953, comprises WL413/X-68, WF881/X-55, WL361/X-71 and WF776/X-54. After a fairly lengthy RAF service, the latter aircraft was one of a small number of T.7s exported to France.
(Crown Copyright, PRB 7017)

The single-engine performance of the Meteor could be lethal if not properly controlled and the instructors at Driffield were for some time split into two schools of thought as to how to deal with it. One thought that the asymmetric flying should be practised with an engine flamed-out altogether, whilst the other maintained that for safety reasons it should be left idling, and thus available for immediate use in an emergency. After about one year at Driffield, 203 AFS adopted the latter method as standard practice, after several fatal accidents had proved the point, several of which were made worse than they might have been by the habit of some instructors and pupils leaving the airbrakes out on final approach, and then trying to overshoot in this configuration.

In addition to insisting on the engine-idling method of training, after consultation again with the Central Flying School, a final approach R/T call of '3 greens, airbrakes in', was introduced, and resulted in a significant reduction in the accident rate, though not before a tragic accident had occured at Middleton St George with 205 AFS, the second Meteor Advanced Flying School, which had been formed to satisfy the pilot needs of the Meteor night-fighter squadrons.

On a Saturday afternoon in the summer of 1950, when most of the station had stood-down for the weekend, there was a limited flying programme in progress. A pupil was sent solo to catch up on single-engine practice and all went well for a while. After about thirty minutes, the pupil was recalled, as usual by air traffic and came in for what should have been his final single-engine landing (with the 'dead' engine flamed-out). He made a good approach and touchdown, but to the consternation of the controller, he called 'Rolling' and opened up the throttles. Not surprisingly, with only one engine responding, he careered off the runway, missed the bulk fuel installation by a small margin and crashed through the wall of the Officers Mess, breaking his neck and writing-off his own car in the process!

Another incident at Middleton St George, though this time with a happier ending, highlighted the old problem of getting a Meteor out of a spin. A QFI and his pupil had completed some high-speed runs in a T.7 and climbed to 20,000 feet to do some spins. Having demonstrated two, the instructor handed control to his pupil, who entered a right-hand spin. After two or three turns, he initiated recovery action to no avail and the instructor was also unable to do anything with the now totally out of control aeroplane. He jettisoned the canopy and ordered his pupil to bale out before following him and unfortunately hitting the tailplane and breaking both his shoulder and his collar-bone. Despite this, he was able to deploy his parachute (as had his pupil), but could not prevent himself from drifting towards a large herd of cows in the corner of a field, eventually landing of the back of a bullock!

By the start of the fifties, Flying Training Command had several hundred Meteors operating in ten Advanced Flying Schools, and to support them, and continue the pupils training before posting to squadrons, several Meteor Operational Conversion Units had been set up within Fighter Command. These included 226 OCU at Stradishall, which trained day fighter pilots, 228 and 238 OCUs at Leeming and Colerne (later North Luffenham) respectively, for the night fighter crews and 231 OCU at Bassingbourn which did the photo-reconnaissance training.

Opposite page: **A picturesque shot of a T.7 from the Central Flying School at Little Rissington, banking over the Cotswold countryside during a sortie on 15 May 1952. Only seven months later this aircraft went to the Royal Netherlands Air Force.** *(Crown Copyright, PRB 4558)*

However, a major shake-up in flying training came about in 1954, with the introduction of the Provost/Vampire scheme, whereby all jet pilots did their basic training on the Provost T.1 and converted to jets on the Vampire T.11, before proceeding direct to the OCUs. This eliminated the need for the Advanced Flying Training Schools, which were disbanded in favour of new Flying Training Schools. Initially, two of these, No.8 at Driffield and No.12 at Weston Zoyland retained Meteors, but as the Vampires became available in greater numbers, they too converted to the newer type, although the Meteor later enjoyed a brief final fling with 4 FTS at Worksop during 1956 and 1957.

One further unit which continued to use the Meteor T.7 in its intended role for several years after the introduction of the Vampire, was the Central Flying School at Little Rissington, which was responsible for the training of all the RAF's qualified flying instructors. The unit was sub-divided into several squadrons, and at Little Rissington, one of the hangars was shared by 2 Squadron, which operated around eighteen Vampire T.11s, and 3 Squadron, which during the late fifties, had a complement of three Canberra T.4s and three or four Meteor T.7s. In addition to their training commitment, CFS were very proud of their long tradition of aerobatic prowess and for several years flew a team of four Meteors, maintaining a tradition started by 203 AFS in the early days. By 1965 though, the need for Meteor QFIs had disappeared, and the CFS strength was down to just one aircraft, which later was maintained purely for display purposes and subsequently teamed up with a Vampire to form the well-known *Vintage Pair* team, which today has no less than three Meteors on strength at the CFS's present Scampton headquarters.

Below: **The Jet Conversion Unit at Binbrook was initiated to convert bomber pilots, used to flying Lincolns etc onto the all-jet Canberra by way of Meteor T.7s and then Meteor F.4s. The unit's F.4s VT142 and VT179, two T.7s including WG942, and Canberra B.2 WD951 were drawn up for inspection in January 1952 when this photograph was taken.** *(Flight 26731s)*

WS757
447
WK663
HX O
WH422
HX S
WG946
Y 72
WK914
H

Opposite page, top to bottom:

The final style of Meteor night-fighter camouflage is shown on this NF.14, WS757, at Little Rissington in August 1960, which belonged to 228 OCU at Leeming. *(Ray Deacon)*

With blackened gun ports from a recent firing exercise, Meteor F.8 WK663 awaits her next pilot at Stradishall. She belongs to 226 OCU, which trained the bulk of Meteor day fighter pilots. *(via M.Fopp)*

Included amongst dozens of Meteors in the Coronation Review at Odiham in June 1953, was T.7 WG946 from 206 AFS, at Oakington. It serves to illustrate the single-letter coding style for flying schools, adopted after the RAF abandoned the three-letter codes in vogue immediately after the war. *(MAP)*

Meteor F.8 WK914 taxies out at Kemble in 1967, on its way back to its unit, the College of Air Warfare at Strubby. After its retirement from active service, '914 reposed on the fire dump at Manston for some time, before being rescued for restoration by the Medway Branch of the Royal Aeronautical Society.
(Ray Deacon)

Above: **During the early sixties, the RAFFC Meteor squadron at Strubby, provided an aerobatic team for several UK air shows, and three of their F.8s are seen here in 1962. They are, top to bottom, WL190, WL181 and WH301, and it is interesting to note that no two aircraft wear the same colour scheme.**
(Crown Copyright PRB 23965)

Another long-term operator of the Meteor was the Royal Air Force Flying College, which had its origins in the Empire Flying School at Hullavington in Wiltshire. This unit began flying Meteors (among many other types), very early in its career, but the severe limitations of the very short runways at Hullavington, together with the crowded airspace in the area, necessitated a move to Manby in Lincolnshire during 1949, coupled with a change of title to the RAF Flying College. The year-long flying course at the RAFFC was for senior officers of the RAF, USAF and Commonwealth air forces who were specially selected and destined for higher responsibilities.

In addition to studying all facets of air operations, students were expected to fly sorties on fighters (Meteors and Vampires), bombers (Lincolns and Canberras) and transports (Hastings) and be able to operate all their appropriate weapon systems etc, using the ranges at Donna Nook and Wainfleet. By 1954, the Meteor F.8 was available on the unit and extensive use was made of it for rocket-firing practice; for most of the Meteor pilots it was their first meeting with an aircraft fitted with an ejection seat, which necessitated additional training on a test-rig at Farnborough. At about this time, it became apparent that many of the officers selected for the course were not in full current flying practice or instrument rated on jet aircraft, so it was decided to form a third squadron at Manby to meet this requirement. Thus in 1955, No.3 (Meteor) Squadron was set-up and immediately moved to the nearby satellite airfield at Strubby to ease the strain on facilities at the home base, before commencing a series of different courses of instruction of varying lengths, to suit the requirements of the customer.

It was not long before the Air Ministry agreed that all senior officers taking up flying appointments after desk-jobs should undertake a rigorous refresher training course at Strubby, and the unit later became known as the School of Refresher Flying. Even foreign air forces used this facility by inter-government agreement and on one occasion in the autumn of 1955, both Israeli and Egyptian pilots were under training simultaneously at Strubby! Needless to say, they were assigned to different flights within the squadron and rarely flew solos on the same day - all aircraft in the squadron flew unarmed! The RAFFC later became the College of Air Warfare, still at the same base, and the refresher flying element at Strubby continued to fly Meteors until the mid-sixties.

Even this was not quite the end for the Meteor in a crew training role. With the availability of surplus NF.14s in the late fifties, supplanted from the operational squadrons by the Javelin, it was decided to use them as navigator trainers, replacing Vampire NF.10s at 2 Air Navigation School at Thorney Island in Hampshire. Known as NF(T).14s, they were operated successfully in this role for several years, being passed on to 1 ANS at Stradishall in early 1962, when the Thorney Island unit went over exclusively to training the 'heavy' navigators in Valettas and Varsities. At Stradishall, the Meteors, supplemented by a few T.7s for pilot conversion, soldiered on until the late autumn of 1965, when they were finally replaced by the Dominie.

The Central Fighter Establishment, although part of Fighter Command, had a vital training role in teaching pilots the tactics necessary to carry out all aspects of air fighting, and was sub-divided into several sections, such as the Air Fighting Development Squadron, The Day Fighter Leaders School and the All Weather Fighter Conversion School. The unit's long association with the Meteor began in 1945, when it received F.3s at its base at Tangmere, subsequently operating every mark of Meteor with the exception of the PR.10 and NF.13 mainly from its more well-known home at West Raynham in Norfolk. Although supplanted by the Hunter and later the Lightning from the late fifties, Meteors continued with the CFE in a communications role, until the time the unit ceased to exist in the early sixties, by which time its remnants were operating from Coltishall.

There were many other units which used the Meteor in an aggressive role, amongst which were the Central Gunnery School (later renamed the Fighter Weapons School), which operated mainly F.4s and F.8s out of Leconfield for many years and the Guided Weapons Development Squadron at Valley in Anglesey, which operated T.7s in a supporting role, but was also briefly involved with the trials of the Fairey Fireflash guided missile, using modified NF.11s, before they were sent out to Woomera.

Below: **At Benson's Battle of Britain display in September 1964, the static display was graced by Meteor NF(T).14 WS797/O from 1 ANS Stradishall, which was just a year away from retiring them. She sports day-glo stripes on nose, engine nacelles and rear fuselage, plus panels on tailplane and under wing.** *(via Roy Bonser)*

Top: A scene from the static line up at RAF Cottesmore's Battle of Britain Open Day on 19 September 1959. Meteor T.7 WL349/Y clearly indicates its allegiance to the Fighter Command Instrument Rating Flight, which it is believed was based at West Raynham. *(C J Salter)*

Middle: In addition to NF(T).14s, 2 ANS at Thorney Island also operated several T.7s, including WL349, seen at Little Rissington in 1962. It carries the school's red diamond markings either side of the roundel. *(R Deacon)*

Above: With the retirement from the front-line squadrons of the NF.14s, several were modified for navigator training as NF(T).14s, and WS744/A was one of ten such examples (coded A to L, less E) in use with 2 ANS at RAF Thorney Island, in August 1961. Of these, K and L were silver/day-glo, but on the others day-glo panels have been added to the standard camouflage pattern; the unit's red diamond markings flank the fuselage roundel and the code was repeated on the nose-wheel door, above the landing light. *(C.J.Salter)*

By 1957, huge numbers of Meteors, especially T.7s and F.8s had been made redundant from the squadrons and from training units, by the advent of more advanced types. Many of the aircraft were fairly new, in fact the last new T.7s and F.8s were only built in 1954, and a major programme was started to up-date the equipment of the many second-line units still operating a motley collection of considerably more aged machinery. One of the most urgent requirements was to provide the RAF with an effective target-tug, and a great many Meteor F.8s were modified to F(TT).8 standard by the addition of a hook incorporated into the ventral tank, which was operated by depressing the camera button on the control column; (quite a number of T.7s were similarly modified).

In this guise, and with a new paint scheme incorporating black and yellow striped undersides to make the aircraft conspicuous to gunners on the ground, the target-tugs served with Armament Practice Schools at Acklington in the UK and Sylt in West Germany, requirements in the Near East being looked after by a unit at Nicosia in Cyprus. In addition, a great many Target Towing Flights were established, where the Meteor replaced such venerable types as the Beaufighter, and several Station Flights within the UK included one or two target-tugs in their inventory. In fact, this model was destined to be the last in regular use in the RAF, when No.1 Tactical Weapons Unit at Brawdy in West Wales, retired its last aircraft in October 1982, the one remaining single-seater (together with a T.7 for continuation training), which was still on strength at that time, being the survivor of what had been a substantial Meteor Flight within 1 TWU's forerunner, 229 OCU at Chivenor - the major Hunter Conversion Unit. It is worth noting, that where a target towing unit was tasked with additional roles, such as airfield defence, the underside stripes were deleted.

The target-towing F.8 was not ideal however, since it was limited to picking up banner targets from the runway before take-off, and jettisoning them over the airfield again before landing, and a more flexible system was fitted to a conversion of the NF.11, known as the TT.20. On this aircraft, a wind-driven winch was mounted on the starboard wing, and a variety of different targets could be carried on a rear fuselage mounting, and let-out and recovered in flight. Although the majority of the TT.20s went to the Royal Navy, several saw service with the RAF, especially with the combined 3/4 CAACU, a civilian manned anti-aircraft co-operation unit at Exeter, which flew the type until it disbanded in 1970.

Photographs on the opposite page:

Top: 'Yankee' and 'Tango' of the Day Fighter Leaders School get smartly airborne from their home base at West Raynham. Neither is camouflaged, but both carry red noses and tails to distinguish them from other elements of the Central Fighter Establishment.
(Crown Copyright photograph, PRB 8813)

Bottom: Meteor NF.14 WS745 was a visitor to Bovingdon in 1958. She belonged to the CFE at West Raynham and had been noted there in August 1957 operating alongside WS751/K and WS722 – the first production NF.14 – possibly coded L. The significance of the 'EC' element of the code is unknown. *(MAP)*

Captions to the photographs on this page:

Top: The Armament Practice School at Sylt operated several Meteors, including this F(TT).8 WL109, which is seen here awaiting scrapping at 33MU Lyneham in 1962, along with others from the unit, including WK988/K, WK740/M, WA926/V and WL121/X. In the background is Meteor T.7 WA609/S ex 228 OCU. *(MAP)*

Above: NF.11 WD767 was the prototype TT.20 conversion, commencing trials with AWA early 1957. It went to the A&AEE in December 1960 and did RADOP trials between 6/62 and 6/67 - probably in conjunction with RAE Llanbedr, where the photograph was taken. To Woomera 1970 and Mildura Air Museum 10.7.75. *(MAP)*

WK986
FC
CS

WE876

Above: **Meteor NF.14 WS777 was last flown by 12 Group Communications Flight at Coltishall. After a spell in store at 33MU it went to Buchan as 7813M and later dumped at Leuchars.** *(MAP)*

Opposite page, top: **The Fighter Command Communications Squadron at Bovingdon had quite an impressive fleet of Meteors, most of them, like F.8 WK986 seen here at Bovingdon's Armed Forces Day event in May 1960, were coded with the unit's initial letters. They were frequently flown by high-ranking officers and thus kept in superb condition.** *(MAP)*

Opposite page, middle: **The Church Fenton Station Flight F.8 WE876, carried the markings of the resident fighter squadrons, 19, 72 and 85 when seen in March 1958.** *(via M.Fopp)*

Opposite page, bottom: **The Bomber Command Communications Squadron was based at Booker, being the nearest RAF airfield to the High Wycombe Headquarters. However, being a fairly small airfield, the Meteor element was detached to nearby Benson, where these two aircraft, WH205 and WL405, both T.7s, were caught by the camera on 25 March 1960.** *(Roger Moore)*

Returning to the arrival of the Vampire T.11s in 1954, the Meteor T.7s ousted by it from the Advanced Flying Schools, were issued to dozens of units both at home and abroad to act as communications aircraft, general 'hacks' for carrying urgent small items of mail and spares etc, and even as VIP transports. There were very few units which did not have at least one Meteor on the strength of its station flight during this period and many were used by the Bomber, Coastal and especially Fighter Command Communications Squadrons based at Booker and Bovingdon in Buckinghamshire. The FCCS started with F.4s in 1947, usually flown by staff officers from the nearby Command HQ at Bentley Priory in Middlesex on visits to the many fighter stations and sector HQs around the country. Both the T.7 and F.8 followed, the latter including at least one example maintained solely for the use of the Commander-in-Chief, and carrying his initials. Towards the end of its existence, in 1960, the FCCS acquired an NF.14.

The Bomber Command unit were the only operators of jet aircraft ever to use the airfield at Booker, which was very close to the HQ at High Wycombe, although the limitations imposed by the only short runway forced the Meteors to move to Benson until they were phased out in favour of the more sedate Anson and Pembroke. The many Group Communication Flights which flew the Meteor also operated from some interesting locations, such as Newton, where 12 GCF happily operated from the grass airfield for several years.

A unique unit in the RAF which also acquired a few Meteor T.7s and F.8s was the Thum Flight at Woodvale on the coast between Blackpool and Liverpool. This used mainly Mosquito and Spitfire aircraft to gather meteorological information for weather forecasting, but with the coming of rather more sophisticated methods of doing the work, was rendered unnecessary and disbanded.

The other major users of the Meteor to be considered are the Air Ministry (later MoD Procurement Executive) establishments at Boscombe Down, Bedford, Farnborough, Pershore and West Freugh, all of which used varying numbers and marks for trials work. Boscombe

Down, under the auspices of the Aeroplane and Armament Experimental Establishment, was naturally involved in the acceptance trials of every mark and modification of the Meteor over a great many years, in addition to carrying out tests with various items of equipment. Similar trials work carried out at other airfields included blind landing experiments at Bedford and radar work at Pershore, which at one stage resulted in an NF.11 being fitted with a TSR.2 nose-cone for work with that aircraft's radar.

By an extraordinary quirk of fate, the very last Meteor in RAE trials use, T.7 XF274, was destroyed in an accident on 14 February 1975, which was very reminiscent of the early troubles with the RAF's training programme on the type. During an asymmetric approach at Farnborough the aircraft started to climb out and banked towards the dead engine. It rotated further into a roll and yawed as it descended, before striking the ground in a cartwheel motion and killing both the crew, one of whom had only recently qualified on the type, with the other being out of current practice.

Also at Farnborough for many years, was the Empire Test Pilots School, which existed to provide service test pilots conversant with all types of flying in all classes of aeroplane, for both the UK and overseas forces. The ETPS acquired its first Meteor, an F.1, in 1945 and went on to fly most marks, not finally retiring its last T.7 until 1965.

Before leaving the Meteor's normal service use, mention should be made of its use within Bomber Command. At the beginning of the 1950s, that Bomber Command suddenly took an enormous technological leap forward, from the Lincolns and Washingtons which had been its mainstay, onto the jet-age Canberra, and they were faced with the situation of having large numbers of bomber crews who were not conversant with jets, and who could not be absorbed into the already fully stretched AFS scheme within Flying Training Command. The short-term solution was to equip a Jet Conversion Unit (also referred to as Jet Conversion Flights or Jet Training Flights) at several of the bomber bases, and thus carry out in-house conversion, there being no-dual control Canberras available at that time. Consequently, T.7s were issued to units at Binbrook, Coningsby, Hemswell and Marham for a fairly brief period, until the initial stumbling block had been overcome.

Opposite page, top: **T.7 WA669 became famous in later years as a member of the 'Vintage Pair', but it belonged to the Handling Squadron at Boscombe Down when it made this visit to Little Rissington in 1966.** *(Ray Deacon)*

Opposite page, middle: **The Empire Test Pilots School at Farnborough used Meteors of several marks over the years, including T.7s WH231/8 and this one WF822, caught by the camera on a visit to Little Rissington in 1965.** *(Ray Deacon)*

Opposite page, bottom: **Many Meteors served as ground instructional airframes and this scene at 10 SoTT Kirkham in Nov 57 is typical. The aircraft are 7139M (WE949/E ex 615 Sqn), 7137M (VZ544/C ex-74 Sqn), 7138M (WH366/V ex 64 Sqn), though in reality they should have been painted as 7319, 7317 and 7318M respectively! As for the intrepid erk . . .** *(Roy Montgomery)*

Below: **The last Meteor flown by the RAE at Farnborough was this smart T.7 XF274, which sadly came to grief there on 14 February 1975. This photograph was taken in 1973.** *(MAP)*

WA669
C
7139M

The Meteor, in common with many other types, saw continued use for many years after its flying days were over, as a ground instructional airframe for the training of mechanics and fitters. As early as 1950, F.3s and F.4s were being allocated for this purpose, and were to be followed by large numbers of F.8s, with a sprinkling of FR.9s and night-fighters in this unglamorous but important task. Their uses varied from being simply hulks for practising airframe repairs, to fully serviceable, but unflown airframes for engine-running and taxying practice. The main users were No 1 School of Technical Training at Halton, No 2 (Cosford), 4 (St Athan), 5 (Locking), 10 (Kirkham) and 12 (Melksham), plus the officers training school at Henlow, which later moved to Cranwell taking a Meteor with it.

These places were a haven for aircraft enthusiasts, with the majority of the long retired aircraft retaining the markings of their last squadrons, many of which had themselves long since ceased to exist. Eventually however, the march of time even overtook the Meteor in this role, and apart from a few examples retained for display at the main gates of RAF stations or with Air Training Corps squadrons, this large fleet went to the scrap-yard in the early sixties.

Other retired aircraft, not required by the training schools, were put into long-term storage at the MUs, notably by 5 MU at Kemble, and 33 MU at Lyneham, the vast majority of these being T.7s and night fighters, with a few single-seaters. With the run-down of the Lyneham unit, its Meteors were gradually pushed outside and scrapped, and were all gone by the time the MU closed permanently in 1966. Kemble however, continued to receive the occasional influx of aircraft, especially around the end of 1969 and 1970, when the last major service users gave up their aircraft as 85 Squadron at Binbrook went over entirely to the Canberra for its target facilities work, and the CAACUs at Exeter and Woodvale disbanded, followed shortly by the Royal Navy TT.20s from Hurn and Hal Far.

Once again, the aircraft mostly went for scrap between 1972 and 1975, but in the latter year several aircraft re-appeared to fly again. All TT.20s, one was sold to a private owner in the United States and flown out via Biggin Hill during June, and five more were flown to France during November and December to act as spares for the small fleet maintained for trials purposes by the Centre d'Essais en Vol at Bretigny - France's equivalent of Boscombe Down. Of the less fortunate aircraft, many were issued to station fire sections for them to practice their skills on, the only items deemed to still be of practical use being the engines, of which a great many were saved for use in mobile snow-blowers, a role in which they still serve today.

Very few Meteors, apart from the Gloster demonstrators, were ever flown in private hands and although today there are plans to restore several examples to flying condition, those that have appeared so far have all been night-fighters.

Below: **The graveyard at 5MU RAF Kemble in 1961, with Meteor NF.14s in various stages of dismemberment. The nearest aircraft is WS833, wearing the markings of its last service user, 72 Squadron at Church Fenton, and behind it can be seen WS743 still in 85 Squadron marks and with a very weathered fin code 'M'. The aircraft coded P was WS724 of 60 Squadron and behind that is another ex-85 Squadron machine WS740 coded K.** *(Ray Deacon)*

Top: **Yet another of the many Meteors put out for scrapping by 33 MU at Lyneham in 1962, was this T.7, WL429, still carrying the familiar RAF College at Cranwell blue band around the rear fuselage.** *(Military Aircraft Photographs)*

Above: **Meteor PR.10 WH570 dismantled at 33 MU Lyneham in 1961. This aircraft last served with 2 TAF Communications Flight at Buckeburg.** *(Military Aircraft Photographs)*

Below: **One of the later clearouts at 33 MU Lyneham, in 1963, produced a number of NF.14s, including WS811/O of 64 Squadron, WS848 of FCCS - the last production aircraft and three 152 Squadron machines: WS735/X, WS783/T and WS789/R.** *(Via David Sargent)*

The prototype NF.14, WM261, was converted from an NF.11 and first flew under its new guise on 23 October 1953. After being used at the A & AEE at Boscombe Down for canopy jettison tests, it was sold to Ferranti at Turnhouse, near Edinburgh, for use as both a flying test-bed for their products, and as a company 'hack' as G-ARCX. In fact they flew it very little, its certificate of airworthiness frequently lapsing and then being renewed for short periods, and it was finally passed on to the Royal Scottish Museum of Flight at East Fortune for display.

Not so fortunate were the other two civilian NF.14s. The first of these was the former WS829, which at one time served with 238 OCU, and was bought by Rolls-Royce at Hucknall as a company run-about and operated by them as G-ASLW, in an attractive blue and white colour scheme for a few years, until bought in mid-1969 by the Target Towing Aircraft Company of Blackbushe in Hampshire. This organisation also bought WS804 from the RAE at Bedford at the same time, and registered it as G-AXNE. Both aircraft were subsequently painted with the titles 'Enterprise Films'.

Thereafter, their fate becomes somewhat obscure, and has been the subject of considerable speculation over the years. On 5 September 1969, both aircraft were flown to Exeter, going on to Bordeaux two days later. By the 23rd of that month, G-AXNE had turned up in Senegal, the other aircraft having apparently ditched somewhere in the Mediterranean. Nothing more is known of the survivor. Today, one NF.11 still flies in private hands in the United States, and another has recently been put back into the air at Hurn. Owned by Mike Carlton, who also has a T.7 awaiting its turn in the restoration queue, WM167 now bears 141 Squadron markings and the civil registration G-LOSM.

Opposite page, top: **An attractive photo of an attractive aeroplane. G-ASLW was an NF.14, which had served with the RAF as WS829, before being bought by Rolls-Royce for use as a communications aircraft at their Hucknall base. It later left the country during 1969 en route for Africa in the hands of another company, and its subsequent fate is unknown.** *(Rolls-Royce HP17169)*

Opposite page, middle: **Destined for a strange fate, NF.14 WS804 of the RAE at Bedford, was operating temporarily from Fairford when this shot was taken in 1966. Three years later it was sold onto the civil market as G-AXNE and was last heard of in Senegal in September 1969 under circumstances shrouded in secrecy. The 'Epner' motif on the nose was presumably acquired following a loan or exchange visit to the French Military Test Pilots School, Ecole du Personnel Navigant d' Essais et de Reception.** *(Ray Deacon)*

Opposite page, bottom: **After service use, T.T.20 WM167 went to the Warbirds Collection. They demodded it to NF.11 standard and restored it to flying condition. It passed to the Brencham collection in mid-84, was promptly registered G-LOSM, painted in 141 Squadron markings and flown for the first time in public at the TV South show at Hurn in August 84.** *(C.J.Salter)*

This page below: **The prototype Meteor NF.14 was WM261, originally built as an NF.11. Its trials over it was sold to Ferranti, registered as G-ARCX, and based at Turnhouse for many years. It is seen here at an RAF Leuchars display and is now in the museum at East Fortune.** *(via Roy Bonser)*

WS804
M
G-LOSM
WM167

Above: **Navalised Meteor F.3 EE387, lands on HMS *Illustrious* during trials in 1948. It can be seen that it has caught the last wire on the deck and is still airborne; another few feet higher on its approach, and the pilot would have had to open up and go round again.** *(Photograph by courtesy of the Fleet Air Arm Museum)*

Below: **Note the 'A' frame arrestor hook on the navalised F.3, EE337. Following extensive modifications to the brakes, engines and undercarriage it was handed over to A & AEE for a series of simulated carrier landing trials. It is seen here during its later service with 778 Squadron at Ford. It was scrapped in 1955.** *(Military Aircraft Photographs)*

5

Naval Meteors

Although the Meteor is, perhaps naturally, remembered primarily as a Royal Air Force aircraft, its not inconsiderable use by the Fleet Air Arm should not be forgotten. The Royal Navy first showed an interest in the type in 1945 when, on 11 August, DG202/G was flown to Abbotsinch, where it was dismantled and taken by lighter to the carrier HMS *Pretoria Castle* in the Firth of Clyde.

For several days, the F.9/40 was used for deck handling trials, after which it was returned to Moreton Valence, the next version to feature in the Navy's use being the F.3. In 1948, Glosters were asked by the Admiralty to prepare Meteors for a programme of test flying from carriers; there is some doubt as to whether two or three aircraft were actually used. At Moreton Valence, EE337 and EE387 (EE317 is quoted as the possible third aircraft), were stripped of armament and all other unnecessary equipment and fitted with Sea Hornet type 'A' frame arrestor hooks under the rear fuselage. Strengthening straps were fitted around the fuselage to take the shock of the arrested landings, and the main undercarriage, which was also strengthened, was refitted without the main doors, since it was thought they might foul the arrestor cables. Finally, the braking system was improved and uprated Derwent 5s were fitted.

Simulated carrier landings were practised at Boscombe Down, followed by a brief period on HMS *Illustrious* and thirty-two landings on HMS *Implacable* between April and June 1948. All landings had to be made with the canopy closed - contrary to normal naval practice - due to the high noise level with it open, and maximum speed during the tests was restricted to 253 knots. Nevertheless, the Navy was well pleased with the Meteor and thought it very easy to handle, but by this time the Supermarine Attacker was being prepared as the service's first jet fighter and the F.3s were passed to second-line

Below: **About to get airborne from Ford's runway 25 in the summer of 1953, is this T.7, WL335 from 702 Squadron. Like so many of its Royal Navy compatriots, it was to end its days in the grand clearout of Brawdy's Meteor graveyard in 1965.** *(MAP)*

training units, with at least one of the aircraft serving with 778 Squadron and later 771 Squadron at Ford and Lee-on-Solent respectively, before going for scrap at Arbroath in 1955.

The first mark of Meteor to see substantial use, and that which was destined to serve in the greatest numbers, was the T.7. With the advent of high performance aircraft like the Attacker, Sea Fury and later Sea Hawk, the Navy was anxious to update its pilot training organisation which unlike today, was entirely separate from the RAF. Consequently, a total of forty-three Meteor T.7s was ordered in 1948, with deliveries commencing that same year to both 702 and 759 Squadrons at Ford and Culdrose, where they were used in a very similar training programme to that being followed by the Advanced Flying Schools in the RAF. In the early stages of its career, the T.7 was also used by 703 Squadron, which was a trials unit based at Ford.

This page, top: **A trio of Royal Navy T.7s, left to right WL336, WS104 and WL353, which do not appear to have been allocated to the same unit, so the formation was possibly mounted by an AHU or the manufacturer.** *(FAA Museum)*

Opposite page top: **This semi-derelict all black T.7 WL353 wears a code within the later range used by the Hal Far based 728 Squadron.'861' sits forlornly in the Navy scrapyard compound at Brawdy in August 1968. Code is in white and under-wing tanks are silver.** *(Barry Lewis)*

Below: **One of Hal Far's duty fire crew inspects 728 Squadron's T.7 WA600/576-HF following an incident which was probably prompted by a faulty nose-wheel. Damage seems slight though and no doubt was quickly repaired and soon flying again.** *(Fleet Air Arm Museum)*

By 1953, Meteor training had been concentrated on 759 Squadron, which had an establishment of fourteen aircraft, and increasing pressure on the facilities and airspace at Culdrose brought about a move to Lossiemouth in Scotland on 30 October. The move was not without incident however, as one of the aircraft failed to arrive and was thought to have ditched somewhere in the Moray Firth. Although the squadron's task continued much as before, it was to be fairly short-lived, for the Navy also adopted the Vampire as its standard training aircraft, and the Meteors were relegated to other duties as required by the various station flights that acquired them.

The majority of the survivors were issued to the various target facilities units as jet conversion and continuation training aircraft, in particular, 728 Squadron at Hal Far in Malta and the civilian-manned Airwork Fleet Requirements Units at St Davids (a satellite of Brawdy), which operated mainly with Sea Hornets and Sea Venoms, and later moved to Hurn near Bournemouth. This unit flew a variety of aircraft, such as Sea Furies, Sea Hawks and Scimitars, but its Meteors outlasted them all, serving right up until the time the unit closed in 1970. As the T.7s were gradually retired during the late '50s and early '60s with the shrinking Fleet Air Arm, they were delivered to the Aircraft Holding Unit at Brawdy for storage and subsequent scrapping in the late summer of 1965.

Below: **Hurn Airwork FRU Meteor T.7 WL350 has had day-glo red areas applied to its nose, 'T' band and engine intakes. She had acquired the code 044 by September 1968 and day-glo red under-wing fuel drop-tanks.** *(via Roy Bonser)*

One mark of Meteor which was used more by the Royal Navy than by any other service, was the TT.20 target-tug. In 1957, Armstrong Whitworth at Bitteswell, received a contract from the Navy to convert surplus RAF NF.11s to the new role, and the first aircraft was handed over to the Admiralty for conversion in May of that year. Ultimately, twenty-five TT.20s were operated, with a further four planned conversions not being proceeded with, as the airframes were found to be unsuitable. The conversion work was carried out not only at Armstrong Whitworth, but also at the Gloster works at Moreton Valence, the Royal Naval Aircraft Yard at Sydenham and the Aircraft Holding Unit at Lossiemouth.

The TT.20 entered service early in 1958, with aircraft going to the Lossiemouth Handling Squadron, which was in fact based at the satellite airfield at Milltown, and 728 Squadron in Malta, which received five aircraft on 26 March. The majority of the type saw service with this unit at one time or another, and it kept them until it disbanded on 31 May 1967. The Hurn FRU also received TT.20s in May 1958 and they became a very familiar sight along the south coast with lime green day-glo and black striped undersides, until the last one was flown away to Kemble for storage on 19 February 1971. One or two were also flown by the station flights at Brawdy and Yeovilton, and most ended their days at Sydenham, where they were cocooned for a year or two before being scrapped. In common with most Navy Meteors, the TT.20 had a remarkably good safety record, only one aircraft being written off during the types thirteen years of service. This was WD711, which whilst serving with 728 Squadron on a night exercise on 14 October 1960, crashed into the sea off the north east coast of Malta.

Undoubtedly the least known Navy Meteors are the U.15 and U.16 drones, which were operated exclusively by 728B Squadron from both Hal Far and Llanbedr, from 1959 to 1961. At least fourteen U.15s and four U.16s are known to have been used, and they were identical to others of their type, apart from the addition of squadron codes on some aircraft. When the Fleet Air Arm left all drone flying in the hands of the RAE, the survivors were returned to Llanbedr.

One further Meteor which had connections with the Royal Navy, although it was never on their charge, was F.4 EE531. After the carrier trials with the F.3s, the Navy briefly considered using the F.4 as a shipboard fighter, and EE531 was sent to Heston Aircraft on 14 August 1946 to be modified for wing-folding experiments, following which it was used for further ground tests unconnected with the Navy.

Opposite page, top: **A nice shot of an Airwork FRU Meteor TT.20, WM159/040, which shows the winch gear beneath the rear fuselage and the small serial presentation.** *(David Sargent)*

Second from top: **WD649/043, another TT.20 of the Hurn-based Airwork FRU, appears to be smartly turned out with silver topsides and black and yellow-cum-lime green undersides. Note the painted radome.** *(David Sargent)*

Third from top: **Black T.7 WL332 was in use with the Hurn FRU in September 1968; along with another black machine, WS103, which had various day-glo red panels. Note the new, as yet unpainted canopy.** *(Barry Lewis)*

Opposite page, bottom: **Meteor TT.20 WD592 spent several years in store following its service use by 728 Squadron at Hal Far. It was sold to a private owner in the USA, and is seen here at Biggin Hill 16.1.75 awaiting the call to depart as N94749 (small regn. on fin)** *(Barry Lewis)*

This page, below: **In the hangar during Brawdy's 1966 Navy Day was T.7 WS104, the code 937 reflecting time spent with Lossiemouth Station Flight. Possibly earmarked for use by Brawdy's S/F, it was standing outside, unused, two years later, in these same marks.** *(Barry Lewis)*

040
ROYAL NAVY

043
ROYAL NAVY
NO SMOKING

ROYAL NAVY
WL332

864
HF
ROYAL NAVY

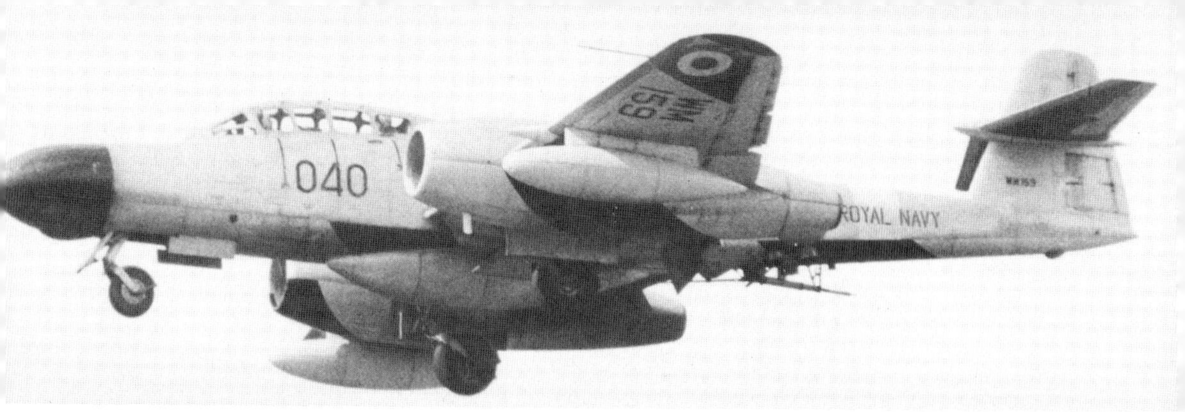

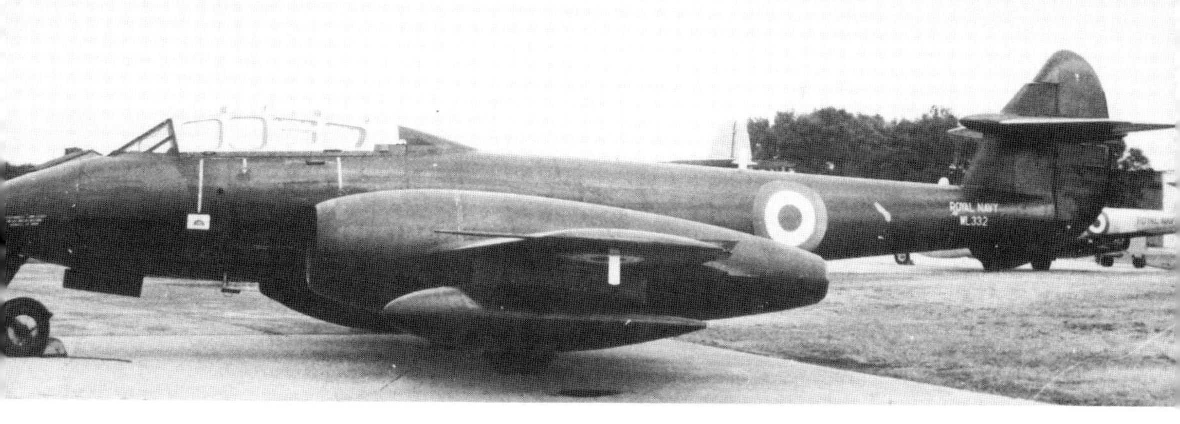

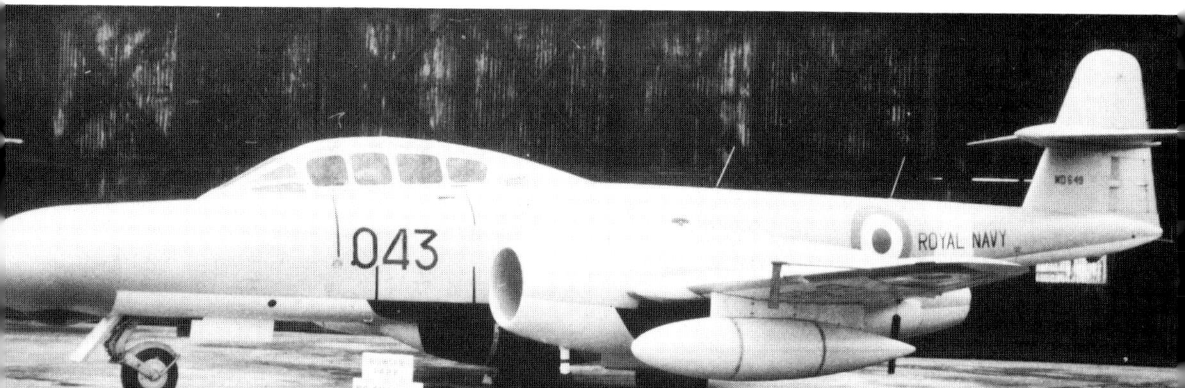

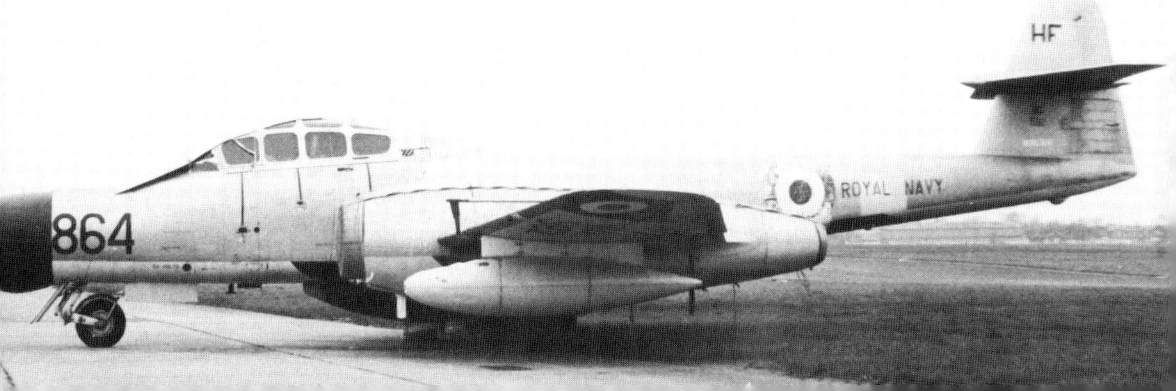

6

Flying Test-Beds

With an aircraft built in such large numbers as the Meteor was, it is not surprising that a great many were used for trials purposes by both the services and industry. Indeed, all the aircraft used for the bewildering array of armament and equipment trials throughout the type's long career, would fill a book on their own. However, the Meteor's use as an engine test-bed, and in ejection seat and missile development, warrants closer examination.

Rolls-Royce 'borrowed' several of the early marks of Meteor for development work on the Derwent, and in later years went on to fit other marks with a wide-range of both centrifugal and axial-flow turbojets, but unique amongst all these aircraft was F.1 EE227, which on 20 September 1945, became the first turbo-propeller aircraft to fly in the world.

EE227 had already seen service with 616 Squadron, after which it was used for a while at Farnborough for stability trials, involving the removal of the top-half of the fin and rudder. Subsequently put back to production standard, it was delivered to Rolls-Royce at Hucknall, near Derby, on 7 March 1945 to have the RB.50 Trent turbo-prop engines installed. The actual engine installation was quite straightforward, although the all-up weight of the aeroplane was increased by just over 2,000 lbs, and the 7 ft 11 ins diameter propellers necessitated increasing the length of the undercarriage to provide adequate ground clearance. All armament was removed and small fins added to the tailplanes to assist with directional stability. The first flight was made from Church Broughton, on the other side of Derby from the Rolls-Royce works, by Eric Greenwood, although the test programme soon moved back to Hucknall. Handling was found to be most unsatisfactory and the aircraft was grounded for a time while solutions were sought. Eventually, cropped propellers of only 4 ft 10½ ins diameter were fitted, together with a smaller diameter jet-pipe to increase thrust, and trials recommenced, including simulated deck landings at Boscombe Down. By the end of October, the Trents were removed, Rolls-Royce having no further need for flight-trials with it, and the aircraft was sent to Farnborough and broken up. *See page 89, colour section.*

By the time the F.4 began to enter service, Rolls were looking at the possibilities of fitting jet engines with afterburners. This system, also referred to as re-heat, entails the fitting of a burner ring in the jet-pipe, downstream from the engine itself, and igniting fuel there to give dramatic increases in thrust, although at the expense of enormously increased fuel consumption. It was first tried on F.4 RA435, which had previously been used for Derwent 5 development, and which first flew with the afterburners in April 1949, later being shown at the SBAC show at Farnborough in that year. The following year, another F.4, VT196, carried on the tests, both with the Derwent 5 and the Derwent 8, and showed some dramatic increases in climb performance, getting to 20,000 feet in three minutes instead of the usual four.

Several Meteor F.4s built in the batch RA473 to RA493, had specially modified centre-sections to facilitate their use as flying test-beds, and two of these, RA490 and RA491, saw extensive use with Rolls-Royce. The first aircraft was fitted with Metropolitan-Vickers F.2/4 Beryl axial-flow turbojets, of the type intended for use on the Saunders-Roe SRA.1 flying-boat fighter, but only managed to fly with these engines twice, since at the end of the second flight the hydraulics failed and the resulting wheels-up landing by Gloster's Bill Waterton severely damaged it.

However, the aircraft was then sent to the National Gas Turbine Establishment, were it was repaired and fitted with a pair of Rolls-Royce Nene engines for a scheme to reduce the aircraft's landing speed by deflecting some of the jet efflux downwards at an angle of sixty degrees to the line of flight. The aircraft was modified by Westland Aircraft, with the Nenes being mounted ahead of the front wing-spar, resulting in a most unusual nose-heavy appearance. To balance any instability this might have caused, an F.8 rear fuselage and tail were fitted, together with PR.10 outer wing panels. The jet deflectors

Top: **Meteor F.4 RA435 was used quite briefly by Rolls-Royce for afterburner experiments, as evidenced by the extended nacelles. It was then returned to standard configuration and normal RAF service.** *(Rolls-Royce H3338)*

Above: **RA490 was an F.4, built specifically for use as a test vehicle, and is seen mounting Nene engines positioned forward of the wing leading edges and fitted with jet blast deflectors. Note the F.8 type tail unit, with finlets on the horizontal stabiliser.** *(via M.Fopp)*

protruded from the bottom of the nacelles, level with the main undercarriage, and tests started at Farnborough in August 1954. It was found that air speeds as low as sixty-five knots could be achieved (a reduction of ten knots on the normal figure), but after many hours flying the idea was dropped, due largely to the weight penalty incurred.

RA491 was delivered by road to Hucknall in November 1948, and fitted with a pair of Avon RA.2 axial-flow turbojets before being returned to Moreton Valence for flight tests. Later, the RA.2s were replaced by RA.3s, and the Avons again demonstrated a dramatic increase in the Meteor's performance, enabling it to climb to 40,000 feet in less than three minutes. After flying a little under one hundred hours with the Avons, RA491 was sold to the French Government for use as a test-bed for the SNECMA Atar engine. Modifications were carried out at Air Service Training at Hamble, and included considerably enlarged nacelles and the substitution of an F.8 front fuselage and cockpit. In this configuration, the aircraft flew again in October 1951.

At the beginning of the fifties, Rolls-Royce were experimenting with expendable turbo-jets for guided missiles and drones, and required a test-bed for the resultant Soar lightweight engine.

Once again, the Meteor fitted the bill, this time in the shape of F.8 WA982 which was delivered from Farnborough to Hucknall in November 1952, and spent the next four months being modified. The engines were mounted at the wing-tips, drawing their fuel from the ventral tank via a pressure system fitted in the wings. In fact, the aircraft flew on Derwent trials for some time, until the Soars were installed in February 1954, the first flight with them being made on the 25th of that month. Although the Soar programme did not, ultimately, progress very far, the Meteor continued to fly with them until the winter of 1956/57, before going to Flight Refuelling for drone conversion, which entailed fitting standard F.8 wings, since the highly modified fuel system was not suitable for the U.16.

Undoubtedly the most heavily modified of all the Rolls-Royce Meteors was VZ608, an FR.9, which was delivered to them in March 1951 and used for Derwent 8 trials before being fitted with afterburners and later thrust reversers for ground tests only. However, in the summer of 1954, it was decided to use the aircraft for flight-testing the RB.108, which was a fairly small engine designed to provide lift thrust for vertical take-off and landing aircraft. For normal flight, the Meteor retained its Derwents, but the main fuel tank bay aft of the cockpit was modified to take a single RB.108, angled at thirty degrees to the line of flight, with provision for titlting fore and aft. Air for the engine was drawn through a dorsal intake behind the cockpit, and the exhaust came through a hole in the area once occupied by the ventral tank.

With all this fuel capacity removed, the Meteor was limited to a maximum of thirty minutes flight time, using permanently attached underwing tanks to feed all three engines. After initial trials, the aircraft was fitted with a replica of the air intake intended for the Short SC.1, the experimental vertical take-off aircraft designed around the RB.108, and flown again from Tangmere in May 1956 prior to being re-delivered to Hucknall, Miles Aircraft at Shoreham having carried out the new work. Naturally, the Meteor could not be taken-off and landed anything but conventionally, the idea simply being to test the operation of the RB.108 in the air. On completion of the tests, the aircraft languished on the dump at Hucknall for some time, until rescued by the Newark Air Museum, with whom it resides today as not only the sole surviving FR.9, but also the only Rolls-Royce test-bed extant.

Opposite page, top: **Sunbathing at Hucknall is Meteor FR.9 VZ608, acquired by Rolls-Royce as a flying test-bed, then heavily modified to accept an RB.108 lift engine in the centre fuselage - note the air intake behind the cockpit. Today this aircraft survives in the Newark Air Museum as the only example of its mark in this country.** *(Rolls-Royce HP.2104)*

Opposite page, lower photograph: **WA982 was the F.8 loaned to Rolls-Royce for flight-testing the Soar expendable engines, which were mounted on the tips of the aircraft's modified wings. When the trials were completed it was passed to Flight Refuelling Limited and converted to a U.16.** *(Rolls-Royce HN.1236)*

Below: **The enormous nacelles on this Meteor F.4 RA491 gave away the presence of Avon turbojets, which made this machine one of the most powerful Meteors to fly. Following its use with Rolls-Royce it was de-modified and sold to France.** *(Rolls-Royce HH.131)*

Another aero-engine company to use Meteors was Armstrong Siddeley Motors, whose flight-test establishment operated out of Bitteswell aerodrome, Leics. In 1953 they acquired an F.8 VZ517, to test their *Screamer* rocket engine. The engine and its liquid-oxygen tank were fitted in a specially strengthened ventral tank, with a wide-cut gasoline fuel tank in the ammunition bay behind the cockpit. As a precaution against overheating of the Meteor's under-fuselage, a stainless-steel heat shield was fitted just aft of the rocket's exhaust.

Another Meteor used by the company was another F.8 WA820, which was in fact the most powerful Meteor ever to fly and was used by Flt Lt Rob Prickett for his F.A.I. confirmed time-to-height records of 31st August 1951. It was fitted with a pair of Sapphire axial-flow turbojets rated at 7,600 lbs thrust each – about double the Meteor's normal power – and to absorb this, required considerable strengthening, especially to the wings.

The company which has used Meteors for far longer than any other is without doubt, Martin-Baker, who first acquired one in November 1945 to test their new ejection seat, which before then had only been tried from the low-speed Boulton Paul Defiant they were operating from Wittering. The Meteor was an F.3, EE416, and work was immediately put in hand to enable it to accept the ejection seats in what amounted to a second cockpit. Using the space originally occupied by the ammunition bay, new bulkheads were fitted, and the fuselage floor strengthened to withstand the loads imposed by the ejection gun; all this work being carried out at Oakley airfield near Thame in Buckinghamshire, in close consultation with Gloster's stress department. On completion, the aircraft was delivered to Martin-Baker's own airfield at nearby Chalgrove in Oxfordshire, and a test ejection was carried out on the ground on 8 June 1946. On 14 June, the first ejection was made in flight (again using a dummy), and several more were made before the first live ejection on 24 July. Carried out by Martin-Baker's own Bernard Lynch, the ejection was perfect, and he subsequently went on to make more than thirty more live tests.

A second F.3, EE415, was also allocated to the company as a photographic chase aircraft, with cameras installed behind the cockpit, but it was little used due to unsatisfactory results, as was EE479, another F.3, which was acquired for seat tests but never completely modified.

In 1952, EE416 was replaced by a T.7, WA634, which was modified in the same way, although this time, the trials seats were fitted in the rear cockpit. With the work completed, the aircraft was sent back to Glosters to have an F.8 style rear fuselage and tail fitted, and subsequently carried out its first test from Chalgrove on 31 August 1953. One of its most significant tests was that carried out on 3 September 1955, when Sqn Ldr John Fifield ejected from the Meteor while it was travelling along the runway at 120 mph. This was using the modified mark 3 seat, which was the first to enable ground-level ejections to be safely carried out.

The next major progression in seat technology brought about the advent of the rocket-assisted model, which again was first tried out from WA634, this time by Sqn Ldr Peter Howard of the Institute of Aviation Medicine, on 13 March 1962, from a height of 250 feet. The following month, the Meteor was retired from active use, and replaced by another, identical model, WA638. The original T.7 was later passed to the museum at RAF St Athan, while WA638 and later still WL419, continued their work at Chalgrove. In fact, both aircraft were still present in 1984, although by this time flying was limited to around two hours a month in WL419.

Perhaps the strangest test Meteor of all was WK935, an F.8 modified by Armstrong Whitworth at Baginton to carry a second pilot lying in the prone position in a greatly extended nose. The idea was that the pilot could better withstand increasing 'g' forces in this position, which would also give the aircraft a smaller cross-section and thus decrease drag. It took two years to modify the Meteor, the first flight taking place on 10 February 1954, after which it was delivered to Farnborough for official trials. It was during this time that the aircraft was flown from the prone-position cockpit by Mark Lambert of 'Flight', who describes it thus:

'You can't eject in any direction lying down. The only way out of the prone Meteor was to slip feet-first off the rear end of the couch and through the floor. One trusted that 'g' would be acting normally at the crucial moment. To depart in a hurry, the pilot first pulled a lever to jettison the ventral fuel tank and to retract the nosewheel, if it was extended. Both would be bad news to a passing body. He was then to pull a plunger to make an hydraulic jack force the leg portion of the couch down into the airstream so that he was hanging over the abyss, so to speak. A final lever under the couch was to release the body to fall out of the aircraft and a long static line would open the parachute'.

'The Meteor's brakes were strictly 1940s vintage and should they show signs of failing, the prone pilot would be uncomfortably close

Above: **The unique prone-pilot Meteor was a conversion of F.8 WK935. After completion of its flight trials it found its way into the Colerne collection, where it was photographed in July 1972. It later spent some time at St.Athan and is now in the care of the Aerospace Museum at Cosford.** *(S.G.Richards)*

Opposite page, bottom: **Seen in the Martin-Baker hangar at Chalgrove in September 1976 is the ex- ETPS and RAE Meteor T.7 WA638. The modifications to the rear cockpit to allow test ejections can clearly be seen, as can the F.8-type tail unit.** *(Author)*

Below: **The best known Martin-Baker Meteor T.7 is WA634, seen at the company airfield at Chalgrove. Here too, the modifications to the rear cockpit area to permit test ejections from the rear seat are evident.** *(via M.Fopp)*

to the ensuing accident. Ditto if the nosewheel failed to extend. In either case, the prone pilot was to manipulate the next-of-kin levers and earn his caterpillar. No-one ever had to try it, but it was a reasonable compromise system under all the circumstances. The Vampire was probably a lot harder to get out of and certainly took a lot of pilots with it on a visit to the sub-soil'.

'To make discomfort absolutely certain, the prone Meteor was not pressurised, and the draughty nosewheel bay formed part of the front cockpit, which made it unbelievably cold in hard weather. Those familiar with the disgracefully crude Meteor T.7 two-seater will vividly remember flying at 40,000 feet in winter with cockpit temperatures around -30°C and a pathetic heater'.

The airborne characteristics of WK935 were compared with the standard F.8:

'Above 20,000 feet' - (in a normal aircraft) -

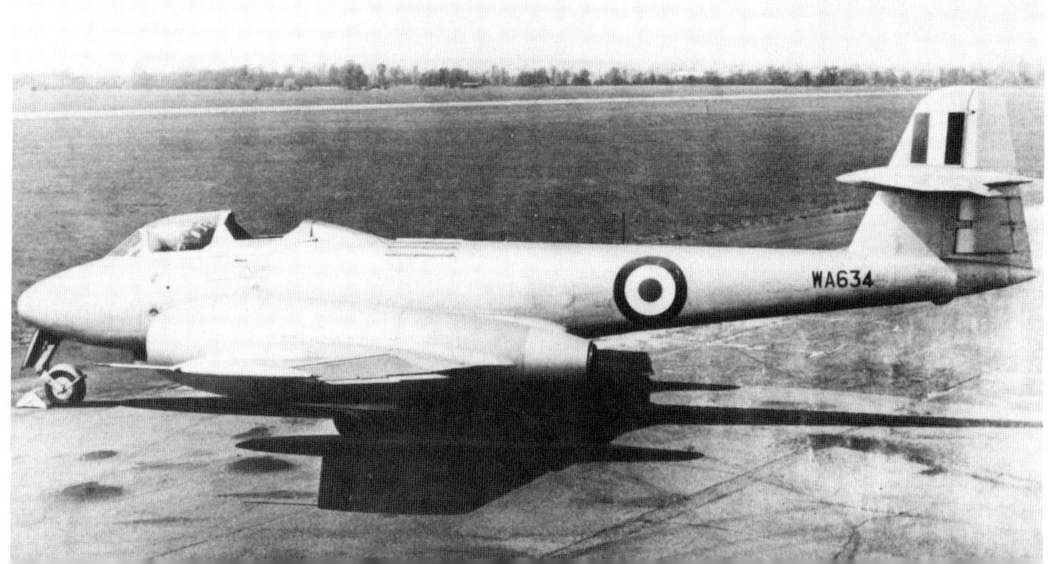

'we usually left the throttles wide open and kept our position in battle formations by playing the cross-over turns and using height. We could not turn very tightly at high altitude and spent most of the time either rumbling and nodding on the edge of the stall or trying to hold off compressibility. At Mach 0·76 the nose would try to rise and by the time we had two hands on the stick to hold it down, 'the Mach' proper would grab hold at around 0·79. The ailerons would twitch violently and the Meteor would rock uncontrollably from side to side and buck hard until we managed to slow down again. Airbrakes and 'g' made it worse. We could improve the turning performance by popping 10° of flap if we could get to the lever at full arm's stretch while pulling several 'g' and move it exactly the right amount'.

'None of this changed significantly in the prone position, except that it was impossible to look sideways, let alone rearwards and that would be fatal for a fighter pilot. I was more relaxed than usual, not having to tense leg and stomach muscles hard whenever the grey-out threatened'.

The arrival of the g-suit, which holds off the effects of tight manoeuvering in a combat aircraft, rendered the prone-pilot experiment invalid, although the Meteor somehow managed to survive and is today another of the Cosford exhibits.

The Meteor also played a small but significant part in the development of the first generation of air-to-air guided missiles. de Havilland, the builders of the Firestreak infra-red homer, used at least two F.8s and one NF.11 from their Hatfield base, mainly testing electronic equipment such as the nose-radar intended for a Firestreak carrying version of the Hawker Hunter. The de Havilland Meteors were all painted in a distinctive black overall colour scheme.

Several NF.11s were also used for live firing trials with the Fairey Fireflash missile, for which they were modified to carry one missile on each wingtip. One or two had the additional electronic equipment housed in modified shape nose radomes and, painted white overall, were sent to the Woomera range in Australia for the bulk of the trials.

Overseas, very few operators of the Meteor used it experimentally, although the French continue to conduct radar tests in their small fleet of NF.11s and NF.14s, and in earlier years, used at least one for trials with the S-600 ramjet engines mounted under the wings, and others as launch vehicles for parachute targets over the Sahara missile ranges.

Below: **Meteor NF.11 WM232 was used by de Havilland Propellers at Hatfield for trials associated with the Firestreak missile, during which it was painted black overall.** *(via M.Fopp)*

Bottom: **The CEV at Bretigny, which is roughly France's equivalent to the A&AEE at Boscombe Down, continues to fly Meteors on a variety of experimental duties. This Meteor NF.11, the first of the batch to be delivered, was seen at Bretigny's Open Day in September 1982, with an interesting nose modification.** *(MAP)*

7

In Foreign Markings

After the end of the Second World War, a market very soon arose for a jet fighter to replace the war-surplus machinery which was being used in large numbers. Surprisingly, although the United States had two excellent machines available in the Lockheed F-80 Shooting Star and the Republic F-84 Thunderjet, they seemed at the time to be more anxious to dispose of the hundreds of P-47 Thunderbolts and P-51 Mustangs which their own forces no longer required. In addition, political pressure prevented the later types being offered abroad.

Glosters were able to step in with the Meteor, and sold many hundreds around the world before the type's approaching obsolesence and the availability of the later Hunter and Sabre in particular, caused the market to dry up for them. The first export customer was the Argentine Republic, which ordered 100 F.4s on 5 May 1947, for £32,800 each. In order to speed delivery, the first fifty aircraft were taken from existing RAF contracts, with the second fifty being started as Argentine machines. They were taken to Argentina by sea, re-assembled and tested by Gloster pilots; the entire fleet were in service by January 1949.

The Meteors were flown mainly by Fighter-Bomber Groups 2 and 3 from Moron air base, and were used by both sides during the 1955 revolution, largely on ground attack missions. By 1956, the Argentine Government was looking for Sabres to replace them, but a lack of finance forced the postponement of these plans, and the Meteors soldiered on in decreasing numbers until at least the end of 1970, when seven aircraft appeared at a flying display. The last aircraft were struck off charge in the second half of 1971 when replaced by Dassault Mirage IIIs.

Shortly after the signing of the Argentine contract, the Netherlands ordered F.4s, eventually receiving thirty-eight of that mark, before progressing to the T.7 and F.8 and becoming Gloster's best customer for the Meteor. In addition twenty-seven ex-RAF F.4s were added to the fleet, which operated from the bases at Twenthe, Soesterberg and Leeuwarden. However, with large numbers of F.8s required, Fokker Aircraft acquired a manufacturing licence from Glosters and built a total of 155 aircraft. All the Dutch Meteors had been replaced in the fighter role by 1956, chiefly by the Hunter, although a few continued in service as target-tugs for a year or two longer, with ten T.7s going to the Naval Air Arm for a time.

Belgium followed a similar approach to the Netherlands with its re-equipment programme, again opting for the Meteor in March 1949, with an order for forty-eight F.4s, all of which were delivered by September of that year. The pattern then continued with large orders for both the T.7 and F.8, and once again, the latter mark was built under licence, this time by Avions Fairey, who produced over two hundred. The fighter wings at Brustem, Bierset, Chievres and Beauvechain flew the type, and after the advent of the Hunter, many were passed to Target Tug Flights.

Belgium also re-equipped its nightfighter force with the Meteor, and bought twenty-four ex-RAF NF.11s in 1957 for use with 10 and 11 Squadrons at Beauvechain. They continued in use until 1959.

Between 1948 and 1974, France acquired a total of sixty-seven Meteors of various marks, beginning with two F.4s, both of which were used as test-beds with the Centre d'Essais en Vol at Bretigny. This establishment, which approximates to the A & AEE at Boscombe Down, also uses the T.7, NF.11, NF.13 and NF.14 in varying numbers, mainly for radio, radar and missile tests and as chase aircraft, and in 1983 they were still flying several NF.11s and the NF.14. All but two of the French aircraft (the exceptions being ex-Syrian T.7s), were ex-RAF, and the six NF.11s bought in 1974, which were actually TT.20s with the towing equipment removed, were the last Meteor exports of all, by a very large margin.

Yet another European country to join the queue for Meteors was Denmark, which signed for twenty F.4s in 1949. These aircraft originally served with the 3rd Air Flotilla of the Danish Naval Air Arm, before it was amalgamated with

Photographs on this page, from top to bottom:

Argentine Meteor F.4 I-065 was one of the new-build examples supplied in 1948. *(MAP)*

I-24 was the fourth F.4 supplied to the Royal Netherlands Air Force, and is seen at Moreton Valence prior to delivery. *(via M.Fopp)*

Preserved R.Neths A.F. Meteor T.7 I-19 seen at Deelen in June 1978, carried a 322 Squadron badge on the rudder. *(S.G.Richards)*

Opposite page photographs, top to bottom:

EF-48 was the last of forty-eight F.4s ordered by the Belgian Air Force in 1949. *(M.Fopp)*

RAF NF.11 WD777 was diverted to the Belgian A.F. as EN-3, coded KT-G of 10Sm. *(M.Fopp)*

Retired Belgian NF.11 EN-18 at Oostende 1958 hoping to be civilianised as OO-ARO. *(D.Gray)*

Belgian F.8 EG-234 sits at Coxyde in '61. *(DMS)*

EN3
G
ND
F
EN 18
EG·234
D

Below: **Forty-one Meteor NF.11s from surplus RAF stocks were supplied to the Armée de l'Air for 30 Escadre, during 1954-55 and were used until the Vautour became available. A small number are still in use today by the CEV for trials and chase duties. In this rare photograph, of the 30 Escadre flight-line at Tours, the aircraft just starting to taxi is coded 30-FB, while next in line is NF11-22/30-FF.** *(ECP Armées)*

Bottom: **Towards the end of 1974, six TT.20s, devoid of winching gear, were purchased from 5MU's store at Kemble, by France, for spares use by their NF.11/NF.14 fleet at Bretigny. The aircraft involved were WD649, WD652, WD780, WM242, WM255 and WM293 and all were flown out using the registration marks F-ZABD. By October 1975 the shells of these aircraft had been sold as scrap.** *(M.Fopp)*

Opposite page, top: The final pair of Syrian F.8s, 418 (right) and 419 (left), formate over southern England on a pre-delivery test-flight. Both had previously been on RAF charge; 418 was ex-WE965 of 609 Sqn and 419 was ex-WH260, of 616 Sqn. In December 1955 they were bought by Glosters for re-sale, going to Flight Refuelling Limited for overhaul and repainting prior to delivery via Le Bourget 7.5.56. *(via M.A.Fopp)*

Above: Danish F.4 472 is being prepared for a pre-delivery test-flight at Moreton Valence in 1950. VZ438 was the first production F.8 and in the background is Egyptian F.4 1401. *(MAP)*

Below: Soon to be on its way to Denmark's 724 Squadron at Karup, is 488, an F.8 parked at Moreton Valence in 1951, in a smart coat of green and grey camouflage. *(MAP)*

This page, from top to bottom:

On a rain-soaked apron at Moreton Valence in 1956, Meteor T.7 1441 awaits delivery to the Egyptian Air Force. Prior to this it had been used by the RAF as WG994. *(M.Fopp)*

The Syrian Air Force bought a total of 19 ex-RAF Meteor F.8s. 109 and 111 are seen here at Moreton Valence in 1953. Note the repeated serial number, in arabic, on both the underwing and belly tanks. *(M.Fopp)*

Three Meteor T.7s from the Danish Air Force conversion unit at Karup, photographed from a fourth. Denmark took delivery of nine T.7s. *(M.Fopp)*

Danish Air Force Meteor NF.11 518, from 723 Squadron at Aalborg on a visit to Bovingdon. The cleanness of the aircraft suggests that it may have been on delivery; in any event, this machine was later converted to TT.20 standard and stripped of its camouflage. *(M.Fopp)*

This page, from top to bottom:

This 1956 photograph clearly illustrates the Israeli practice of censorship. Luckily, the serial 17 – itself at variance with the acknowledged delivery serial range – is visible on the nose-wheel door. The significance of the markings on nose and intake rims is unknown. *(IDF)*

Israeli Meteor F.8 '10' is a further example of post-delivery re-serialling. *(via M.Fopp)*

Israeli Meteor NF.13 '157' was in the museum at Be'er Sheva in the early 'eighties, in really good condition. It too has had a change of serial from the time of delivery in the late 'fifties. *(S.Howe via M.Fopp)*

Australian Meteor F.8s of 77 Squadron taxi out for take-off on an escort mission, providing cover for U.S. bombers, over North Korea. The lead aircraft, A77-616 is piloted by the unit C.O., Sqn Ldr R.C.Cresswell, with A77-559 following close behind. *(RAAF via R.Bonser)*

the Air Force in October 1950. They were followed by comparatively small numbers of the T.7 and F.8, which went to the same station at Karup, and by twenty NF.11s, which went to Aalborg to replace the F.4s in December 1952. They remained in use until 1958, when all but six were scrapped, the survivors being returned to Armstrong Whitworth at Baginton for conversion to TT.20 standard and re-delivery to Denmark, four eventually finding their way onto the Swedish civil register.

The Meteor also found favour in the Middle East, with Egypt selecting it with an order for F.4s in 1948. Twelve aircraft were delivered during 1950, and were later followed by T.7s, F.8s and NF.13s, although not without brief interruptions due to various arms embargoes placed by the British Government, which in fact held down the final number of F.8s to reach Egypt.

Egyptian Meteors fought during the Suez crisis in October and November 1956, with at least two being lost during air battles. All had been withdrawn from use with the advent of Russian types in 1958.

Syria also ordered the type at around the same time as Egypt, although no F.4s were involved. Two T.7s and nineteen F.8s for one squadron, were later followed by two FR.9s and six NF.13s; all the Syrian aircraft being ex-RAF stock. Very little is known of their service use, but again, they were replaced by Russian aircraft in the late fifties.

Sandwiched between these two Arab countries Israel too joined the Meteor club, eventually acquiring thirty-two aircraft comprising T.7s, F.8s, FR.9s and NF.13s, delivered between 1953 and 1958. The T.7s were in fact the first jet aircraft ever used by the Israeli Air Force, and the first three aircraft carried the names *Ben Gurion Sufa* (Storm), *Sa'ar* (gale) and *Barak* (lightning). In addition to the normal training role, the T.7s were also fitted for photo-reconnaissance work and target towing. The F.8s, although primarily intended for ground-attack, for which they were fitted with rocket-rails, also scored several air-to-air combat successes against Egyptian Vampires. On 1 September 1955, a single Meteor shot down two out of a formation of four Vampires which had invaded Israeli airspace from Northern Gaza, and in the following year, during the Sinai Campaign, braces of Vampires were downed on two further occasions. Israeli F.8s were fitted with later M2E ejection seats and locally produced cannons.

After replacement by Dassault Mystères, the Meteors served as operational trainers and target-tugs until well into the sixties, with one NF.13 reported as being airworthy until at least the late seventies.

Despite the Meteor's limited combat success in the Middle East, it is undoubtedly best remembered for its almost legendary war service in Korea with the Royal Australian Air Force. In late 1950, F.8s began to arrive to re-equip 77 Squadron, which at that time was flying the P-51 Mustang from Iwakuni in South Korea as part of the United Nations Forces established when the North invaded the South in June of that year.

Since the Mustang was hopelessly outclassed by the opposing MiG-15, some priority was given to getting the Gloster fighter to the war-zone, and deliveries were made direct to Korea. The squadron officially became operational on them on Friday 4 May 1951, the delay being caused by American insistence that they be fitted with radio altimeters and compasses. Despite doubts expressed in many quarters, it was at first decided to use the Meteor as an interceptor, and its baptism of fire came on 29 August 1951, when eight aircraft were on a sweep over the Chongju area at 35,000 feet. They were engaged by a large number of MiGs which easily out-manoeuvred them, and when the Meteors were finally able to withdraw, one had been shot down, and two others seriously damaged for no loss to the enemy.

A second encounter on 5 September when six Meteors were attacked by twelve MiGs, although not resulting in any losses, proved the British type's unsuitability for the fighter role. It was found that only three gun-firing opportunities had arisen for them throughout the engagement, due to their inferior manoeuvring, and as a result, 77 Squadron was immediately taken off fighter sweeps, its role being changed to B-29 escort and flying combat air patrols. Finally, on 1 December, the Meteor got its revenge, when Flg Off Bruce Gorgerly, flying A77-17, shot down a MiG-15 over Sunchon. In the same combat, another was claimed as a probable, but the squadron lost three Meteors, and were withdrawn from escort and CAP work completely.

When Wing Commander Susans took over command of the squadron in that December, he got official approval to have his Meteors modified for ground-attack work, convinced that this would be its forte. With the necessary underwing rocket and bomb rails fitted, the first such mission was flown on 8 January 1952 and was completely successful. From then on until the ceasefire on 27 July 1953, 77 Squadron ranged far and wide on low-level fighter-bomber and ground attack missions, giving a good account of itself, and even claiming the occasional MiG in air-to-air combat, where the lower levels were more in the Meteor's favour. Nevertheless, losses from ground fire were considerable, and by the

Top of page:
22 (City of Sydney) Squadron RAAF, at Richmond, operated this F.8, A77-855 in 1959. The shot shows the modifications typical of late production and long-serving models, such as the larger diameter air intakes and all-clear canopy. Note the Squadron badge beneath the cockpit. *(RAAF photograph)*

Above right: **These four RAAF Meteor F.8s are believed to belong to 23 (City of Brisbane) Squadron, based at Amberley. The lead aircraft is A77-873, and like the others, a veteran of operations with 77 Squadron in Korea. This particular aircraft was later converted to U.21A standard and was eventually struck off the inventory after it succumbed to a missile on the Woomera ranges.** *(RAAF photograph)*

cessation of hostilities, the squadron had flown 4,836 missions for the loss of thirty-two Meteor pilots. Against that, it could claim the destruction of 1,500 vehicles, sixteen bridges, 3,700 buildings and six enemy aircraft. A little known fact is that a number of Royal Air Force exchange pilots flew missions with the squadron.

In December 1954, 77 Squadron returned to Australia, the aircraft travelling on the carrier HMS *Vengeance.* They joined 78 Wing at Williamstown, which consisted of 75 Squadron with Meteors and Vampires, 76 with Vampires only and 77 still with Meteors. While there, the wing operated an official Meteor aerobatic team, using three aircraft, and known as *The Meteorites.* However, in 1955, Commonwealth Sabres began to re-equip 78 Wing, and the Meteors were passed on to units of the Citizen Air Force (the equivalent to the R.Aux.AF). 22 (City of Sydney) Squadron at Richmond and 23 (City of Brisbane) Squadron at Amberley, operated until declared non-flying units in June 1960, after which the Meteors went the way of so many of their UK counterparts, by largely being converted to U.21 target drones for use at Edinburgh Field in support of the Woomera missile ranges.

The Woomera unit (the Weapons Research Establishment), also operated a great many U.15s shipped out from England, and several TT.20s, but all these retained their RAF identities. One NF.11 was operated by them in full RAAF markings as A77-3, this being scrapped in 1956.

Top: **This Brazilian Meteor F.8 at Santa Cruz in 1971 has clearly been painted as 4399, yet all available sources quote the serial range of the F.8s as 4400 to 4459. Any ideas anyone? Note the underwing rocket rails.** *(MAP)*

Above: **This aircraft is believed to be EE429, the F.4 loaned to the S. African A. F. from 1946 to 1949, and photographed in that country, possibly at Dunnottar.** *(via Roy Bonser)*

Below: **Stylish markings were worn by several of the Brazilian Air Force T.7s, including this 'TF-7' 4301, originally destined for RAF use as WS143, but seen inside the airship hangar at Santa Cruz in 1970.** *(MAP)*

Opposite page, bottom: **After the Ecuadorian Air Force had finally retired its Meteor FR.9s in the mid-'seventies, FF-123 was displayed in the Parque Aeronautica in Quito, where it was photographed in July 1978. The serial suggests that the original batch of 701 to 712 has been renumbered at some point; the badge of Combat Wing 21 appears on the fuselage and that of Escuadrón de Combate 2111 'Aguilas' on the nose, over a smart paint scheme.** *(S.N.Simms)*

Above: **Ecuador received twelve refurbished ex-RAF Meteor FR.9s and based them at Taura; a few were still in use in 1975.'712' was WH555 in RAF service and left the UK on delivery on 19 November 1954.** *(M.Fopp)*

At about the time of the Meteor's finest hour in Korea, Brazil had become sufficiently interested in it to place an order and eventually received ten T.7s and sixty F.8s, which were mainly flown by the 1° Grupo, several surviving in use as 'hacks' well into the sixties. Also in South America, the FR.9 found favour with Ecuador, who bought twelve ex-RAF examples in 1954, for operation by Escuadron de Combate 2111 with some remaining in use until the early seventies.

Apart from these countries which all bought the Meteor for first-line use, several other aquired a few examples for test or trial purposes. As early as February 1944, an F.1 was sent to Muroc AFB on loan to the United States in exchange for a P-59 Airacomet; the aircraft was returned the following year.

1945 also saw New Zealand acquire their sole example, when an F.3 EE395 was sent out to become NZ6001. After a brief flying career, it was relegated to instructional use and survives to this day. The South African Air Force borrowed another F.3 EE429, and kept it for just over three years before returning it to the UK in July 1949.

Several aircraft were loaned to various organisations in Canada, notably for winterisation trials, but 421 Squadron Royal Canadian Air Force, flew two T.7s for a period in 1953, which were supplied by the RAF and eventually returned to them. Two years later, in 1955, the Royal Swedish Air Force ordered three Meteor T.7s for evaluation by the private company, Swedair as target-tugs. One of these aircraft was of particular interest, in that it had originally been built as the private-venture ground-attack fighter G-AMCJ in 1950, before becoming a T.7, G-ANSO, in 1954. *See page 91, colour section.*

The bright yellow T.7s were later joined by four ex-Danish Air Force TT.20s, but all the Meteors had been retired in the late sixties. Two of the TT.20s were overhauled in 1968 and sold to a German firm the following year, but by February 1970 they were up for sale again in Brussels, after which their history became obscure.

WA669

WF791

8

Survivors

When RAF Brawdy retired its two remaining Meteors at the end of October 1982, it brought to an end a service career spanning over thirty years; a figure unsurpassed by any other type of Royal Air Force aircraft. However, despite this, there are still eight airworthy Meteors in Great Britain, with the prospect of at least one more to join them.

Within the Royal Air Force, the *Vintage Pair* display team has maintained a T.7 alongside a Vampire T.11 for many years at Leeming in Yorkshire; the Brawdy aircraft were added to the strength when that station finished with them.

The *Vintage Pair* is actually part of the Examining Wing of the Central Flying School, and moved with them to Scampton, near Lincoln in the early autumn of 1984.

The problems of keeping thirty-plus year old aircraft flying are obviously many, and Chief Technician 'Mal' Myers, who heads the servicing team on the *Vintage Pair,* recently explained both something of his difficulties, and the operating policy which has been developed to keep the machines in the air for as far into the future as possible.

'The team is restricted to performing at fifty shows every year, in addition to which, a certain amount of flying time must also be devoted to necessary aircrew training and post rectification test flying, etc. The airframes are stress limited to a maximum of +2½G and -0.5G, but despite all the care and sparing use of flying time, at the start of the 1984 season, WF791 had used up 99¾% of its total fatigue life, and can obviously only be used for short transit flights and when the need demands. No firm decision has yet been taken on this aeroplane's final fate when the time comes to ground it for good'.

'The other T.7, WA669, which has returned to full use with the team this year, has 5% of its fatigue life remaining, which is, at current rates of utilisation, good for around six more years, although it is hoped that a way can be found to extend this still further. Spare parts are not really too much of a problem at present, although in the long term, we may get into difficulties with the engines'.

'Our third Meteor is F.8 VZ467, which is currently stored at RAF Shawbury. This aircraft has a lot of airframe life left - 16% in fact - but is suffering from corrosion, and this is being treated with a trial hot air system while a decision on its future is thrashed out'.

'As far as other available airframes are concerned, although Llanbedr's T.7, WA662, may yield some spares when it is retired, it too is passed 99% of its life, and will therefore be of very little use to us. The RAE will undoubtedly fly the remaining hours off and dispose of it themselves'.

'The aircraft we really have our eyes on are the two Martin-Baker T.7s, WA638 and WL419, kept at Chalgrove, both of which are only at about half life. Their flying is virtually restricted to what is absolutely necessary to enable the company pilot to keep current on the type, and only one aircraft is maintained in an airworthy state at any one time. It is to be hoped that, once they have sorted out a replacement aircraft for testing their ejection seats, a deal can be struck to bring the Meteors into the care of the *Vintage Pair'*.

On the aircrew side, the *Vintage Pair* Meteors are usually the mount of Sqn Ldr Bruce McDonald, who has flown them for a great many years and displays an obvious affection for his 'Meat-boxes'. It was Squadron Leader MacDonald who took WF791 to Cranwell in March 1983 to celebrate the type's fortieth anniversary by re-enacting the

Opposite page, top: **The 'Vintage Pair' in action. Vampire T.11 XH304 peels away from Meteor T.7 WA669.** *(Air Portraits via S.G.Richards)*

Opposite page, bottom: **'Vintage Pair' Meteor T.7 WF791 has been a popular visitor to a great many displays in recent years, and is seen here parked in the active aircraft area at the 1979 Greenham Common Air Tattoo.** *(D.M.Sargent)*

first flight of the F.9/40. On this occasion, the front seat was occupied by Air Chief Marshal Sir Keith Williamson, the Chief of Air Staff, and among other dignitaries present, was Michael Daunt, who made the first flight all those years ago.

Another station which can still boast three airworthy Meteors, is the Royal Aircraft Establishment at Llanbedr on the west coast of Wales. For some twenty-five years now, Meteor drones have been flown from here in support of missile trials from the Aberporth range, the army range at Ty Croes on Anglesey (now closed) and for RAF fighter squadrons flying on missile practice sorties from Valley. By the beginning of the eighties, the Meteor population was down to five, being further reduced by the destruction of a D.16 on an early trial of the Skyflash missile from an RAF Phantom and then by the passing of the NF.11 to the *Vintage Pair* for spares.

Above: **An open day at RAF Valley in August 1977 brought about a meeting of Brawdy's VZ467/01 and Llanbedr's D.16 WK800. The former aircraft wears the blue/white markings of 615 (County of Surrey 'Churchill's Own') Sqn., Royal Auxiliary Air Force, even though VZ467 did not serve with the unit.** *(S.G.Richards)*

Below left: **The F.9/40 made its first flight from RAF Cranwell on 5 March 1943 and exactly 40 years later, Meteor T.7 WF791 re-enacted the occasion from the same aerodrome, crewed by ACM Sir Keith Williamson and Sqn Ldr Bruce MacDonald.** *(RAF Cranwell 152/83).*

Below: **Sir Keith Williamson was afterwards interviewed in the company of Michael Daunt, who had made the original flight in DG206/G.** *(Crown Copyright, RAF Cranwell, 154/83)*

Above: **The three surviving Llanbedr Meteors bask serenely on the ramp in 1982. T.7 WA662 is flanked by D.16s WH453/L and WK800/Z, which have different intake standards. All Meteor drones had the capability to be flown conventionally, and frequently did so.** *(photograph by RAE Llanbedr)*

Below: **Still looking smart in its red and yellow scheme, D.16 WK800 poses for the camera in 1982. A very historic aeroplane, '800 served the Royal Australian Air Force in Korea as A77-876, was converted to a U.21 and finally returned to the UK as a D.16 in 1971. It is to be hoped that '800 will be preserved when its flying days are over, rather than suffer the ignominious fate of all the other drones.** *(RAE Llanbedr)*

Thus today, just the T.7 and two D.16s remain, and the days of all of them are numbered. The T.7 WA662 is now almost at the end of its fatigue life, and will be disposed of shortly, while the two drones WH453 and WK800 are expected to continue in service for some time yet, before being destroyed. It will be a great shame if neither of them can be saved for preservation to represent Britain's drone programme, especially WK800, which was originally a Royal Australian Air Force machine, and which saw service with 77 Squadron in Korea. In the early part of 1985 this aircraft was still in the throes of a major overhaul and modification programme with Marshalls at Cambridge.

At Chalgrove in Oxfordshire, Martin-Baker still keep a T.7 in flying condition for the occassional ejector seat trial. Currently, WL419 is the flyer, with WA638 used as a source of spares. Both aircraft are heavily modified hybrids, using the space normally occupied by the rear seat for the ejections, and both are fitted with F.8 type tail units. By virtue of its modest performance, the Meteor is now of limited value for such tests, the ultimate plan being to replace the aircraft, possibly with a Canberra.

After one or two false starts, there is now one Meteor flying in private hands again in this country with a second in prospect. At the recent auction of the effects of the Southend aircraft museum, T.7 VZ638 was purchased by Mike Carlton along with a Sea Hawk, and taken to Hurn airport near Bournemouth for restoration to flying condition. It has since been registered to his company, Brencham Ltd, as G-JETM, and before too long will hopefully be gracing the skies again in company with TT.20 WM167, recently purchased from the Warbirds of GB collection at Blackbushe, and now flying again as G-LOSM. *See page 57.*

Apart from the fliers, a great many Meteors survive in aircraft museums and at the entrances to RAF stations throughout the country. Some of the best examples are to be seen at the St Athan museum, which has no less than four aircraft: the air speed record breaking F.4, an ex-Martin-Baker T.7, an F.8 and an NF.14, all beautifully restored. The Newark Air Museum has an F.4, an NF.14 and the sole surviving examples of the FR.9 and NF.12, and the wonderful museum at Duxford has an F.8 and an NF.11/NF.12 hybrid which was rescued from the dump at RAF Bedford and is now resplendent in a fresh coat of night-fighter camouflage. Other museums including Meteors in their collections include those at East Fortune, Hendon, Yeovilton, Lasham, Baginton, Flixton, Sunderland, Torbay, North Weald, Rhoose and of course, Cosford, where the original F.9/40 keeps company with the prone-pilot F.8 and an NF.14. Both the Cosford and St Athan museums are part of the RAF Museum collection.

Among the RAF stations which keep single examples as gate guardians, are Kemble, Odiham and Neatishead with F.8s, Digby, Innsworth, Locking and Quedgeley with T.7s and Carlisle, Ely, Leeming, North Luffenham and Watton with NF.14s. Details of all survivors will be found in the production appendix.

Overseas, Meteors still fly in France and the United States. At Bretigny, near Paris, the CEV maintains a fleet of three NF.11s and an NF.14 for a variety of test purposes. Many of them are heavily modified and seem set for several more years service. The only airworthy Meteor on the American continent is N94749, a TT.20 bought by Al Letcher from Kemble in the summer of 1975, and now based at Mojave and flown in a striking red and white colour scheme.

The Israeli Air Force museum at Be'er Sheva has an NF.13 which is reputed to be maintained in an airworthy condition, but all the other overseas survivors are firmly grounded. Argentina has kept three F.4s at various locations, including one in a museum in Buenos Aires and the other South American survivors are five F.8s in various locations in Brazil. In Europe, Meteors have been preserved by Belgium (five F.8s), Denmark (two F.4s, one T.7, two F.8s and one NF.11), France (one NF.11), Netherlands (one F.4, two T.7s and three F.8s) and Sweden (two T.7s).

Below:
Meteor F.8 WH364 has been restored to its original 601 Squadron, Royal Auxiliary Air Force markings and has been a familiar sight on the gate of RAF Kemble, in Gloucestershire, for many years. This photograph was taken in May 1975. *(Author)*

This page: top to bottom -

Meteor TT.20 WM167, which survived to fly again in 1984 as G-LOSM, was in use by RAE Llanbedr for various trials when photographed in September of 1976. See page 57. *(MAP)*

Sole-surviving Meteor NF.12 WS692 originally served with 72 Sqn, then became 7605M (but wrongly painted as 7065M) at Henlow. It later moved to RAF Cranwell from where it was acquired by the Newark Air Museum. *(John Kyte)*

Meteor F.4 EE531 was kept at Lasham by the RAE for many years before acquisition by the Midland Air Museum for display at Baginton. *(S.G.Richards)*

Meteor NF.14 WS776, in the marks of its first service user, 25 Squadron, has been on the gate at RAF North Luffenham for many years. Photographed in June 1978. *(B.J.White)*

Further afield, one or two T.7s and F.8s are thought to remain in use with the Singapore Air Force as instructional airframes, and New Zealand still has the unique F.3 NZ6001 in an Auckland museum. However, by far the largest collection outside the United Kingdom, is to be found in Australia. The RAAF museum at Point Cook has a T.7 as has the Moorabbin collection. F.8s reside with museums in Camden and Canberra, and TT.20s at Mildura and Queensland. Other aircraft guard the gates at Regents Park, Wagga-Wagga and Williamstown.

Of almost 4,000 Meteors built, just under 120 remain today around the world. Regrettably, no example of the F.1 has survived, despite the great importance of the mark in British aviation history, and of the other marks, the PR.10 and U.15 are extinct. Several aircraft are, even today, in extreme danger of yielding to the scrap merchant's torch or being allowed to pass into limbo in some other way. One of Britain's only four surviving Meteor F.4s is still to be seen rotting at the Defence NBC School at Winterbourne Gunner in Dorset, its owners seemingly oblivious to its historical value and as already mentioned, the D.16 may soon pass into history. The F.3 exists in this country only as a nose section in the Science Museum, and the very last NF.12 was only saved at the eleventh hour by the Newark Air Museum - there is no room for complacency.

See page 93 for colour section photo captions.

Above: **Surviving Belgian Meteor F.8 EG 79 is the gate-guardian at Brustem airfield: codes are S2-R. Note the original-style canopy.** *(Author)*

Below: **Preserved Dutch Meteor F.4 I-69 was photographed at Soesterberg 1976.** *(S.Richards)*

Meteor Photo Album

See page 93 for colour section caption details

WH291
01
VZ467
F
F

SVENSK FLYGTJANST AB
STOCKHOLM
SE-DCC

ROYAL NAVY

747
NF14-747
WD790
ROYAL NAVY

Photo Album

Captions to colour illustrations on pages 89 to 92

Page 89, top: Meteor F.3 EE275/YQ-Q of 616 Squadron, seen at Lubeck in Germany in 1945. This particular aircraft was later passed to 263 Squadron and towards the end of its life, saw service with several training units, before being scrapped in 1955. *(RAF Museum P100278)*

Page 89, bottom: The unique Trent-powered Meteor F.1 EE227, seen in flight with the original large diameter propellers. This aircraft was the first in the world to fly solely on turbo-prop power. *(RAF Museum P100286)*

Page 90, top: A nice shot of 85 Squadron Meteor F.8 WH291 taxying past the tower at Hatfield during the annual open day on 5th July 1969. Note the repetition of the squadron colours on the wing-tips. *(via Roy Bonser)*

Page 90, middle: Meteor F.8 VZ467 has had a long and varied career, and by the late 'sixties, was towing targets for 229 OCU at Chivenor. They took it with them when they moved to Brawdy to become 1 TWU, and soon had it re-camouflaged and put in 615 Squadron markings (with whom it actually never served). Known affectionately as *Winston,* '467 was finally retired in October 1982, along with Brawdy's T.7 WA669 *Clementine,* and both aircraft were flown to Leeming to join the 'Vintage Pair' fleet. *(Author)*

Page 90, bottom: RAE Llanbedr Meteor U.16s are a comparatively rare sight, but the station can usually be relied on to provide an example for the static park at the neighbouring RAF Valley open day. WA991/F attended one such event in the mid-'seventies. *(S. G. Richards)*

Page 91, top: SE-DDC was originally built as the Ground Attack Fighter G-7-1, then converted to the company demonstrator T.7 G-ANSO before being sold to Swedair. It now resides in a museum at Ugglarp. *(via R. Bonser)*

Page 91, middle: Royal Navy Meteor T.7 WS103 was in use with the Airwork FRU when photographed at Hurn in July 1969.

Page 91, bottom: Meteor T.7 WF816 survived as a squadron 'hack' with 23 Squadron at Leuchars until well into the 'sixties, finally ending its days with the Manston Fire School. *(via Roy Bonser)*

Opposite page, top: Originally built for and issued to the RAF as WS747, this Meteor NF.14 served with 264 Squadron prior to overhaul and sale to France for use by their CEV, a research establishment akin to the British A & AEE. It was photographed in September 1982 and is thought to be still in use. *(via John Grech)*

Opposite page, middle: The Radar Research Establishment at Pershore used the hybrid WD790 for a variety of trials, including testing the radar intended for the TSR.2, hence the odd nose radome. It still belonged to them when photographed at Wittering in August 1974, and later spent time at Llanbedr and Bedford, before being broken-up at Leeming to keep the 'Vintage Pair' aircraft going. *(Author)*

Opposite page, bottom: This uncoded Meteor TT.20 WD780 of the Airwork FRU was in use at Hurn on 25th July 1969. *(Barry Lewis)*

Immediately below: EE307 was quite an early F.3 and was photographed at Finningley in about 1947. The 'RAW' code letters denote its use by 616 Squadron. *(via S.G.Richards)*

EE457

UB J

A6 B
RA444

Early Birds

Captions to photographs on opposite page:

Top: **A delightful study of Meteor F.3 EE457, which was kept by Glosters for a while, before being issued to 222 Squadron who wrote it off in October 1947.** *(Chas E. Brown via R. Bonser)*

Middle, upper left: **63 Squadron re-equipped with Meteor F.4s in June 1948. One of its old F.3s, EE384, was sent to Cardington for ground trials to investigate the effects of jet-blast on various different surfaces. It still carried codes UB-J in October 1949.** *(Ron Clarke)*

Middle, lower left: **An anonymous F.4 guarding RAF Hornchurch. It is in fact VW790, which had served with the RAE at Farnborough; it was later given to an ATC unit at Benfleet when Hornchurch closed down.** *(MAP)*

Middle, upper right: **No. 1 SoTT at Halton, acquired this F.3 just after Christmas 1954, and changed its serial from EE339 to 7166M. Four years later it appeared to have outlived its usefulness in that humble role.** *(A. Thorpe)*

Middle, lower right: **The markings adopted by 611 (West Lancashire) Squadron, R.Aux.A.F, for their Meteors, were red and yellow segmented diamonds on a black background, and they are shown here to advantage on a retired F.4, painted as 'M7221'. The true identity of this aircraft is RA449, which was sent to 8 School of Technical Training at Weeton, Lancs, in June 1955 to eventually guard the gate. Allocated the maintenance serial 7221M, this machine never actually served with 611 Squadron, but was doubtless painted in their marks due to the local association. The photo was taken on 15 November 1962.** *(Ron Clarke)*

Bottom: **F.4 RA444 of 257 Squadron, up from Horsham St. Faith on 22 June 1948. On the nose it bears the unit's emblem of a Burmese chinthe.** *(Crown Copyright: PRB R1586)*

This page, top: **74 Squadron pilots pose for the camera with their F.4s, at Horsham St. Faith near Norwich in the late 'forties. The Squadron's tiger head emblem appears on the extreme nose, and the second aircraft has blackened cannon ports, a sure sign of recent gun firing.** *(D. Todd)*

This page, top: After serving the CFE, RA476 was taken on charge by the Exhibition Pool at Olympia 31.5.49 and in this connection is seen here as part of a Battle of Britain Exhibition in Horse Guards Parade, London in 1954. It was allocated the maintenance airframe serial 7361M on 18 June 1956. *(via David M. Sargent)*

This page, below: A curious mixture of roundel styles are displayed on this F.4, VW261, which belongs to 609 Squadron, R.Aux.A.F., based at Church Fenton. She carries the squadron badge on the engine cowlings, and yellow crosses on a blue rectangle each side of the fuselage roundel. After later service with various Advanced Flying Schools, '261 was destroyed in a flying accident on 3 December 1953. 609 Squadron operated F.4s alongside their F.8s, for just a few months in 1951. *(Philip Murton)*

Opposite page, top: Bearing the yellow and black checks of 63 Squadron from Thorney Island, is Meteor F.4 VT242, photographed in 1950 shortly before the unit re-equipped with the F.8 and moved to Waterbeach. *(MAP)*

Opposite, second from top: The final service user of F.4 VT229, was 209 AFS at Weston Zoyland, from where it was struck off charge in April 1954. After a spell in the museum at Colerne and then a lengthy period in the open at Duxford, it later passed into the care of the Newark Air Museum. *(Roy Bonser)*

Opposite, third from top: A line-up of F.4s belonging to 1 Squadron and headed by VT265, which survived longer than most of its mark, to see R.Aux.A.F. and AFS service. *(Roy Bonser)*

Opposite, bottom: An F.3 belonging to 500 Squadron at West Malling displays the four-letter codes popular in the early post-war years. The photo was taken in 1950. *(via Ron Clarke)*

VT265

EE420
B-RAA

Sevens

This page, top: **T.7 VW422 proudly displays the bordered rectangles of 25 Squadron, at a time when the unit was operating Meteor NF.12/14s.** *(via David M. Sargent)*

This page, bottom: **611 Squadron's Meteor T.7, WA718, is well sealed and wrapped against the elements at 12 MU Kirkbride. More fortunate than most of that unit's inmates, it was later returned to active service and was not finally retired until 1968.** *(MAP)*

Opposite page, top: **This smart T.7 VZ637/P proudly bears the blue rectangles with red lightning flash marking of 502 (Ulster) Squadron Royal Auxiliary Air Force, a Vampire-equipped unit. Also on the nose is the squadron badge.** *(MAP via David M. Sargent)*

Middle, upper left: **WG987/T-Z was used by 79 Squadron, at a time when its main equipment was Meteor FR.9s.** *(MAP via David M. Sargent)*

Middle, upper right: **WH127 was employed by no less than nine different service units before finally being soc in October '63. It is seen here in 610 (County of Chester) Squadron, Royal Auxiliary Air Force colours. Note the wing tips too.** *(I. G. Stott, via C. J. Salter)*

Middle, lower left and right: **WA612 in two guises –** *left,* **on New Years Day in 1954, wearing the colours and code Z, of 63 Squadron at Waterbeach** *(H. Orme),* **and** *right,* **a few years later, it is in use by 111 Squadron, at a time when they were better known as 'The Black Arrows'.** *(MAP via David M. Sargent)*

Opposite page, bottom: **Camouflaged Meteor T.7s were rare, and WL380 was first issued to Horsham St. Faith's-based 74 Squadron, whose black and yellow markings adorn.** *(via M. Fopp)*

P
VZ637

T Z

L

S
WA612

WA733
Q
WF769
XA825
WC979
WA659

Opposite page, top: WA733, clearly in the 66 Squadron markings of the period, at Acklington in 1960. Curiously, the record card for '733 makes no mention of service with this unit or Acklington Station Flight, so it may have been 'borrowed', with no official transfer taking place. *(Military Aircraft Photographs)*

Opposite, second from top: WF769/Q was a fore-runner to WA733 (above). It too, served the Hunter-equipped 66 Squadron, but was SOC in 1958. *(MAP, via David M. Sargent)*

Opposite, third from top: Another squadron 'hack' was 64 Squadron's WG979. It was used when the unit operated Javelins from Duxford, but was scrapped in 1962. *(via David M. Sargent)*

Opposite, bottom: WA659 is wearing 33 Squadron markings and is thought to have been in use during the unit's early days with the Javelin. 33 operated FAW.7s, but note that it is a T.3 in the background. *(via David M. Sargent)*

This page, top: A very rare photograph of a Meteor T.7 attached to 234 Squadron – a Sabre squadron at Oldenburg in Germany. The aircraft is probably VW485 and carries their black and red markings. *(RAF Museum P10182)*

This page, bottom: Typical of many Station Flight Meteors, is this one from Leuchars, positioned in that base's static display for the 1958 Battle of Britain Day show, (20.9.58). It has the standard silver finish with yellow bands around the rear fuselage and over the wings, plus the addition of black and yellow target-tug stripes underneath. The squadron markings are those of the two units resident at Leuchars at that time, 43 and 151. *(David Gray)*

WL403
O K
WH186
72
WL468

Opposite page, top: **WL403 passed to the CFS after service with 215 AFS and 8 FTS. It is painted in the early silver and yellow trainer-band scheme.** *(MAP via David M. Sargent)*

Opposite page, middle: **In the static aircraft park at Abingdon's 1961 Battle of Britain display, is Meteor T.7 WH186 from 5 FTS at Oakington. She is in the latter-day scheme for her breed of silver with large day-glo patches on nose, tail and wings.** *(MAP)*

Opposite page, bottom: **T.7 WL468 belonged to the RAE at Farnborough when this photo was taken. She has 'day-glo' red applied to the nose, rear fuselage and fin, wing tips and wing leading edges and is unusual in having yellow/black target-towing stripes on the under surfaces.** *(via Roy Bonser)*

Above: **By contrast with the photo at the top of the opposite page, WH166 was wearing a later CFS scheme when seen at its Little Rissington base in 1965. The aircraft flew until September 1969, when it was retired to RAF Digby to guard the gate.** *(Ray Deacon)*

Below: **In 1973, near the end of its service career, Chivenor's 229 OCU T.7 WL349 was decorated with 28 Squadron markings. It is seen here in August 1974, in storage at 5 MU Kemble – having been grounded the previous January. Note the code 'Z' on the nose-wheel door. It survived to be preserved at Staverton Airport.** *(Barry Lewis)*

Hybrids

VW411 was a hybrid Meteor: a basic T.7 with an F.8 tail unit and an FR.9 nose. It was used by various government establishments. The top photograph *(MAP)* **was taken at Cranfield, in 1964 and it appears to have an overall (light?) blue scheme; whereas, at the Gaydon Battle of Britain show on 17 September 1966, it had a Royal Blue scheme with white outline to roundels and fin flash. The Scorpion motif on the fin is thought to be that of the Royal Netherlands Air Force base at Soesterberg – possibly acquired as a result of a trials visit.** *(C. J. Salter)*

Left:
WL405 is a T.7 with an FR.9 nose, an inscription 'Royal Aircraft Establishment' and badge on front fuselage, plus day-glo areas on an otherwise overall silver paint scheme. *(via Keith Woodcock)*

Eights

Opposite page, bottom: **Another T.7 with FR.9 nose was WA690. It had an A&AEE Boscombe Down inscription on the fuselage top and an emblem on the fin, when visiting Little Rissington 1965.** *(Ray Deacon)*

The early 'fifties saw the introduction of the F.8s in large numbers, to both front line and auxiliary units. Examples are: *Top:* **WA780/G of 66 Squadron circa 1953** *(via K.Woodcock);* *Middle left:* **WH505 of 611 (County of Lancaster) Sqn, R.Aux.A.F. still fitted with the early canopy.** *(via D.M.Sargent)* *Bottom:* **WK673 used solely by 54 Sqn.** *(MAP, via D.M.Sargent)*

Below: **Two Meteor F.8s from Nicosia Station Flight at 35,000 feet over Ethiopia, during a non-stop flight from Khartoum to Aden in 1953, – one of them is WK946.** *(via M.Fopp)*

Above: 616 Squadron, which had pioneered the introduction of the Meteor, operated F.8s between 1951 and 1957. WH456/L only saw service with 616, and was eventually consigned to scrap in May 1958. *(MAP, via D.M. Sargent)*

Below: A few Meteor F.8s were used as 'hacks' by squadrons that flew more advanced machines. WH450, which was on view at the West Malling Battle of Britain show in September 1956, displayed obvious allegiance to 153 Squadron, who were flying Meteor NF.12s/NF.14s at the time. *(Military Aircraft Photographs)*

Opposite, bottom: Finally, another hack was WK941 of 33 Squadron, which almost certainly served the unit during its brief Meteor night-fighter era at Leeming from September 1957 to July 1958. *(via David M. Sargent)*

Opposite page, top: It is thought that this 66 Squadron 'hack', WH512/U, was active around 1957; a time when 66 was equipped with Hunter F.6s at Acklington. The T.7 in the background, VW487, was allocated to 29 Squadron for a time, which, coincidentally, flew Meteor night-fighters, from Acklington, during this period. *(MAP, via David M. Sargent)*

Opposite, second from top: This photograph of 1 Squadron F.8s WL176/P and WH288/S was taken very late in their Meteor era; probably in 1954 or '55 – note the glossy camouflage and white centres to the red-outlined fuselage bands. This Tangmere unit fully converted to Hunter 5s by the end of July'55. *(via David M.Sargent)*

Opposite, third from top: Following the closure of the Advanced Flying Schools, the Meteor did not see particularly widespread service with the Flying Training Schools. However, WA763/18 was one of the fair-sized fleet operated for a while by 4FTS from Worksop, Notts. *(M. Fopp)*

U
WH512

18
WA763

WK941

Above: Meteor F(TT).8 WA963/D was taken on charge by No.1 SoTT, Halton, in March 1956. It wears the marks of the Armament Practice Station at Acklington. Note the paint scheme on the tailplane and wing-tips. The serial has been lined through and 7321M applied – the latter conflicts with the 'M' serial quoted in the production history. *(David M. Sargent)*

Below: 12 MU Kirkbride in April 1958 and Meteor F.8 WF661/G, late of 609 Squadron at Church Fenton, points its tail to the sky after removal of its nose undercarriage. Keeping it company are three of its old squadron compatriots, including WE871/E. *(David Gray)*

Opposite page, top: Several ex R.Aux.A.F. machines found temporary homes with RAF training schools. 7294M, ex WF759/U of 600 Squadron was photographed at Halton on 14 September 1957. *(via David M. Sargent)*

Opposite, second from top: The arrival of the Hunters ousted the Meteor from front-line service. Many were immediately scrapped but Biggin-Hill-based 41 Squadron's WL112/M found temporary refuge at No.1 SoTT, Halton, as 7259M. *(via David M. Sargent)*

Opposite, third from top: Another 12MU scene and R.Aux.A.F. casualty WA776/S awaits the breakers torch in April 1958. Last flown by 610 Squadron from Hooton Park, it still bears their black and white markings on both the fuselage side and the wing-tips. *(David Gray)*

Opposite page, bottom: After service with front-line units, WH443 was used for 'hack' duties by the NF.12/14 equipped 25 Squadron. W/o in January 1956, it found its way to the Civil Defence Training Centre at Falfield, Glos., where it was snapped in June '68. *(D.M.Sargent)*

U

M

M
S
WA776

A

Top: Some F.8s soldiered on, despite the arrival of superior machines for first-line duties. WH404, although officially on charge to 25 Squadron, was displayed at the Sculthorpe Armed Forces Day event on 16 May 1959, wearing the station badge and initials of the RAF Waterbeach C.O., Gp Cpt J. G. Topham, DSO, OBE, DFC & Bar. *(C. J. Salter)*

Below: F.8 WL166 taxies out from Kemble's apron on a late winter's afternoon in 1962, on her way back to the RAF Flying College at Strubby. By contrast with the photograph at the foot of the opposite page, she has large day-glo areas over glossy camouflage finish. *(Ray Deacon)*

Opposite page, top: Another development in the late 'fifties was the formation of 'TT' flights at most of the front-line fighter bases. F(TT).8 VZ521/3 was officially on the books of the Hunter F.6 equipped and Church Fenton based, 19 Squadron, but is thought in practice to have been in the care of the Station's Target Towing Flight, circa 1958. *(MAP, via David M. Sargent)*

Opposite, second from top: F(TT).8 WK817/2 was officially assigned to Leconfield Station Flight around 1960, when 19 Squadron were using Hunter F.6s and 72 Squadron had Javelin FAW.4/5s. *(MAP, via David M. Sargent)*

Opposite, third from top: At Waterbeach, Target Facility duties for the co-located 25 Squadron Meteor NF.12/14s and 56 Squadron Hunters were undertaken by a number of F(TT).8 coded in the range T1 to T6. WK918/T1 was, strictly speaking, on 25 Squadron's books. Circa late 1958. *(MAP, via D. M. Sargent)*

Opposite, bottom: Strubby was something of a 'Mecca' for Meteor buffs. This nicely turned-out F.8 WK712, is thought to have been in use by the Jet Refresher Squadron, when photographed in July '60. *(I. W. O'Neill via D. Sargent)*

3
VZ521
2
WK817
WK712

Above: Meteor F.8 WL108 is thought to have been 'hacked' around by 1 Squadron from Wattisham circa 1962/63. Note the fuselage and nose markings. *(MAP, via D. M. Sargent)*

Below: WH286/A seen in F(TT).8 guise, belonged to 229 OCU at Chivenor at the time of the August 1969 Open Day. It has a Light Grey top with day-glo stripes and panels on fuselage and wing and tailplane, plus black/yellow striped undersides. It went on to become the final D.16 conversion in May 1972, though, not surprisingly, it has not survived. *(Author)*

Opposite page, top: 85 Squadron operated as a Target Facilities unit between 1963 and 1970, most of the time from Binbrook. Here WK654/X is on the approach to its base in July 1967 – the black/red unit marks clearly displayed. The style of the 'W' in the serial would suggest a local re-paint job at some stage. *(D. M. Sargent)*

Opposite, second from top: A Wednesday afternoon at Middleton St. George in August 1960, and F.8 WL130 gives away no clues as to the identity of its operator. Officially on the books of the Javelin-equipped 33 Squadron, it actually operated from the Station Flight hangar along with T.7 WF813. *(C. J. Salter)*

Opposite, third from top: WE876, an F(TT).8 of 1574 Flight in Singapore, displays the black tail carried by that unit at the time leading up to its disbandment. *(MAP, via David M. Sargent)*

Opposite, bottom: 5 CAACU operated a small fleet of Meteors from Woodvale, and although F.8 WH453 is reported to have been coded 'L' at some stage during its career with this unit, it was not evident when this photograph was taken, in September 1969. *(Barry Lewis)*

WK654
WL130
WE876

Y
VS975
A N

Nines

Above: When the Fighter Reconnaissance Flight at Khormaksar gave up its Meteors, this FR.9, WH546, was put on display inside the camp area. It eventually became an instructional airframe in 1963 before passing out of the RAF's hands. *(Ray Deacon)*

Opposite page, top: Meteor FR.9 VZ603 displays the markings of 79 Squadron, and from the pennant below the cockpit, was evidently the squadron commander's favoured mount. *(MAP, via David M. Sargent)*

Opposite, second from top: FR.9 of 8 Squadron, at rest at Khormaksar in 1958. *(MAP)*

Tens

Opposite, third from top: Meteor PR.10 VS975/A-N from 541 Squadron, RAF Germany on a visit to Benson. She carries the original camouflage of Light Grey upper surfaces and Cerulean Blue under surfaces. *(I. W. O'Neill via D. Sargent)*

Opposite, bottom: This PR.10, WB167, seen during 1956, was destined never to see any squadron service. After spending several years in storage at various MUs, it was allocated to the Far East Air Force, but again put into storage on arrival and eventually scrapped in March 1960, with what must have been very few hours 'on the clock' indeed. *(MAP)*

This page, below: Plugged in to the 'trolley-acc' and ready to go at Tengah at the end of 1960 is 81 Squadron PR.10 WB166. *(Roy Montgomery)*

Elevens

Above: The second prototype Meteor NF.11 was WA547. *(MAP, via David M.Sargent)*

This page, below: The first unit to receive NF.11s was 29 Squadron at Tangmere in August 1951. This rare shot shows WD792/U in 29's famous 'XXX' marks and unit badge under the cockpit, probably taken at a 1956 Battle of Britain event. *(D. C. Davis via D. M. Sargent)*

Opposite page: Following the formation of four UK-based squadrons in 1951, deliveries commenced to 2nd TAF units, 68 and 87 Squadrons at Wahn in March 1952, and 96 and 256 Squadrons in the Autumn of that year.

Opposite, top: WD680/B served 68 Squadron faithfully until consigned to scrap in November 1958. *(via David M. Sargent)*

Opposite, second from top: WD673/F of 87 Squadron poses for a standard side-on photo. *(MAP via David M. Sargent)*

Opposite, third from top: Ahlhorn-based WD784 displays 96 Squadron marks and code 'F', though it is believed to have once been coded 'L-F'. It was eventually scrapped in February 1959. *(via David M. Sargent)*

Opposite, bottom: WD585 was the first production NF.11 and after use by the CFE went to 256 Squadron as 'B'. It is seen here landing at Aalborg in Denmark on a visit from its base at Ahlhorn — the fin bullet is painted red. '585 would later become a TT.20 in the hands of the Royal Navy. *(RAF Museum P9482)*

B
WD680

F
WD673

F

A
WM152

WD791

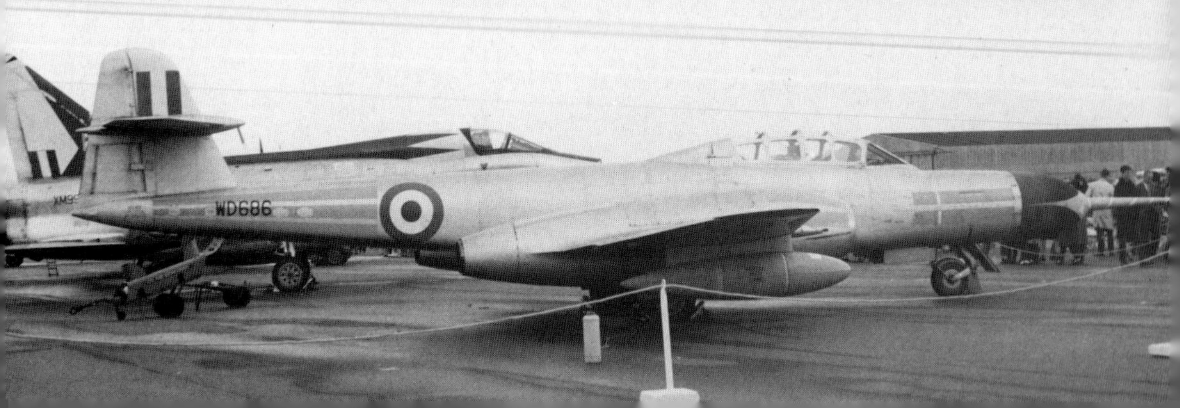
WD686

In January 1959, 5 and 11 Squadrons, in 2 TAF were the last units to be equipped with the NF.11. Fifteen months later they were superceded by Javelins and most made their way back to the UK for scrapping.

This page, above: 11 Squadron's WM238/Y avoided the axe for a while and did a stint as a static test airframe at AWA's Whitley plant. *(I. W. O'Neill, via David M. Sargent)*

Opposite, third down: WD791, modded to NF.12 standard, was on MoS charge, operated by Ferranti and from the TRE at Defford when she visited Bovingdon. *(MAP)*

Opposite page top: 5 Squadron NF.11 WD752/H was at Hullavington 15 July 1961, and WD771 with 11 Squadron fuselage marks can be seen in the background. *(Robin Forbes)*

Opposite bottom: WD686, complete with long nose probe, was shown statically at Cottesmore's Battle of Britain show in September 1965. It was said to be from RAE Bedford, who operated from Thurleigh. *(Barry Lewis)*

Opposite, second down: 228 OCU at Leeming converted a lot of the night fighter crews, Its work done, WM142/A sits it out awaiting the scrapman probably at Lyneham. *(MAP, via DMS)*

This page, bottom: The Empire Test Pilots School at Farnborough operated a number of NF.11s including WD769/1 and this one, WD765/5. *(MAP, via David M. Sargent)*

WD687
WS700
D
WS806
WS729

Twelves

Opposite page, top: **WD687 was built as an NF.11, modded to NF.12 standard and spent all its active life at the A & AEE Boscombe Down, before retiring to the Fire School at Stansted, where it was photographed in October 1961.** *(C. J. Salter)*

Opposite, second from top: **72 Squadron operated a mixture of NF.12/14s at Church Fenton from February 1956 until mid-1959, but WS700/D was lost in 1958 in a mid-air collision with WS782.** *(MAP via D. Sargent)*

Thirteens

This page, top: **39 Squadron NF.13 WM322/A on short finals to land at its Luqa, Malta base, in the mid-'fifties.** *(Author's collection)*

Fourteens

Opposite, third from top: **264 Squadron received a mix of NF.12/14s at Linton in October 1954 and they flew them until renumbered 33 Squadron in 1957. 264's WS806/D, is featured, but in the background is an NF.14 coded 'HMT', which was flown by 264's CO, Sqn Ldr H.M.H. Tudor.** *(MAP via David M. Sargent)*

Bottom, left: **WS729/A wears the distinctive fuselage colours and bat motif of West Malling-based 153 Squadron.** *(David M. Sargent)*

Bottom, right: **In July 1958, 153 Squadron was renumbered 25 Squadron at Waterbeach and several of their aircraft were repainted in 25's colours. Here is WS729 again – the fuselage bands and fin motif have been changed, but the code style is still very much à la 153 Squadron. 25's original NF.14s had a full border to the fuselage bands and a light code superimposed on a small diameter black circle, on the fin – though this is thought to have changed later to a simple white fin code letter.** *(via DMS)*

Above: In the early 'sixties, amongst the NF.14s being gradually dismantled at 5MU was WS724 coded P. The code and fuselage markings were appropriate to the style applied by 72 Squadron, excepting that the fuselage marking had been modified to include a 60 Squadron-style flash. 72 Squadron were the last unit to fly NF.14s operationally in the UK, officially disbanding at Church Fenton in June 1959. It is thought that some of their aircraft and possibly the air-crew, moved to Leeming at the time of the disbandment, to form the nucleus of the new Meteor NF.14-equipped 60 Squadron. They presumably used these aircraft to work up with, then took delivery of newly refurbished machines later in the Summer, which the crews then ferried out to Tengah–in fact WS754 and WS800 were seen by Roy Montgomery, staging through Nicosia on 19 September, without codes or colours. If this proves to be what happened, then it is likely that the newly reformed squadron at Leeming modified the old 72 Squadron colours to something near to those traditionally worn by 60 Squadron – but outlined in a dark colour (green?) rather than white. The record cards do not appear to mention the service of WS724 and others with this newly-formed unit, so can anyone else confirm our theory? *(D.M.Sargent)*

Below: When 60 Squadron finally gave up its Meteors in September 1961, NF.14 WS787, which had made the RAF's last operational NF.14 sortie, on 17 August '61, was preserved near the Tengah main gate, as seen in this May 1962 photograph. Note the white surround to the fuselage colours. *(Ron Clarke)*

Opposite page, top: WS798/R shows the style of coding adopted by the Leeming-based 228 OCU NF.14s. *(via David M. Sargent)*

Opposite, second from top: For its 1957 Armed Forces Day, Bovingdon persuaded Duxford's 64 Squadron to send this NF.14 for static display. The code 'S' appears on the fin in a barely discernible script. *(MAP)*

Opposite, third from top: WS829/Z – probably ex-AWOCU, out in the open at 33 MU. This aircraft went on to Rolls-Royce as G-ASLW. In the background is WS733/Z of 64 Squadron. *(MAP, via David M. Sargent)*

Opposite, bottom: WS833/A bears the fuselage colours of Church Fenton-based 72 Squadron and the initials of their CO, Wg Cdr Maurice Shaw. *(MAP, via David M. Sargent)*

R
WS798

WS840

WS829

MS
WS833

WS777
WS832
W
WS838
XS734
WS845
6

Captions to photographs on page 124, opposite:

Top: **After a period guarding the gate at the radar station at Buchan following its use by 12 Group Communications Flight, NF.14 WS777 was acquired by Leuchars, who repainted it in this rather odd scheme, with the station lion on the nose. It did not survive for long after this 1969 shot — the fire section apparently took a fancy to it.** *(Military Aircraft Photographs)*

Second from top: **Wearing a most odd colour scheme (perhaps a hang-over from its time with the AWOCU), is NF.14 WS832/W, seen in 1962, when it was on the strength of the RAE at Llanbedr. Today it is in the safe hands of the Solway Aviation Group at Carlisle airport.** *(MAP)*

Third from top: **One of several star items at the 'Battle of Britain' show at Gaydon on 14.9.68 was WS838, an all-yellow NF.14 sporting an A & AEE badge on the fin.** *(C. J. Salter)*

Bottom: **NF.14 WS845 was one of the ETPS fleet at Farnborough, and is seen at Stansted in August 1963 awaiting the attention of the fire-fighting school trainees.** *(David Gray)*

This page, top: **Visiting Newcastle's Woolsington airport, is NF.14 WS775/V from No.13 Group Communications Flight at Ouston. It is in immaculate condition and carries the final style of camouflage applied to these machines.** *(MAP)*

Tugs

Below: **In long-term cocooned storage at RNAY Sydenham, Belfast, is Meteor TT.20 WD706. Unusually, this aircraft was later taken out of storage and returned to the RAF for further service with 3/4 CAACU at Exeter.** *(MAP)*

Target Tugs

Above: 3/4 CAACU operated a number of TT.20s, out of Exeter in the '60s. WD679/T was actually w/o following an overshoot there on 16 July 1968. Note the difference in rear fuselage paint scheme to 'Z' in the bottom photograph. *(N. Franklin via D. Sargent)*

Below: 1574 Flight's WD623, a TT.20 sits on the steel-plate dispersal at Changi, Singapore during 1966. In the latter days of this unit's existence, their aircraft were given black fins and rudders. *(Military Aircraft Photographs)*

Bottom: Kemble in August 1974 and Meteor TT.20s recently retired by the FRU at Hurn (ie WD649) and 3/4 CAACU at Exeter (ie WM293/Z) await disposal, together with a solitary T.7, WL345. *(S. G. Richards)*

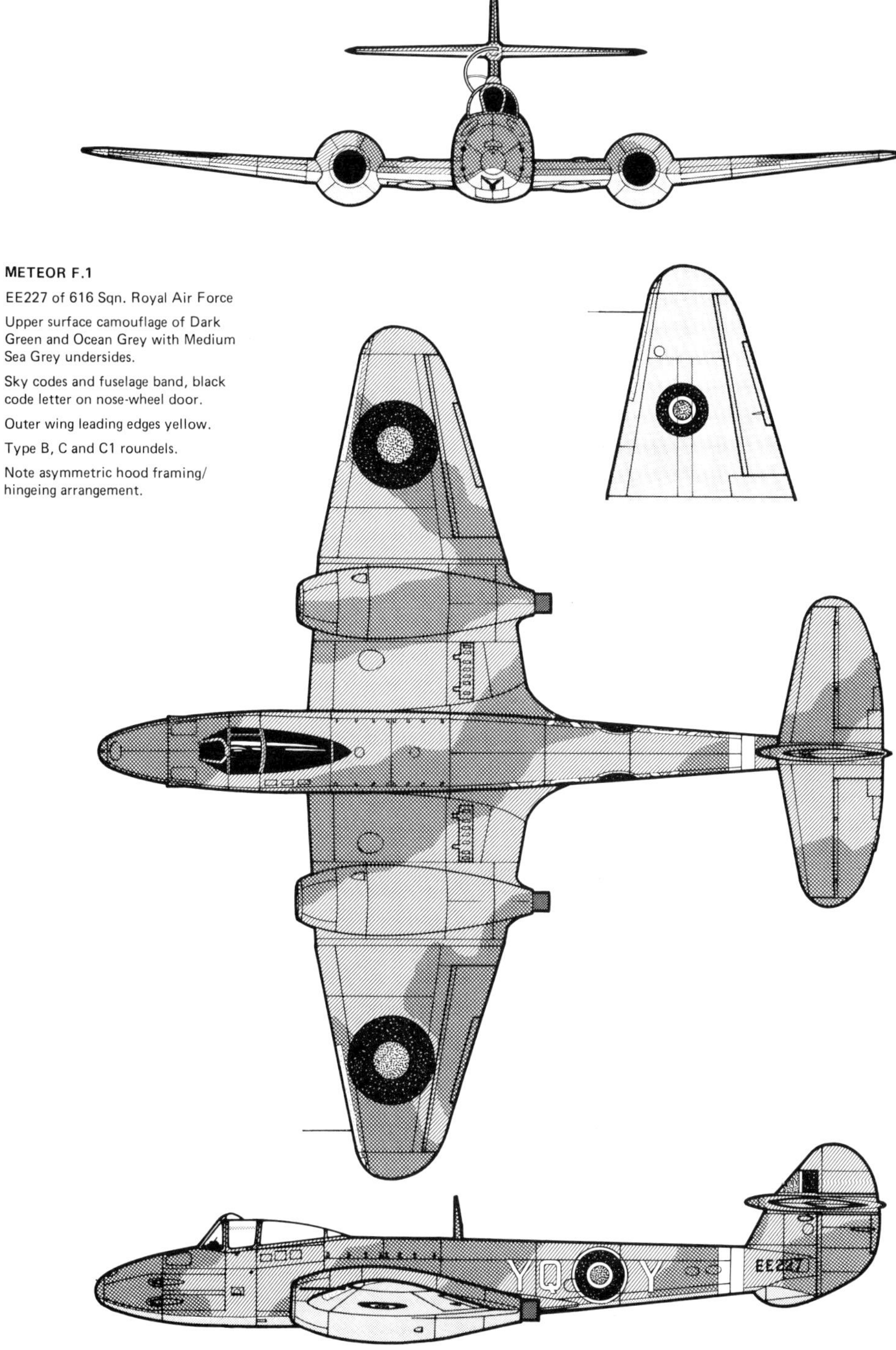

METEOR F.1

EE227 of 616 Sqn. Royal Air Force

Upper surface camouflage of Dark Green and Ocean Grey with Medium Sea Grey undersides.

Sky codes and fuselage band, black code letter on nose-wheel door.

Outer wing leading edges yellow.

Type B, C and C1 roundels.

Note asymmetric hood framing/hingeing arrangement.

KW

METEOR F.3

EE286 of 245 Sqn. Royal Air Force

Upper surface camouflage of Dark Green and Ocean Grey with Medium Sea Grey undersides.

Sky codes and fuselage band with code letter repeated on nose-wheel door in black.

Outer wing leading edges yellow.

Type C and C1 roundels.

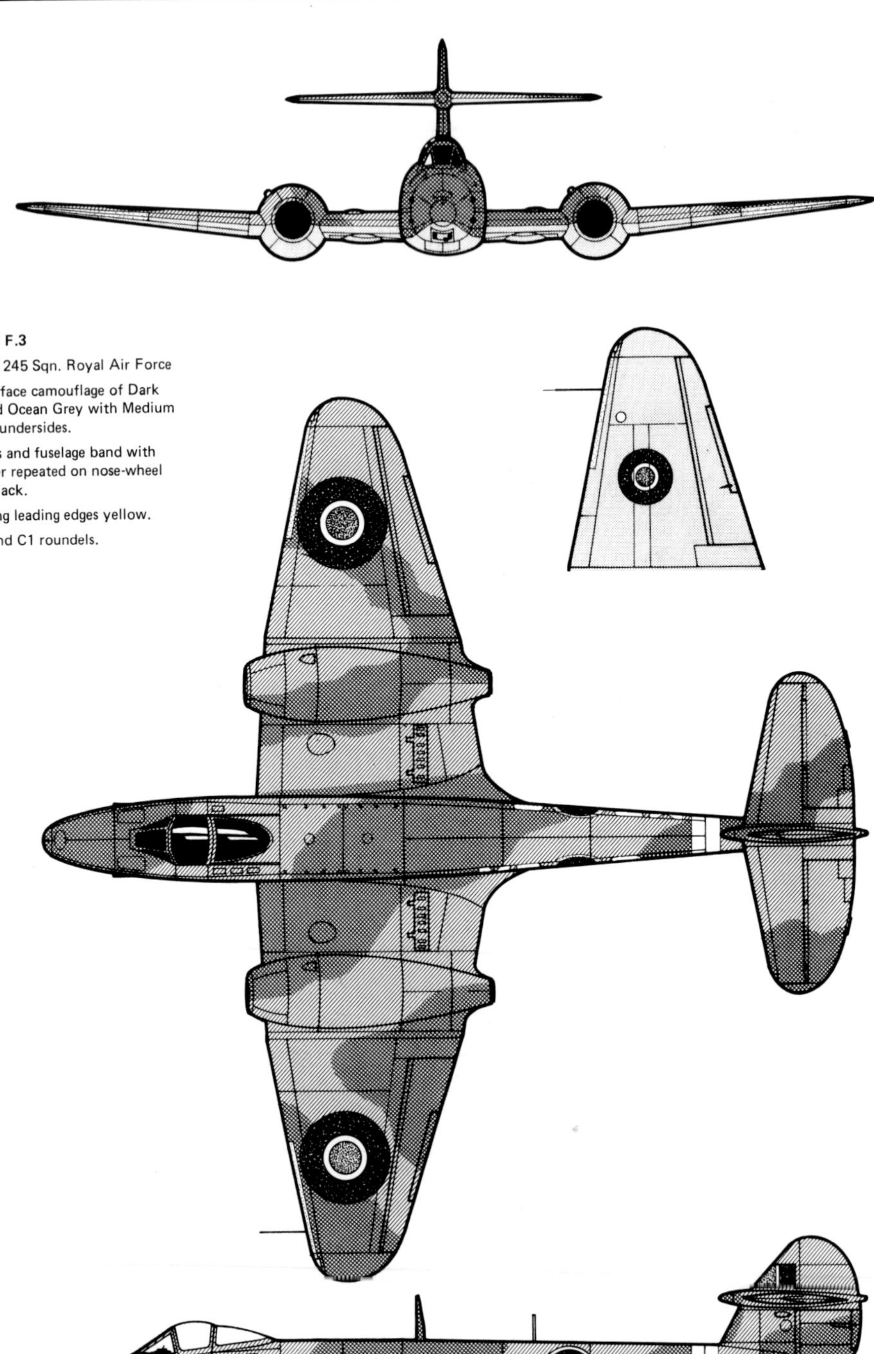

KW

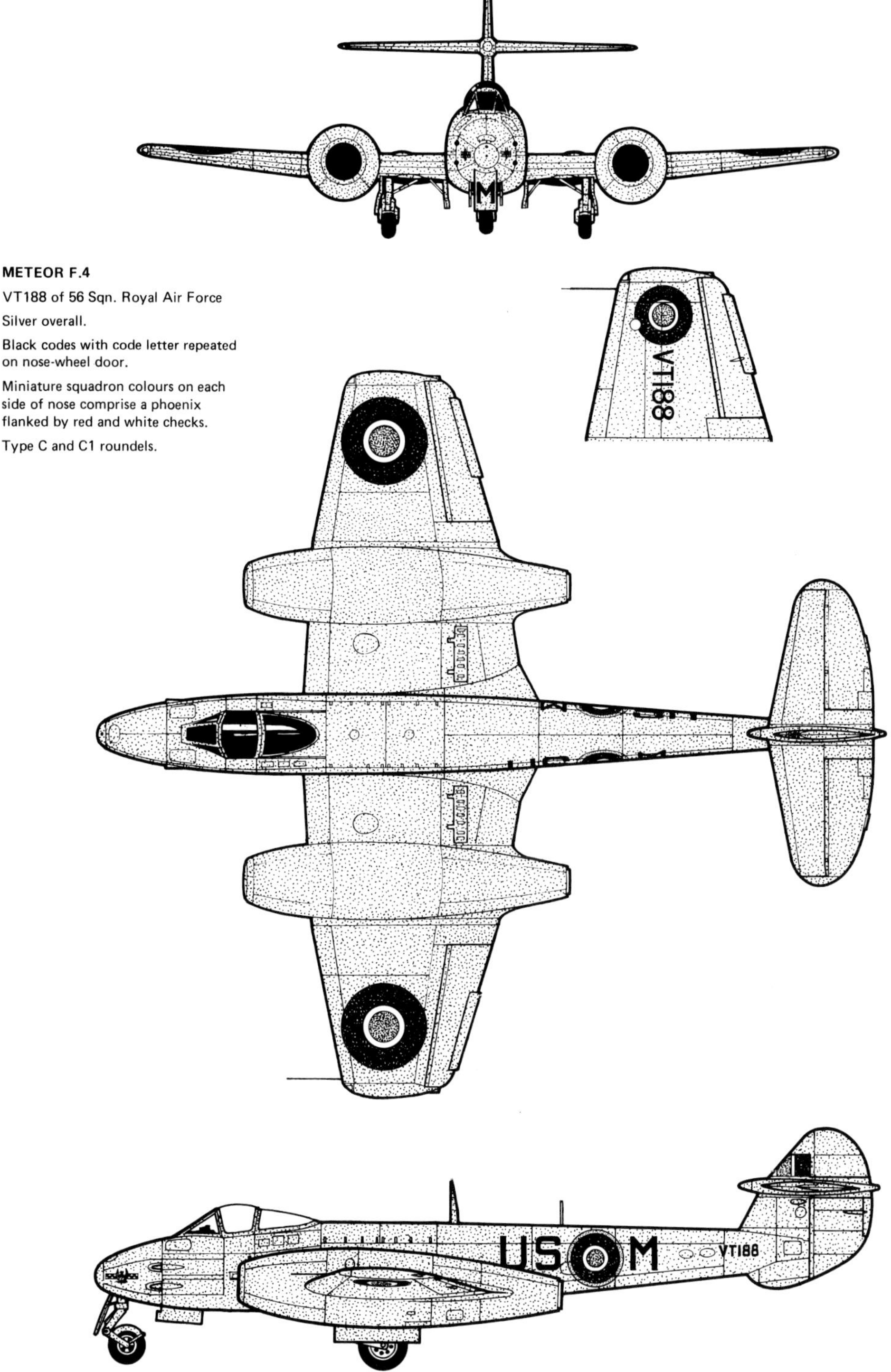

METEOR F.4

VT188 of 56 Sqn. Royal Air Force

Silver overall.

Black codes with code letter repeated on nose-wheel door.

Miniature squadron colours on each side of nose comprise a phoenix flanked by red and white checks.

Type C and C1 roundels.

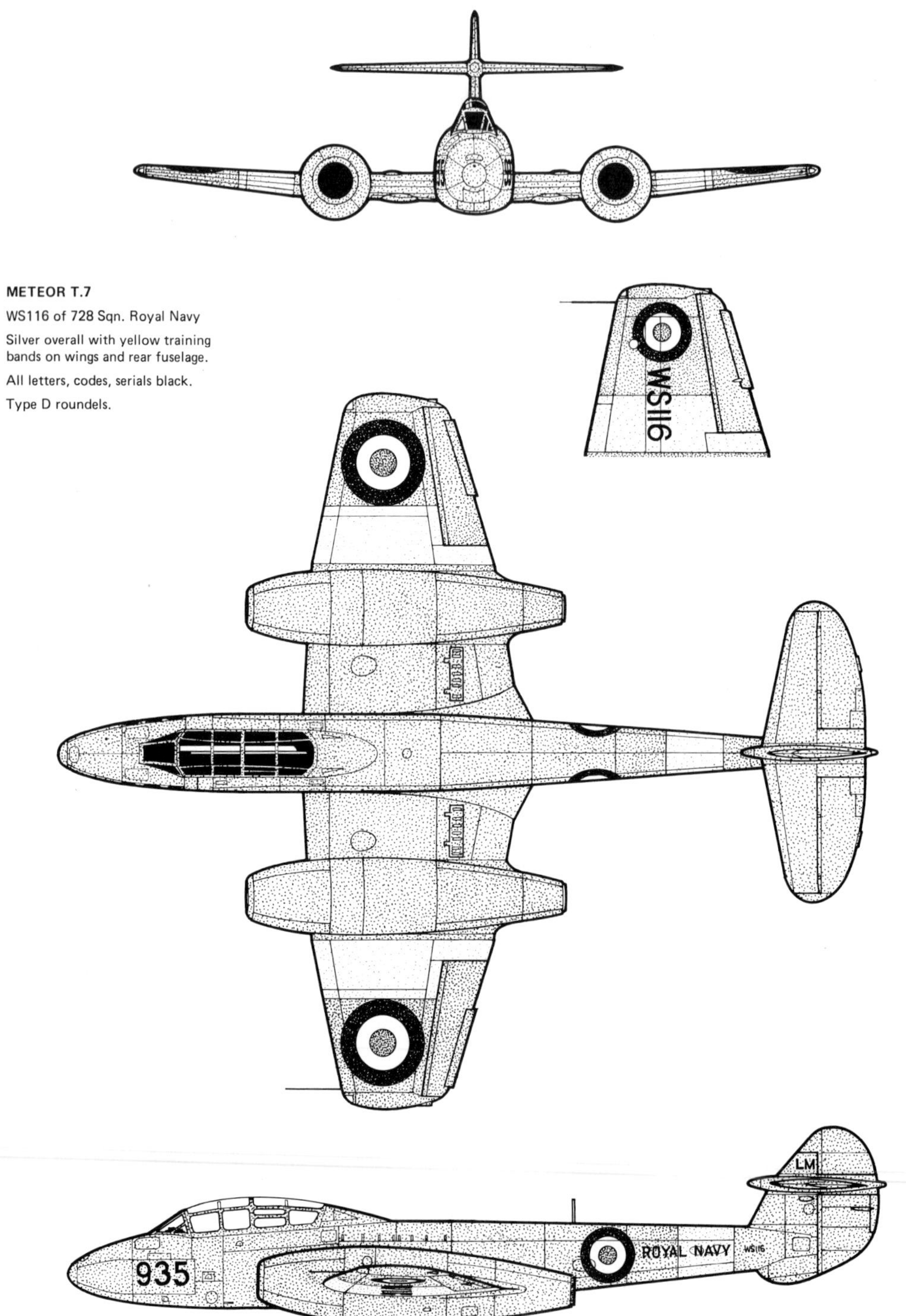

METEOR T.7

WS116 of 728 Sqn. Royal Navy

Silver overall with yellow training bands on wings and rear fuselage.

All letters, codes, serials black.

Type D roundels.

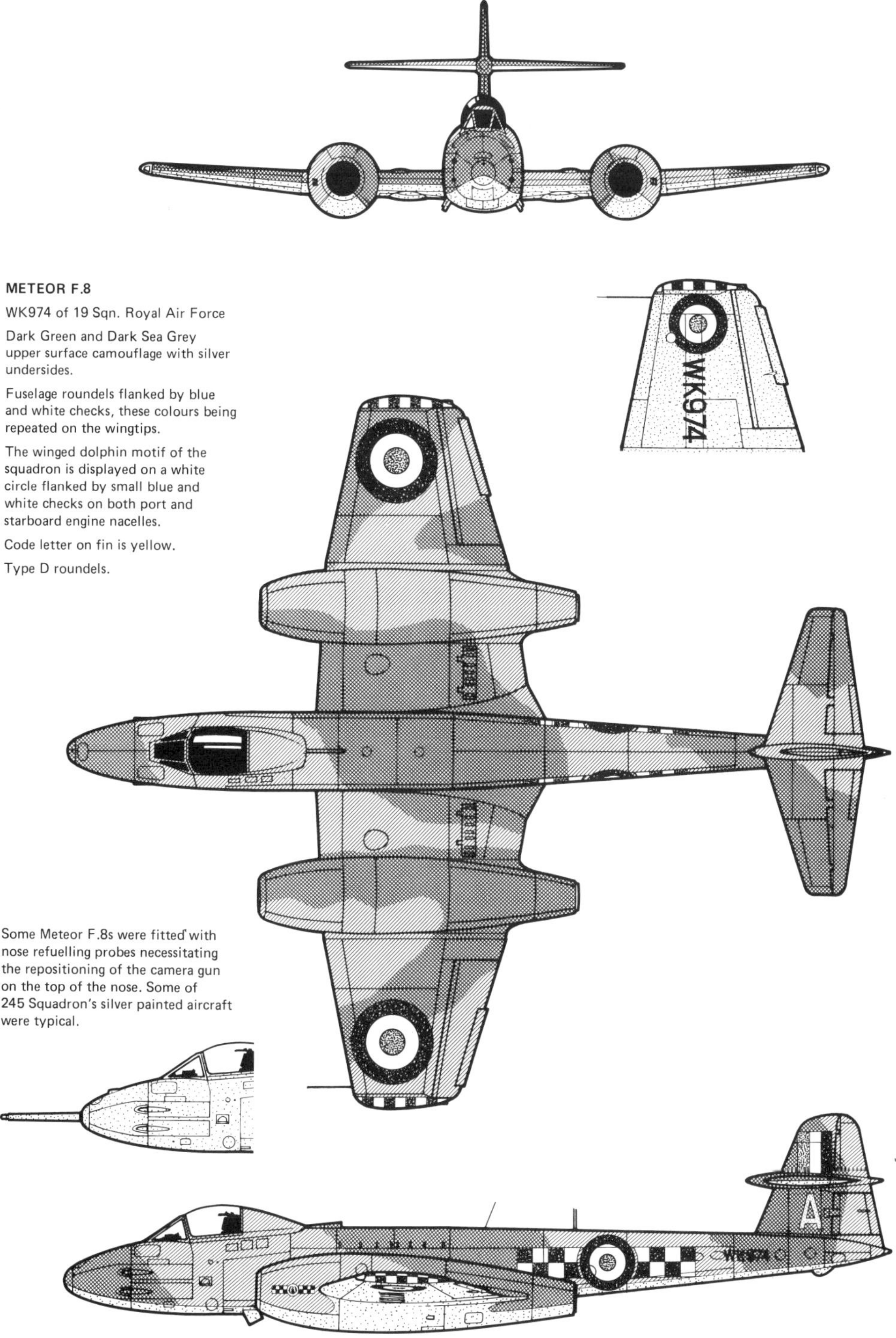

METEOR F.8

WK974 of 19 Sqn. Royal Air Force

Dark Green and Dark Sea Grey upper surface camouflage with silver undersides.

Fuselage roundels flanked by blue and white checks, these colours being repeated on the wingtips.

The winged dolphin motif of the squadron is displayed on a white circle flanked by small blue and white checks on both port and starboard engine nacelles.

Code letter on fin is yellow.

Type D roundels.

Some Meteor F.8s were fitted with nose refuelling probes necessitating the repositioning of the camera gun on the top of the nose. Some of 245 Squadron's silver painted aircraft were typical.

KW

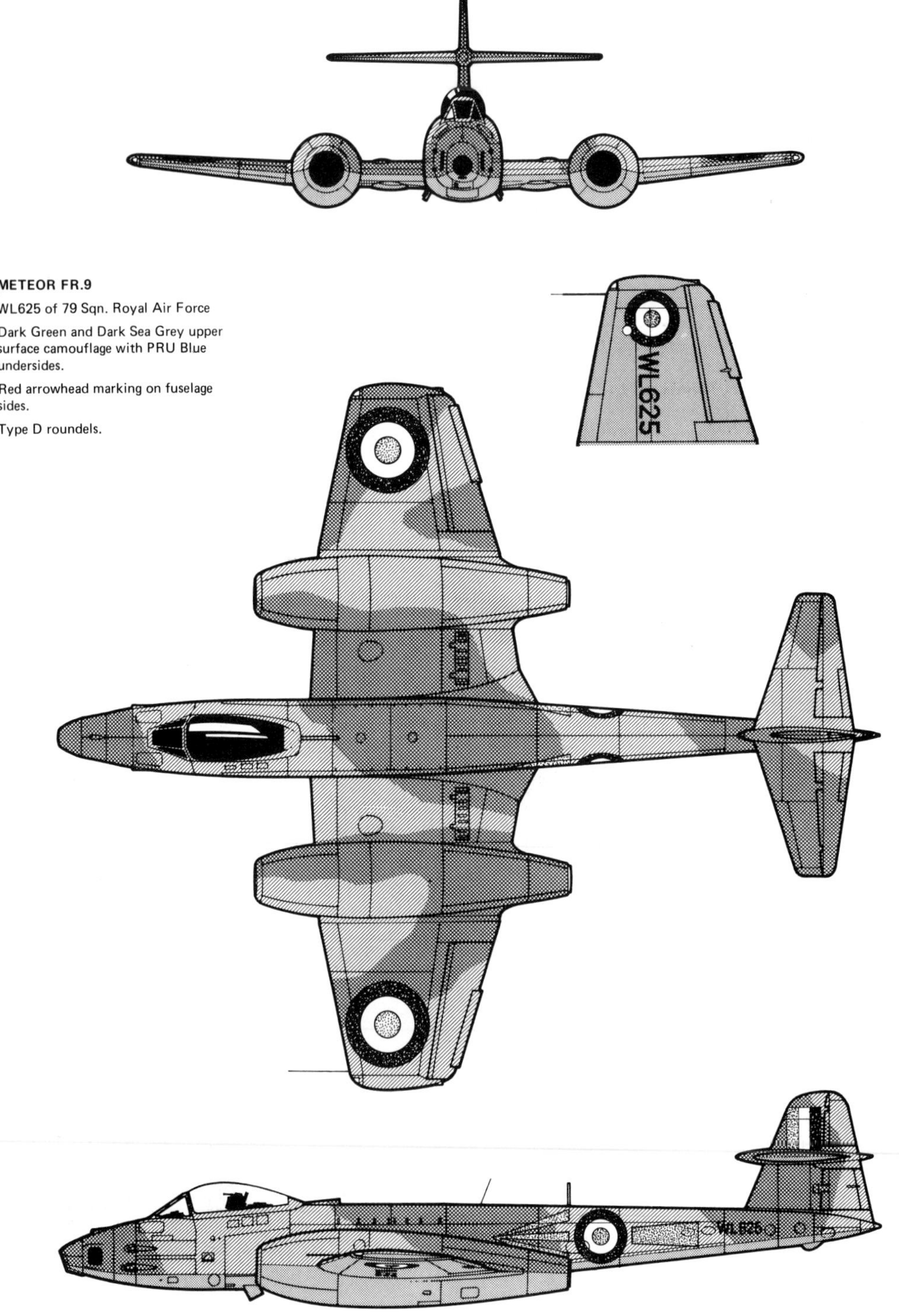

METEOR FR.9

WL625 of 79 Sqn. Royal Air Force

Dark Green and Dark Sea Grey upper surface camouflage with PRU Blue undersides.

Red arrowhead marking on fuselage sides.

Type D roundels.

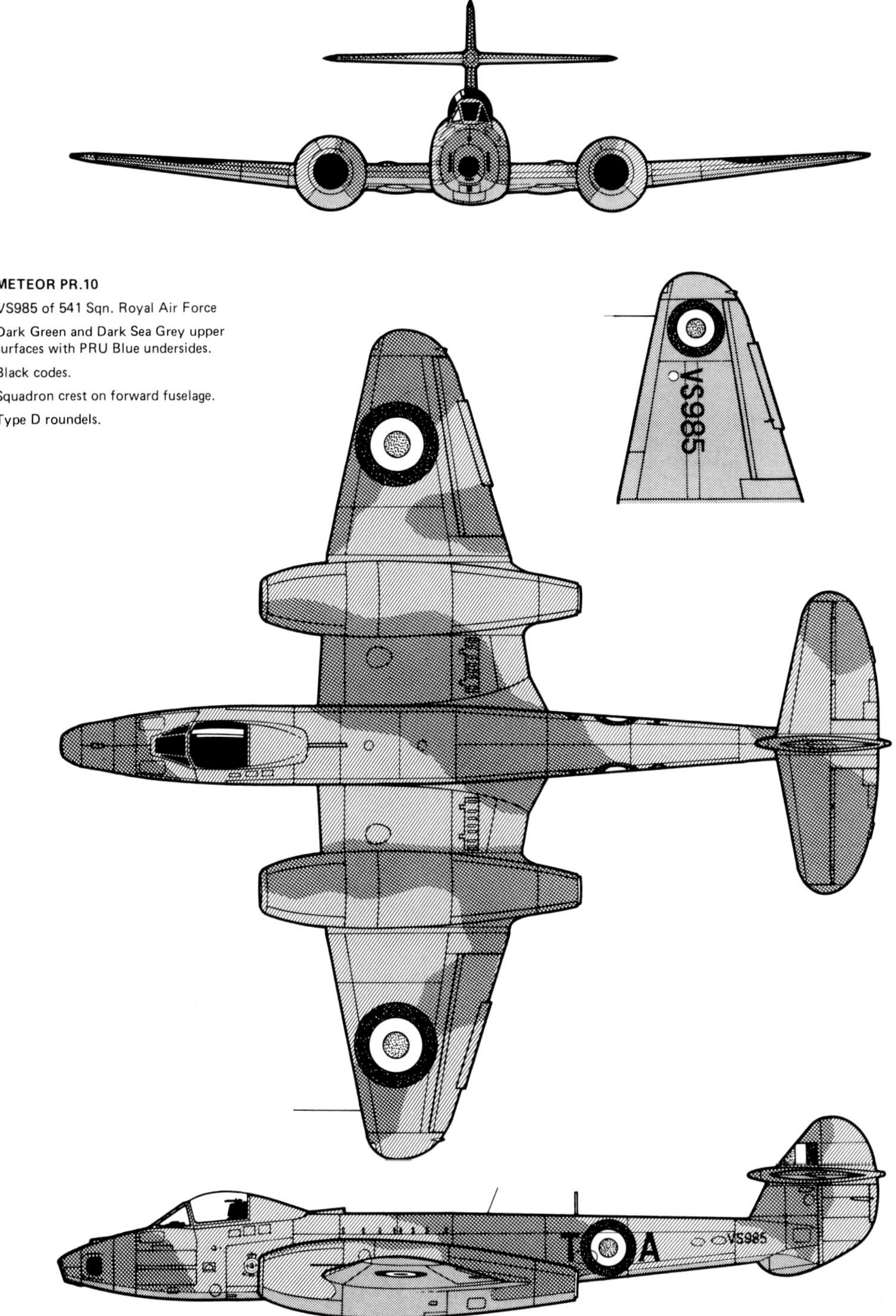

METEOR PR.10

VS985 of 541 Sqn. Royal Air Force

Dark Green and Dark Sea Grey upper surfaces with PRU Blue undersides.

Black codes.

Squadron crest on forward fuselage.

Type D roundels.

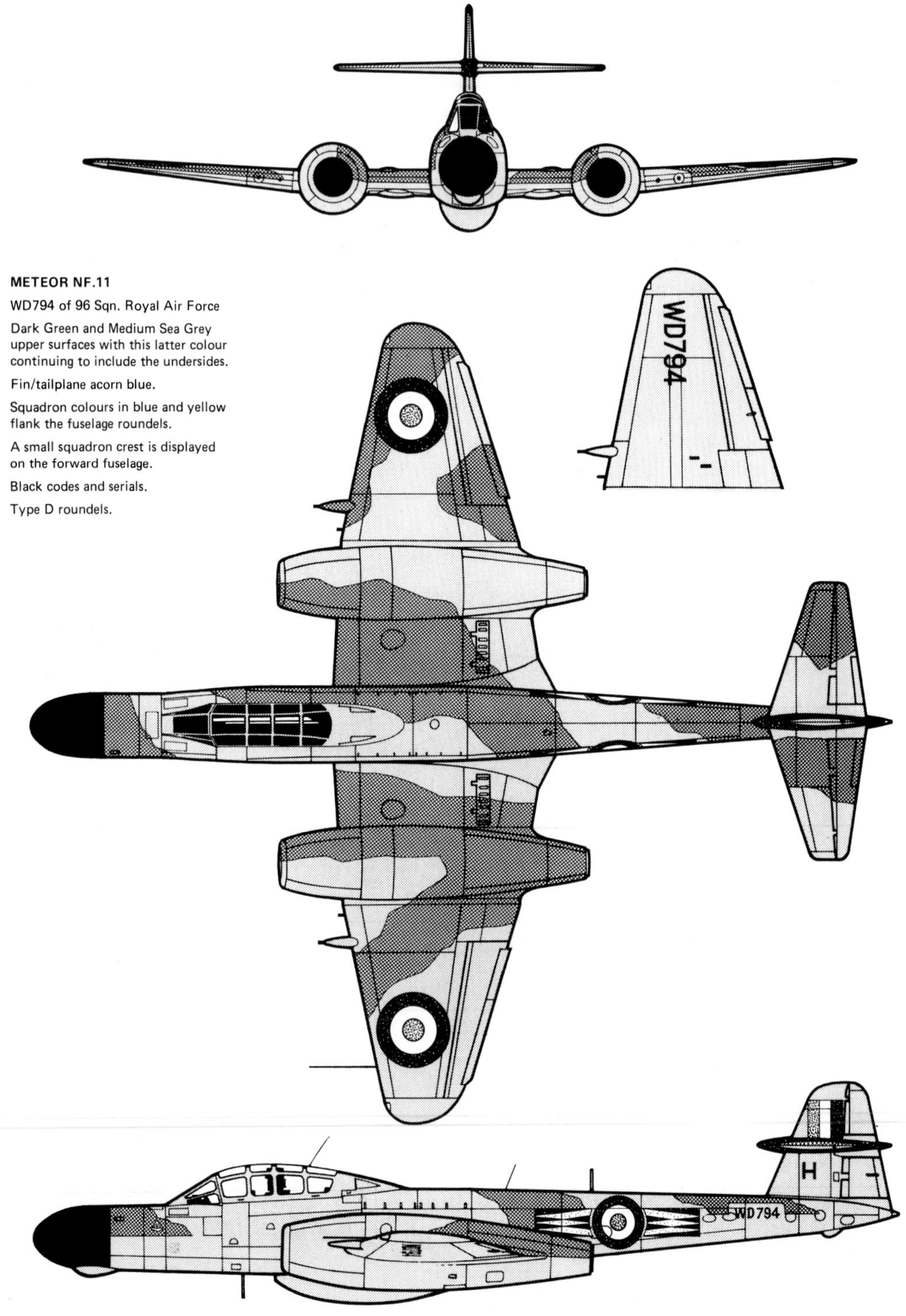

METEOR NF.11

WD794 of 96 Sqn. Royal Air Force

Dark Green and Medium Sea Grey upper surfaces with this latter colour continuing to include the undersides.

Fin/tailplane acorn blue.

Squadron colours in blue and yellow flank the fuselage roundels.

A small squadron crest is displayed on the forward fuselage.

Black codes and serials.

Type D roundels.

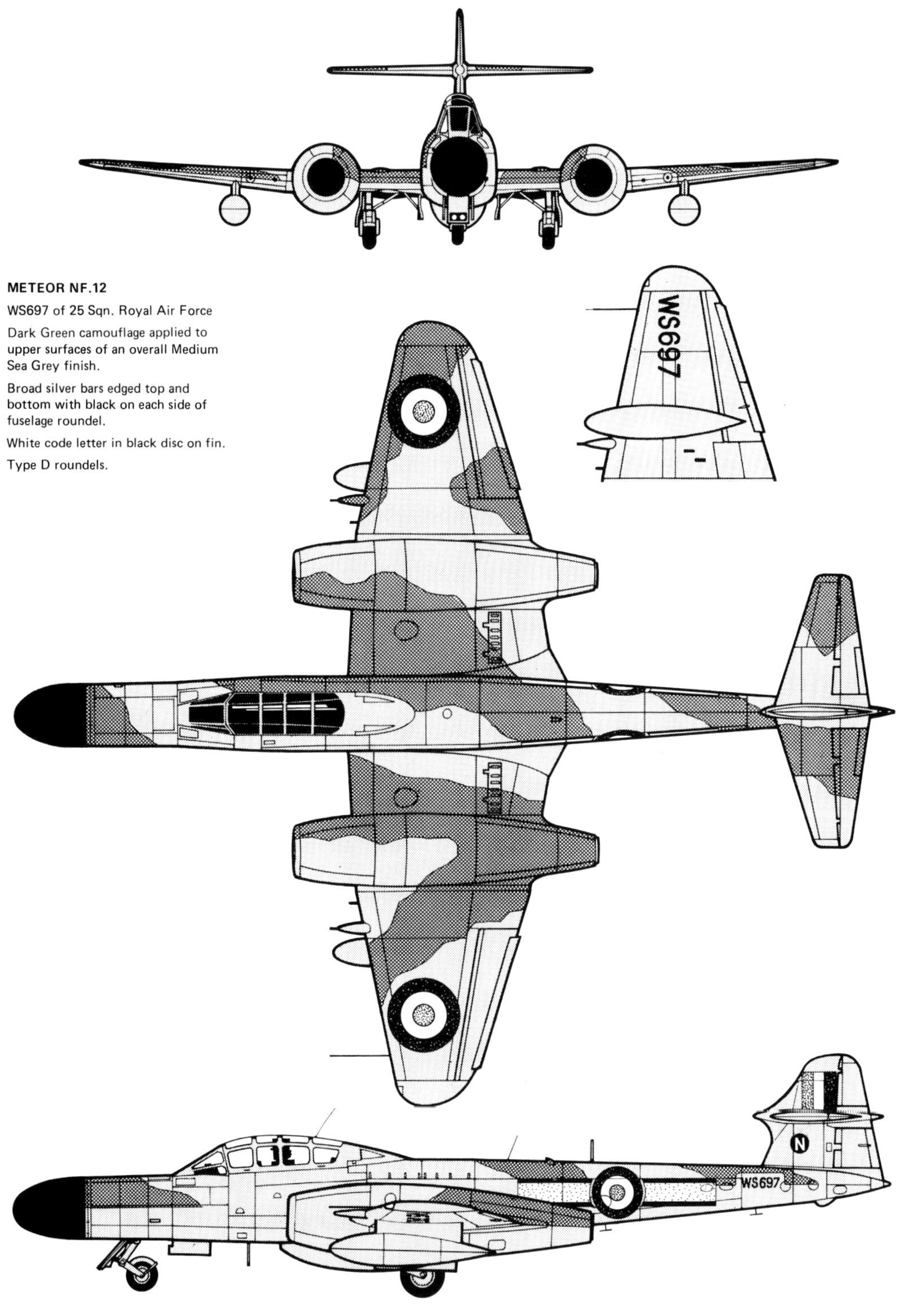

METEOR NF.12

WS697 of 25 Sqn. Royal Air Force

Dark Green camouflage applied to upper surfaces of an overall Medium Sea Grey finish.

Broad silver bars edged top and bottom with black on each side of fuselage roundel.

White code letter in black disc on fin.

Type D roundels.

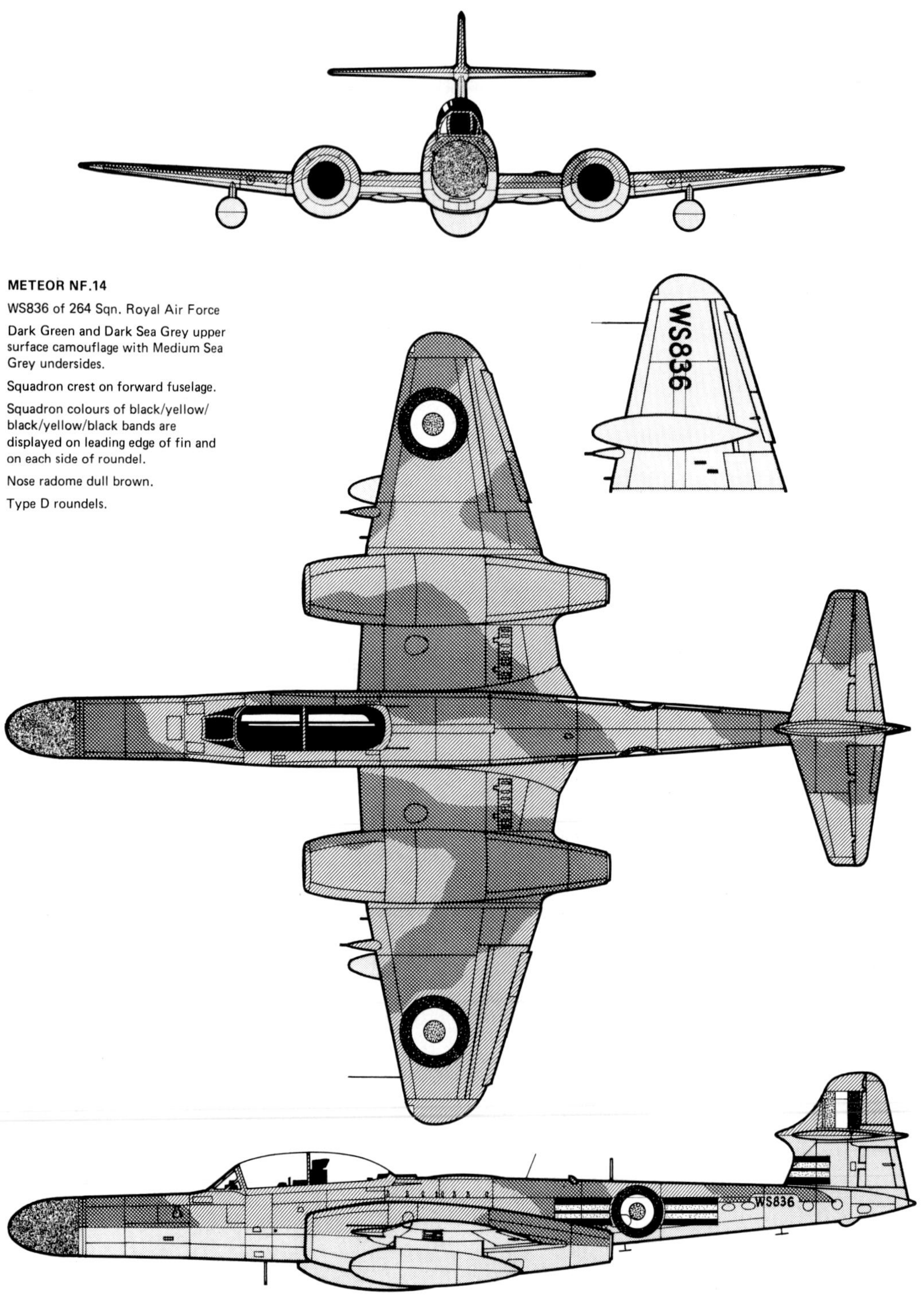

METEOR NF.14

WS836 of 264 Sqn. Royal Air Force

Dark Green and Dark Sea Grey upper surface camouflage with Medium Sea Grey undersides.

Squadron crest on forward fuselage.

Squadron colours of black/yellow/black/yellow/black bands are displayed on leading edge of fin and on each side of roundel.

Nose radome dull brown.

Type D roundels.

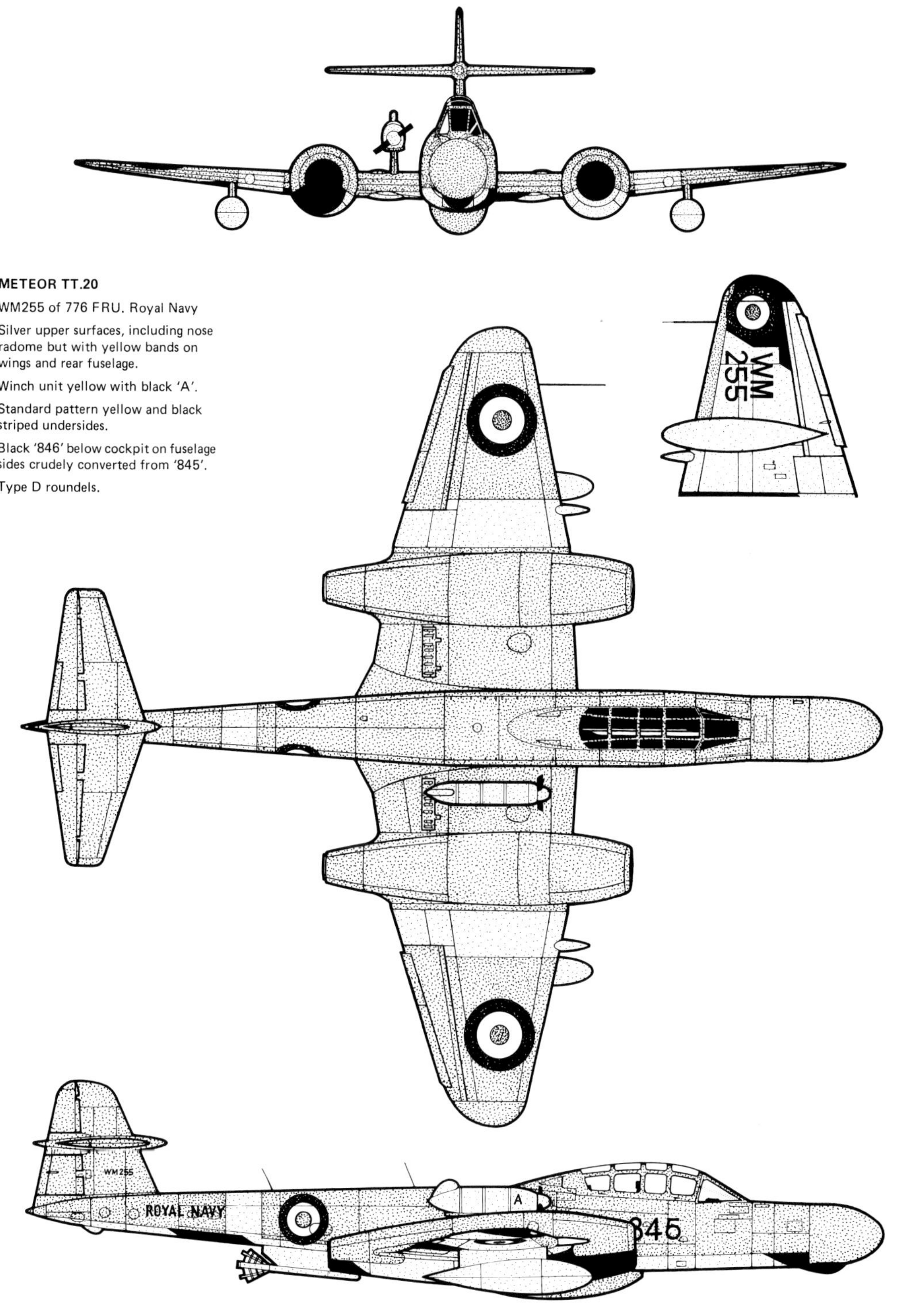

METEOR TT.20

WM255 of 776 FRU. Royal Navy

Silver upper surfaces, including nose radome but with yellow bands on wings and rear fuselage.

Winch unit yellow with black 'A'.

Standard pattern yellow and black striped undersides.

Black '846' below cockpit on fuselage sides crudely converted from '845'.

Type D roundels.

KW

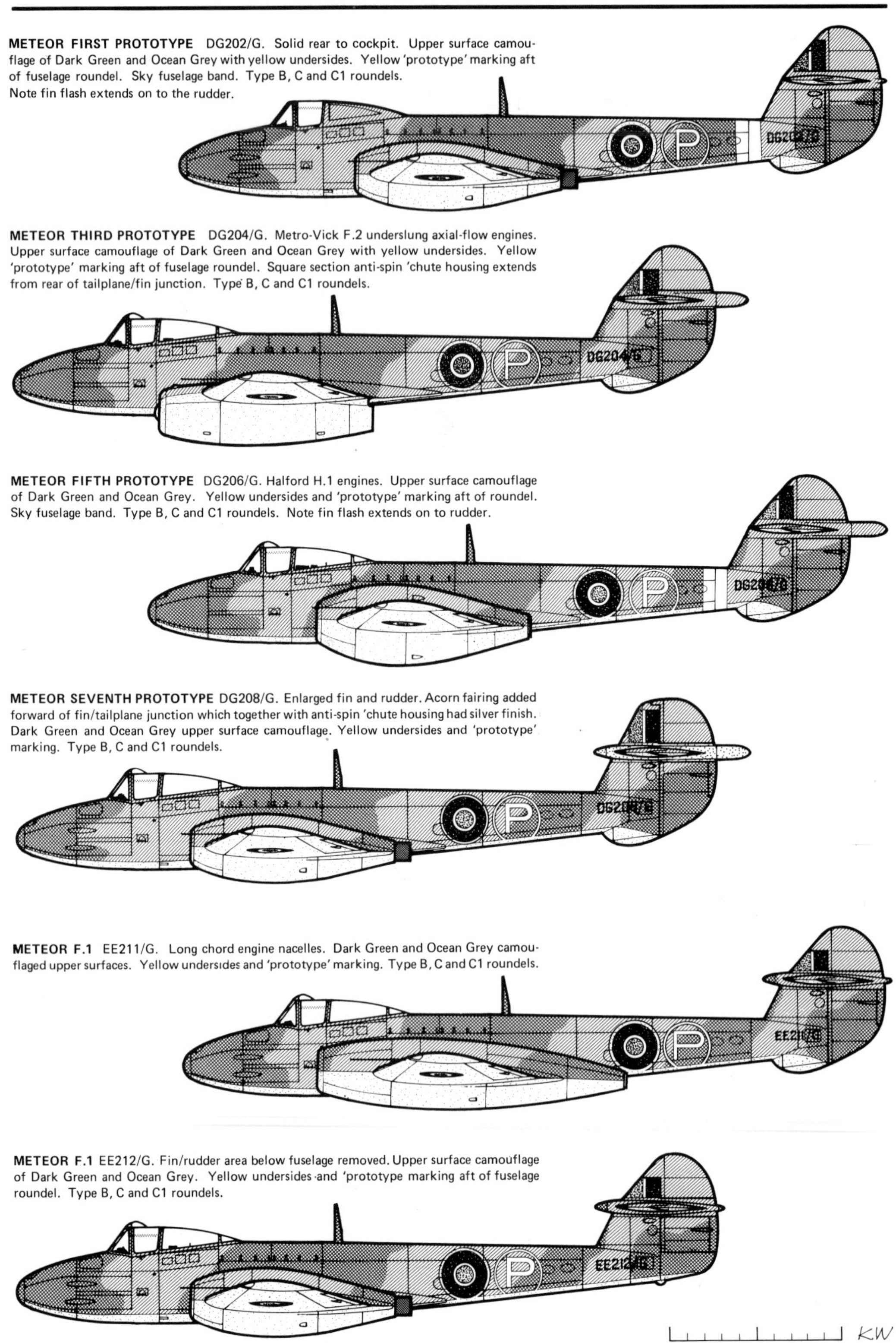

METEOR FIRST PROTOTYPE DG202/G. Solid rear to cockpit. Upper surface camouflage of Dark Green and Ocean Grey with yellow undersides. Yellow 'prototype' marking aft of fuselage roundel. Sky fuselage band. Type B, C and C1 roundels. Note fin flash extends on to the rudder.

METEOR THIRD PROTOTYPE DG204/G. Metro-Vick F.2 underslung axial-flow engines. Upper surface camouflage of Dark Green and Ocean Grey with yellow undersides. Yellow 'prototype' marking aft of fuselage roundel. Square section anti-spin 'chute housing extends from rear of tailplane/fin junction. Type B, C and C1 roundels.

METEOR FIFTH PROTOTYPE DG206/G. Halford H.1 engines. Upper surface camouflage of Dark Green and Ocean Grey. Yellow undersides and 'prototype' marking aft of roundel. Sky fuselage band. Type B, C and C1 roundels. Note fin flash extends on to rudder.

METEOR SEVENTH PROTOTYPE DG208/G. Enlarged fin and rudder. Acorn fairing added forward of fin/tailplane junction which together with anti-spin 'chute housing had silver finish. Dark Green and Ocean Grey upper surface camouflage. Yellow undersides and 'prototype' marking. Type B, C and C1 roundels.

METEOR F.1 EE211/G. Long chord engine nacelles. Dark Green and Ocean Grey camouflaged upper surfaces. Yellow undersides and 'prototype' marking. Type B, C and C1 roundels.

METEOR F.1 EE212/G. Fin/rudder area below fuselage removed. Upper surface camouflage of Dark Green and Ocean Grey. Yellow undersides and 'prototype marking aft of fuselage roundel. Type B, C and C1 roundels.

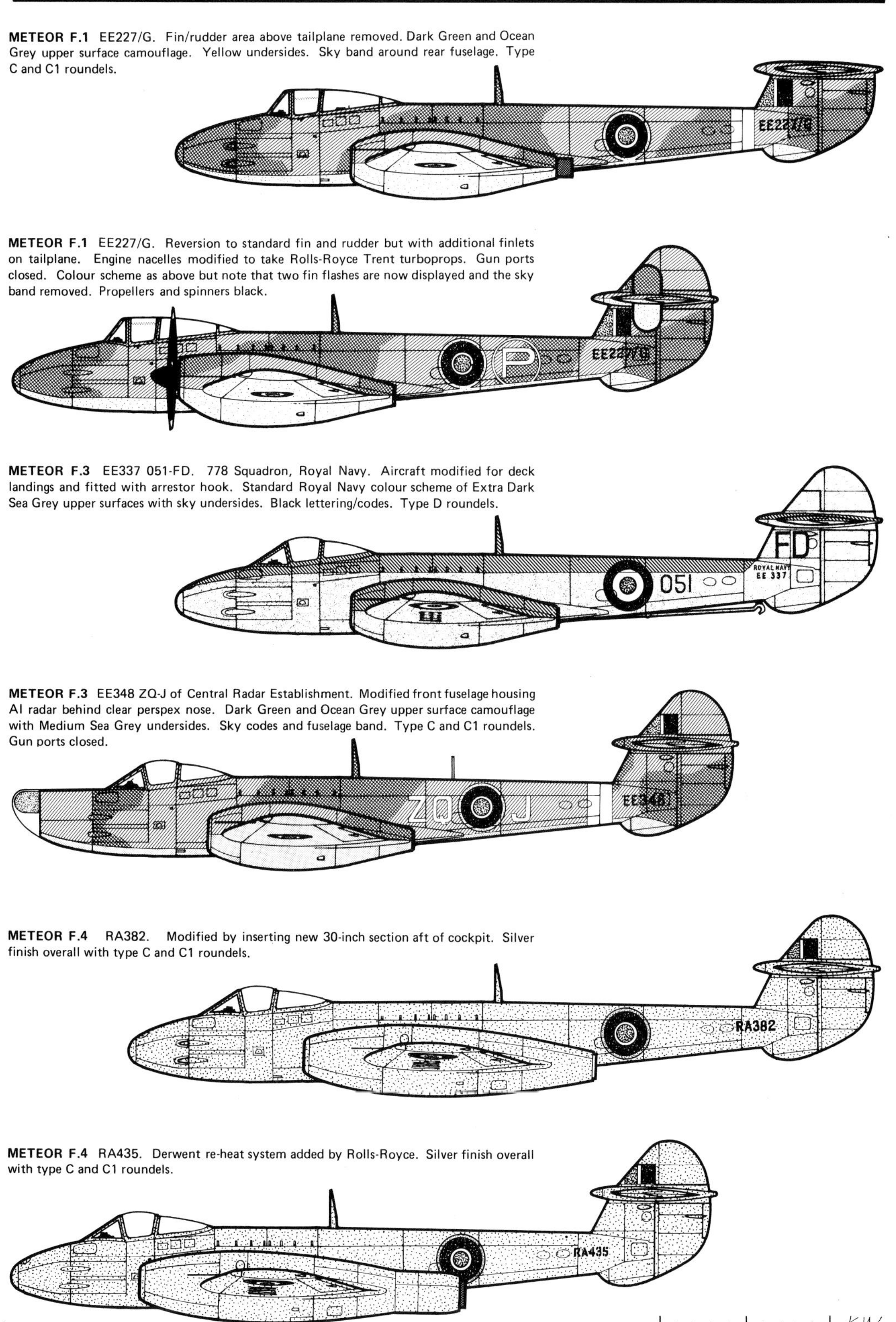

METEOR F.1 EE227/G. Fin/rudder area above tailplane removed. Dark Green and Ocean Grey upper surface camouflage. Yellow undersides. Sky band around rear fuselage. Type C and C1 roundels.

METEOR F.1 EE227/G. Reversion to standard fin and rudder but with additional finlets on tailplane. Engine nacelles modified to take Rolls-Royce Trent turboprops. Gun ports closed. Colour scheme as above but note that two fin flashes are now displayed and the sky band removed. Propellers and spinners black.

METEOR F.3 EE337 051-FD. 778 Squadron, Royal Navy. Aircraft modified for deck landings and fitted with arrestor hook. Standard Royal Navy colour scheme of Extra Dark Sea Grey upper surfaces with sky undersides. Black lettering/codes. Type D roundels.

METEOR F.3 EE348 ZQ-J of Central Radar Establishment. Modified front fuselage housing AI radar behind clear perspex nose. Dark Green and Ocean Grey upper surface camouflage with Medium Sea Grey undersides. Sky codes and fuselage band. Type C and C1 roundels. Gun ports closed.

METEOR F.4 RA382. Modified by inserting new 30-inch section aft of cockpit. Silver finish overall with type C and C1 roundels.

METEOR F.4 RA435. Derwent re-heat system added by Rolls-Royce. Silver finish overall with type C and C1 roundels.

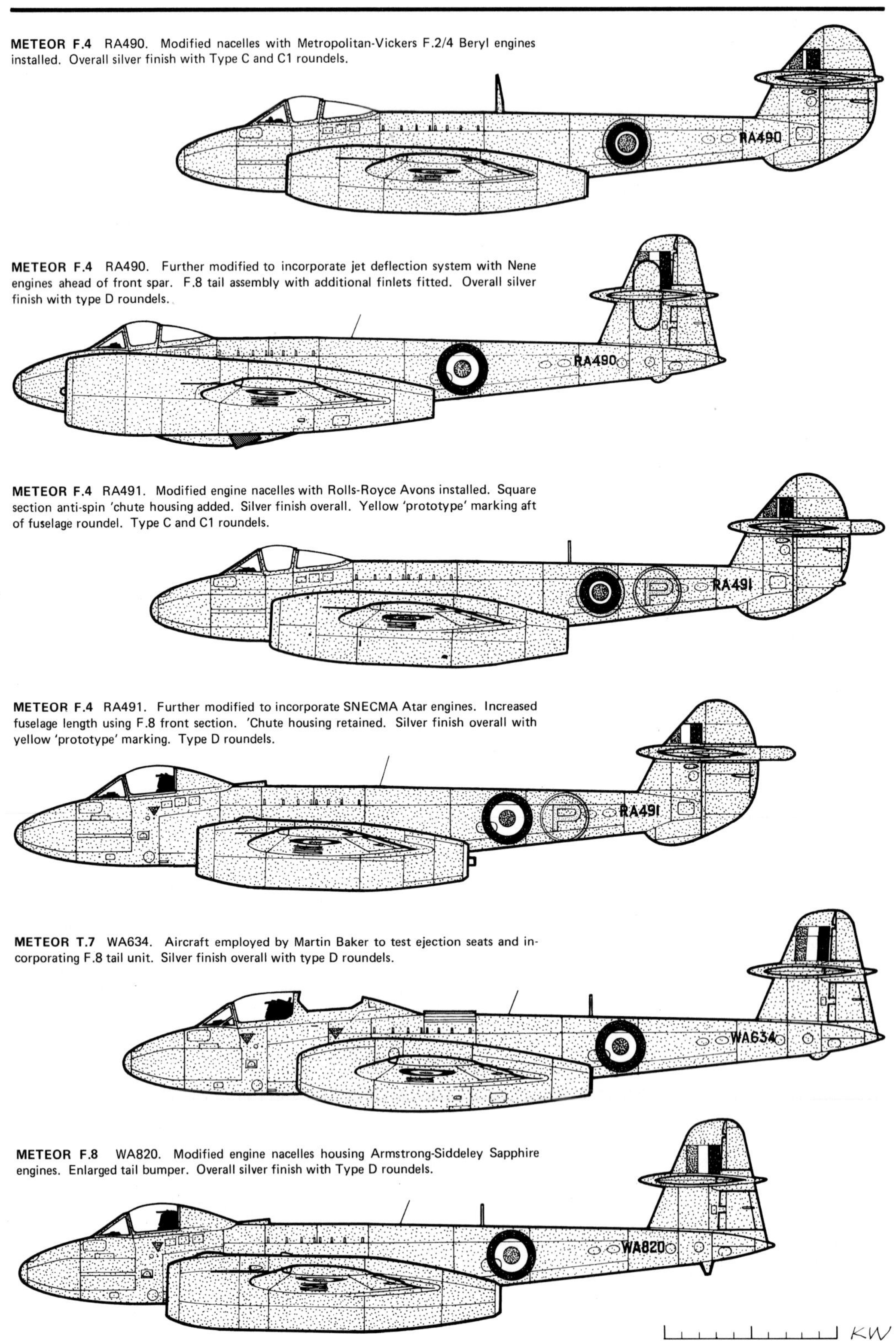

METEOR F.4 RA490. Modified nacelles with Metropolitan-Vickers F.2/4 Beryl engines installed. Overall silver finish with Type C and C1 roundels.

METEOR F.4 RA490. Further modified to incorporate jet deflection system with Nene engines ahead of front spar. F.8 tail assembly with additional finlets fitted. Overall silver finish with type D roundels.

METEOR F.4 RA491. Modified engine nacelles with Rolls-Royce Avons installed. Square section anti-spin 'chute housing added. Silver finish overall. Yellow 'prototype' marking aft of fuselage roundel. Type C and C1 roundels.

METEOR F.4 RA491. Further modified to incorporate SNECMA Atar engines. Increased fuselage length using F.8 front section. 'Chute housing retained. Silver finish overall with yellow 'prototype' marking. Type D roundels.

METEOR T.7 WA634. Aircraft employed by Martin Baker to test ejection seats and incorporating F.8 tail unit. Silver finish overall with type D roundels.

METEOR F.8 WA820. Modified engine nacelles housing Armstrong-Siddeley Sapphire engines. Enlarged tail bumper. Overall silver finish with Type D roundels.

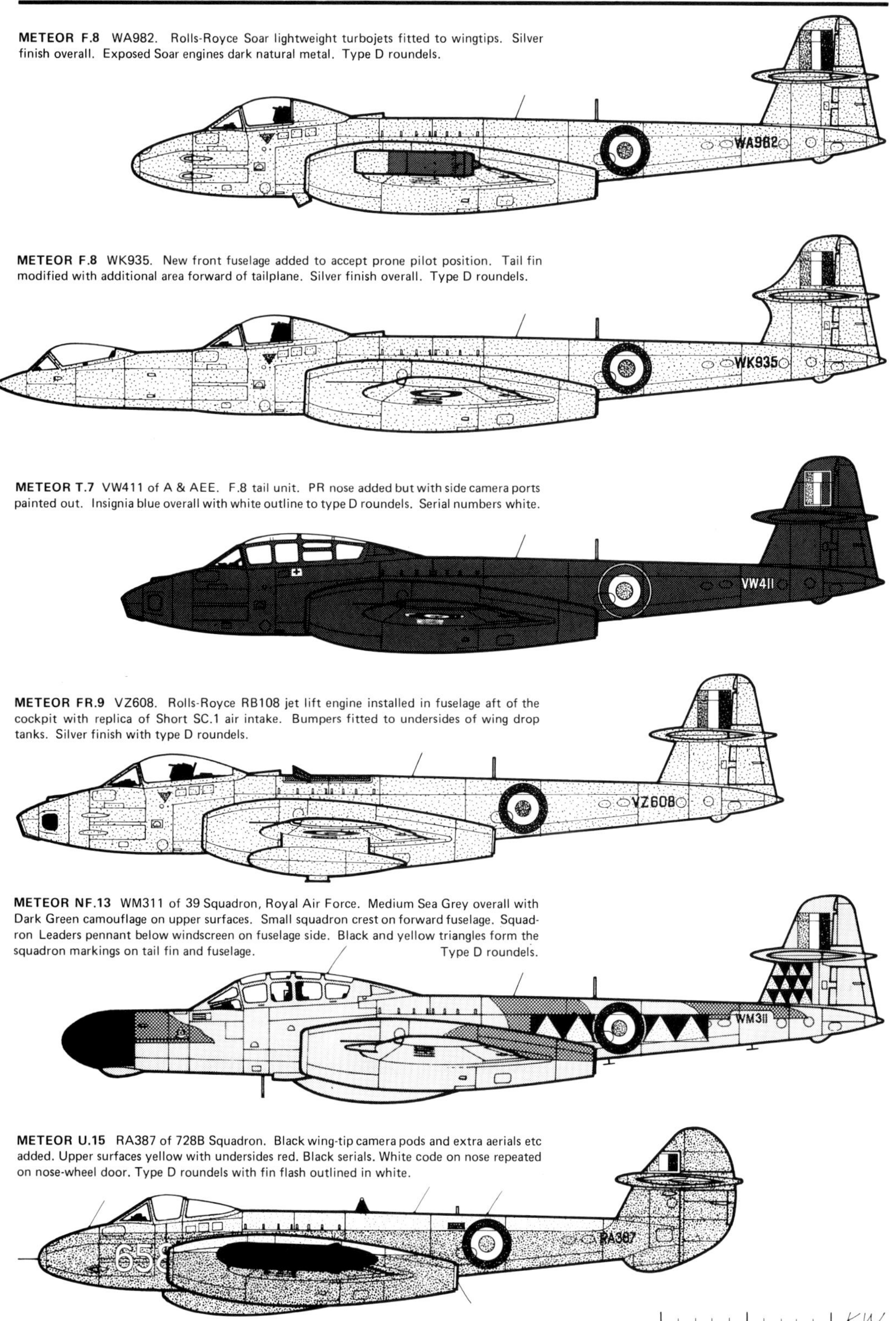

METEOR F.8 WA982. Rolls-Royce Soar lightweight turbojets fitted to wingtips. Silver finish overall. Exposed Soar engines dark natural metal. Type D roundels.

METEOR F.8 WK935. New front fuselage added to accept prone pilot position. Tail fin modified with additional area forward of tailplane. Silver finish overall. Type D roundels.

METEOR T.7 VW411 of A & AEE. F.8 tail unit. PR nose added but with side camera ports painted out. Insignia blue overall with white outline to type D roundels. Serial numbers white.

METEOR FR.9 VZ608. Rolls-Royce RB108 jet lift engine installed in fuselage aft of the cockpit with replica of Short SC.1 air intake. Bumpers fitted to undersides of wing drop tanks. Silver finish with type D roundels.

METEOR NF.13 WM311 of 39 Squadron, Royal Air Force. Medium Sea Grey overall with Dark Green camouflage on upper surfaces. Small squadron crest on forward fuselage. Squadron Leaders pennant below windscreen on fuselage side. Black and yellow triangles form the squadron markings on tail fin and fuselage. Type D roundels.

METEOR U.15 RA387 of 728B Squadron. Black wing-tip camera pods and extra aerials etc added. Upper surfaces yellow with undersides red. Black serials. White code on nose repeated on nose-wheel door. Type D roundels with fin flash outlined in white.

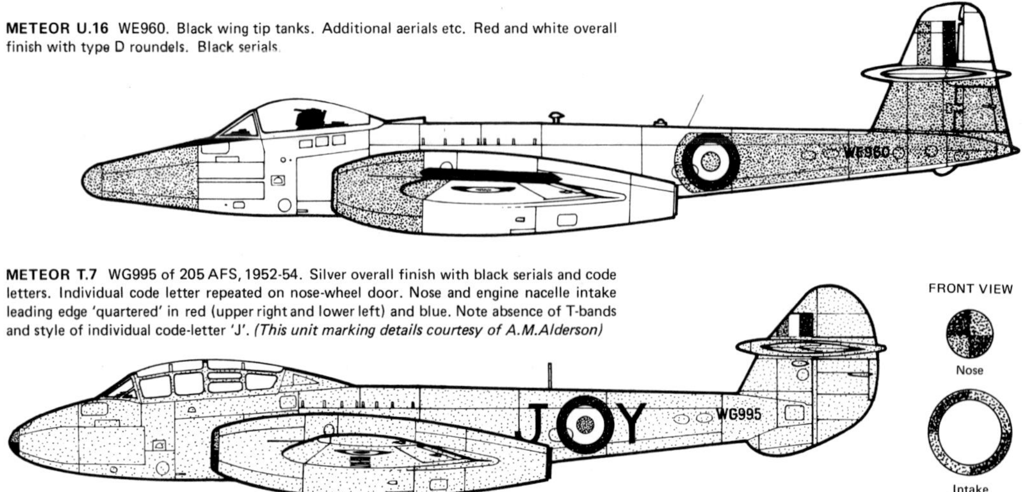

METEOR U.16 WE960. Black wing tip tanks. Additional aerials etc. Red and white overall finish with type D roundels. Black serials.

METEOR T.7 WG995 of 205 AFS, 1952-54. Silver overall finish with black serials and code letters. Individual code letter repeated on nose-wheel door. Nose and engine nacelle intake leading edge 'quartered' in red (upper right and lower left) and blue. Note absence of T-bands and style of individual code-letter 'J'. *(This unit marking details courtesy of A.M.Alderson)*

205 Advanced Flying School operated a fleet of Meteor F.4s and T.7s at Middleton St George during the early 1950s. The markings went through three phases: a single letter code, a two-letter code (as above) and finally a number code, but this was only part of a complicated system.

From mid to late 1950 - aircraft wore only a single letter code, forward of the roundel, but occasionally only on the nose-wheel door. F.4 aircraft codes had a bar over the letter, T.7s did not. Aircraft were apparently divided into two squadrons, with yellow noses and black noses respectively.

From early 1951 to mid-1951 a reorganisation resulted in a division into four squadrons - red, yellow, black and blue, and from Spring '51 the engine nacelle leading edges were also painted in the appropriate colours.

From mid-1951 a code letter - placed aft of the roundel - was introduced to indicate the squadron, in addition to the coloured noses and engines: M on the red squadron aircraft, O - yellow, R - black and W - blue.

Later in 1951, a fifth squadron appeared, coded X and with white noses, but these soon disappeared and at the very end of 1951 two more came into use - Y with red and blue noses etc and Z using yellow and black. All six continued until mid-1954 when the unit was renamed 4 FTS.

From mid- to late 1954, numbers, forward of the roundel, were used instead of code letters, and the colours were retained. Red aircraft were coded in the 10's, yellow in the 20's, black in 30's, blue in 40's, red/blue in the 50's and yellow/black in the 60's. One exception was WA663/18 which had the nose and engine nacelles divided into black and white eighths.

All aircraft were silver for a long time. Yellow bands first appeared on new aircraft in 1952, e.g. WL343/M-B, and were added to all aircraft with the number codes in 1954. Vampires replaced the Meteors at the end of 1954.

Meteor F.8: Wheels and Flaps detail

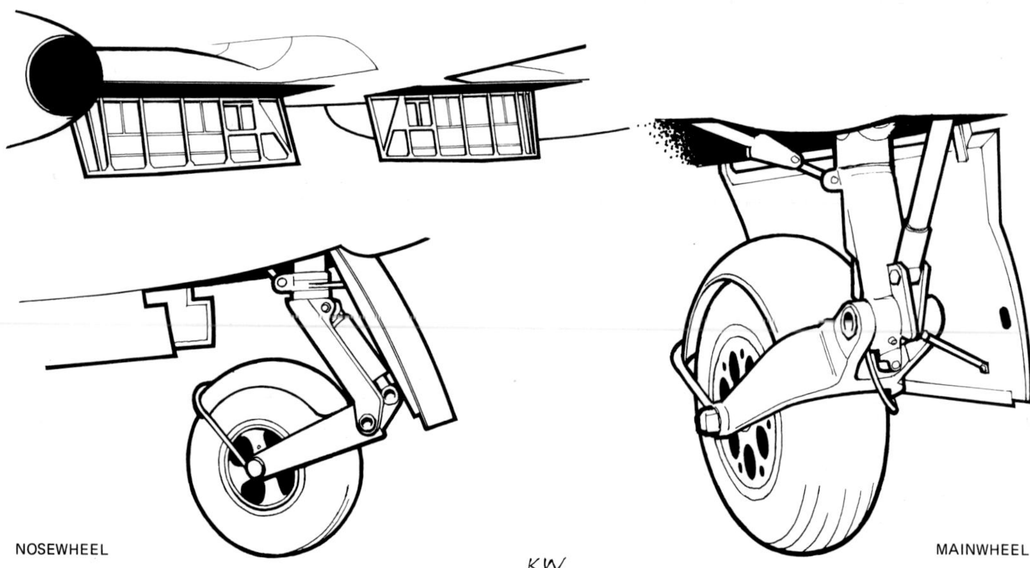

Meteor F.8 Cockpit Interior

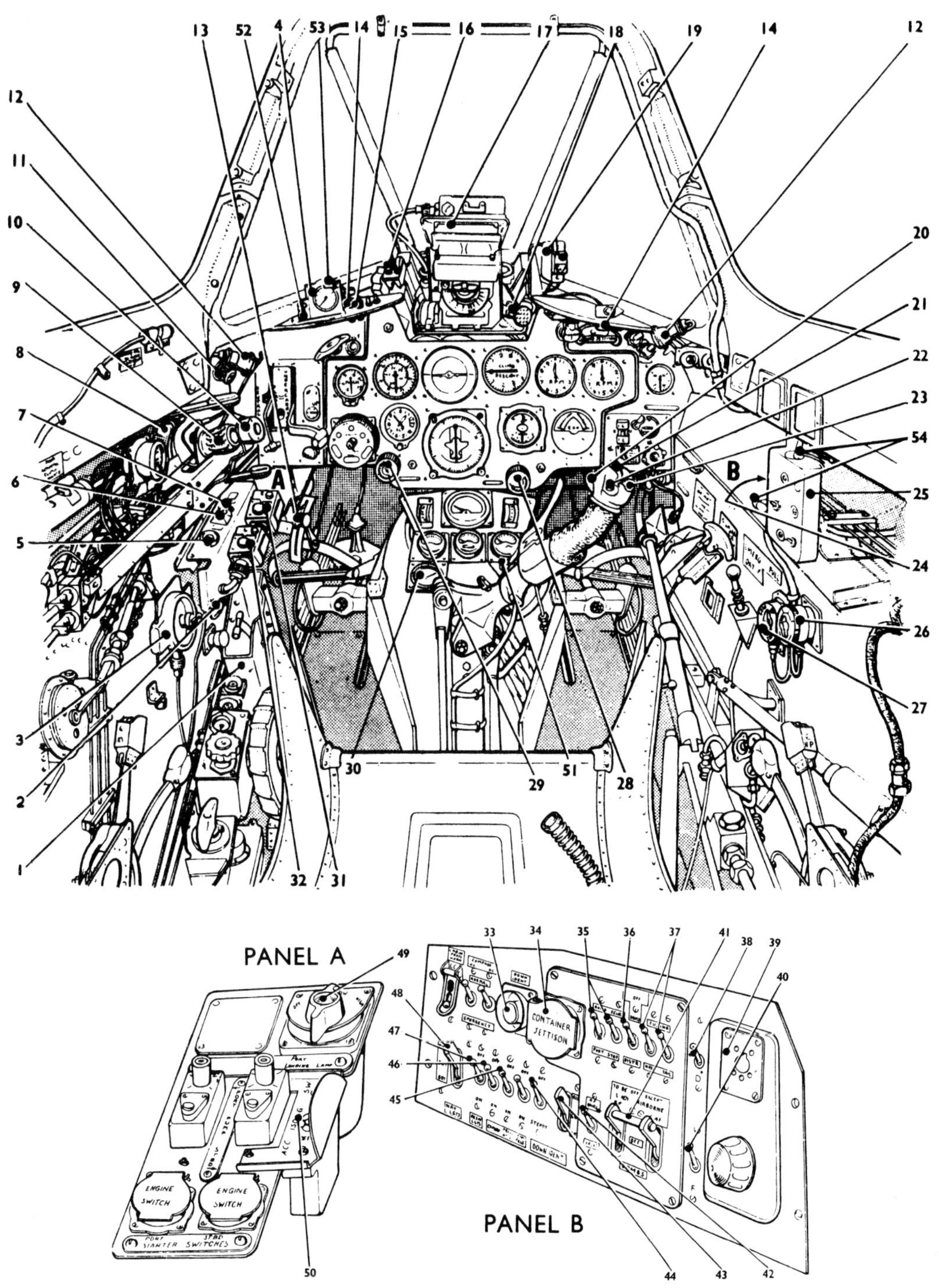

Key to Meteor F.8 Cockpit Interior

See illustration on previous page.

The key emphasises the operational and miscellaneous equipment. The engine and flying controls and instruments are fairly well known and more easily accessed.

1 Map Case
2 Trimmer Lamp
3 Camera Footage Indicator
4 DME Range Meter
5 Radio 'G Manual' Switch
6 Radio 'G Auto' Switch
7 Radio Set Selector Switch
8 Brake Gauge Lamp
9 Gyro Gun Sight Range Control
10 Radio 'Press-to-Speak' Switch
11 Ancillary Lamps Dimmer Switch
12 Ultra-Violet Interior Flood Lamps
13 Bomb/Tank Manual Jettison Lever
14 Instrument Panel Lamps
15 Emergency Lamp
16 Gyro Gun Sight Control Switch
17 Retractable Gyro Gun Sight
18 Gun Sight Emergency Retraction
19 Gun Sight Master Circuit Breaker
20 Gun Firing Trigger
21 Gun Firing Safety Catch
22 Cine Camera Switch
23 Bomb or Rocket Firing Switch
24 Emergency Lamp Switch
25 DME Control Unit
26 Gun Sight 'Rocket/Guns' Switch
27 Gun Sight Selector Dimmer
28 Instrument Panel Lamps Dim Switch
29 Ultra-Violet Lamps Dimmer Switch
30 Clock
31 VHF Radio Controller (No.1 Set)
32 VHF Radio Controller (No.2 Set)
33 Downward Ident Lamps Push Switch
34 Bomb Container Jettison Switch
35 Bomb Selector Switches
36 Bomb Distributor Switch
37 Bomb Fuzing Switches
38 Radio IFF Distress Switch
39 Radio IFF Controller
40 Radio IFF On/Off Switch
41 Bomb/Rocket Firing Selector Switch
42 Rocket Pair/Salvo Selector Switch
43 Downward Ident Lamps Switch
44 Downward Ident Lamps Steady Sw.
45 Pressure Head Heater Switch
46 Camera Master Switch
47 Recognition Lamp Switch
48 Navigation Lamps Switch
49 Landing Lamp Switch
50 Accumulator Isolating Switch
51 Generator Failure Warning Lamps
52 DME Range Meter Lamps Switch
53 DME Range Meter Lamp
54 DME Control Unit Lamps (2)

Key to Meteor F.1 Cockpit Interior

See illustration on opposite page.

It is believed that the items prefixed with a 'D' and 'L' in the illustration refer to Dimmer switches and Lamps respectively.

1 High Pressure Fuel Cock Controls
2 Balance Cock Control
3 Elevator Trimmer Handwheel
4 Rudder Trimmer Handwheel
5 Camera Footage Indicator
6 B/A Switch
7 Dummy Socket (item 5 plug stowage)
8 Engine Relighting Switches
9 Triple Pressure Gauge
10 TR.1143 Controller
11 Throttle Controls
12 Map Case
13 Low Pressure Fuel Warning Lights
14 Alighting Gear Emergency Release
15 Alighting Gear Selector Lever
16 Flap Selector Lever
17 Alighting Gear Emergency Release
18 Undercarriage Indicator
20 Direct Vision Panel
21 Undercarriage Warning Lamp
22 Spare Bulb Stowage
23 Instrument Flying Panel
24 Reflector Gun Sight
25 Exhaust Temperature Gauge
26 RPM Indicators
27 Fire Extinguisher Push Buttons
28 Fuel Contents Gauge
29 Identification Switchbox
30 Hood Jettison Handle
31 ARI.5025 Destruction Push Buttons
32 Cutout Warning Lamp
33 Rounds Counter
34 Identification Lamp Selector Switch
35 Navigation Lamp Switch
36 Harness Release Lever
37 Pressure Head Heater Switch
38 Resin Lamp Switch
40 ARI.5025 On Off Switch
41 ARI.5025 Distress Switch
42 ARI.5025 Controller
43 Tank Pump Test Push Switches
44 Tank Pump Test Socket
45 Emergency Hand Pump
46 Vacuum Change Over Cock
47 Low Pressure Fuel Cock Controls
48 High Pressure Oxygen Stop Valve
49 Seat Raising Lever
50 Compass Switch
51 Gun Sight Switch
52 Camera Switch
53 Gun 'Wobble' Button
54 Brake Lever
55 Fuel Contents Selector Buttons
56 Pressure Cabin Altimeter
57 Micro Telephone Socket
58 Burner Pressure Gauge
59 Oxygen Regulator
60 Oil Pressure Gauges
61 Cabin Pressure & Ventilation Control
62 Compass Indicator
63 Rudder Pedal Adjuster
64 Flap Indicator
65 Clock
66 Landing Lamp Switch
67 Supercharger Safety Switches
68 Starter Push Switches
69 Oxygen Economiser
70 Brake Bottle Pressure Gauge
71 Demisting Control
72 Air Pressure Warning Lamp
73 Air Temperature Gauge
74 Hooding Deflation Valve

Meteor F.1 Cockpit Interior

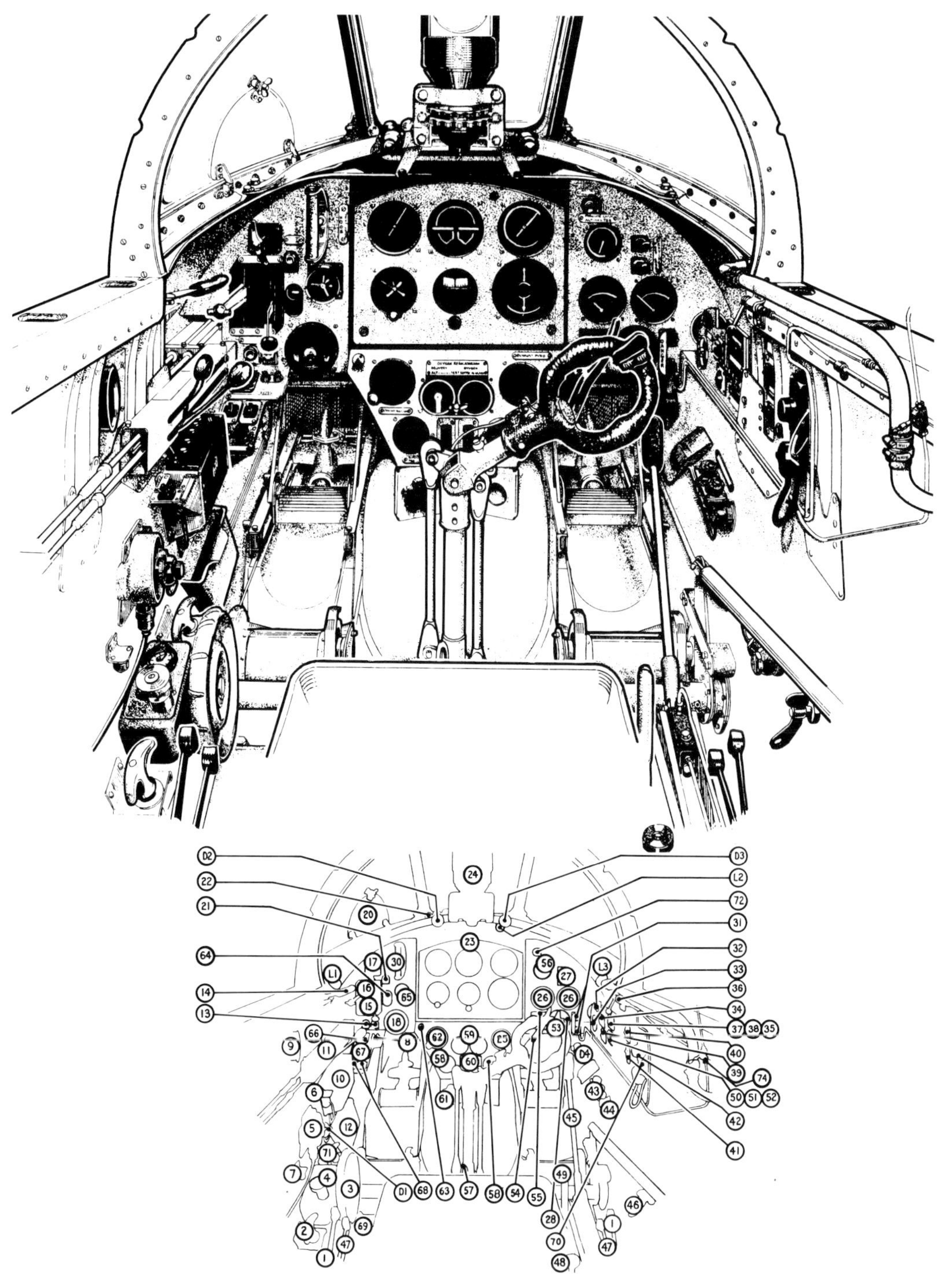

Appendix A

British Service Operators of the Meteor

ROYAL AIR FORCE SQUADRONS WHICH USED THE METEOR AS MAIN EQUIPMENT

1 F.3 Oct 46 Tangmere; Harvards and Oxfords only from Aug 47 until F.4s received Jun 48; F.8 Sep 50. The squadron code letters JX were used from 1946 until 1950, when, in common with most other units, the system was changed to one of single letters only. Re-equipped with Hunter F.5 in Sep 55.

2 FR.9 and PR.10 Dec 50 Buckeburg; FR.9 only from Jun 51; Gutersloh May 52; Wahn Jul 53. Aircraft coded in a two letter sequence, beginning with the letter B. Re-equipped with Swift FR.5 Jun 56 at Geilenkirchen.

5 NF.11 Jan 59 Laarbruch. Re-equipped with Javelin FAW.5 Aug 60.

8 FR.9 (with Venoms) Jan 58 Khormaksar; Meteor element detached to become separate flight Aug 59 to Aug 60. Re-equipped with Hunter FR.10 (and FGA.9) Apr 61.

11 NF.11 Jan 59 Geilenkirchen. Re-equipped with Javelin FAW.4 1960.

13 PR.10 Jan 52 Fayid; Abu Sueir Jan 55; Akrotiri Feb 56. Re-equipped with Canberra PR.7, the last Meteor left Nov 56.

19 F.4 Jan 51 at Church Fenton; F.8 Apr 51. Re-equipped with Hunter F.6 early 1957.

25 NF.12 and NF.14 Jan 54 West Malling; Tangmere Sep 57; Waterbeach Jul 58 (153 Sqn re-numbered). Re-equipped with Javelin FAW.7 Mar 59.

29 NF.11 Aug 51 Tangmere; Acklington Jan 57; to NF.11 and NF.12 1957. Re-equipped with Javelin FAW.6 Dec 57.

33 NF.14 Oct 57 Leeming. Re-equipped with Javelin FAW.7 and moved to Middleton St George Jul 58, although the last Meteor did not leave until Aug 58.

34 F.8 Jul 54 Tangmere. Re-equipped with Hunter F.5 in Feb 56.

39 NF.13 Mar 53 Fayid; Luqa Jan 55. 69 (Canberra) Sqn took over the number in Jun 58.

41 F.4 Jan 51 Church Fenton; Biggin Hill Mar 51; F.8 Apr 51. Re-equipped with Hunter F.5 Aug 55.

43 F.4 Feb 49 Tangmere; F.8 Oct 50; Leuchars Nov 50. Code SW carried until 1951. Re-equipped with Hunter F.1 Jul 54.

45 F.8 Mar 55 Butterworth (with Vampires). Sqn re-equipped Venom FB.1 Oct 55.

46 NF.12 and NF.14 Aug 54 Odiham. Re-equipped with Javelin FAW.1 Feb 56.

54 F.8 Apr 52 Odiham. Re-equipped with Hunter F.1 in Mar 55.

56 F.3 Apr 46 Bentwaters; Boxted Sep 46; Wattisham Nov 46; Duxford Apr 47; Thorney Island Mar 48; F.4 Jun 48; Waterbeach May 50; F.8 Dec 50. The squadron code ON used until 1947, when it was changed to US until the change to single codes in 1950. Re-equipped with Swift F.1 in Feb 54.

60 NF.14 Oct 59 Tengah (aircraft were collected from Leeming). Re-equipped with Javelin FAW.9 Sep 61

63 F.3 Apr 48 Thorney Island; F.4 Jun 48; F.8 1950. Waterbeach May 50; Code UB used until 1950. Re-equipped with Hunter F.6 1956.

64 F.8 Apr 51 Linton-on-Ouse; Duxford Aug 51; to NF.12 and NF.14 Sep 56. Re-equipped with the Javelin FAW.7 Sep 58.

65 F.8 Apr 51 Linton-on-Ouse; Duxford Aug 51. Re-equipped with Hunter F.6 Mar 57.

66 F.3 Mar 47 Duxford; F 4 May 48; Linton-on-Ouse Oct 49; F.8 Jan 51. Code HU used until 1949, then LZ until the change to F.8s. Re-equipped in Jan 54 with Sabre F.4.

68 NF.11 Jan 52 Wahn; Laarbruch Jul 57. Unit re-numbered 5 Sqn in Jan 59.

72 F.8 Jul 52 North Weald; Church Fenton Jul 53; NF.12 and NF.14 Dec 55. Re-equipped with the Javelin FAW.4 in Jun 59.

74 F.3 May 45 Colerne; Bentwaters Sep 46; Horsham St Faith Oct 46; F.4 Dec 47 (last F.3 left Mar 48); F.8 Oct 50. Code AD used until 1951. Re-equipped with Hunter F.4 Mar 57.

79 FR.9 Nov 51 Gutersloh; Buckeburg Jul 54; moved to Laarbruch, then Gutersloh. Re-equipped with Swift FR.5 Aug 56.

81 PR.10 Dec 53 Seletar; Tengah Mar 58. Canberras added to the unit in 1958, the last Meteor retiring from service in Jul 61.

85 NF.11 Oct 51 West Malling; NF.12 Aug 53; NF.14 May 54; Church Fenton Sep 57 with NF.12 and NF.14. Re-equipped with Javelin FAW.2 Nov 58 by re-numbering 89 Sqn at Stradishall. F(TT)8 Mar 63 Binbrook (with Canberras). Meteors retired at the end of 1969.

87 NF.11 Jan 52 Wahn. Re-equipped with the Javelin FAW.1 Aug 57 at Bruggen.

92 F.3 Jan 47 Acklington; Duxford Feb 47; F.4 May 48; Linton-on-Ouse Oct 49; F.8 Oct 50. The code DL used until the introduction of the F.8s, when it was changed to 8L. Two letter codes dropped in 1951. Re-equipped with Sabre F.4 in Feb 54.

96 NF.11 Oct 52 Ahlhorn. For a short time, the unit used a two-letter code beginning with the letter L. Re-numbered 3 Sqn Jan 59 and re-equipped with Javelin FAW.4 at Geilenkirchen.

111 F.8 Dec 53 North Weald. Re-equipped with the Hunter F.4 in Jun 55.

124 F.3 Aug 45 Molesworth; Bentwaters Oct 45. Code ON used. Re-numbered 56 Sqn Apr 46.

125 NF.11 Mar 55 Stradishall. Re-equipped with the Venom NF.3 in Jan 56.

141 NF.11 Sep 51 Coltishall. Re-equipped with Venom NF.3 Jun 55.

151 NF.11 Apr 53 Leuchars (with Vampire NF.10); Meteors only in 1954. Re-equipped with Venom NF.3 in Sep 55.

152 NF.12 and NF.14 Jun 54 Wattisham. Disbanded Jul 58 at Stradishall.

153 NF.12 and NF.14 Feb 55 West Malling; Waterbeach Sep 57. Re-numbered 25 Sqn in Jun 58.

208 FR.9 Mar 51 Fayid; Abu Sueir Oct 51; Hal Far Jan 56; Akrotiri Mar 56; Takali Aug 56. Unit re-equipped with Hunter F.6 at Tangmere Jan 58.

219 NF.13 Mar 51 Kabrit. Disbanded Sep 54.

222 F.3 Oct 45 Fairwood Common; Boxted Jun 46; Exeter Jun 46; Weston Zoyland Jul 46; Tangmere Oct 46; Lubeck May 47; Tangmere Jun 47; F.4 Dec 47; Lubeck Jun 48; Thorney Island Jul 48; Waterbeach Mar 50; Leuchars May 50; F.8 Sep 50. Used the code ZD until the mid-'fifties. Re-equipped with Hunter F.1 in Dec 54.

234 F.3 Feb 46 Molesworth; Boxted Mar 46. Code FX used. Re-numbered 266 Sqn in Sep 46.

245 F.3 Aug 45 Colerne; Bentwaters Jun 46; Horsham St Faith Oct 46; F.4 1948; F.8 Aug 50; Stradishall Jun 55. Code MR used until 1951. Re-equipped with Hunter F.4 Apr 57.

247 F.8 May 51 Odiham. Re-equipped with Hunter F.1 Jun 55.

256 NF.11 Nov 52 Ahlhorn; Geilenkirchen Feb 58. Re-numbered as 11 Sqn Jan 59.

257 F.3 Sep 46 Church Fenton; Horsham St Faith Sep 47; F.4 1948; F.8 1950; Wattisham Oct 50. Used the code A6 until the end of 1950. Re-equipped with Hunter F.2 Nov 54.

263 F.3 Sep 45 Acklington; Church Fenton Sep 45; Boxted Jun 46; Horsham St Faith Sep 46; To F.4 1948; F.8 1950; Wattisham Oct 50. Code HE used until 1950. Re-equipped with Hunter F.2 Jan 55, (last Meteor left in Feb 55).

264 NF.11 Dec 51 Linton-on-Ouse; NF.12 and NF.14 Oct 54; Middleton St George Mar 57. Re-numbered 33 Sqn Oct 57 at Leeming.

266 F.3 Sep 46 Boxted; Acklington Sep 46; Wattisham Nov 46; Tangmere Apr 47; Lubeck Apr 47; Tangmere Jun 47; F.4 Feb 48. Code FX used. Unit re-numbered 43 Sqn Feb 49.

500 F.3 Jul 48 West Malling; F.4 Jul 51; F.8 Nov 51. Used the code RAA until 1950, when it was changed to S7 for the last year of codes. Squadron was disbanded in Feb 57.

501 F.8 1953 Filton. Disbanded Feb 57.

504 F.3 Apr 45 Colerne. Re-numbered 245 Sqn Aug 45 F.4 Oct 49 Wymeswold; F.8 Mar 52. The F.3s used the code TM; F.4s used RAD until 1951. Squadron disbanded in Feb 57.

527 NF.11 Watton Jun 53 to Aug 55 (with other types)

541 F.3 1946 Benson (with other types). Disbanded. PR.10 Dec 50 Benson; Buckeburg Jun 51; Laarbruch Nov 54; Wunsdorf Nov 55. Used the code WY until changed to a two-letter code starting with the letter A in 1951. Disbanded Sep 57.

600 F.4 Mar 50 Biggin Hill; F.8 Nov 51. Code LJ used until the end of 1953. Disbanded Mar 57.

601 F.8 Aug 52 North Weald. Disbanded Mar 57.

604 F.8 Aug 52 North Weald. Disbanded Feb 57.

609 F.4 and F.8 Jan 51 Church Fenton; F.8 only from late 1951. Disbanded Feb 57.

610 F.4 Apr 51 Hooton Park; F.8 Sep 51. Squadron disbanded in Feb 57.

611 F.4 May 51 Woodvale; Hooton Park Jul 51; F.8 Dec 51. Disbanded Feb 57.

615 F.4 Sep 50 Biggin Hill; F.8 Sep 51. Code V6 was used until 1951. Disbanded Feb 57.

616 F.1 Jul 44 Culmhead; Manston Jul 44; Colerne Jan 45; F.3 Jan 45; Andrewsfield Feb 45; Gilze-Rijen Mar 45; B.109/Quackenbruck Apr 45; Lubeck May 45. Disbanded Aug 45. F.3 Dec 48 Finningley F.4 Apr 50; F.8 Dec 51; Worksop May 55. The code YQ was used in 1944 and 1945, changing to RAW for a short time in 1948, before reverting to YQ until all codes were dropped in 1951. The Sqn was finally disbanded in Feb 57.

In addition to their main equipment, virtually all these squadrons also operated one or more T.7s for continuation training, communications, target towing etc. These aircraft frequently continued in use long after the squadrons had re-equipped with more modern types, and were later joined by redundant F.8s in the same roles. The last front-line squadron to use Meteors in this way was 29 at Akrotiri in Cyprus, which retired its remaining two F.8s and single T.7 in November 1965.

OTHER FRONT-LINE SQUADRONS WITH METEORS ON INVENTORY FOR 'HACK' DUTIES

3 (Sabres, Geilenkirchen); 6 (Canberras, Akrotiri); 14 (Venoms, Fassberg); 16 (Venoms, Celle); 20 (Sabres, later Hunters, Ahlhorn); 23 (Javelins, Coltishall and Leuchars); 26 (Sabres, Oldenburg); 28 (Vampires, Kai Tak); 32 (Vampires, Nicosia); 67 (Sabres, Wildenrath); 71 (Sabres, Wildenrath), 73 (Vampires, Nicosia), 89 (Venoms, Stradishall); 93 (Vampires, Celle); 94 (Vampires, Celle); 98 (Vampires, Fassberg); 100 (Canberras, Wittering); 112 (Sabres, Bruggen); 118 (Vampires, Fassberg); 130 (Sabres, Bruggen); 145 (Venoms, Celle); 185 (Vampires, Habbaniya); 187 (a ferry unit at Aston Down, which 'acquired' a few FR.9s for a period in August and September 1953 for the annual Battle of Britain day celebrations); 213 (Canberras, Ahlhorn); 249 (Vampires, Deversoir); 502 (Vampires, Aldergrove); 603 (Vampires, Turnhouse); 605 (Vampires, Honiley); 607 (Vampires, Ouston); 608 (Vampires, Middleton St George); 612 (Vampires, Edzell); 613 (Vampires, Ringway); 614 (Vampires, Llandow).

METEOR AIRCREW TRAINING ESTABLISHMENTS

Advanced Flying Schools

202 AFS T.7 (with Vampires) Feb 51 Valley. Aircraft used code P. Re-numbered 7 FTS Jun 54.

203 AFS F.4 and T.7 1949 Driffield. Used the codes FMJ and FMK, later changed to O and X. Re-numbered 8 FTS Jun 54.

205 AFS F.4 and T.7 Sep 50 Middleton St George; moved to Worksop. Used the code Z. Unit became 4 FTS in Jun 54.

206 AFS F.4 and T.7 Oakington. Used the code Y.

207 AFS F.4 and T.7 Full Sutton. Disbanded 1954.

208 AFS F.4 and T.7 Merryfield. Disbanded 1954.

209 AFS F.4 and T.7 Weston Zoyland. Used the codes N and S. Re-numbered 12 FTS Jun 54.

210 AFS F.4 and T.7 Tarrant Rushton. Disbanded 1954

211 AFS F.4 and T.7 Worksop (with Vampires). The Meteor element absorbed into 4 FTS Jun 56.

215 AFS F.4 and T.7 Finningley 1952. Disbanded.

Conversion Units and Operational Conversion Units

1335 CU F.3 Colerne; Molesworth Jan 46. Code XL used. To Bentwater to become 226 OCU.

226 OCU F.3 Bentwaters; moved to Stradishall and acquired F.4s and T.7s, with F.8s and FR.9s later. Used the codes HX, KD and KR.

228 OCU NF.11 Jul 52 Leeming; NF.14 later. Meteors left in 1960 when it became the Javelin OCU.

229 OCU T.7 (with Vampires) Leuchars; Chivenor Mar 51. Used the code ES for a time. Became the Hunter OCU, but continued to operate Meteors until the unit moved to Brawdy in Sep 74, when it became 1 TWU.

231 OCU T.7, FR.9 and PR.10 Nov 51 Bassingbourn; Merryfield Jul 55. Became an all Canberra unit in Oct 56.

233 OCU T.7 and F.8 (with Vampires and Hunters) Pembrey. Meteors used in a non-training role only.

237 OCU PR.10 Apr 51 Benson; Bassingbourn Oct 51. Combined with 231 OCU Dec 51.

238 OCU NF.12 and NF.14 1955 Colerne; to North Luffenham Jan 57. Disbanded Jun 58.

Flying Training Schools

4 FTS F.4 and T.7 Jun 54 Middleton St George; Worksop Jun 56; F.8 1956. Became an all-Vampire unit in Dec 57.

5 FTS T.7 Oakington. Became a multi-engine school with Varsities.
8 FTS T.7 Jun 54 Driffield. Became an all-Vampire unit at Swinderby.
12 FTS T.7 Jun 54 Weston Zoyland. Disbanded.
19 FTS T.7 Cranwell. Used the code FAG. Became the RAF College.

Air Navigation Schools
1 ANS NF(T).14 and T.7 early 62 Stradishall. Re-equipped with Dominie T.1 autumn 65, although the last Meteor did not leave until late October.
2 ANS NF(T).14 and T.7 Jun 59 Thorney Island. Meteor element absorbed by 1 ANS early 62.

OTHER ROYAL AIR FORCE METEOR OPERATORS

1 GWDS T.7 Valley. Weapons trials unit equipped with Javelins.
1 OFU T.7 Jul 50 Chivenor; Abingdon 1951.
1 (P)RFU T.7 1951. Aircraft used code FDA.
1 TWU T.7 and F.8 1974 Brawdy. A Hunter and Hawk unit which retired the RAF's last Meteors in late 1982.
1 GCF (Group Communications Flt). T.7 Lindholme
2 TAF Com Flt T.7, FR.9 and PR.10 Buckeburg.
3 GCF T.7
3/4CAACU T.7 and TT.20 Jan 62 Exeter. Disbanded in 1970.
5CAACU T.7, F(TT).8 Llanbedr. Woodvale Jan 58. TT.20 1970. Disbanded Sep 71.
6 JSTU T.7 Valley. Became 1 GWDS in 1957.
11 GCF F.8 Martlesham Heath.
12 GCF F.8 Newton; to Coltishall. T.7 and NF.14.
13 GCF T.7 and NF.14 Ouston.
23 GCF T.7 Cranfield.
25 GCF T.7 Manby.
26 APC T.7 and F.8 Nicosia.
32 OTU No details known.
41 GCF T.7
81 GCF T.7 Colerne.
83 GCF T.7
101 FRS F.4 and T.7 Finningley.
102 FRS No details known, although it operated T.7s
103 FRS No details known, although it operated T.7s
205 GCF T.7 Abu Sueir. Became Abu Sueir Stn Flt.
1574 Flt T.7, F(TT).8 and TT.20 Nov 59 Changi. Unit disbanded at the end of 1970.
1689 Flt T.7 Benson 1950.

Abu Sueir Station Flight: T.7
Acklington Station Flight: T.7
Aden Protectorate Reconnaissance Flight: FR.9 Khormaksar. This is the same unit known in official records as the FR Flight.
Aden Communications Squadron: T.7 Khormaksar.
AFDS (part of CFE): F.3 and T.7. Used for communications, although virtually every mark of Meteor served with the various elements of the CFE. Aircraft used the code AF at one time.
Ahlhorn Station Flight: T.7
AIEU: T.7 Martlesham Heath.
Air Attache, Paris: F.8 Le Bourget.
AMSDU: F.4 Wattisham Aug to Nov 47.
APC Seletar: T.7.
APS Acklington: T.7 and F.8 from about 1950 to 1957. Used code WH. This unit also frequently referred to as 1 APS.
APS Sylt: T.7 and F(TT).8
AWDS (part of CFE): NF.14 West Raynham.
AWFCS (part of CFE): F.8 West Raynham. This unit at one time carried the 'shadow' squadron number 219.
ATF Sylt: T.7
BAFO Communications Squadron: Another title for 2 TAF Communications Flight at Buckeburg.
BCCF: T.7 Booker.
BCCS: T.7 1960 Benson.
Benson Station Flight: T.7
BFAP Station Flight: T.7 Khormaksar. Also known as the Khormaksar Station Flight.
Biggin Hill Station Flight: T.7 and F.8 from at least Apr 54 to Sep 57.
Binbrook Station Flight: T.7
Bruggen Station Flight: T.7
B & TT Flight: F.8 Seletar.
Caledonian Sector Flight: F.8 from at least 1952 to 1956, at Turnhouse.
CFE: F.3 Jul 45 Tangmere. Moved to West Raynham, and operated all marks of Meteor except the PR.10, NF.13 and TT.20 until their last T.7 was retired in 1963.
CFS: F.3 and T.7 1951 Little Rissington. Aircraft used code FDJ, later O. One T.7 was retained for display flying from 1970 onwards, and moved with the unit to Cranwell, Leeming and Scampton.
CGS: F.3 and F.4 1950 Leconfield. Later joined by T.7 and F.8 and re-named FWS in 1956. Aircraft used the codes FJT, FJV and FJX.
Changi TT Flight: T.7 and F(TT).8.
Church Fenton Station Flight: T.7 and F.8 from at least 1950 to 1960.
CNS: T.7 Hullavington 1949.
Coastal Command Communications Flt: T.7 Bovingdon
Colerne Communications Squadron: T.7 and F.8.
Coltishall Station Flight: T.7 and F.8.
Coningsby Station Flight: T.7
College of Air Warfare: T.7 and F.8 Manby and Strubby until 1966.
Cranwell Station Flight: T.7
CSDE: FR.9 Wittering.
CSE: NF.12 1957 Watton.
Development Squadron: NF.12 Watton. Probably part of the CSE.
DFLS (part of CFE): F.3 and other mks, West Raynham
Duxford Station Flight: T.7 and F.8 from at least 1953 to 1958.
EAAS: T.7 Hullavington. Used code FGC. Became the RAFFC at Manby in 1949.
EANS: Hullavington. Used code FGG. Became the CNS in 1949.
Eastern Sector Flight: F.4 Oct 46 Horsham St Faith; F.8 Jan 50 to Oct 57.
ECFS: F.3 Hullavington. Used code FCW; Became the EFS in 1946.
EFS: F.3 1946 Hullavington. Later acquired F.4 and T.7, and became part of the RAFFC at Manby in 1949. Used code FCS.
Fassberg Station Flight: T.7
FCCS: F.4 1947 Bovingdon; T.7 and F.8 circa 1950; NF.14 1960. Meteors retired in 1961. The unit coded all its aircraft FCCS, and was responsible for the C in C Fighter Command's own F.8.
FCIRS: T.7 West Raynham
FEAF Examining Squadron: T.7 Seletar.
FE Communications Squadron: T.7. Became the FE Training Squadron.
FE Training Squadron: T.7
FR Flight: FR.9 1959 Khormaksar. Disbanded 1960.
FSS: T.7 Benson from at least 1953 to 1960, during which time it became known as the FTU.
FTU: see FSS above.
FWS: T.7, F.8 and NF.12 Leconfield.
Gaydon Station Flight: T.7
Geilenkirchen Station Flight: T.7 and F.8.
Gutersloh Meteor Flight: T.7
Habbaniya Station Flight: F.8
Handling Squadron: T.7 and F.8 Boscombe Down, with the T.7 staying until 1966. Earlier marks, including F.4s, served with a Handling Sqn at Manby, but whether or not this was the same unit it not known.
Hemswell Station Flight: T.7
High Speed Flight: F.4 1945 and 1946 Tangmere.
Hooton Park Station Flight: F.8
Horsham St Faith Station Flight: T.7 and F.8 from at least Dec 1950 to May 57.
ITF BAFO: T.7
ITF Nicosia: T.7
ITF Shallufa: T.7
ITF Tangmere: T.7 1950; moved to West Raynham. Also referred to as the ITS.
Jet Conversion Flight Binbrook: F.4 and T.7
JCU Coningsby: T.7 circa 1953/54.
JCU Hemswell: T.7
JCU Marham: T.7
JSTU (Joint Service Trials Unit): NF.11
JTF Lyneham: T.7
Kai Tak TT Flight: T.7. Also known as Kai Tak SHQ.
Khormaksar Station Flight: T.7 and FR.9.
Laarbruch Station Flight: T.7
Leconfield Station Flight: T.7 up to at least Sep 60.
Leuchars Station Flight: T.7 and F.8.
Levant Communications Flight: T.7 and F.8.
Linton-on-Ouse Conversion Flight: T.7
Linton-on-Ouse Station Flight: T.7 and F.8.
Malta Communications & TT Squadron: T.7 and F.8 circa 1956 to 1959, Takali.
MEAF Communication Flt/Sqn: T.7 Khormaksar.
Metropolitan Sector Flight: F.3 May 46 North Weald. Later acquired F.8s and moved to West Malling.
Middleton St George Station Flight: T.7 until at least Sep 60.
Middle Wallop Station Flight: F.3 Jul 46 to Mar 47.
Nicosia Station Flight/TT Flight: T.7 and F.8.
Northern Sector Flight: F.4 and F.8 from Dec 50 to (C) Nov 57.
North Weald Station Flight: T.7 and F.8.
Odiham Station Flight: T.7 and F.8 until about 1959.
Oldenburg Station Flight: T.7
Ouston Station Flight: F.8
PC & S Squadron Aden: T.7 Khormaksar.
PRDU: FR.3 Benson 1946.
RAF College: T.7 Cranwell.
RAF Flying College T.7 and F.8 Manby and Strubby.
Scampton Station Flight: T.7
Scottish Sector Flight: F.8 Leuchars.
SHQ Butterworth: F.8
SHQ Seletar: T.7 and F.8
Southern Sector Flight: F.3 Mar 47 Middle Wallop. Later moved to Tangmere and Biggin Hill and flew F.8s.
SRF: T.7 and F.8 Strubby until 1966. Was officially 3 Squadron of the RAFFC.
Stradishall Station Flight: T.7 and F.8.
Tangmere Station Flight: F.3 Oct 52 to Feb 56; T.7, F.8 Jun 54 to at least 1956.
Target Facilities Squadron: F.8 Binbrook. Became 85 Squadron in Mar 63.
Thorney Island Station Flight: T.7
THUM Flight: F.8 Woodvale; Disbanded May 59.
TT Flight North Front: F.8 Gibraltar.
TT Flight Seletar: T.7
TT Flight Takali: T.7. Probably a reference to the MC & TTS.
Turnhouse Communications Flight: F.8 in 1957/58.
Upwood Station Flight: T.7
Wahn Station Flight: T.7
Waterbeach Station Flight: T.7 and F.8 between 1956 and 1959 at least.
Wattisham Station Flight: T.7 and F.8 still in use 1960
Western Sector Communications Flight: F.8
West Malling Station Flight: F.3, F(TT).8 in use Sep 60.
West Raynham Station Flight: T.7
Wildenrath Station Flight: T.7. Also known as the Wildenrath Meteor Flight.
Wittering Station Flight: T.7
Wroughton Station Flight: T.7
Wunsdorf Meteor Flight: T.7
Wymeswold Station Flight: F.8 from at least Nov 55 to May 57.
Wyton Station Flight: T.7
Yorkshire Sector Flight: F.8. Linton-on-Ouse. Became the Northern Sector Flight Dec 50.

The units listed above, are in the main, those to which the aircraft were officially allocated. It should be realised that the situation is considerably complicated by the then common practice of units borrowing aircraft, with no official transfer taking place. Thus it may well be that further operators of the Meteor have yet to come to light.

Another common practice was that of applying the markings of the locally based squadrons to station flight aircraft. This was particularly prevalent at the fighter units, where it was often the case that the Meteors would carry the badges or flashes of several different units, such as 43 and 151 Squadrons at Leuchars, who shared space on several aircraft.

Many station, wing and even sometimes squadron, commanders, acquired their own Meteors, which were often decorated with their initials although they remained on the strength of either one of the local squadrons, or of the station flight. Likewise, high-ranking officers in charge of commands or groups had similar machines, which were usually looked after by the nearest group or command communication flight and appeared on their books.

Where unit titles have been abbreviated, they are presented in the form by which they were commonly known. Many were simply not spoken in shortened form (e.g. the Royal Air Force College was never called the 'RAFC'), and are thus presented in full. An explanation of the abbreviations can be found on page 163.

MAINTENANCE UNITS HANDLING METEORS AND TRAINING SCHOOLS USING GROUNDED AIRFRAMES

5 MU Kemble: Storage and disposal unit until late '70s
6 MU Brize Norton: Receipt and modification Feb 48 to Oct 51.
12 MU Kirkbridge: Storage and disposal.
20 MU Aston Down: Storage/preparation for overseas.
29 MU High Ercall: Receipt.
33 MU Lyneham: Storage, preparation for overseas and disposal.
38 MU Llandow: Receipt.
390 MU Seletar: Storage and disposal.
1 S of TT Halton.
2 S of TT Cosford.
4 S of TT St Athan.
5 S of TT Locking.
10 S of TT Kirkham.
12 S of TT Melksham.
RAF Henlow.

ROYAL NAVY UNITS

700 Sqn TT.20 1958 Yeovilton. Disbanded Jun 60.
702 Sqn T.7 1948 Ford.
728 Sqn T.7 1952 Lossiemouth; Hal Far Mar 58; TT.20 Mar 58. Disbanded May 67.
728(B) Sqn U.15 and U.16 1959 Hal Far. Meteors had gone by 1961.
736 Sqn T.7 1953 Lossiemouth.
759 Sqn T.7 Apr 52 Culdrose; Lossiemouth Oct 53. Re-equipped with Hunter T.8.
771 Sqn T.7 1949 Lee-on-Solent.
778 Sqn F.3 1948 Ford. Meteors left approx 1954.
Airwork FRU: T.7 and TT.20 May 58 Hurn. Disbanded May 70. This unit was officially 776 FRU, but the number was never used.
Airwork FRU: T.7 St Davids. Disbanded 1958.
Brawdy Station Flight//TT Flight: T.7 and TT.20.
Ford Station Flight: T.7 1951, TT.20 1958.
Handling Squadron: TT.20 1958 Milltown. Disbanded in Jan 62.
Lossiemouth Station Flight: T.7 from at least 1955 to 1959.
Yeovilton Station Flight T.7 and TT.20.
AHU Brawdy: Repair and storage.
AHU Lossiemouth: Repair and storage.
NARIU Lee-on-Solent: Modification unit.
RNAY Fleetlands: Overhaul and repair.
RNAY Sydenham: Modification and storage.

AIR MINISTRY, MoD AND OTHER GOVERNMENT ESTABLISHMENTS

A & AEE Every mark of Meteor from 1944 until the late 1960s. Boscombe Down.
BLEU T.7 Bedford/Thurleigh.
CRD F.1 1944; F.3 Defford.
ETPS F.1 Apr 45; F.3, F.4, T.7, F.8, NF.11 and NF.14 until about 1965. Cranfield, then Farnborough.
IAM T.7 Farnborough.
NGTE F.1, F.4 and T.7 Farnborough.
RAE Bedford: T.7, F.8 and NF.14 until late 1960s.
RAE Farnborough: F.1, F.3, F.4, T.7, F.8 until 1973.
RAE Llanbedr: T.7, U.15, U.16, D.16, NF.14 and the TT.20. Three Meteors still in use in 1984.
RAE West Freugh: T.7
RRE NF.11 and NF.14 Pershore.
TRE F.4, F.8 and NF.11 Defford.

Appendix B

Overseas Operators of the Meteor

ARGENTINA

100 F.4s delivered between May 1947 and January 1949, serials I-001 to I-100, the first 50 ex-RAF, second 50 being new build. Serial prefix later changed from I to C.

Operated by Fighter-Bomber Groups 2 and 3 of Air Brigade 7 at Moron.

Survivors: C-019, I-025 (Moron); C-041 (Buenos Aires)

AUSTRALIA

One ex-RAF F.3 delivered 1947. A77-1

Nine ex-RAF T.7 delivered between 1951 and 1955.

Ninety-four ex-RAF F.8 delivered between 1951 and 1953. See Production Lists for serial details.

One ex-RAF NF.11 delivered Aug 53. A77-3.

Operating Units:

1 APU F.3 Jun 46 Laverton, w/o 14.2.47.

22 (City of Sydney) Sqn; T.7 and F.8 1955 Richmond. Unit reduced to non-flying status Jun 60.

23 (City of Brisbane) Sqn: T.7 and F.8 1955 Amberley. Unit reduced to non-flying status Jun 60.

38 Sqn Comms Flight: T.7 and F.8 1960 Richmond.

77 Sqn T.7 and F.8 May 51 Iwakuni. Moved to Kimpo. Williamtown Dec 54. Re-equipped with Sabres during 1955.

75 Sqn T.7 and F.8 (with Vampires) Dec 54 Williamtown. Re-equipped with Sabres during 1955.

The F.8s later converted to U.21 drones, were operated by 1 and 2 Air Trials Units from Edinburgh Field from 1961 to 1970, alongside a few T.7s and the NF.11.

Survivors: see production appendix.

BELGIUM

F.4 Forty-eight new Gloster-built examples delivered 1949. Serials EF-1 to EF-48. Twenty of these were later converted by Avions Fairey to T.7 standard (see under T.7) and others to Israel.

T.7 Forty-three aircraft, acquired in several batches between 1948 and 1957. ED-1 to ED-3 newly built by Glosters, delivered 1948. ED-4 to ED-12 unused ex-RAF aircraft, delivered 1951-53. ED-13 to ED-42 converted from Belgian F.4s by Avions Fairey. ED-33 to ED-37 second batch of unused ex-RAF aircraft. ED-38 to ED-43 batch of six used ex-RAF aircraft.

F.8 240 aircraft delivered from various sources, as under: EG-1 to EG-145 Fokker-built, delivered 1950-54. EG-146 to EG-150 ex-RAF, delivered via Fokker 1951. EG-151 to EG-180 thirty aircraft assembled by Avions Fairey from components built by Fokker. EG-201 to EG-223 ex-RAF aircraft delivered 1950/51. EG-224 to EG-260 were assembled by Avions Fairey from Gloster-built parts.

NF.11 Twenty-four aircraft, delivered in two batches of twelve (in 1952 and 1956). Several operated with both Belgian serials on fuselage and their ex-RAF identity under the wings. Serials EN-1 to EN-24. Survivors withdrawn 1958 and languished at Oostende with temporary civil registrations.

Operating Units:

1 Wing, Beauvechain:
- 4 Sqn: T.7 and F.8.
- 10 Sqn: T.7 and F.8, NF.11 1957. Used the code KT.
- 11 Sqn: T.7 and F.8, NF.11 1957. Used the code ND.
- 349 Sqn: F.4, later T.7 and F.8. Used the code GR.
- 350 Sqn: F.4, later T.7 and F.8. Used the code MN.
- Wing re-equipped with Hunter F.4 and F.6 during 1955-56, except for 10 and 11 Squadrons, which received the CF-100 in 1959.

5 Wing, Sylt:
- 24 Sqn: F(TT).8, renamed TTF in 1954.

7 Wing, Chievres:
- 7 Sqn: T.7 and F.8. Used the code 7J.
- 8 Sqn: T.7 and F.8.
- 9 Sqn: T.7 and F.8. Used the code S2.
- Wing re-equipped with Hunter F.4 and F.6

9 Wing, Bierset:
- 22 Sqn: T.7 and F.8. 26 Sqn: T.7 and F.8
- Wing re-equipped with Hunter F.4 and F.6.

13 Wing, Brustem, later Koksijde:
- 25 Sqn: T.7 and F.8. 29 Sqn: T.7 and F.8
- 33 Sqn: T.7 and F.8

Fighter School: T.7

TTF Koksijde: F(TT).8.

TTF Solenzara: F(TT).8.

TTF Sylt: F(TT).8. Used the code B2.

Survivors: EG-18 (Chièvres); EG-79 (Brustem); EG-162 (Dinant); EG-224 (Brussels); EG-247 (Brussels).

BRAZIL

Ten T.7 delivered 1953. Serials 4300 to 4309, believed to be ex-RAF allocations WS142 to WS151.

Sixty F.8 delivered 1953. Serials 4400 to 4459, of which 4455 to 4459 were ex-Egyptian Air Force 1415, 1419, 1420, 1421 and 1423 respectively.

Operated by two squadrons of the 1st Grupo de Caca, Santa Cruz. Replaced by Mirage IIIE.

Survivors: 4401 (Rezende-Rio); 4411 (Goiania-Go); 4438 (Galaleo); 4441 (Santa Cruz); 4460 (Rio).

CANADA

One F.4 loaned to CNAE Uplands: VT196.

Two F.7 used for a short time in 1953 by 421 Sqn at Odiham. Serials WA740 and WA742, both returned to the RAF.

DENMARK

Twenty F.4 delivered during 1949 and 1950. Serials 461 to 480.

Nine T.7 delivered 1951. Serials 261 to 269.

Twenty F.8 delivered 1951. Serials 481 to 500.

Twenty NF.11 delivered in 1952 and 1953. Serials 501 to 520, with 504, 508, 512, 517, 518 and 519 later being converted to TT.20 standard. (These aircraft were allocated RAF serials WM384 to WM403. to WM403).

Operating Units:

3 Air Flotilla: F.4 1949 Karup. Became 723 Sqn in Jan 51.

723 Sqn: F.4 Jan 51 Karup; NF.11 1942 Aalborg. Re-equipped with F-86D Sabre.

724 Sqn: F.4 1951 Karup; F.8 1951.

Flying School/Conversion Unit: F.4 and T.7 Karup.

Survivors: 265 (Karup); 461 (Copenhagen); 469 (Skrydstrup); 491 (Karup); 499 (Karup); 504 (Aalborg).

EGYPT

Twelve F.4 delivered 1950. Serials 1401 to 1412.

Six T.7 delivered between 1949 and 1955. Serials 1400, 1413, 1414 and 1439 to 1441, with the last three being ex-RAF.

Twelve F.8 delivered between 1952 and 1955. Serials 1415 to 1426, all ex-RAF.

Six ex-RAF NF.13 del'd 1955. Serials 1427 to 1432.

ECUADOR

Twelve FR.9 delivered 1954 and 1955. Serials 701 to 712 all ex-RAF. Later reserialled with FF prefixes, examples being FF-116, FF-119, FF-123.

Operated by 21 Squadron at Taura until about 1971/72.

Survivors: FF-123 at Quito.

FRANCE

Two ex-RAF F.4 delivered in 1948 and 1952. EE523 became F-WEPQ, RA491 retained its British serial.

Fourteen T.7, serials 91 and 92 new aircraft (diverted from Syrian order) delivered February 1951; F-BEAR (ex WA607) delivered 1955; F1 to F11 (for EC 30) ex-RAF stocks delivered in 1956.

Forty-one NF.11 delivered 1954-55. NF11-1 to NF11-9 for CEV and NF11-10 to NF11-41 for EC 30, all ex-RAF stocks.

Two NF.13 delivered 1956. Serials 364, 365, ex-RAF.

Two NF.14, NF14-747 (ex WS747) delivered 28.8.55 and NF14-796 (ex WS796) delivered 20.10.55.

Six TT.20 (de-modded) delivered 1974 for spares use. All used the ferry serial F-ZABD and were ex-RAF.

Operating Units:

30 Escadre: NF.11 1953 Tours. Re-equipped with the Vautour IIN in 1957/58. The wing consisted of three squadrons, with all aircraft coded with the wing number, followed by a two-letter sequence, the first of which denoted the squadron, (e.g. aircraft belonging to Esc.1/30 used the letter O). Also used a few T.7s.

CEV (Centre d'Essais en Vol): T.7, NF.11, NF.13 and NF.14, with the NF.11 and NF.14 surviving in use in 1984. In recent years, these aircraft have adopted a two-letter code system commencing with B.

Preserved: NF.11-24 (Musée de l'Air).

ISRAEL

Six T.7 delivered Jun 53. Serials 2162 to 2165 from Glosters, plus 4X-FNB and one from Avions Fairey.

ISRAEL *continued*

Eleven F.8 delivered 1953 and 1954. Serials 2166 to 2169 and 2172 to 2178, of which 2176 and 2178 were all ex-Egyptian.

Seven FR.9 delivered 1954 and 1955. Serials 211 to 217, all being ex-RAF.

Six NF.13 delivered 1956 to 1958, all ex-RAF. Serials 4X-FNA, 4X-FNB, 4X-FND left 5.9.56 on delivery. 4X-FNC, 4X-FNE, 4X-FNF spent prolonged period in storage (i.e. until after the Suez incident) at Bitteswell) before departing on delivery 21.3.58. Dates quoted in the production lists are thought to be those when the airframe passed from the RAF to AWA.

At some time during their service, Israeli Meteors were reserialled, examples being F.8 106 and NF.13 157.

Survivors: NF.13 157 (Be'er Sheva); 4X-BET (Lodd).

NETHERLANDS

Sixty-five F.4 delivered from 1948. Serials I-21 to I-58 new build and I-59 to I-86 ex-RAF.

Forty-three T.7 delivered between 1949 and 1956. Serials I-1 (formerly G-AKPK) to I-20, I-87 to I-100 and I-256 to I-264. Ten aircraft later transferred from the air force to the navy as serials 131 to 140.

160 F.8 delivered between 1951 and 1954. Serials I-90 to I-94 ex-RAF, and I-101 to I-255 Fokker built.

Operating Units:

322 Sqn: F.4 1948 Soesterberg; F.8 1951. Re-equipped with Hunter F.4 in 1956.

323 Sqn: F.4 Leeuwarden; F.8. Re-equipped with the Hunter F.4 in 1956.

324 Sqn: F.8 Leeuwarden. Re-equipped with the Hunter F.4.

325 Sqn: F.8 Leeuwarden. Re-equipped with the Hunter F.4.

326 Sqn: F.4 Leeuwarden; F.8.

327 Sqn: F.4 Soesterberg; F.8. Re-equipped with the Hunter F.4.

328 Sqn: F.8 Soesterberg.

Fighter School: F.4 Twenthe.

Survivors: I-19 (Gilze-Rijen); I-69 (Soesterberg); I-177 (Gilze-Rijen); I-187 (Soesterberg); I-189 (Schiphol); 'I-320' (Beek).

NEW ZEALAND

One F.3 delivered 1945. Serial NZ6001 ex-RAF EE395. Became instructional airframe INST147 at Hobsonville in 1947.

SOUTH AFRICA

One F.3 delivered Mar 46, ex-RAF EE429. Returned to Britain in Jul 49.

SWEDEN

Three T.7 delivered between 1955 and 1959 and operated as target-tugs by Swedair. Registered SE-CAS ex-WF833, SE-CAT ex-WH128 and SE-DCC ex-G-ANSO.

Four TT.20 delivered in the early sixties, all ex-Danish Air Force. Registered SE-DCF ex-512, SE-DCG ex-517, SE-DCH ex-508 and SE-DCI ex-519. All were withdrawn from use by late 1966.

Survivors: SE-CAS (Malmslatt); SE-DCC (Ugglarp).

SYRIA

Two T.7 delivered Jun 50 at Moreton Valence, but not taken up and diverted to France (serials 91 and 92). Two further ex-RAF aircraft, also serialled 91 and 92 delivered in Nov 52.

Nineteen F.8 delivered in 1952 and 1953. Serials 101 to 112 and 413 to 419 - the latter batch were ex-RAF WA785, WL174, WK868, WK984, WH503, WE965 and WH260 respectively and were delivered between 26.3.56 and 7.5.56.

Two FR.9 delivered in 1956. Serials 480 and 481, ex-RAF WB133 and WK972 respectively, both delivered 17.7.56.

Six NF.13 delivered 1954. Serials 471 to 476, ex-RAF.

All surviving Meteors were replaced by MiG-15 and MiG-17 aircraft in the late fifties.

UNITED STATES

One F.1 delivered Feb 44 for evaluation at Muroc Field. Serial EE210/G, later returned to GAC.

One TT.20 acquired by Al Letcher in Jun 75 and based at Mojave. Registered N94749, ex-WD592.

Appendix C

Meteor Production and Individual Histories

SUMMARY OF PRODUCTION FOR ROYAL AIR FORCE & ROYAL NAVY

plus Company Demonstrators

Model	Number built	Remarks
F.9/40	8	GAC-built; ordered 6.2.41.
F.1	20	GAC-built; ordered 8.8.41. Delivered 7/9.44.
F.3	210	GAC-built. Delivered 12.44 to 4.46.
F.4	490	GAC-built up to VW791; AWA-built from VZ386. Delivered 5.45 to 4.50.
T.7	641	GAC-built. First batch ordered 2.8.47, last 28.4.51. Delivered 12.48 to 7.54.
F.8 (inc GAF)	1090	GAC-built except for the following AWA-built batches VZ518 to 569, WA755 to WB112, WE852 to 902, WF639 to 688, all WH series with gaps, also WK707 to 756 and WK906 to 935. First batch ordered 4.9.49 last batch ordered 15.1.51. Delivered 8.50 to 5.54.
FR.9	126	GAC-built. First batch was ordered 2.8.47, last 17.8.51. Delivered 7.50 to 8.52.
PR.10	59	GAC-built. First batch was ordered 22.11.46, last 8.8.50 Delivered 12.50 to 4.52.
NF.11	318	AWA-built. Delivered 10.50 to 1953.
NF.12	100	AWA-built. Del. 1953/54.
NF.13	40	AWA-built. Delivered 1953.
NF.14	100	AWA-built. Delivered 3.54. to 5.55.

GLOSTER F.9/40

DG202/G f/f 24.7.43 Barford St John. Rolls-Royce. Deck trials HMS *Pretoria Castle*. Moreton Valence. To 5 STT Locking as 5758M. Yatesbury 1.51, to gate 3.58. To Cosford Aerospace museum.
DG203/G f/f 9.11.43 Moreton Valence.
DG204/G f/f 13.11.32 Farnborough. w/o 1.4.44.
DG205/G f/f 12.6.43 Barford St John. w/o Moreton Valence 27.4.44.
DG206/G f/f 5.3.43 Cranwell. NGTE. Scrap.
DG207/G f/f 24.7.45 Moreton Valence. DH Hatfield. (F.2 prototype).
DG208/G f/f 20.1.44 Moreton Valence. DH Hatfield. To 5 STT 5.11.46 as 5826M.
DG209/G f/f 18.4.44 Moreton Valence. Rolls-Royce. RAE Farnborough. Scrap 13.7.46.
DG210/G Construction not proceeded with.
DG211/G Construction not proceeded with.
DG212/G Construction not proceeded with.
DG213/G Construction not proceeded with.

METEOR F.1

EE210 f/f 12.1.44. RAE. Loaned to US 18.2.44, Muroc Field. GAC 24.4.45. RAE Farnborough 17.5.45. To Melksham 5.3.46 as 5837M.
EE211 f/f 16.4.44. RAE. To 2 STT Cosford 12.4.46 as 5927M. Scrap 4.56.
EE212 f/f 15.4.44. F.3 aerodynamic prototype. A & AEE. To 14 STT 23.5.46 as 5943M. Scrap 14.9.50.
EE213 RAE Farnborough. A & AEE. To 11 STT on 11.1.46 as 5790M.
EE214 RAE Farnborough. CRD Defford. To 11 STT 17.1.46 as 5798M. Scrap 15.12.49.
EE215 A & AEE. 616 Sqn. CRD Flt. Power Jets. soc 29.11.47.
EE216 CRD Farnborough. 616 Sqn. 1335 CU (XL-A). To 1 STT 27.9.45 as 5676M.
EE217 CRD. 616 Sqn. 1335 CU. GAC. 39 MU. To 2 STT 5.12.45 as 5752M.
EE218 616 Sqn. 1335 CU. To 1 STT as 5677M. To Cosford. soc 27.5.49.
EE219 616 Sqn (YQ-D/YQ-N). To 11 STT 17.1.46 as 5799M.
EE220 616 Sqn (YQ-G). 1335 CU. To Locking on 21.9.45 as 5678M.
EE221 616 Sqn. GAC. AID Jets. 39 MU. To 2 STT as 6544M. Scrap 14.9.50.
EE222 616 Sqn. w/o 29.8.44, forced landing out of fuel at Plucksgutter, Kent.
EE223 GAC. CRD. A & AEE. Rolls-Royce. Scrap 6.46
EE224 616 Sqn. Ground accident 17.8.44; re-cat w/o 20.9.44, hit by cannon shells from EE225 while on the ground at Manston.
EE225 616 Sqn. 1335 CU. To 5 STT 29.3.45 as 5094M
EE226 616 Sqn. w/o 15.8.44, stalled and spun-in on approach, near Ashford.
EE227 616 Sqn (YQ-Y). RAE Farnborough. Rolls-Royce. Conv to Trent Meteor. A & AEE. Rolls-Royce. RAE Farnborough for fire tests. Scrap end 1948. soc 29.6.49.
EE228 616 Sqn. 1335 CU (XL-E). GAC. To 5 STT on 8.2.46 as 5816M.
EE229 616 Sqn (YQ-W). 1335 CU. Church Fenton Stn Flt to St Athan 12.6.47, became 6356M.

METEOR F.2

See F.9/40 DG207/G

METEOR F.3

EE230 A & AEE. soc 31.5.49.
EE231 616 Sqn. 1335 CU. To 4 STT 30.6.55 as 5785M
EE232 616 Sqn. 1335 CU. CFE. To 11 STT as 5789M.
EE233 616 Sqn. 1335 CU (XL-E). To Henlow on 10.10.45 as 5711M.
EE234 616 Sqn (YQ-O). 1335 CU. To 5229M 28.4.45, after accident.
EE235 616 Sqn (YQ-H). 1335 CU. CFE (RA). To 2 STT 10.1.46 as 5781M.
EE236 616 Sqn. 1335 CU. ECFS. To 11 STT 12.1.46 as 5786M.
EE237 616 Sqn. 1335 CU. To Henlow 10.10.45 as 5712M.
EE238 616 Sqn. 1335 CU. w/o 18.5.45, Farnborough, lost control in a roll.
EE239 616 Sqn. 1335 CU. ECFS. To 11 STT 12.1.46 as 5787M.
EE240 616 Sqn. 1335 CU. CFE. To 2 STT 10.1.46 as 5782M.
EE241 616 Sqn. 1335 CU. To 2 STT 10.1.46 as 5783M
EE242 616 Sqn. 1335 CU. To 11 STT 12.1.46 as 5791M.
EE243 616 Sqn (YQ-F). AFDU/CFE (MD). To 2 STT 18.1.46 as 5784M.
EE244 616 Sqn. 1335 CU (XL-U/XL-Z). Damaged during take-off 29.3.45, to 11 STT 12.1.46 as 5788M.
EE245 616 Sqn (YQ-C). 263 Sqn (HE-C). 222 Sqn. 234 Sqn. 266 Sqn. w/o 9.2.48.
EE246 616 Sqn (YQ-A). ML Aviation. RAE Farnborough. To PEE ranges Shoeburyness 4.12.50.
EE247 616 Sqn. 263 Sqn. 222 Sqn (ZD-P). 1 Sqn. 222 Sqn. 245 Sqn. 56 Sqn. To 1 STT 8.7.48 as 6573M.
EE248 616 Sqn (YQ-C). CFE. 263 Sqn (HE-C). 66 Sqn. 56 Sqn. 206 AFS. To 12 STT 16.2.55 as 7184M.
EE249 616 Sqn. 263 Sqn (HE-N). FCCS. Scrap 8.10.55
EE250 616 Sqn. 263 Sqn. To 2 STT 18.2.47 as 6271M.
EE251 Handling Sqn. To 11 STT 8.3.46 as 5838M.
EE252 616 Sqn. w/o 29.4.45, mid-air collision with EE273.
EE253 616 Sqn. 257 Sqn (A6-E). 616 Sqn. 206 AFS. 210 AFS. Scrap 22.6.56.
EE254 616 Sqn. 234 Sqn (FX-J). 266 Sqn (FX-J). 616 Sqn. To 1 STT 23.5.52 as 6961M.
EE269 A & AEE. 500 Sqn (RAA-D). To Bentley Priory 23.5.51 as 6866M.
EE270 616 Sqn. 222 Sqn (ZD-F). 245 Sqn (MR-H). 74 Sqn. 245 Sqn. 66 Sqn (HI-H). 222 Sqn. Scrap 18.1.55.
EE271 616 Sqn. 245 Sqn. 56 Sqn (ON-H/US-H). To 1 STT 8.7.48 as 6572M.
EE272 616 Sqn. 257 Sqn. 263 Sqn (HE-M). 500 Sqn. 206 AFS. Scrap 9.7.56.
EE273 616 Sqn. w/o 29.4.45, mid-air collision with EE252.
EE274 616 Sqn. 263 Sqn (HE-P/HE-X). 257 Sqn. To 2 STT 15.4.48 as 6546M.
EE275 616 Sqn (YQ-Q). 263 Sqn (HE-Q). 74 Sqn. 226 OCU. 206 AFS. 210 AFS. Scrap 11.8.55.
EE276 616 Sqn (YQ-T). 263 Sqn (HE-R). 616 Sqn. To 4 STT 16.5.52 as 6978M.
EE277 616 Sqn. 234 Sqn. 266 Sqn (FX-H). 222 Sqn. Scrap 17.11.55.
EE278 616 Sqn. 263 Sqn (HE-T). 257 Sqn (A6-A). 222 Sqn. SHQ Thorney Island. 1 Sqn. 206 AFS. To 1 STT 28.12.54. as 7165M.
EE279 504 Sqn. 616 Sqn. 263 Sqn (HE-G). 74 Sqn. 226 OCU. To 1 STT 15.5.52 as 6962M.
EE280 504 Sqn. w/o 23.8.45, mid-air collision with EE283 near Weston-super-Mare.
EE281 CFE. 226 OCU. w/o 28.1.48.
EE282 504 Sqn. 245 Sqn. 222 Sqn. A & AEE. CFS. 206 AFS. Scrap 18.10.55.
EE283 504 Sqn (RAA-P). 245 Sqn. 500 Sqn. 205 AFS soc 2.7.52.
EE284 504 Sqn. 245 Sqn. 1 Sqn. 66 Sqn. 222 Sqn. Scrap 20.4.56.
EE285 504 Sqn. 616 Sqn. 257 Sqn. 263 Sqn (HE-A). soc 29.9.48.
EE286 504 Sqn. 245 Sqn (MR-Q). 1335 CU. To 11 STT 31.1.46 as 5804M.
EE287 504 Sqn. 245 Sqn. 266 Sqn. 63 Sqn. CFS. 206 AFS. 210 AFS. To PEE 20.4.56.
EE288 (Last aircraft built to carry the security letter G after its serial number). 504 Sqn. w/o 8.6.45, spun-in at Colerne.
EE289 504 Sqn. 245 Sqn. 600 Sqn. To 1 STT 27.5.52 as 6963M.
EE290 234 Sqn (FX-A). 266 Sqn. 500 Sqn. w/o 14.10.50.
EE291 CRD Power Jets. w/o 21.7.45 during display for Power Jets at Whetstone, Leics, killing test-pilot P.J. Moffet.
EE292 504 Sqn. 245 Sqn (MR-D). 257 Sqn (A6-D). 266 Sqn. 63 Sqn (UB-F). 206AFS. To 1 STT 18.1.54 as 7127M.
EE293 504 Sqn. 245 Sqn. w/o 23.4.46.
EE294 616 Sqn. 504 Sqn. 245 Sqn. 257 Sqn. 266 Sqn. Scrap 5.5.48.
EE295 504 Sqn. 245 Sqn. 222 Sqn. w/o 1.7.46.
EE296 616 Sqn. 504 Sqn. 245 Sqn. 1335 CU. 226 OCU. w/o 25.3.47.
EE297 504 Sqn. 245 Sqn. w/o out of fuel 18.12.47.
EE298 504 Sqn. 245 Sqn. w/o 16.1.46.
EE299 504 Sqn. 245 Sqn. 226 OCU. soc 25.2.49.
EE300 616 Sqn. 263 Sqn. 616 Sqn. To 8 STT 5.5.52 as 6965M.
EE301 616 Sqn. 263 Sqn (HE-X). soc 22.6.47.
EE302 504 Sqn. 245 Sqn. w/o 8.10.45, spun in near Frome, Somerset.
EE303 504 Sqn. 245 Sqn. 222 Sqn. 245 Sqn. w/o on 18.12.47.
EE304 504 Sqn. 245 Sqn. 222 Sqn. Tangmere Stn Flt. 222 Sqn. Scrap 26.5.55.
EE305 504 Sqn. 245 Sqn. 74 Sqn. 500 Sqn. 206 AFS. Scrap 22.6.56.
EE306 74 Sqn (4D-N). CGS (FJV-O). To 8 STT on 22.5.52 as 6966M.
EE307 74 Sqn. 263 Sqn. 74 Sqn. 616 Sqn (RAW-O). To 4 STT 6.5.52 as 6979M.
EE308 74 Sqn. w/o 24.7.45, hit trees during a low flypast at Colerne.
EE309 74 Sqn. 263 Sqn. 74 Sqn. HQ Metropolitan Sector. 226 OCU. To 6718M 2.2.50.
EE310 74 Sqn. 263 Sqn. 74 Sqn. 206 AFS. 210 AFS. To PEE 16.4.56.
EE311 Turbo Research Co, Ontario. w/o 29.6.46, ditched in Helen Bay Lake.
EE312 74 Sqn. 222 Sqn. w/o 2.7.46.
EE313 1335 CU. w/o 28.11.45, spun in, Kimbolton.
EE314 GAC. CGS. To 8 STT 19.5.52 as 6867M. To 2 STT, then 4 STT.
EE315 1335 CU. To 11 STT 31.1.46 as 5808M.
EE316 1335 CU. w/o 20.11.45, missing without trace on unauthorised flight.
EE317 504 Sqn. To 1 STT 1.2.46 as 5806M.
EE318 1335 CU. To 2 STT 1.2.46 as 5807M.
EE331 1335 CU. To 2 STT 22.2.46 as 5825M.
EE332 74 Sqn. 222 Sqn. 234 Sqn. 91 Sqn (DL-E). 266 Sqn. 92 Sqn. 226 OCU. 206 AFS. w/o 4.1.52.
EE333 74 Sqn. w/o 8.7.47.
EE334 74 Sqn. w/o 10.7.46.
EE335 74 Sqn. w/o 2.1.46.
EE336 Loan to Dominion for tropical trials at Khartoum. A & AEE. To 2 STT 17.11.47 as 6487M.
EE337 GAC. RAE Farnborough. To RN 31.3.52. 778 Sqn. Scrap 1955.
EE338 PRDU Benson. w/o 10.10.46.
EE339 Rolls-Royce. NGTE. 500 Sqn. To 1 STT on 29.12.54 as 7166M.
EE340 74 Sqn. 206 AFS. Scrap 22.6.56.
EE341 74 Sqn (4D-G). 56 Sqn. 206 AFS. 210 AFS. Scrap 22.6.56.
EE342 74 Sqn. 222 Sqn. 616 Sqn. 206 AFS. 210 AFS. Scrap 19.3.54.
EE343 74 Sqn. 263 Sqn. 74 Sqn. w/o 11.11.46.
EE344 74 Sqn. w/o 20.12.45.
EE345 74 Sqn. 263 Sqn. 74 Sqn. 245 Sqn. 63 Sqn. 500 Sqn. To PEE 8.3.56.
EE346 74 Sqn. w/o 19.7.46.
EE347 1335 CU. w/o 15.10.45.
EE348 CFE. 500 Sqn. 616 Sqn (RAW-D). To 4 STT 24.4.52 as 6975M.

METEOR F.3 *continued*

EE349 1335 CU. 56 Sqn. 66 Sqn. 56 Sqn. 500 Sqn. To PEE 16.4.56.

EE350 A & AEE. TFU Defford. To 4 STT 9.5.52 as 6980M.

EE351 1335 CU. A & AEE. Hit by truck being uncrated at Port Said 31.5.47 and damaged beyond repair. To Farnborough dump. soc 31.7.48.

EE352 1335 CU. 74 Sqn. 263 Sqn. 257 Sqn (A6-G). 66 Sqn (HI-A). 500 Sqn (RAA-A, later S7-A). To 1 STT 29.12.54 as 7167M.

EE353 1335 CU. 226 OCU. 263 Sqn. 257 Sqn. 74 Sqn. w/o 24.9.47.

EE354 1335 CU (XL-H). CFE/FIS. 263 Sqn. 74 Sqn. 63 Sqn (UB-B). Fairey Aviation, Cranfield. To 2 STT 23.5.52 as 6971M.

EE355 1335 CU. 500 Sqn. 206 AFS. Scrap 18.10.55.

EE356 1335 CU. CGS (FJT-J). To 2 STT 20.5.52 as 6972M.

EE357 1335 CU (HB). 226 OCU (HFO-N). 245 Sqn. Eastern Sector (HBW). 245 Sqn. 56 Sqn. w/o 16.8.49.

EE358 74 Sqn. 263 Sqn. 74 Sqn. 257 Sqn (A6-K). 206 AFS. To 1 STT 18.1.54 as 7128M.

EE359 GAC. EFS (FCW-J). 616 Sqn. To 12 STT on 16.2.55 as 7185M.

EE360 GAC. Conv to F.4 prototype. To 1 STT on 28.5.51 as 6867M.

EE361 Rolls-Royce. GAC. To 1 STT 19.2.48 as 6511M Recalled 5.6.48 but fuselage only could be found at Halton and aircraft presumed soc.

EE362 124 Sqn (ON-C). 56 Sqn. w/o 23.8.46.

EE363 124 Sqn. 56 Sqn. w/o 17.5.46.

EE364 124 Sqn. 56 Sqn. w/o 18.12.47 by 66 Sqn.

EE365 124 Sqn (ON-N). 56 Sqn. soc 5.8.49.

EE366 124 Sqn. 56 Sqn. soc 5.8.49 as 6686M.

EE367 124 Sqn. 56 Sqn. Loan to GAC as Argentine pilot trainer. 1 Sqn. 226 OCU. To 1 STT 9.5.52 as 6964M.

EE368 124 Sqn. 222 Sqn. 1 Sqn. 66 Sqn. 206 AFS. Scrap 18.10.55.

EE369 124 Sqn. 66 Sqn. To 1 STT 2.9.48 as 6593M.

EE384 124 Sqn. 66 Sqn (HI-F). 63 Sqn (UB-J). To RAE Cardington for runway and jet blast tests. Scrap 16.2.56.

EE385 124 Sqn. 56 Sqn. w/o 23.10.47.

EE386 124 Sqn. 222 Sqn (ZD-M). 616 Sqn. Scrap 18.10.55.

EE387 TSU Defford. A & AEE. GAC. To RN. Scrap 1955 as A2295.

EE388 245 Sqn. 222 Sqn. 1 Sqn. 222 Sqn. 92 Sqn (DL-C). To 4 STT 6.5.52 as 6981M.

EE389 124 Sqn (ON-Y). 56 Sqn. Duxford Stn Flt. To 12 STT 16.2.55 as 7186M.

EE390 124 Sqn. w/o 15.1.46.

EE391 124 Sqn. 56 Sqn (ON-T). To 5 STT 8.7.48 as 6574M.

EE392 124 Sqn. w/o 15.1.46.

EE393 124 Sqn. 56 Sqn. 226 OCU. 616 Sqn. To PEE 10.4.56.

EE394 124 Sqn. GAC. A & AEE. 222 Sqn. soc 5.8.49.

EE395 Loan to New Zealand. soc 15.3.50 and sold as NZ6001. To ground instructional airframe at Hobsonville as INST 147 in 1961. To Auckland museum.

EE396 ETPS Cranfield. Lubeck. Scrap 27.3.50.

EE397 ETPS Boscombe Down. 206 AFS. To 1 STT 29.12.54 as 7168M.

EE398 ETPS. 206 AFS. 210 AFS. Scrap 22.6.56.

EE399 124 Sqn. 66 Sqn. w/o 23.2.48.

EE400 124 Sqn (ON-H). 56 Sqn. 500 Sqn. To Cranwell 14.12.50 as 6817M. soc 10.2.53.

EE401 74 Sqn. Middle Wallop Stn Flt (HK/MK/BKO). Southern Sector. 222 Sqn. 206 AFS w/o 9.9.52.

EE402 39 MU. To 2 STT 3.10.45 as 5839M.

EE403 Church Fenton (PLB). 500 Sqn (RAA-E, later S7-E). RAE Farnborough. To PEE 9.2.55.

EE404 Acklington Stn Flt (HR). 263 Sqn (HE-D). w/o 5.12.47.

EE405 39 MU. To 11 STT 23.3.46 as 5897M. Hednesford 23.2.55. Bridgnorth gate. Scrapped.

EE406 39 MU. To 11 STT 23.3.46 as 5898M. West Kirby 23.2.55.

EE407 39 MU. To 11 STT 29.3.46 as 5924M. 2 STT 6.4.48.

EE408 CFE. Scrap 30.8.54.

EE409 541 Sqn. 2 STT. 234 Sqn. 91 Sqn. 92 Sqn (DL-F). w/o 14.8.47.

EE410 541 Sqn. 234 Sqn. 266 Sqn. 66 Sqn. soc 21.11.47.

EE411 541 Sqn. 234 Sqn (FX-V). 266 Sqn (FX-V). w/o 16.6.47.

EE412 245 Sqn. 222 Sqn. 1 Sqn. 222 Sqn. 206 AFS. 210 AFS. 206 AFS. To PEE 23.3.56.

EE413 EANS (FGG-I). To 4 STT 24.4.52 as 6976M.

EE414 234 Sqn (FX-D). 91 Sqn. 92 Sqn. 206 AFS (M-17). Scrap 24.6.52.

EE415 Martin-Baker. Scrapped.

EE416 Martin-Baker. Scrapped, nose to Science Museum.

EE417 263 Sqn.

EE418 1335 CU (HBG). Power Jets.

EE419 245 Sqn (MR-V). CFS. 206 AFS. To Coltishall as 7247M. Burnt 1969.

EE420 222 Sqn. 500 Sqn (RAA-B, later S7-B).

EE421 222 Sqn. 1 Sqn (JX-A). 257 Sqn (A6-B). 263 Sqn (HE-H). Wattisham Stn Flt. CFS.

EE422 222 Sqn.

EE423 222 Sqn (ZD-K/ZD-L).

EE424 222 Sqn. 1 Sqn. 222 Sqn. 500 Sqn. 206 AFS. soc 25.10.55 to Coltishall for display as 7248M. To Manston dump.

EE425 222 Sqn. 1 Sqn. 222 Sqn. 266 Sqn. 63 Sqn (UB-G). 206 AFS. 210 AFS. 206 AFS. To PEE 16.2.56.

EE426 FCCS. CFS (FDJ-G). 206 AFS. Scrap 10.4.56.

EE427 GAC. Transferred to RAAF 6.1.49. 1 APU at Laverton as A77-1. w/o 14.2.47, due to a heavy landing at Darwin.

EE428 CFE. 74 Sqn. 245 Sqn. 266 Sqn. 63 Sqn. 500 Sqn. To 2 STT 18.5.52 as 6973M. 4 STT 30.6.55.

EE429 GAC. Loan to South African Air Force 23.3.46 to 11.7.49. To Henlow 29.7.49 as 6684M.

EE444 CFE. w/o 19.7.46.

EE445 RAE Farnborough. soc 30.6.50.

EE446 CFE. To Henlow 23.5.47 as 6341M.

EE447 222 Sqn. 500 Sqn (RAA-K, later S7-K). To 8 STT 15.5.52 as 6969M.

EE448 222 Sqn. w/o 1.2.46.

EE449 234 Sqn (FX-N). 91 Sqn. 92 Sqn (DL-E). 206 AFS. Scrap 17.11.55.

EE450 222 Sqn (ZD-K). w/o in ground accident on 22.12.47.

EE451 CFE. 206 AFS (W-20). 210 AFS. Scrap 17.11.55

EE452 Allocated to the RAAF but not taken up. 234 Sqn. 91 Sqn. 92 Sqn. 206 AFS. Scrap 20.4.56.

EE453 Allocated to the RAAF but not taken up. 234 Sqn (FX-H). 91 Sqn. 92 Sqn. w/o 19.3.48.

EE454 GAC/ETPS test aircraft ('Britannia'). Allocated to 2 STT as 6712M but not taken up. To School of Air/Land Warfare 29.3.50.

EE455 GAC/ETPS test aircraft ('Forever Amber'). soc at Farnborough 1.1.54.

EE456 Handling Sqn, Hullavington. w/o 12.2.46.

EE457 GAC. 222 Sqn (ZD-Q). w/o 7.10.47.

EE458 1335 CU. 222 Sqn. 1 Sqn (JX-B). To Chigwell CTTB 1.3.47 as 6277M.

EE459 1335 CU. 74 Sqn (4D-S). 56 Sqn (ON-S, later US-S). To 8 STT 26.5.52 as 6970M.

EE460 263 Sqn (HE-H). A & AEE. GAC for Argentine training. 500 Sqn. 206 AFS. Scrap 11.8.55.

EE461 254 Sqn. 91 Sqn. 92 Sqn. 1 Sqn. w/o 24.9.48.

EE462 74 Sqn (4D-L). 206 AFS. 210 AFS. w/o on 14.10.53.

EE463 263 Sqn. 616 Sqn. 206 AFS. 210 AFS. soc 30.11.55.

EE464 124 Sqn (ON-F). 66 Sqn. CFE. To 10 STT 13.5.52 as 6974M.

EE465 ECFS. 616 Sqn. 206 AFS. w/o 30.6.52.

EE466 ECFS. w/o 9.8.46.

EE467 ECFS. EFS. Scrap 10.9.47.

EE468 124 Sqn (ON-B). 66 Sqn. To 6563M 1.6.48.

EE469 245 Sqn. 500 Sqn (RAA-G). To 4 STT 16.5.52 as 6982M. 10 STT 2.5.55.

EE470 GAC for Argentine training. 263 Sqn. 245 Sqn. 245 Sqn. Eastern Sector. 63 Sqn (UB-H). 616 Sqn. 206 AFS. To 1 STT 5.11.52 as 7109M.

EE471 245 Sqn. Scrap 15.1.52.

EE472 1335 CU. CFE. 92 Sqn (DL-A). 222 Sqn. 616 Sqn (YQ-T). w/o 8.1.50.

EE473 1335 CU. 74 Sqn. 245 Sqn. 74 Sqn. 226 OCU. Scrap 18.10.55.

EE474 1335 CU. 226 OCU. 222 Sqn. CFS. Scrap on 18.10.55.

EE475 234 Sqn. 266 Sqn. soc 16.9.48.

EE476 RAE Farnborough. Scrap 12.7.54.

EE477 ECFS. EFS. w/o 30.7.47.

EE478 74 Sqn. 226 OCU. 206 AFS. To 1 STT 29.12.54 as 7169M.

EE479 Martin-Baker. 206 AFS. To 1 STT 29.12.54 as 7170M.

EE480 NGTE. To 4 STT 9.5.52 as 6983M.

EE481 222 Sqn (ZD-U), 63 Sqn. To 1 STT 29.12.54 as 7171M.

EE482 North Weald (RWO). 92 Sqn. Metropolitan Sector. Scrap 18.10.55.

EE483 226 OCU. 222 Sqn. To 4 STT 9.5.52 as 6984M.

EE484 245 Sqn. w/o 15.4.47.

EE485 234 Sqn. 245 Sqn. 56 Sqn. Scrap 7.5.48.

EE486 234 Sqn. 266 Sqn. 91 Sqn. 92 Sqn. 226 OCU. To 4 STT 24.4.52 as 6977M.

EE487 234 Sqn. 266 Sqn (FX-W). Scrap 17.11.55.

EE488 245 Sqn (MR-A). Scrap 20.4.56.

EE489 56 Sqn. 66 Sqn. To Oakington 30.10.51 as 6913M.

EE490 CGS. w/o 13.9.46.

EE491 ETPS Cranfield. 206 AFS. w/o 13.8.52.

EE492 A & AEE. ML Aviation. 206 AFS. 210 AFS. Scrap 17.11.55.

EE493 GAC. ECFS. To 5 STT 2.10.48 as 6604M.

METEOR F.4

G-AIDC GAC. w/o in Belgium 4.47.

EE517 GAC. Rolls-Royce. GAC. 226 OCU. 207 AFS. Scrapped 8.7.54 at Rufforth.

EE518 w/o 9.5.46 before delivery and used for spares

EE519 GAC. To PEE 9.2.55.

EE520 A & AEE. GAC (Used for ground tests only, never flown).

EE521 Handling Sqn, Hullavington. CGS. 207 AFS. F/R for conv to U.15 15.9.54.

EE522 GAC. NGTE. ML Aviation. NGTE. Gutersloh Station Flight. TRE.

EE523 GAC. To France as F-WEPQ 23.7.48

EE524 610 Sqn. 215 AFS. F/R for conversion to U.15 22.3.54.

EE525 GAC. A & AEE. 207 AFS. w/o 12.4.54.

EE526 GAC. To Argentina as I-042.

EE527 To Argentina as I-027.

EE528 HSF Tangmere. 205 AFS. w/o 26.9.52.

EE529 HSF Tangmere. 205 AFS. 215 AFS. 207 AFS. Scrap 6.7.54.

EE530 HSF Tangmere. A & AEE. RAE Farnborough. Scrap 14.2.58. (Aircraft was converted by the RAE at some stage to a T.7).

EE531 GAC. A & AEE. Scrap 25.8.53, but retrieved as 7090M for ground trials at Lasham. To Midland Air Museum.

EE532 To Argentina as I-025. Preserved at Moron.

EE533 To Argentina as I-047.

EE534 To Argentina as I-044.

EE535 To Argentina as I-028.

EE536 To Argentina as I-049.

EE537 To Argentina as I-029.

EE538 w/o 13.9.46 before delivery.

EE539 To Argentina as I-048.

EE540 To Argentina as I-043.

EE541 To Argentina as I-050.

EE542 To Argentina as I-030.

EE543 To Argentina as I-046.

EE544 To Argentina as I-021.

EE545 GAC. To RNAS Bramcote as A2332 23.10.53. Scrap 13.10.55.

EE546 To Argentina as I-020.

EE547 To Argentina as I-045.

EE548 To Argentina as I-024.

EE549 HSF. FCCS (JMR). CFE. To RAF Museum Cranwell 10.6.52. Fulbeck store 4.6.58 as 7008M. Innsworth gate. RAFM Hendon, RAFM St Athan.

EE550 HSF. 615 Sqn (V6-R). w/o 6.1.51.

EE551 To Argentina as I-015.

EE552 To Argentina as I-022.

EE553 To Argentina as I-019, later C-019. Preserved.

EE554 To Argentina as I-017.

EE568 RAE Farnborough. w/o 30.8.48.

EE569 To Argentina as I-016.

EE570 To Argentina as I-013.

EE571 To Argentina as I-018.

EE572 To Argentina as I-026.

EE573 GAC. Defford. Fairey Aviation. RAE Farnborough. Scrap 6.5.58 (as a T.7).

EE574 To Argentina as I-034.

EE575 To Argentina as I-014.

EE576 To Argentina as I-023.

EE577 To Argentina as I-036.

EE578 CFE. w/o 5.5.47.

EE579 CFE. Flying accident 24.10.46. Allocated to 2 STT 21.12.46 as 6228M but not taken up.

EE580 To Argentina as I-035. w/o 7.60.

EE581 To Argentina as I-032.

EE582 To Argentina as I-033.

EE583 To Argentina as I-037, later C-037.

EE584 257 Sqn. 504 Sqn. w/o 7.7.51.

EE585 To Argentina as I-030. w/o 5.60.

EE586 To Argentina as I-041, later C-041. Preserved Buenos Aires Museum.

EE587 To Argentina as I-038.

EE588 To Argentina as I-031.

EE589 To Argentina as I-040.

EE590 CGS. 203 AFS. 207 AFS. Scrap 28.5.54.

EE591 CFE. 56 Sqn (N). 226 OCU. 215 AFS. Scrap 21.5.54.

EE592 CFE. 92 Sqn. 205 AFS. w/o 17.4.51.

EE593 203 AFS. 205 AFS. 203 AFS. w/o 30.5.53.

EE594 RAE Farnborough. Andover Stn Flt. Flying accident 21.12.49 to Horsham St Faith as 6732M on 24.5.50. Scrap 5.9.50.

EE595 ACFE Singapore. GAC. 205 AFS. Scrap 8.10.53.

EE596 ACFE Singapore. GAC. Bovingdon. 207 AFS. Scrap 14.6.54.

EE597 Rolls-Royce. RAE Farnborough. To Henlow 7.9.53 as 7099M.

EE598 GAC. Defford. 19 Sqn. 207 AFS. Scrap 1.6.55.

EE599 RAE Farnborough. 205 AFS. w/o 30.11.50.

RA365 CGS. 203 AFS/8 FTS. w/o 20.9.54.

RA366 245 Sqn. 66 Sqn. 19 Sqn. 215 AFS. 206 AFS. 209 AFS/12 FTS. To MoS 31.3.56.

RA367 CGS. 205 AFS. F/R for conv to U.15 10.6.55.

RA368 66 Sqn. 19 Sqn. 611 Sqn. 206 AFS. 209 AFS/12 FTS. soc 8.1.55.

RA369 504 Sqn. 215 AFS. w/o 24.7.52.

RA370 To Argentina as I-007.

RA371 1 Sqn (JX-D). 63 Sqn (V). Manby. 500 Sqn (S7-E). 207 AFS. F/R for conv to U.15 7.7.55.

RA372 226 OCU. w/o 12.4.50.

RA373 203 AFS (FMJ-W). 215 AFS. To MoS 9.3.56. U.15 (X) w/o 4.5.60.

RA374 203 AFS/226 OCU. w/o 21.3.50.

RA375 257 Sqn. 504 Sqn. 215 AFS (64). To Mos 28.3.56. F/R for conv to U.15 (F). 728 (B) Sqn. (658). Destroyed Llanbedr 6.5.60.

RA376 203 AFS. 215 AFS. w/o 11.8.52.

RA377 CFE. 226 OCU. 209 AFS/12 FTS. To Scrap 24.9.54.

RA378 205 AFS/4 FTS. Scrap 3.2.55.

RA379 600 Sqn (LJ-V). 203 AFS/8 FTS. To Scrap 28.7.55.

RA380 203 AFS. w/o 15.7.52.

RA381 RAE Farnborough. 600 Sqn. 226 OCU. 215 AFS. 207 AFS. Scrap 7.5.54.

RA382 A & AEE, (trials as first 'long-nose' F.4). w/o 5.3.49.

RA383 203 AFS. w/o 20.9.50.

RA384 To Argentina as I-001.

RA385 To Argentina as I-008.

RA386 To Argentina as I-002.

RA387 RAE Farnborough. 1 Sqn. 203 AFS/8 FTS. F/R for conv to U.15 31.3.56. 728 Sqn (658).

RA388 To Argentina as I-003.

RA389 To Argentina as I-004.

RA390 To Argentina as I-005.

RA391 To Argentina as I-006.

RA392 To Argentina as I-009.

RA393 To Argentina as I-010.

RA394 GAC.

RA395 To Argentina as I-011.

RA396 To Argentina as I-012.

RA397 A & AEE. 203 AFS. 5 CAACU. F/R for conv to U.15 28.3.56 (O). w/o 29.7.59.

RA398 Handling Sqn, Hullavington. 92 Sqn. 226 OCU. 207 AFS. F/R for conv to U.15 16.5.55.

RA413 CFE. 92 Sqn. Duxford Stn Flt. 226 OCU. 209 AFS/12 FTS (82). Scrap 7.4.55.

METEOR F.4 *continued*

RA414 245 Sqn (MR-H). 263 Sqn. w/o 26.6.49.

RA415 CFE. 92 Sqn. 257 Sqn. 615 Sqn. 500 Sqn. 226 OCU. F/R for conv to U.15 22.4.58 (L). w/o 5.9.58.

RA416 CFE. 203 AFS/226 OCU (KR-R). Flying accident 10.10.51, to 205 AFS as 6937M 20.11.51.

RA417 GAC. F/R for conv to U.15 12.7.54. RAAF. soc 31.1.59.

RA418 w/o during delivery flight to CFE 7.7.47.

RA419 226 OCU. Tangmere Stn Flt. 63 Sqn. Waterbeach Stn Flt. 226 OCU. 209 AFS/12 FTS. w/o 13.5.54

RA420 A & AEE. Rolls-Royce. A & AEE. F/R for conv to U.15 20.7.54 (T). w/o 19.2.62.

RA421 RCAF Edmonton. WEE. Defford. Conv to U.15. w/o 1.7.55 at Tarrant Rushton.

RA422 203 AFS. w/o 17.8.50.

RA423 CFE. 66 Sqn. 226 OCU. 600 Sqn (LJ-L). Training Flt. 203 AFS/8 FTS. Scrap 26.4.55.

RA424 GAC. RAE Farnborough. Scrap 23.11.55.

RA425 AMSDU Wattisham. 43 Sqn (SW-P). 63 Sqn (P). 226 OCU. 207 AFS. 8 FTS. w/o 13.6.55.

RA426 CFE. 263 Sqn (HE-J). 203 AFS. w/o 20.12.51

RA427 74 Sqn. 263 Sqn. 206 AFS. 215 AFS. w/o 31.12.53.

RA428 203 AFS. 226 OCU. 203 AFS/8 FTS. w/o 30.6.54.

RA429 CFE. 616 Sqn (YQ-H). 215 AFS. 205 AFS. w/o 20.8.52.

RA430 Rolls-Royce. 215 AFS. F/R for conv to U.15 13.9.54.

RA431 203 AFS. 226 OCU. w/o 28.12.50.

RA432 257 Sqn. 215 AFS. F/R for conv to U.15 28.3.56 (T). w/o 25.4.60.

RA433 CFE. CGS. 215 AFS. F/R for conv to U.15 4.7.55.

RA434 66 Sqn. 111 Sqn. 56 Sqn (US-Q). 205 AFS. To 4 STT 16.7.54 as 7130M. 10 STT 2.5.55.

RA435 Rolls-Royce. 215 AFS. 209 AFS. To 2 STT 5.7.54 as 7131M. 4 STT 30.6.55.

RA436 92 Sqn. 226 OCU. 203 AFS. 209 AFS/12 FTS w/o 21.6.54.

RA437 43 Sqn. 63 Sqn. 226 OCU. FS Finningley. 207 AFS. 12 FTS. Scrap 4.11.54.

RA438 A & AEE. F/R for conv. to U.15 23.7.54.

RA439 74 Sqn (ZD-F/4D-F). 263 Sqn. CGS. 215 AFS. F/R for conv to U.15 31.3.56 (V). w/o 9.12.59.

RA440 66 Sqn. CFE. 226 OCU. 203 AFS. 209 AFS/ 12 FTS. Scrap 10.9.54.

RA441 263 Sqn. 207 AFS. F/R for conv to U.15 13.4.55.

RA442 226 OCU. 222 Sqn (ZD-T). 215 AFS. 12 FTS. F/R for conv to U.15 28.3.56 (J). w/o 23.4.59.

RA443 222 Sqn. 266 Sqn. w/o 12.7.48.

RA444 257 Sqn (A6-B). 205 AFS/4 FTS. Scrap 19.7.54

RA445 257 Sqn. To 5 STT 13.12.48 as 6621M. soc 30.5.50.

RA446 263 Sqn (HE-L). 207 AFS. Scrap 1.6.54.

RA447 257 Sqn. w/o 5.8.48.

RA448 74 Sqn. 66 Sqn. 19 Sqn. 12 Grp Com Flt. 215 AFS. w/o 15.5.53.

RA449 1 Sqn. 205 AFS/4 FTS. To 8 STT 30.6.55 as 7221M. Put on gate in 611 Sqn markings.

RA450 222 Sqn. 66 Sqn. 222 Sqn. w/o 26.8.48.

RA451 74 Sqn. w/o 14.12.49.

RA452 FCCS. w/o 19.4.49.

RA453 CFE. w/o 17.1.49.

RA454 CFE. 245 Sqn. 141 Sqn. 226 OCU. 215 AFS. F/R for conv to U.15 2.5.55.

RA455 CFE. w/o 26.9.49.

RA456 CFE. 245 Sqn. 611 Sqn. 205 AFS/4 FTS. To 8 STT 29.6.55 as 7222M.

RA457 245 Sqn. 610 Sqn. 205 AFS. F/R for conv to U.15 8.10.54. w/o 31.1.59 at Woomera.

RA473 266 Sqn. CFE. FCCS. 257 Sqn. 74 Sqn (ZD-C). 263 Sqn. 245 Sqn. 500 Sqn (S7-O). 203 AFS. F/R for conv to U.15 7.4.55.

RA474 228 OCU. 226 OCU. 263 Sqn (HE-P). 500 Sqn. 226 OCU. 206 AFS. 209 AFS. 207 AFS. Scrap 31.1.55

RA475 CFE. 206 AFS. w/o 3.9.53.

RA476 CFE. Exhibition Pool, Olympia 31.5.49. To 7361M 18.6.56.

RA477 CFE. w/o 4.6.48.

RA478 CFE. CGS. 207 AFS. Scrap 14.6.50.

RA479 A & AEE. RAE Farnborough. Conv to U.15 (E).

RA480 257 Sqn (A6-F). 205 AFS. w/o 29.4.52.

RA481 222 Sqn. 66 Sqn (HI-E). 222 Sqn. w/o 14.7.49.

RA482 38 MU. w/o 16.3.48.

RA483 92 Sqn. 66 Sqn. 226 OCU. w/o 30.6.52.

RA484 GAC. A & AEE. 226 OCU. 205 AFS/4 FTS. Scrap 31.10.50.

RA485 74 Sqn. 263 Sqn. 207 AFS. 12 FTS. To Scrap 3.12.54.

RA486 A & AEE. 245 Sqn. RAFFC. w/o 29.6.52.

RA487 245 Sqn (MR-M). 66 Sqn. w/o 7.12.50.

RA488 257 Sqn. w/o 19.3.48.

RA489 263 Sqn. 43 Sqn (SW-N). 92 Sqn (DL-N). 226 OCU. 206 AFS. 203 AFS/8 FTS. Scrap 26.10.54.

RA490 GAC. NGTE. RAE Farnborough.

RA491 GAC. NGTE. Allocated 6879M at Cranwell, but not taken up. AST Hamble. To France 28.9.51.

RA492 226 OCU (HX-W). 206 AFS. 203 AFS/8 FTS. Scrap 7.11.55.

VT102 266 Sqn. 1 Grp Com Flt. 615 Sqn (V6-S). w/o 30.4.51.

VT103 Handling Sqn. 66 Sqn. 43 Sqn. 1 Sqn. 205 AFS w/o 19.4.51.

VT104 266 Sqn (FX-W). 92 Sqn. 19 Sqn. 611 Sqn. 203 AFS. 215 AFS. F/R for conv to U.15 8.7.55. 728 (B) Sqn (656).

VT105 222 Sqn. CFE. 205 AFS. 206 AFS. F/R for conv to U.15 20.7.55.

VT106 74 Sqn (4D-D). 600 Sqn (LJ-E/LJ-F). F/R for conv to U.15 13.6.55.

VT107 222 Sqn. 266 OCU. CFE. 610 Sqn. 206 AFS (65). 205 AFS/4 FTS. 12 FTS. F/R for conv to U.15 28.3.56. 728(B) Sqn (657). Dest by missile 4.10.61.

VT108 RAE Farnborough. w/o 29.4.48.

VT109 245 Sqn (MR-C). 66 Sqn. 41 Sqn. 600 Sqn. 215 AFS. 205 AFS/4 FTS. Scrap 9.8.54.

VT110 222 Sqn. 226 OCU/203 AFS (FMJ-N). RAFFC F/R for conv to U.15 2.5.55 (A). 728 (B) Sqn (655). w/o 29.3.60.

VT111 263 Sqn (HE-J). Rolls-Royce. 66 Sqn. 41 Sqn. 615 Sqn. 215 AFS. Scrap 20.4.54.

VT112 266 Sqn. 266 OCU. CFE. 616 Sqn. 215 AFS. F/R for conv to U.15 6.7.55.

VT113 263 Sqn. 257 Sqn. CFE. 616 Sqn. RAFFC. F/R for conv to U.15 10.6.55.

VT114 266 Sqn. 43 Sqn. 205 AFS. w/o 20.11.51.

VT115 CFE. 616 Sqn. 205 AFS/4 FTS. w/o 2.2.55.

VT116 263 Sqn. w/o 7.3.49.

VT117 CFE. Eastern Sector. Newton. 207 AFS. To Scrap 30.6.54.

VT118 263 Sqn. RAFFC. F/R for conv to U.15 6.6.55

VT119 263 Sqn. w/o 13.5.49.

VT120 257 Sqn. 263 Sqn. Biggin Hill Stn Flt. 226 OCU 209 AFS. Scrap 6.5.54.

VT121 263 Sqn. 245 Sqn. 66 Sqn. 19 Sqn. 611 Sqn. w/o 22.7.51.

VT122 257 Sqn (A6-C). 74 Sqn. 66 Sqn (LZ-B). 19 Sqn. 207 AFS. Scrap 30.4.54.

VT123 257 Sqn. 245 Sqn. w/o 5.1.49.

VT124 245 Sqn. w/o 23.11.49.

VT125 245 Sqn (MR-B). 266 Sqn. 205 AFS. 203 AFS. 8 FTS. To 8 STT 31.8.55 as 7223M.

VT126 245 Sqn. w/o 4.5.48.

VT127 245 Sqn. 92 Sqn (DL-Z). 65 Sqn. 203 AFS. w/o 16.9.52.

VT128 245 Sqn. 263 Sqn. 205 AFS/4 FTS. 12 FTS. To Chivenor 6.4.55 as 7204M.

VT129 245 Sqn (MR-N). Eastern Sector. Coltishall Stn Flt. 203 AFS. w/o 26.3.52.

VT130 74 Sqn. 609 Sqn. 610 Sqn. 206 AFS. F/R for conv to U.15 13.6.55.

VT131 66 Sqn. w/o 17.4.50.

VT132 266 Sqn (FX-P). 43 Sqn (SW-Z). 92 Sqn. 226 OCU. 205 AFS/4 FTS. Scrap 26.11.54.

VT133 74 Sqn (4D-J). CGS. 215 AFS. w/o 18.2.52.

VT134 266 Sqn. 43 Sqn. 92 Sqn. 64 Sqn. 226 OCU. 205 AFS/4 FTS. To 8 STT 15.8.55 as 7224M.

VT135 266 Sqn. APS. 226 OCU. 215 AFS. F/R for conv to U.15 26.3.56 (L). w/o 18.12.58 Harlech beach.

VT136 263 Sqn. w/o 22.9.48.

VT137 257 Sqn. w/o 30.8.49.

VT138 66 Sqn. 92 Sqn. 64 Sqn. 215 AFS. w/o 20.5.53.

VT139 66 Sqn. 226 OCU. 215 AFS. 207 AFS. F/R for conv to U.15 27.6.55.

VT140 1 Sqn. w/o 28.2.49, lost at sea.

VT141 EFS. CGS. RAFFC. w/o 22.7.52.

VT142 66 Sqn. Duxford Stn Flt. JCU Binbrook. JCU Hemswell. JCU Coningsby. F/R for conv to U.15 on 18.7.55.

VT143 92 Sqn. w/o 10.7.48.

VT144 CFE. w/o 4.9.48.

VT145 EFS. 504 Sqn. 203 AFS. 215 AFS. w/o 12.5.52.

VT146 EFS. 1 Sqn. w/o 19.4.50.

VT147 92 Sqn. Duxford Stn Flt. 92 Sqn. 41 Sqn. 215 AFS. Scrap 11.3.54.

VT148 257 Sqn. w/o 23.6.49.

VT149 66 Sqn. w/o 30.9.48.

VT150 GAC. A & AEE. RAE Farnborough. Conv to F.8 prototype.

VT168 66 Sqn. 263 Sqn (HE-E). 207 AFS (20-P). F/R for conv to U.15 15.10.54. soc Woomera 31.1.59.

VT169 257 Sqn. 504 Sqn. 500 Sqn (S7-F). 203 AFS. Flying accident 17.3.53. Scrap 30.4.53.

VT170 92 Sqn. 226 OCU. 1 Sqn. 205 AFS. w/o 11.12.50.

VT171 92 Sqn. 41 Sqn. 600 Sqn. 209 AFS. w/o 26.3.54.

VT172 1 Sqn. w/o 14.9.48.

VT173 1 Sqn. w/o 26.5.50.

VT174 92 Sqn (DL-U). 65 Sqn. 29 Sqn. Scrap 10.11.52.

VT175 92 Sqn (DL-V). 226 OCU. 257 Sqn. 615 Sqn. F/R for conv to U.15 6.7.55.

VT176 226 OCU. 203 AFS. w/o 21.5.52.

VT177 92 Sqn. 41 Sqn. 615 Sqn. 500 Sqn. 615 Sqn. 214 AFS. 206 AFS. 215 AFS. F/R for con to U.15 5.5.55.

VT178 66 Sqn. Duxford Stn Flt. 1 Sqn (JX-B). CGS. 209 AFS/12 FTS. Scrap 30.11.54.

VT179 1 Sqn. JCU Binbrook. JCU Hemswell. JCU Coningsby. F/R for conv to U.15 29.6.55.

VT180 1 Sqn. Scrap 3.8.50.

VT181 1 Sqn. 203 AFS. w/o 9.6.52.

VT182 1 Sqn. 615 Sqn (V6-A). 207 AFS. 206 AFS. MoS 31.3.56.

VT183 56 Sqn (US-D). 609 Sqn. 610 Sqn (N). 203 AFS/8 FTS. w/o 11.6.54.

VT184 Southern Sector. 222 Sqn (ZD-Q). CGS. 205 AFS. F/R for conv to U.15 30.6.55.

VT185 Metropolitan Sector. w/o 24.4.50.

VT186 56 Sqn (Q). 226 OCU. w/o 27.4.51.

VT187 Eastern Sector. 257 Sqn (A6-L). 74 Sqn. 245 Sqn. 611 Sqn (E). F/R for conv to U.15 31.8.55.

VT188 56 Sqn (US-M, later M). 609 Sqn. 610 Sqn.; w/o 6.9.51.;

VT189 56 Sqn (T). 226 OCU. w/o 28.5.51.

VT190 CFE. 203 AFS. w/o 20.4.51.

VT191 56 Sqn (US-Q, later P). 609 Sqn. 207 AFS. F/R for conv to U.15 16.6.55.

VT192 74 Sqn (4D-C/4D-K). 611 Sqn. 206 AFS. F/R for conv to U.15 12.5.55.

VT193 56 Sqn. w/o 14.2.49.

VT194 56 Sqn (R). 207 AFS. w/o 17.5.54.

VT195 56 Sqn. APS. 226 OCU. 205 AFS/4 FTS. w/o 7.7.54.

VT196 Rolls-Royce. Div of Mech Eng, Ottawa. Ret to UK and damaged in wheels-up landing at Aston Down 11.6.58 and conv to U.15 (U). Last flight by any U.15 on 9.2.63.

VT197 63 Sqn. 222 Sqn. 56 Sqn. 500 Sqn. 203 AFS. F/R for conv to U.15 3.8.55.

VT198 63 Sqn (UB-B). w/o 28.8.50.

VT199 63 Sqn. 56 Sqn (U). 215 AFS. w/o 27.3.52.

VT213 63 Sqn. w/o 4.7.50.

VT214 63 Sqn (UB-E, later E). 226 OCU. 209 AFS/ 12 FTS (77). Scrap 20.9.54.

VT215 EFS. RAFFC. 207 AFS. 8 STT. Scrap 15.2.55

VT216 506 Sqn (TM-H). w/o 9.8.50.

VT217 EFS. RAFFC. w/o 28.2.50.

VT218 222 Sqn (ZD-R). 226 OCU. 205 AFS. 206 AFS. Scrap 18.12.52.

VT219 222 Sqn. 1 Sqn. 63 Sqn (UB-C, later C). 215 AFS. F/R for conv to U.15 14.4.55.

VT220 CFE. 226 OCU. 206 AFS. F/R for conv to U.15 1.7.55.

VT221 CBE Marham. w/o 14.9.49.

VT222 CFE. 205 AFS. F/R for conv to U.15 19.4.55.

VT223 63 Sqn. 222 Sqn. 205 AFS/4 FTS. 8 FTS. To Scrap 29.4.55.

VT224 CFE. 226 OCU. 215 AFS. w/o 22.10.52.

VT225 63 Sqn (G). 207 AFS. Scrap 6.7.54.

VT226 63 Sqn (UB-A). 616 Sqn. 205 AFS. F/R for conv to U.15 30.9.55. 1 A/C Depot.

VT227 266 Sqn. 43 Sqn. 257 Sqn. Flying accident on 19.8.49. Scrap 27.3.50.

VT228 CFE. 222 Sqn. Scrap 5.8.49.

VT229 Lubeck. Yorkshire Sector. 616 Sqn. 207 AFS. 209 AFS (60). soc for scrap 27.3.54, but became 7151M. To Colerne, Duxford & Newark Air Museums.

VT230 CFE. 222 Sqn. 63 Sqn. CFE (DFLS). 609 Sqn. 206 AFS. F/R for conv to U.15 5.7.55.

VT231 245 Sqn. 66 Sqn. 65 Sqn. 205 AFS/4 FTS. w/o 3.8.54.

VT232 CFE. 222 Sqn. 56 Sqn (US-N). 504 Sqn. 205 AFS/4 FTS. w/o 15.11.54.

VT233 CFE. 222 Sqn (ZD-S). w/o 22.4.49.

VT234 CFE. w/o 9.5.50.

VT235 CFE. 245 Sqn. 611 Sqn. 203 AFS. 206 AFS/ 8 FTS. w/o 14.4.55.

VT236 CFE. 609 Sqn. 610 Sqn. 209 AFS. 12 FTS. Scrap 21.4.55.

VT237 92 Sqn. 203 AFS. w/o 13.5.52.

VT238 266 Sqn (FX-R). 43 Sqn. w/o 25.11.49.

VT239 257 Sqn. 205 AFS. w/o 19.6.51.

VT240 263 Sqn (HE-M). 245 Sqn. 141 Sqn. 203 AFS. w/o 9.4.54.

VT241 GAC. RRE.

VT242 43 Sqn (SW-X). 63 Sqn. 226 OCU. 203 AFS/8 FTS. Scrap 13.10.54.

VT243 1 Sqn. 63 Sqn. 609 Sqn. 610 Sqn. 203 AFS/8 FTS. F/R for conv to U.15 28.3.56. 728 (B) Sqn.

VT244 56 Sqn. 203 AFS. w/o 13.9.51.

VT245 43 Sqn. 92 Sqn. 226 OCU. 205 AFS. w/o 6.11.52.

VT246 203 AFS/226 OCU. w/o 27.6.51.

VT247 222 Sqn. w/o 2.9.49.

VT256 266 Sqn. 43 Sqn. 63 Sqn. 226 OCU. 215 AFS. F/R for conv to U.15 6.9.55.

VT257 43 Sqn (SW-T). w/o 19.12.49.

VT258 63 Sqn. w/o 25.9.49.

VT259 RAE Farnborough. F/R for conv to U.15 24.11.55.

VT260 203 AFS/12 FTS (67). soc 21.6.54. To Defence NBC School, Winterbourne Gunner.

VT261 66 Sqn. 92 Sqn. w/o 16.1.50.

VT262 CFE. 63 Sqn. 609 Sqn. 610 Sqn. 203 AFS. F/R for conv to U.15 11.7.55.

VT263 56 Sqn (K). 226 OCU. 8 FTS. w/o 15.6.55.

VT264 CGS. 215 AFS. w/o 22.7.52.

VT265 1 Sqn (JX-G). 615 Sqn. 500 Sqn. 209 AFS. w/o 2.2.53.

VT266 Duxford Stn Flt. 66 Sqn (HI-X). 92 Sqn. Duxford Stn Flt. Yorkshire Sector (ES). Linton-on-Ouse Stn Flt. 64 Sqn. 209 AFS. w/o 18.6.53.

VT267 Handling Sqn. 226 OCU. w/o 21.3.50.

VT268 257 Sqn (A6-B). Eastern Sector. 74 Sqn. 12 Grp Com Flt. 12 FTS. F/R for conv to U.15 28.3.56.

VT269 92 Sqn. w/o 8.1.49.

VT270 Tangmere Stn Flt. 1 Sqn. 615 Sqn (V6-B). 203 AFS. F/R for conv to U.15 19.4.55.

VT271 CGS. 209 AFS. Scrap 28.4.54.

VT272 263 Sqn (HE-K). 257 Sqn. 205 AFS/4 FTS (61). 12 FTS. Scrap 15.6.55.

VT273 245 Sqn. 263 Sqn. 207 AFS. Scrap 8.7.54.

VT274 222 Sqn. CGS. 215 AFS/12 FTS. Scrap 21.6.54

VT275 66 Sqn. 64 Sqn. 600 Sqn. w/o 18.6.51.

VT276 43 Sqn. w/o 25.11.49.

VT277 66 Sqn. To 4 STT 4.12.50 as 6813M.

VT278 Rolls-Royce. 56 Sqn (Y). 226 OCU. w/o 25.10.51.

VT279 203 AFS/226 OCU. 204 AFS/4 FTS. 12 FTS. Scrap 8.6.55.

VT280 GAC. 222 Sqn. 63 Sqn (UB-K). 203 AFS. w/o 20.12.51.

VT281 245 Sqn. 266 Sqn. 600 Sqn (LJ-V). w/o 18.6.51.

VT282 74 Sqn (4D-T). 263 Sqn. 205 AFS. JCU Marham. F/R for conv to U.15 28.3.56 (Z). 728 (B) Sqn. Shot down 8.9.60.

VT283 54 Sqn. 600 Sqn. 203 AFS. w/o 14.3.52.

VT284 1 Sqn (JX-E). Tangmere Stn Flt. 1 Sqn. 63 Sqn. 226 OCU. 206 AFS. 203 AFS/8 FTS. Scrap 5.8.55

VT285 257 Sqn. 615 Sqn. 500 Sqn. 209 AFS/12 FTS. w/o 31.8.54.

VT286 92 Sqn (DL-R). 64 Sqn. 226 OCU. 215 AFS. F/R for conv to U.15 7.6.55.

VT287 63 Sqn. 56 Sqn (US-S). 615 Sqn. 610 Sqn. 203 AFS. 8 FTS. Scrap 11.8.55.

VT288 1 Sqn. 63 Sqn. RAFFC. 500 Sqn (J). 215 AFS. 203 AFS. Scrap 26.4.54.

METEOR F.4 *continued*

VT289 CFE. 611 Sqn. 206 AFS. F/R for conv to U.15 26.7.55.

VT290 245 Sqn. 66 Sqn. 64 Sqn. JCU Coningsby. w/o 17.8.53.

VT291 1 Sqn. 43 Sqn. 92 Sqn. 226 OCU. 12 FTS. F/R for conv to U.15 28.3.45 (S). 728(B) Sqn (659). Aircraft destroyed by missile 5.10.61.

VT292 203 AFS. 226 OCU. 206 AFS. 203 AFS/8 FTS Scrap 29.4.55.

VT293 245 Sqn (MR-A). 226 OCU (KR-K). 205 AFS. 206 AFS. w/o 3.11.53.

VT294 245 Sqn. 66 Sqn. 19 Sqn. 611 Sqn. 205 AFS. F/R for conv to U.15 1.7.55.

VT303 74 Sqn (4D-L). 203 AFS (O-R/O-27). 209 AFS. w/o 14.10.53.

VT304 56 Sqn (O). 226 OCU. FS Finningley. 207 AFS. 209 AFS. w/o 12.3.53.

VT305 203 AFS/226 OCU. 209 AFS. w/o 2.11.53.

VT306 CFE. 206 AFS. w/o 2.12.52.

VT307 EFC. RAFFC. 203 AFS. w/o 5.10.51.

VT308 257 Sqn. Yorkshire Sector (ES). 65 Sqn. 203 AFS/8 FTS (X-O/16-O). Scrap 3.11.54.

VT309 63 Sqn (UB-F, later F). Waterbeach Stn Flt. 203 AFS. 209 AFS. w/o 17.3.54.

VT310 Duxford Stn Flt. 92 Sqn (DL-Q). 226 OCU. 206 AFS. F/R for conv to U.15 28.3.56. 728 (B) Sqn.

VT311 203 AFS/8 FTS. MoS 28.3.56.

VT312 CGS. 203 AFS. Scrap 15.1.55.

VT313 203 AFS. 226 OCU. 209 AFS. w/o 12.2.54.

VT314 226 OCU. w/o 8.3.50.

VT315 66 Sqn. w/o 13.1.49.

VT316 66 Sqn. 64 Sqn. 207 AFS. F/R for conv to U.15 13.4.55.

VT317 CGS. 215 AFS (N-O). 209 AFS/12 FTS (72). To 10 STT 31.7.55 as 7225M. Scrapped at Minworth.

VT318 203 AFS. 205 AFS/4 FTS. To 10 STT 31.7.55 as 7226M. Scrapped at Aylesbury.

VT319 56 Sqn (V). 226 OCU. 215 AFS. 207 AFS. F/R for conv to U.15 24.11.54.

VT320 257 Sqn (A6-P). w/o 21.11.49.

VT321 504 Sqn (RAD-G, later TM-G). 215 AFS. w/o 13.2.53.

VT322 74 Sqn (4D-J). 263 Sqn. 207 AFS. To MoS 29.3.56.

VT323 Southern Sector. 205 AFS. 206 AFS. 203 AFS/8 FTS. Scrap 5.1.55.

VT324 226 OCU/203 AFS. 205 AFS. 101 FRS. 205 AFS. w/o 25.9.51.

VT325 226 OCU (KR-N). w/o 5.6.51.

VT326 66 Sqn. 65 Sqn. 203 AFS. w/o 4.3.52.

VT327 504 Sqn. 205 AFS (Z-M)/4 FTS. 8 FTS. To Scrap 11.8.55.

VT328 263 Sqn (HE-J). 611 Sqn. 206 AFS. 203 AFS. 8 FTS. w/o 26.4.55.

VT329 222 Sqn (ZD-U). Northern Sector. 65 Sqn. 209 AFS. F/R for conv to U.15 30.6.55.

VT330 CGS. 500 Sqn (G). 215 AFS. F/R for conv to U.15 20.7.55.

VT331 222 Sqn (ZD-Y). APS. 206 AFS. 203 AFS. To Scrap 31.8.55.

VT332 226 OCU. 203 AFS. 215 AFS. 8 FTS. F/R for conv to U.15 28.3.56 (X). w/o 16.3.60 when radio control lost.

VT333 To Netherlands as I-76.

VT334 504 Sqn. 215 AFS. RAFFC. F/R for conv to U.15 20.7.55.

VT335 CFE. 206 AFS. w/o 29.10.53.

VT336 263 Sqn. 207 AFS. w/o 6.6.52.

VT337 92 Sqn (DL-R). 226 OCU. 205 AFS/4 FTS. Scrap 5.1.55.

VT338 ETPS. GAC. JCU Coningsby. JCU Marham. F/R for conv to U.15 28.3.56 (B). w/o 22.7.59.

VT339 56 Sqn. 226 OCU. w/o 7.12.51.

VT340 Defford. RAE Farnborough. Fairey Aviation.

VT341 222 Sqn (ZD-R). 63 Sqn. 616 Sqn. 215 AFS. w/o 21.11.52.

VT342 Defford. w/o 21.12.50.

VT343 257 Sqn. Eastern Sector. 257 Sqn. w/o 16.5.50

VT344 226 OCU/203 AFS. w/o 17.6.52.

VT345 504 Sqn (RAD-B). w/o 21.4.50.

VT346 63 Sqn (D). 616 Sqn. 203 AFS. Scrap 7.5.54.

VT347 GAC. Conv to FR.5. w/o 15.6.49 on maiden flight.

VW255 205 AFS. w/o 25.1.51.

VW256 600 Sqn (LJ-U). 207 AFS (11-P). To Scrap 25.5.54.

VW257 74 Sqn. 263 Sqn. 245 Sqn. 611 Sqn. 205 AFS. 4 FTS. 12 FTS. Scrap 5.5.55.

VW258 92 Sqn (DL-L). 65 Sqn. 29 Sqn. 209 AFS. 12 FTS. F/R for conv to U.15 28.3.56 (J). 728 (B) Sqn.

VW259 RAFFC. 205 AFS/4 FTS. 12 FTS. To Scrap 10.6.55.

VW260 CFE. 207 AFS. Scrap 7.5.54.

VW261 222 Sqn. 56 Sqn. Waterbeach Stn Flt. 56 Sqn. 609 Sqn. 610 Sqn. 206 AFS. 203 AFS. 215 AFS. w/o 3.12.53.

VW262 56 Sqn. 222 Sqn. CGS. 215 AFS. w/o 15.3.53.

VW263 To Netherlands as I-77.

VW264 To Netherlands as I-72.

VW265 263 Sqn (HE-G). w/o 8.7.50.

VW266 257 Sqn (A6-H). 615 Sqn. 203 AFS. F/R for conv to U.15 13.5.55.

VW267 92 Sqn. w/o 14.5.50.

VW268 205 AFS. w/o 27.10.52.

VW269 Bovingdon. 203 AFS. w/o 24.4.52.

VW270 1 Sqn (JX-D). 610 Sqn. Hooton Park Stn Flt. 207 AFS. Scrap 1.6.54.

VW271 66 Sqn. 205 AFS/4 FTS (80). 12 FTS. Scrap 21.5.55.

VW272 504 Sqn. 205 AFS. 206 AFS. 203 AFS/8 FTS. Scrap 25.4.55.

VW273 266 Sqn. 66 Sqn. 51 Sqn. 600 Sqn. 206 AFS. 215 AFS. F/R for conv to U.15 25.7.55.

VW274 504 Sqn (RAD-F, later TM-F and F). w/o 20.5.52.

VW275 245 Sqn (MR-K). 66 Sqn. 64 Sqn. 615 Sqn. 616 Sqn. 203 AFS. F/R for conv to U.15 8.6.53.

VW276 66 Sqn. 111 Sqn. 66 Sqn. 19 Sqn. 611 Sqn. 610 Sqn. 209 AFS. F/R for conv to U.15 28.3.56 (T). 728 (B) Sqn. w/o 20.7.60 after damage on 7.7.60.

VW277 56 Sqn. w/o 11.3.49.

VW278 CFE. 66 Sqn. 611 Sqn (G). 206 AFS. 203 AFS. 215 AFS. 209 AFS/12 FTS (60). Scrap 16.5.55.

VW279 63 Sqn. w/o 6.7.49.

VW280 56 Sqn (J). 226 OCU. 206 AFS. F/R for conv to U.15 3.8.55 (P). w/o 2.6.60.

VW281 263 Sqn. 205 AFS/4 FTS. 12 FTS. To Scrap 8.6.55.

VW282 CFE (AWDS). 203 AFS. w/o 2.2.52.

VW283 203 AFS/226 OCU. 207 AFS. Scrap 29.4.54.

VW284 74 Sqn. 263 Sqn. 611 Sqn. 205 AFS/4 FTS. Scrap 25.11.54.

VW285 Duxford Stn Flt. 66 Sqn (LZ-A). 41 Sqn. 615 Sqn. 610 Sqn. 205 AFS. F/R for conv to U.15 28.3.56 (X). w/o 16.12.59.

VW286 To Netherlands as I-66.

VW287 203 AFS/226 OCU. w/o 24.4.50.

VW288 To Netherlands as I-71.

VW289 203 AFS/226 OCU (KR-L). w/o 23.2.51.

VW290 FCCS. CGS. 209 AFS/12 FTS. Scrap 17.12.54

VW291 To Netherlands as I-73.

VW292 226 OCU/203 AFS. w/o 28.9.50.

VW293 CFE. A & AEE. RAFFC. F/R for conv to U.15 23.3.56 (M). w/o 21.12.59.

VW294 1 Sqn. 615 Sqn. 500 Sqn. CGS. 215 AFS. Scrap 13.12.52.

VW295 To Netherlands as I-79.

VW296 To Netherlands as I-80.

VW297 226 OCU/203 AFS (FMJ-R). 205 AFS. w/o 24.11.51.

VW298 CFE. 205 AFS. w/o 29.4.52.

VW299 203 AFS. JCU Coningsby. Coningsby Stn Flt. JCU Marham. F/R for conv to U.15 28.3.56 (H). w/o 7.4.60.

VW300 600 Sqn. 207 AFS. 209 AFS. Scrap 5.4.54.

VW301 226 OCU/203 AFS. w/o 5.10.51.

VW302 ETPS. 207 AFS. 12 FTS. w/o 19.11.54.

VW303 ETPS. Dunlop Rubber, Baginton. F/R for conv to U.15 3.5.56.

VW304 600 Sqn. 203 AFS. w/o 20.12.51.

VW305 To Netherlands

VW306 To Netherlands

VW307 To Netherlands

VW308 GAC. AIEU Martlesham Heath. F/R for conv to U.15 1.9.54.

VW309 To Netherlands as I-65.

VW310 To Netherlands as I-74.

VW311 74 Sqn. 205 AFS/4 FTS. 8 FTS. Scrap 7.6.55.

VW312 226 OCU (KR-J). 205 AFS/4 FTS. To Scrap 21.4.55.

VW313 To Netherlands as I-75.

VW314 226 OCU. Flying accident 12.1.51. To Scrap 31.8.51.

VW315 To Netherlands as I-81.

VW316 To Belgium.

VW357 To Belgium.

VW386 Not built

VW387 Not built

VW388 Not built

VW389 Not built

VW780 A & AEE. 222 Sqn (ZD-T). CGS. 209 AFS/12 FTS. To MoS 28.3.56.

VW781 ML Aviation. To F/R for conv to U.15. To RAAF 9.2.56.

VW782 222 Sqn. CFE. w/o 2.2.49.

VW783 257 Sqn (A6-K). w/o 28.6.49.

VW784 CFE. 29 Sqn. 500 Sqn. 203 AFS. w/o 24.7.52

VW785 263 Sqn. 226 OCU. CGS. w/o 15.6.50.

VW786 226 OCU. 222 Sqn. 205 AFS/4 FTS. w/o 18.9.54.

VW787 66 Sqn (HI-A). w/o 5.9.48.

VW788 226 OCU/203 AFS. w/o 2.1.50.

VW789 226 OCU. CFE. w/o 24.2.49.

VW790 RAE Farnborough. A & AEE. To Hornchurch as 7012M 6.2.53. To Benfleet ATC. Scrap at Little Rissington in 1968.

VW791 257 Sqn. CGS. 207 AFS. 12 FTS. To MoS, then F/R for conv to U.15 28.3.56.

VZ386 RAFFC. 205 AFS. F/R for conv to U.15 on 14.6.55.

VZ387 To Netherlands as I-60.

VZ388 To Netherlands as I-62.

VZ389 F/R. Fairey Aviation. Percival Aircraft. F/R for conv to U.15 24.7.54.

VZ390 To Netherlands as I-63.

VZ391 To Netherlands as I-55.

VZ392 Duxford Stn Flt. 92 Sqn. 500 Sqn. 226 OCU. 215 AFS. 207 AFS. 12 FTS. Scrap 28.4.55. (at one time coded N-W).

VZ393 To Netherlands as I-56.

VZ394 To Netherlands as I-78.

VZ395 To Netherlands as I-57.

VZ396 To Netherlands as I-58.

VZ397 To Netherlands as I-59.

VZ398 To Netherlands as I-67.

VZ399 To Netherlands as I-64.

VZ400 To Netherlands as I-61.

VZ401 504 Sqn. 206 AFS. F/R for conv to U.15 21.6.55.

VZ402 To Netherlands as I-68.

VZ403 504 Sqn (RAD-A, later TM-A). 207 AFS. RAE Farnborough. F/R for conv to U.15 13.3.56.

VZ404 504 Sqn. w/o 18.3.51.

VZ405 CFE. 616 Sqn. 206 AFS. w/o 9.9.52.

VZ406 504 Sqn (RAD-E, later TM-E). 206 AFS. w/o 10.8.53.

VZ407 Metropolitan Sector. 203 AFS. F/R for conv to U.15 13.9.54.

VZ408 To Netherlands as I-70.

VZ409 To Netherlands as I-69. To Soesterberg Museum

VZ410 245 Sqn. w/o 13.4.50.

VZ411 600 Sqn (LJ-W). 226 OCU. w/o 1.4.52.

VZ412 600 Sqn (LJ-P). 203 AFS. w/o 23.6.53.

VZ413 56/87 Sqn (W). Waterbeach Stn Flt. 616 Sqn (YQ-J). 264 Sqn. 215 AFS. 209 AFS/12 FTS. Scrap 2.5.55.

VZ414 600 Sqn. 226 OCU. 206 AFS. F/R for conv to U.15 28.6.55.

VZ415 66 Sqn (LZ-J). 65 Sqn. 41 Sqn. 600 Sqn. RAFFC. F/R for conv to U.15 19.3.56 (A). 728 (B) Sqn. Destroyed 3.5.60 by Thunderbird.

VZ416 CFE. 29 Sqn. 85 Sqn. 203 AFS/8 FTS. Scrap 7.10.54.

VZ417 63 Sqn (A). 500 Sqn. 215 AFS. 209 AFS/12 FTS. F/R for conv to U.15 28.3.56. 728 (B) Sqn.

VZ418 600 Sqn. 205 AFS. w/o 10.7.51.

VZ419 CGS. 203 AFS. Scrap 22.5.54.

VZ420 To Egypt.

VZ421 To Egypt.

VZ422 To Egypt.

VZ423 To Egypt.

VZ424 To Egypt.

VZ425 To Egypt.

VZ426 To Egypt.

VZ427 CGS. 203 AFS. w/o 29.1.53.

VZ428 1 Sqn. 615 Sqn (J). 611 Sqn. 215 AFS. w/o 21.11.52.

VZ429 600 Sqn (LJ-Q). 205 AFS/4 FTS. To Scrap 2.12.54.

VZ436 1 Sqn (JX-E). 63 Sqn (T). 609 Sqn. 610 Sqn. 209 AFS. MoS 29.3.56.

VZ437 226 OCU. 206 AFS. 205 AFS/4 FTS. Scrap 19.5.55.

METEOR FR.5

See F.4 VT347.

METEOR T.7

G-AKPK F/F 19.3.48. To R.Neth.AF as I-1, 11.48. To Soesterberg Museum.

G-ANSO Conv from GAF G-7-1 in 1954. To Sweden as SE-DCC. To Ugglarp museum.

EE530 Conv from F.4 7.47. A & AEE. RAE Farnborough. soc 14.2.58.

EE573 Conv from F.4. CS(A) Defford. Fairey Avn, Cranfield. soc 6.5.58.

VW410 F/F 26.10.48. GAC. 47 MU. To RAAF 9.11.51 Became A77-2. soc 6.3.57.

VW411 A & AEE. AIEU Martlesham Heath. RAE Bedford. To PEE Foulness.

VW412 RAE Farnborough. CFE. RAE.

VW413 AWA. A & AEE. RAE Farnborough. 20 MU. Scrap 11.2.58.

VW414 BLEU. Fairey Aviation. Percival. Fairey. ETPS. RAE Bedford.

VW415 203 AFS/226 OCU. 205 AFS. 210 AFS. RAFFC NEA 10.1.57.

VW416 203 AFS/226 OCU (FMK-Q/FMK-J). Driffield 1 Sqn. 54 Sqn. 56 Sqn. 610 Sqn (L). 605 Sqn. Scrap 5.3.58.

VW417 203 AFS. FCCS. 616 Sqn. To R.Neth AF. On static display at Beek as 'I-320'.

VW418 EFS. RAFFC. A & AEE. ETPS (1).

VW419 203 AFS/226 OCU. FRS Finningley. 206 AFS. CFS. 206 AFS. 210 AFS. RAFFC. 8 FTS. w/o 15.12.54.

VW420 203 AFS. Binbrook. JCU Hemswell. JCU C Coningsby. JCU Marham. Scrap 30.7.57.

VW421 205 AFS/4 FTS. 8 FTS (73-X). 203 AFS. 205 AFS. CFS. 4 FTS. Scrap 20.3.62.

VW422 203 AFS/226 OCU (FMK-D). 231 OCU. 25 Sqn (Z). Scrap 30.10.61.

VW423 203 AFS/226 OCU (FMK-E). CGS. FWS. 13 Grp Com Flt. 41 Grp. 13 Grp Com Flt. w/o 4.3.60.

VW424 203 AFS/226 OCU (FMK-F). RAFFC. Handling Sqn. FTU. 12 Grp Com Flt. JTF. 8 FTS. RAFFC. CAW. Scrap 14.12.66.

VW425 203 AFS/226 OCU. Tangmere Stn Flt. F/R. 125 Sqn. 245 Sqn. Scrap 22.5.56.

VW426 203 AFS/226 OCU. FRS. Manby. Scrap 30.10.63.

VW427 203 AFS/226 OCU. 500 Sqn. RAFFC. CAW (R). To fire school at Catterick 14.8.72. Scrap 1974.

VW428 56 Sqn. 257 Sqn. 615 Sqn. 219 Sqn. Scrap 5.3.58.

VW429 CGS. Manby. 203 AFS. 202 AFS. 145 Sqn. 112 Sqn. 130 Sqn. Scrap 31.3.58.

VW430 Horhsam St Faith Stn Flt. 74 Sqn (4D-X). 209 AFS. w/o 12.2.54.

VW431 ITF Tangmere. w/o 14.9.50.

VW432 ITF Tangmere. 72 Sqn. 32 Sqn. 249 Sqn. 208 Sqn. TTF Nicosia. 208 Sqn. w/o 5.4.57.

VW433 CFS. Finningley. 206 AFS. Scrap 11.6.58.

VW434 56 Sqn. w/o 14.10.49.

VW435 CFS. 202 AFS. 101 FRS. 205 AFS. CFS. 205 AFS. 4 FTS. F/R. To Egypt 12.12.55 as 1439.

VW436 702 Sqn.

VW437 CFS. 229 OCU. w/o 20.3.52.

VW438 CFS. 602 Sqn. w/o 23.6.51 at Newport, Fife-hit trees out of fuel.

VW439 203 AFS/226 OCU. CFE. 502 Sqn. 607 Sqn (R). 92 Sqn. To Linton-on-Ouse fire section 8.4.57.

VW440 203 AFS/226 OCU (FMK-H). w/o 30.8.49.

VW441 RAE. soc 27.8.58.

VW442 226 OCU (FMK-C). 65 Sqn. 231 OCU. Hemswell Stn Flt. 231 OCU. 1 Grp Com Flt. BCCS. Allocated to fire fighting training 6.1.59.

VW443 NGTE. DH Firestreak trials camera ship. RAE U.15 trials.

VW444 226 OCU (KD-B). 12 Grp Com Flt. 504 Sqn. 228 OCU. SHQ Seletar. w/o 3.6.57.

VW445 226 OCU. FRS. 208 Sqn. 209 AFŚ. w/o 10.7.53.

VW446 728 Sqn (HF-570). AHU Brawdy. Scrap late 1965.

VW447 759 Sqn (CU-412). 728 Sqn (HF-571). Lossiemouth Stn Flt (LM-935). AHU Brawdy. Scrap 1965.

VW448 226 OCU. w/o 15.11.49.

VW449 226 OCU. FRS. 101 FRS. 202 AFS. 231 OCU. Benson Stn Flt. BCCF. 231 OCU. FTU. w/o 30.12.55.

VW450 CFS. 229 OCU Leuchars. Duxford Stn Flt. w/o 14.12.54.

VW451 A & AEE. Andover. Binbrook Stn Flt. Middleton St George. 102 FRS. 206 AFS. 215 AFS. 205 AFS. 4 FTS. Scrap 31.3.58.

VW452 CS(A). CFE. 613 Sqn (3). 46 Sqn (Z). RAFFC. CAW (S). Catterick dump 14.7.72.

VW453 604 Sqn. ETPS (3). A & AEE. Static airframe Porton Down.

VW454 203 AFS/226 OCU. Tangmere ITS. West Raynham ITS. To 1 STT Halton 27.1.55 as 7163M.

VW455 203 AFS (FMK-M). CFS. w/o 2.4.52.

VW456 203 AFS. 228 OCU. 43 Sqn (X). 43/151 Sqns (X). 29 Sqn (X). Scrap 6.1.64.

VW457 203 AFS. 12 Grp Com Flt. 226 OCU (HX-V/HX-3). 501 Sqn (B). 151 Sqn (K). 60 Sqn. To Catterick dump 1.7.62.

VW458 203 AFS. Flying accident 2.7.49. To Cranwell 29.11.50 as 6800M.

VW459 203 AFS (FMK-A). CGS. 215 AFS. 210 AFS. 8 FTS. Scrap 23.8.57.

VW470 RAE Farnborough. MoS/Airwork. Scrap 22.7.58.

VW471 203 AFS. 12 Grp Com Flt. Coltishall Stn Flt. 23 Sqn. 141 Sqn. 610 Sqn (K). MoS 22.5.58.

VW472 203 AFS (FMK-N). CFS. 211 AFS. CFS. 8 FTS. 216 Sqn. RAFFC. w/o 11.1.60.

VW473 203 AFS. 229 OCU. 56 Sqn. Wattisham Stn Flt. 257 Sqn. 152 Sqn. 56 Sqn. Scrap 1.11.57.

VW474 CGS. Manby. 203 AFS (FMK-L). w/o 11.2.51 off the Yorkshire coast.

VW475 226 OCU. CFS. 202 AFS. To R.Neth AF 10.3.55.

VW476 203 AFS. w/o 27.11.49.

VW477 EAAS. 203 AFS (FMK-J). RAFFC. 4 FTS. Scrap 16.11.62.

VW478 CFE. 228 OCU. CFS. 3/4 CAACU (P). Kemble dump 30.3.73.

VW479 226 OCU. 206 AFS. 203 AFS (FMK-P). 8 FTS Scrap 31.3.58.

VW480 203 AFS/226 OCU (FMK-B). 211 AFS. 4 FTS RAFFC. Scrap 12.11.62.

VW481 CFS. w/o 5.4.50.

VW482 6 Sqn. 78 Wing RAAF. ITF. Levant Com Flt. w/o 1.9.58.

VW483 RAFFC. CGS. 215 AFS. w/o 19.6.53.

VW484 245 Sqn (MR-T). w/o 6.7.50.

VW485 ATF Sylt. 234 Sqn. 130 Sqn. 234 Sqn. 26 Sqn. CFS (26). Scrap 14.12.66.

VW486 Odiham Stn Flt. 54 Sqn. 205 AFS. w/o 17.9.52

VW487 1 Sqn. 29 Sqn. FCCS. TTF Seletar. 1574 Flt. To SAF Changi as instructional airframe 12.1.71.

VW488 43 Sqn (V). 13 Grp Com Flt. w/o 8.8.57.

VW489 263 Sqn (HE-Z/Z). 607 Sqn (Q). 63 Sqn (Q). 25 Sqn. 5 FTS. Scrap 2.12.60.

VZ629 72 Sqn. 226 OCU. 264 Sqn. w/o 26.1.54.

VZ630 Duxford Stn Flt. 66 Sqn. 111 Sqn. FCCS. 111 Sqn. 604 Sqn. MoS (NEA) 17.4.58.

VZ631 257 Sqn. w/o 12.9.50.

VZ632 53 Sqn (UB). 205 AFS. w/o 28.3.52.

VZ633 222 Sqn (ZD-Z). Binbrook Stn Flt. Wittering Stn Flt. 611 Sqn. soc 15.11.57.

VZ634 247 Sqn. 609 Sqn. 141 Sqn. 41 Sqn. Stradishall Stn Flt. Leeming. NEA 15.11.71. Wattisham 26.4.72 for crash rescue training.

VZ635 CGS. CFS. 215 AFS. 12 FTS. Kai Tak SHQ. Scrap 17.11.59.

VZ636 92 Sqn. 614 Sqn (7A-V/V). Scrap 14.2.58.

VZ637 92 Sqn. 502 Sqn (P). 275 Sqn. 13 Grp Com Flt (A). Scrap 30.10.62.

VZ638 500 Sqn (RAA-C). 25 Sqn. 54 Sqn (X). 85 Sqn. FCCS. Biggin Hill Stn Flt. 501 Sqn. 5 FTS. 8 FTS. RAFFC. soc 3.5.65. To Historic Aircraft Museum at Southend, 12.1.72. To Brencham Ltd 1983 as G-JETM.

VZ639 500 Sqn. Takali on loan. 500 Sqn. 501 Sqn. Scrap 25.3.58.

VZ640 616 Sqn. FWS. West Raynham Stn Flt (Z). Scrap 30.10.61.

VZ641 CFE (DFLS). CFE Com Flt. 500 Sqn. 63 Sqn (Z). Scrap 7.7.58.

VZ642 CFS. w/o 3.11.51, hit wires and trees while on approach to Little Rissington.

VZ643 616 Sqn. 607 Sqn. w/o 5.5.52.

VZ644 CFE (DFLS). CFE Com Flt. Linton Stn Flt. 216 Sqn. Thorney Island Stn Flt. 2 ANS. RAFFC. CAW. Scrap 14.12.66.

VZ645 702 Sqn.

VZ646 To Royal Navy late 1949.

VZ647 728 Sqn (HF). Scrapped at Brawdy 1965.

VZ648 759 Sqn (411/CW). 728 Sqn (HF-936). Lossiemouth Stn Flt/736 Sqn. Scrapped at Brawdy in 1965.

VZ649 CFE. 226 OCU. 603 Sqn. 616 Sqn. Scrap 14.2.58.

WA590 CFE. 226 OCU. 211 AFS. Scrap 2.9.57.

WA591 CFE. 203 AFS (FMK-O). 208 AFS. 215 AFS. 12 FTS. RAFFC. 5 FTS. 8 FTS. RAFFC. CAW (U). 5 MU apprentice school 16.8.66 as 7917M. St Athan apprentice school. Woodvale for display 1979.

WA592 501 Sqn. Scampton Stn Flt. To R.Neth AF 9.5.56 as I-322.

WA593 CFE. 226 OCU. RAFFC. To Linton dump 6.5.68.

WA594 501 Sqn. 502 Sqn. To R.Neth AF 20.10.55.

WA595 605 Sqn. w/o 10.5.53.

WA596 249 Sqn. w/o 7.8.53.

WA597 CGS. CFS. 203 AFS. 4 FTS. 8 FTS (52-X). Scrap 30.10.63.

WA598 605 Sqn. 205 AFS/4 FTS. 8 FTS. To Catterick dump 24.8.62.

WA599 APS Acklington. 263 Sqn. 46 Sqn (Z). 601 Sqn. North Weald Stn Flt. Wattisham Stn Flt. Leeming. To Catterick dump 23.3.62.

WA600 702 Sqn. 728 Sqn (HF-573/HF-576).

WA601 601 Sqn. 72 Sqn (Z). 609 Sqn. Scrap 14.2.58.

WA602 ITF Tangmere. 226 OCU. 233 OCU. 1 Sqn. RAFFC. To Little Rissington for fire practice 21.5.68. To Catterick 28.10.68.

WA603 CFE (ITS). w/o 1.2.51, lost hood and aircraft abandoned in spin off Cromer.

WA604 FRS. 203 AFS. 611 Sqn. 228 OCU. w/o 29.5.51 while on approach to Leeming.

WA605 6 Sqn. 13 Sqn. Scrap 13.3.57.

WA606 208 Sqn. w/o 28.2.52.

WA607 1689 Flt. Benson. To GAC 17.12.54. To France 6.4.55 as F-BEAR for ejector seat trials.

WA608 CGS. 203 AFS. 202 AFS. 208 AFS. 209 AFS. w/o 9.2.53.

WA609 1 OFU Chivenor. FTU. 228 OCU (S). Scrap 16.11.62.

WA610 504 Sqn (TM-M). Bruggen Stn Flt. APS Sylt. Bruggen Stn Flt. Scrap 2.11.62.

WA611 32 Sqn. 13 Sqn. 32 Sqn. 249 Sqn. Scrap 16.12.57.

WA612 601 Sqn. 63 Sqn (Z). 111 Sqn (S). Scrap 30.10.61.

WA613 32 Sqn. MEAF Com Sqn. 205 Grp Com Flt, became Abu Sueir Stn Flt. ITF. Scrap 14.2.58.

WA614 FRS Finningley. 203 AFS (FMK-S). w/o 27.9.50.

WA615 504 Sqn. 205 AFS. CFS. 153 Sqn (Z). 25 Sqn (Z). Scrap 2.10.58.

WA616 Missing in transit to MEAF 28.4.50.

WA617 208 Sqn. w/o 29.5.51, undershot at Nicosia.

WA618 73 Sqn. 205 Grp Com Flt. 208 Sqn. AHQ Malta. Scrap 31.12.57.

WA619 RAFFC/19 FTS (FAG-A). Cranwell Stn Flt. IAM Farnborough. Deck 'roller' trials HMS *Ark Royal*. Scrap 30.10.63.

WA620 54 Sqn. 229 OCU. 233 OCU. 604 Sqn. 111 Sqn 601 Sqn (P). 89 Sqn. Scrap 30.10.61.

WA621 226 OCU. w/o 8.9.52.

WA622 213 Sqn. 73 Sqn. 13 Sqn. El Adem store. 12 MU. Scrap 14.2.58.

WA623 To R.Neth AF 3.8.50 as I-8.

WA624 213 Sqn. MEAF Com Sqn. ITF Nicosia. MEAF Com Sqn. Scrap 2.9.57.

WA625 FRS. 203 AFS (FMK-W). w/o 24.11.50.

WA626 To R.Neth AF 3.8.50 as I-9. To MLD 1958.

WA627 249 Sqn. Levant Com Flt. PC & S Sqn, Aden. 8 Sqn. Levant Com Flt. Scrap 19.11.57.

WA628 RAFFC. 41 Sqn. 600 Sqn (S). Scrap 17.4.58.

WA629 56/87 Sqns. CFE (ITS). 602 Sqn. w/o 3.10.54

WA630 RAFFC. 205 AFS. 4 FTS (69). Oakington. To Scrap 16.11.62.

WA631 73 Sqn. w/o 29.6.50.

WA632 203 AFS (FMK-K). 101 FRS. 202 AFS. 207 AFS. w/o 19.1.54.

WA633 To R.Neth AF 3.8.50 as I-10.

WA634 A & AEE. Martin-Baker. wfu 4.62. To St Athan museum.

WA635 RAFFC. 205 AFS. 209 AFS (49). 205 AFS. 209 AFS. 12 FTS. 211 AFS. Scrap 2.9.57.

WA636 IAM Farnborough. w/o 10.4.52.

WA637 613 Sqn (4). Scrap 5.3.58.

WA638 RAE Farnborough. ETPS (3). Martin-Baker. Grounded 1979 and used as spares ship for WL419.

WA639 FRS. 203 AFS. 229 OCU. Waterbeach Stn Flt. Scrap 16.11.62.

WA649 771 Sqn (LP-591).

WA650 Airwork FRU St Davids (BY-003).

WA651

WA652 702 Sqn. Scrapped at Brawdy in 1965.

WA653 203 AFS (FMK-X). JCF Binbrook. 231 OCU. 3 Grp Com Flt. 228 OCU. Scrap 20.3.62.

WA654 RAFFC. 203 AFS (FMK-G). RAFFC. w/o 31.12.53.

WA655 604 Sqn. 601 Sqn. 604 Sqn. 601 Sqn. To Scrap 14.2.58.

WA656 3 Sqn. Gutersloh Meteor Flt. Wildenrath Meteor Flt. 3 Sqn. Scrap 21.2.58.

WA657 16 Sqn. 205 AFS. 4 FTS. Scrap 31.3.58.

WA658 247 Sqn. 229 OCU. 247 Sqn. 229 OCU. 245 Sqn. FWS. AWDS. GWDS. Scrap 14.6.62, to Valley dump.

WA659 Gutersloh. 16 Sqn. 87 Sqn. 16 Sqn. CFS Com Flt. 92 Sqn. 33 Sqn (Y). 74 Sqn. To Manston fire school 19.4.66.

WA660 237 OCU. 237 OCU det, Benson. 231 OCU. CFS. Scrap 31.3.58.

WA661 203 AFS (FMK-Y). 215 AFS. 206 AFS. 203 AFS. 8 FTS. Scrap 8.7.58.

WA662 3 Sqn. Gutersloh Meteor Flt. Wildenrath Meteor Flt. 3 Sqn. FCCS. Short Bros. RAE Llanbedr (K).

WA663 Gutersloh. 26 Sqn. 2 Sqn. 94 Sqn. 207 AFS. 203 AFS. 205 AFS. 4 FTS. 8 FTS (54-X). Scrap 30.7.57

WA664 CFE (ITS). CFS. 211 AFS. Scrap 26.7.57.

WA665 CFE (ITS). 600 Sqn. w/o 24.4.52.

WA666 26 Sqn. 93 Sqn. CFS. 209 AFS. 12 FTS. w/o 10.1.55.

WA667 Thorney Island. 600 Sqn. ITF. 605 Sqn. Scrap 14.5.58.

WA668 CFS. w/o 19.6.50.

WA669 203 AFS (FMK-R). RAFFC. RAF Handling Sqn. CFS (27). 'Vintage Pair'. 1 TWU (02). CFS 'Vintage Pair' 22.10.82.

WA670 56 Sqn (US-A). 501 Sqn. 604 Sqn. w/o 20.3.55

WA671 600 Sqn. 608 Sqn (6T-O/O). Linton Stn Flt. Middleton St George Stn Flt. 111 Sqn. 74 Sqn. RAF Germany. soc crash/rescue training, Wildenrath 4.5.64.

WA672 600 Sqn. 608 Sqn. 609 Sqn (P). 72 Sqn (V). 19 Sqn. 92 Sqn. 32 MU test-rig 1.4.66.

WA673 CFS. 203 AFS (FMK-T). CFS. w/o 30.10.50.

WA674 1 OFU Chivenor. Abingdon. To R.Neth AF 16.9.55 as I-319.

WA675 28 Sqn. SHQ Kai Tak. FE Com Sqn. 81 Sqn. FE Com Cqn. Scrap 9.1.60.

WA676 FEAF Examining Sqn. Seletar. 60 Sqn. 45/33 Sqns. APC. SHQ Seletar. Scrap 17.11.59.

WA677 72 Sqn. 205 AFS. Missing 27.2.51 off the Durham coast.

WA678 CFE (ITS). w/o 1.5.51, spun in while on approach to West Raynham.

WA679 CFS. RAFFC. w/o 16.5.52.

WA680 203 AFS/226 OCU. Binbrook Stn Flt. BCCF Booker. To RAAF 27.7.55, A77-705 allocated but not worn. WRE. RAAF Museum Point Cook 15.1.75 as A77-705.

WA681 60 Sqn. FE Examining Sqn, became FE Trng Sqn (M-58). 60 Sqn. 81 Sqn. Scrap 23.7.59.

WA682 203 AFS (FMK-H). CFS. 210 AFS. FCCS. 605 Sqn. Scrap 5.3.58.

WA683 FE Examining Sqn/Trng Sqn. Kai Tak. FE Trng Sqn. APC. 45/33 Sqns. APC. SHQ Butterworth. Scrap 5.9.57.

WA684 615 Sqn. To Belgian AF 30.11.56 as ED-40.

WA685 2 Sqn. w/o 25.6.52.

WA686 203 AFS. 211 AFS (56). To Martin-Baker for static tests with F.8 front fuselage, 12.7.57.

WA687 615 Sqn. w/o 26.8.51.

WA688 CFS. 203 AFS (FMK-C). CFS. To Belgian AF 9.10.56 as ED-38.

WA689 615 Sqn. 600 Sqn (T). Scrap 14.2.58.

WA690 Boscombe Down. CGS. RAE Farnborough. Folland. A & AEE.

WA691 CFS (O-Y). 203 AFS (FMK-M). CFS. w/o 20.8.52.

WA692 4 Sqn. Belly-landed in error at Wunstorf 2.7.51, to Cranwell as 6900M 29.9.51. To Chivenor 3.55.

WA693 11 Sqn. 2 Sqn. 11 Sqn. Wunstorf Meteor Flt. Fassberg Stn Flt. 5 Sqn. APS Sylt. Scrap 31.3.58.

WA694 CFE (ITS). 207 AFS. 8 FTS (61-X). Scrap 31.3.58.

WA695 2 Sqn. w/o 5.9.50.

WA696 600 Sqn. Colerne Com Sqn. 81 Grp Com Sqn. Scrap 30.10.61.

WA697 541 Sqn. 237 OCU. Binbrook Stn Flt. Benson Stn Flt. Binbrook Stn Flt. JCU Hemswell. 231 OCU. Gaydon Stn Flt. 13 Grp Com Flt. 111 Sqn. 156 (ATC) Sqn, Kidderminster, as 7609M. Catterick 14.12.67. To Scrap 1978.

WA698 CFS. 8 FTS. Scrap 16.8.57.

WA707 205 AFS. CFS. 205 AFS/4 FTS. RAFFC. Scrap 30.10.61.

WA708 CFS. 203 AFS. w/o 10.4.51, abandoned in spin over Yorkshire.

WA709 205 AFS. Boscombe Down.

WA710 541 Sqn. 87 Sqn. Wunstorf Meteor Flt. 87 Sqn. Meteor Trng Flt Wunstorf. 96 Sqn. Scrap 11.12.57.

WA711 205 AFS. w/o 1.5.51, crashed during overshoot at Middleton St George.

WA712 205 AFS. 103 FRS. 207 AFS. 208 AFS. 209 AFS (42). w/o 8.9.53.

WA713 205 AFS. Accident 20.2.51. To Valley 17.5.51 as 6863M.

WA714 205 AFS. CFS. 71 Sqn. Wildenrath Stn Flt. RAE Farnborough. A & AEE.

WA715 205 AFS. w/o 19.1.53.

WA716 203 AFS. 202 AFS. w/o 21.12.51, bellied-in, out of fuel, near Holland Arms, Anglesey.

WA717 205 AFS. 210 AFS. Aden Com Sqn. 8 Sqn. APCS. Command reserve, Khormaksar. 8 Sqn. Khormaksar Stn Flt. Scrap 27.10.59.

WA718 205 AFS. 612 Sqn (T). 611 Sqn (X). RAFFC. CAW (Y). soc 2.8.68 to Woodvale dump. Scrap 11.78.

WA719 205 AFS. w/o 12.1.51, hit railway embankment on single-engine approach to Middleton St George.

WA720 205 AFS. w/o 20.11.51, abandoned in spin and crashed Barnard Castle, Durham.

WA721 501 Sqn. 23 Sqn. 74 Sqn. RAFG for crash/rescue trng 27.8.63.

WA722 63 Sqn. CFE (ITS). 29 Sqn. Scrap 26.6.57.

WA723 600 Sqn. FTU. Scrap 12.11.62.

WA724 1 Sqn. 29 Sqn. 141 Sqn. w/o 19.8.53.

WA725 245 Sqn (L). Horsham St Faith Stn Flt. Leuchars Stn Flt (Y). 151 Sqn. Scrap 16.11.62.

WA726 500 Sqn. w/o 24.2.52.

WA727 203 AFS. 209 AFS. CFS. 12 FTS. 152 Sqn. C(A) 5.2.58.

WA728 203 AFS. 65 Sqn. Scrap 31.5.58

WA729 229 OCU. Tangmere Stn Flt. Scrap 20.5.61.

WA730 205 AFS. 98 Sqn. To Egypt 12.12.55 as 1440.

WA731 To RAAF 8.1.51 as A77-229. Re-serialled as A77-701. WRE.

WA732 To RAAF 8.1.51 as A77-305. Re-serialled as A77-702. 38 Sqn Com Flt. RAAF Museum.

WA733 229 OCU. Odiham Stn Flt. 85 Sqn. AFDS. To Scrap 30.10.63.

WA734 229 OCU. Coltishall Stn Flt. 605 Sqn. w/o 27.3.54.

WA735 229 OCU (ES-W). Leuchars Stn Flt. w/o 8.7.53

WA736 202 AFS. 215 AFS. 211 AFS. Nicosia Stn Flt. Safi store. 29 Sqn. To Topcliffe dump 8.3.66.

WA737 203 AFS (X-52). 8 FTS. Scrap 11.3.58.

WA738 CS (A). Fairey Aviation.

WA739 2 Sqn. 211 AFS. RAFFC. Scrap 31.3.58.

WA740 421 Sqn (RCAF). 226 OCU. Church Fenton Stn Flt. Leconfield Stn Flt (B). 72 Sqn. Scrap 30.10.63.

WA741 CFS (O-D). 209 AFS/12 FTS. RAFFC. Scrap 5.12.57.

WA742 421 Sqn (RCAF). 226 OCU. Wattisham Stn Flt. Waterbeach Stn Flt (A). 56 Sqn. 46 Sqn. 64 Sqn. Scrap 20.12.63.

METEOR T.7 *continued*

WA743 611 Sqn. 610 Sqn (K/L). 4 FTS. RAFFC. To scrap 30.11.62.
WF766 202 AFS. 231 OCU. RAF Handling Sqn. w/o 11.11.60, Farnborough.
WF767 203 AFS. w/o 30.11.51, on night take-off from Driffield.
WF768 203 AFS. 215 AFS. 209 AFS/12 FTS. soc 12.3.58.
WF769 CFS. 12 FTS. Linton Stn Flt. 66 Sqn (Q). soc 13.11.58.
WF770 611 Sqn (W). BFAP Stn Flt. soc 21.12.61.
WF771 ITF. 600 Sqn. 229 OCU. 4 FTS (3). RAFFC. w/o 29.1.62.
WF772 CFS. JCU Marham. 3 Grp Com Flt. 231 OCU. 208 Sqn. Malta Com & TT Sqn. 29 Sqn (Y). To Leuchars dump 15.5.68.
WF773 602 Sqn (W). 231 OCU. Scrap 25.11.57.
WF774 502 Sqn. Linton Conversion Flt. 66 Sqn. w/o 12.12.52.
WF775 500 Sqn. w/o 29.6.53.
WF776 203 AFS (54-X). 205 AFS. 203 AFS. CFS. 12 FTS. To France 29.6.56.
WF777 202 AFS. w/o 4.12.51, engine cut while on approach to Valley.
WF778 613 Sqn (5). Scrap 5.3.58.
WF779 14 Sqn. 541 Sqn. Wunstorf Stn Flt. Scrap 19.5.58, to Martin-Baker for spares recovery.
WF780 202 AFS. FTU. MOA. RAE Farnborough. soc 25.5.66.
WF781 Fairey Aviation, Cranfield.
WF782 HQ BAFO. 112 Sqn (Z/Y). soc 11.3.55.
WF783 609 Sqn. w/o 11.1.55.
WF784 26 Sqn. 130 Sqn. FTU. RAFFC. 5 CAACU. To Quedgeley for display, 20.11.65 (allocated 7895M)
WF785 54 Sqn. 610 Sqn (K). Scrap 14.2.58.
WF786 71 Sqn. w/o 1.5.51, lost hood and abandoned near Bielefeld.
WF787 19 Sqn (X). 23 Sqn ('Athene'). Coltishall Stn Flt. 74 Sqn. To Manston dump 7.4.66.
WF788 202 AFS. 207 AFS. 500 Sqn (L/'Isle of Thanet') Scrap 30.5.58.
WF789 16 Sqn. w/o 7.8.52.
WF790 4 Sqn. w/o 19.8.51, hit ground during aerobatics, East Sutton, Kent.
WF791 26 Sqn. CFS (27). 5 CAACU. 'Vintage Pair'.
WF792 67 Sqn. Gutersloh Meteor Flt. Wildenrath Meteor Flt. w/o 25.9.53.
WF793 502 Sqn. 64 Sqn. 228 OCU. w/o 7.8.52.
WF794 202 AFS. 207 AFS. 211 AFS. Scrap 11.10.57.
WF795 237 OCU. 231 OCU. Gaydon Stn Flt. Levant Stn Flt. ME Com Sqn. Nicosia St. Flt. Scrap 3.12.60.
WF813 98 Sqn. APS. AFDS (U). 264 Sqn. 33 Sqn. 92 Sqn. 72 Sqn. Scrap 16.11.62.
WF814 202 AFS. Allocated to Israel but rejected as unsuitable 14.7.55. To Belgian AF 8.2.57 as ED-43.
WF815 CFE (ITF). ITS. 207 AFS. w/o 1.3.54.
WF816 602 Sqn. 601 Sqn. 604 Sqn. 141 Sqn. 25 Sqn (Y). 41 Sqn. 600 Sqn. Duxford Stn Flt. 65 Sqn. 29 Sqn. 23 Sqn. 85 Sqn. To Manston dump 30.5.68.
WF817 To Belgian AF 3.7.51 as ED-4.
WF818 To Belgian AF 3.7.51 as ED-6.
WF819 19 Sqn. APS (WH-G). Acklington Stn Flt. 29 Sqn. Acklington Stn Flt. 29 Sqn. AFDS. 12 Grp Com Flt. Cat.4 'Rogue' 33 MU 30.11.59. Scrap 1.12.60.
WF820 613 Sqn. 608 Sqn (U). Scrap 5.3.58.
WF821 64 Sqn. Missing 16.5.53.
WF822 RAE Farnborough for NF.11 radar trials. ETPS (11).
WF823 ITF. 504 Sqn. West Raynham. w/o 7.11.52.
WF824 502 Sqn (N). Scrap 14.2.58.
WF825 603 Sqn (X/2). 33 Sqn. RAFFC. CAW. To 2189 (ATC) Sqn, Lyneham, 6.2.69 as 'Z'.
WF826 1689 Flt. FTU. CFS. 1 ANS (Z). To 5 MU as snow-blower 23.2.65. Scrapped 1974.
WF827 To Belgian AF 3.7.51.
WF828 611 Sqn. 610 Sqn. 226 OCU. w/o 6.8.52.
WF829 205 AFS. 4 FTS. RAFFC. soc 14.4.61.
WF830 205 AFS. 4 FTS. RAFFC. Scrap 16.11.62.
WF831 103 FRS. 207 AFS. w/o 26.2.52.
WF832 ITF BAFO. 71 Sqn. Gutersloh Meteor Flt. To France 2.7.53.
WF833 607 Sqn. To GAC 19.8.54. To Sweden as SE-CAS. wfu 4.59. To Malmslatt museum.
WF834 611 Sqn. 72 Sqn (Z). 4 FTS. 5 FTS. 3 CAACU To Bassingbourn dump 19.4.66.
WF835 228 OCU. 5 FTS. w/o 2.10.59.
WF836 118 Sqn. 4 Sqn. 2 Grp Com Flt. 83 Grp Com Flt. 68 Sqn. Laarbruch Stn Flt. soc 10.59.
WF837 612 Sqn. w/o 30.4.54.
WF838 603 Sqn (Y). Scrap 14.2.58.
WF839 Nicosia TTF. TTF Takali. Scrap 31.3.55.
WF840 Manby. CFS. CC Com Flt. Scrap 12.11.62.
WF841 CFE (ITF). Scrap 23.11.53.
WF842 612 Sqn. w/o 17.9.51, spun-in at Newham Farm, Northumberland.
WF843 Scampton Examining Flt. 540 Sqn. JCU. To RAAF 21.6.55 as A77-706. Scrap 23.7.57.
WF844 102 FRS. 206 AFS. CFS. 215 AFS. 209 AFS/12 FTS. RAFFC. Cat.4 'Rogue' 24.8.58.
WF845 ITF. South Cerney. 504 Sqn. Scrap 5.3.58.
WF846 602 Sqn (LO-V/V). Scrap 5.3.58.
WF847 1 OFU. FTU. 12 FTS. RAFFC. Scrap 2.9.57.
WF848 41 Sqn. 85 Sqn. FECS. w/o 21.12.56.
WF849 Nicosia ITF. w/o 7.2.55.
WF850 607 Sqn. 611 Sqn. w/o 11.4.54.
WF851 CFE (ITS). 207 AFS. 12 FTS. CFS. Scrap 31.7.58.
WF852 CFS. w/o 31.12.52.
WF853 Shallufa ITF. Nicosia ITF. soc 4.7.58.
WF854 65 Sqn. w/o 28.5.52.
WF855 213 Sqn. 8 Sqn. soc 6.9.54.
WF856 93 Sqn. To R.Neth AF 9.5.56 as I-323.
WF857 202 AFS. w/o 8.4.53.
WF858 4 Sqn. Wunstorf Meteor Flt. 4 Sqn. 615 Sqn (W). Scrap 14.2.58.
WF859 ITF BAFO. 67 Sqn. Gutersloh Meteor Flt. 87 Sqn. w/o 19.3.52.
WF860 ITF BAFO. 71 Sqn. w/o 2.11.51, crash landed Achtel, Belgium.
WF861 222 Sqn. Leuchars Stn Flt. 222 Sqn. Scrap 16.11.62.
WF862 Wunstorf Meteor Flt. Meteor Trng Flt. 96 Sqn. 256 Sqn. Ahlhorn Stn Flt. Geilenkirchen Stn Flt. Scrap 1.12.60.
WF875 ITF Nicosia. 208 Sqn. w/o 6.11.52.
WF876 25 Sqn. 85 Sqn. w/o 17.11.51, engine cut on approach to West Malling.
WF877 11 Sqn. Wunstorf Meteor Flt. 96 Sqn. F/R. To Torbay Museum 1.2.74.
WF878 205 AFS. w/o 17.4.52.
WF879 ITF Nicosia. RAFFC. JTF Lyneham. RAF Handling Sqn. A & AEE. soc 1.8.66 and dumped at Old Sarum.
WF880 208 AFS. FCCS. Duxford Stn Flt. FCCS. 11 Grp Com Flt. soc 8.10.59.
WF881 203 AFS (X-55). 8 FTS. 211 AFS. Scrap 26.6.57.
WF882 203 AFS. ITF. 73 Sqn. Levant Com Flt. soc 25.3.57.
WF883 FEAF. w/o 17.9.52.
WG935 94 Sqn. 71 Sqn. 2 Sqn. 67 Sqn. Scrap 2.9.57.
WG936 141 Sqn. w/o 22.12.51, engine cut in circuit, Middleton St George.
WG937 CGS. 4 FTS (68). 211 AFS. Scrap 20.11.62.
WG938 1 Sqn. 604 Sqn. Scrap 15.5.58.
WG939 94 Sqn. 256 Sqn. Scrap 31.3.58.
WG940 CGS. FWS. 609 Sqn. 19 Sqn (W). To West Raynham for ground instruction as 7579M 21.10.58.
WG941 185 Sqn. 73 Sqn. ITF. Levant Com Flt. MEAF Com Sqn. soc 4.12.57.
WG942 Binbrook Stn Flt. JCU Binbrook. JCU Hemswell. JCU Coningsby. JCU Marham. Upwood Stn Flt. 100 Sqn. Scrap 5.3.58.
WG943 226 OCU (UU-F). 245 Sqn. Scrap 28.6.57.
WG944 206 AFS. w/o 25.11.52.
WG945 MEAF. ITF. Scrap 7.5.58, to Martin-Baker for spares.
WG946 202 AFS. 109 FRS. 206 AFS (Y-72). 209 AFS/12 FTS. Scrap 12.11.61.
WG947 205 AFS. 231 OCU. w/o 4.11.55.
WG948 614 Sqn. w/o in ground accident 24.2.52.
WG949 151 Sqn. 603 Sqn (Z). Scrap 5.3.58.
WG950 203 AFS (X-65). 8 FTS. Scrap 31.3.58.
WG961 41 Sqn. Odiham Stn Flt. w/o 27.6.57 and dumped at Odiham.
WG962 203 AFS. CFS. CFS (O-P). w/o 26.6.62 on take-off from Little Rissington.
WG963 541 Sqn. Wunstorf Ft. Flt. 79 Sqn (A-Z). Wahn Stn Flt. Bruggen Stn Flt. soc 23.1.58.
WG964 203 AFS. 211 AFS. 203 AFS. 207 AFS. CFS. 8 FTS. HQ Malta Sector. MC & TTS. soc 30.4.62.
WG965 205 AFS. 4 FTS. 8 FTS. Scrap 31.3.58.
WG966 205 AFS. 210 AFS. 209 AFS/12 FTS. Laarbruch Stn Flt. 2 TAF Com Sqn. Scrap 30.10.62.
WG967 60 Sqn. w/o 21.8.53.
WG968 612 Sqn. 209 AFS/12 FTS. RAFFC. soc 5.6.58
WG969 202 AFS. 207 AFS. 12 FTS. CFS. PEE Shoeburyness 10.4.58.
WG970 264 Sqn. 211 AFS. Belgian AF 29.1.57 as ED-42
WG971 206 AFS. w/o 17.6.53.
WG972 231 OCU. w/o 7.4.53.
WG973 5 Sqn. 541 Sqn. 79 Sqn. 112 Sqn. w/o 26.9.54.
WG974 To RAAF 31.10.51 as A77-380. Re-serialled A77-703. 77 Sqn. w/o 20.6.55 on take-off from Williamtown.
WG975 205 AFS. w/o 21.1.52.
WG976 28 Sqn. SHQ Kai Tak. SHQ Seletar. 45/33 Sqns. SHQ Seletar. 81 Sqn. SHQ Seletar. soc 26.5.60.
WG977 To RAAF 31.10.51 as A77-577. Re-serialled as A77-704. 77 Sqn. w/o 6.9.52 during a thunderstorm in Korea.
WG978 206 AFS. w/o 18.12.52.
WG979 207 AFS. CFS. 12 FTS. 64 Sqn. Scrap 24.10.62.
WG980 207 AFS. 208 AFS. 210 AFS. CFS. 12 FTS. FECS. soc 29.3.57.
WG981 206 AFS. 205 AFS. 4 FTS. 12 FTS. CFS. soc to 16 MU Stafford for display as 7417M 18.2.57, with codes 'DT-O'.
WG982 206 AFS. w/o 3.12.53.
WG983 202 AFS (P-29). 207 AFS. 211 AFS. Scrap 2.9.57.
WG984 206 AFS. 209 AFS/12 FTS (N-E). 5 CAACU. Scrap 20.12.63.
WG985 206 AFS, 215 AFS (N). 8 FTS (X-63). Scrap 30.10.62.
WG986 207 AFS. w/o 16.4.52.
WG987 206 AFS. CFS. 79 Sqn (T-Z). Wunstorf Stn Flt. 541 Sqn. 2 Grp Com Flt. 5 FTS. RAF Handling Sqn. Cottesmore dump 1.4.66.
WG988 205 AFS. 209 AFS. w/o 17.4.53.
WG989 206 AFS. w/o 20.4.53.
WG990 203 AFS. 215 AFS. 203 AFS/8 FTS (X-62). Driffield. Scrap 19.7.57.
WG991 614 Sqn (S). Scrap 25.3.58.
WG992 206 AFS. w/o 5.5.52.
WG993 206 AFS. CFS. 8 FTS. 602 Sqn. Scrap 5.3.58.
WG994 206 AFS. 215 AFS. 203 FAS/8 FTS. To Egypt 22.2.56 as 1441.
WG995 205 AFS. 211 AFS. 4 FTS. 23 Grp Com Flt. Scrap 10.11.62.
WG996 20 Sqn. Oldenburg Stn Flt. A & AEE.
WG997 To France 28.2.52.
WG998 To R.Neth AF 12.2.53 as I-304.
WG999 206 AFS. 210 AFS. 209 AFS/12 FTS. 8 FTS (X-66). RAFFC. Scrap 31.3.58.
WH112 207 AFS. 12 FTS. RAFFC. 4 FTS. RAFFC. 13 Grp Com Flt. Scrap 29.10.62.
WH113 213 Sqn. 205 Grp Com Flt. Abu Sueir Stn Flt 13 Sqn. Scrap 5.12.57.
WH114 207 AFS. 215 AFS. 12 FTS (N-A). To Belgian AF 9.11.56 as ED-39.
WH115 208 AFS. 210 AFS. 616 Sqn. 605 Sqn. w/o 16.10.55.
WH116 13 Sqn. w/o 19.12.53.
WH117 71 Sqn. Gutersloh Meteor Flt. Wildenrath Meteor Flt. 71 Sqn. To Belgian AF 30.11.56 as ED-41.
WH118 CFS. Coningsby Stn Flt. Scampton Stn Flt. To RAAF 8.9.55 as A77-707. 23 Sqn. To Moorabin Air Museum 1966.
WH119 237 OCU. 231 OCU. FECS. SHQ Butterworth FECS. 81 Sqn. soc 19.5.60.
WH120 206 AFS. 203 AFS/8 FTS. 616 Sqn (F). Scrap 5.3.58.
WH121 207 AFS. 8 FTS. Scrap 16.11.62.
WH122 206 AFS. 210 AFS. 12 FTS. Scrap 2.9.57.
WH123 215 AFS. Wunstorf Meteor Flt. Wunstorf Stn Flt. 541 Sqn. Laarbruch Stn Flt. 68 Sqn. Laarbruch Stn Flt. Scrap 16.11.62.
WH124 215 AFS. 211 AFS. RAFFC. w/o 15.4.58.
WH125 To R.Neth AF 27.3.53 as I-305.
WH126 207 AFS. 215 AFS. 12 FTS. Scrap 2.8.57.
WH127 237 OCU. 231 OCU. 2 TAF. 610 Sqn (L). 141 Sqn. 41 Sqn. Wattisham Stn Flt. 41 Sqn. 74 Sqn. soc 14.10.63.
WH128 205 AFS. 4 FTS. To GAC 22.2.56. To Sweden 1.3.56 as SE-CAT. w/o 21.1.59 at Visby.
WH129 206 AFS. 210 AFS. 209 AFS/12 FTS. 211 AFS 4 FTS. Scrap 5.3.58.
WH130 203 AFS. w/o 16.7.52.
WH131 CFS. w/o 10.11.53.
WH132 207 AFS. 8 FTS. RAFFC. CFS. RAFFC. CAW (J). To 276 (ATC) Sqn, Chelmsford, 27.7.66 as 7906M.
WH133 207 AFS. 210 AFS. 93 Sqn. 94 Sqn. Scrap 21.2.58.
WH134 205 AFS. 4 FTS. 211 AFS. Scrap 31.3.58.
WH135 215 AFS. To R.Neth AF 14.12.54 as I-316.
WH136 To France 3.3.52.
WH164 215 AFS. 209 AFS/12 FTS. Scrap 22.7.57.
WH165 To R.Neth AF 14.2.52 as I-11.
WH166 208 AFS. 210 AFS. 205 AFS. 4 FTS. Manby. RAFFC. CAW. 5 CAACU. CFS (27). soc 12.9.69. To Digby for display 1.12.69. Allocated 8052M.
WH167 207 AFS. w/o 13.5.52.
WH168 To France 1.7.53.
WH169 207 AFS. 208 AFS. 209 AFS. MEAFCS. RAFFC. w/o 26.9.60, remains to Skylines yard at Sandhurst.
WH170 208 AFS. 209 AFS/12 FTS. 8 FTS. Scrap 22.7.58.
WH171 To Belgian AF 13.4.53 as ED-11.
WH172 206 AFS. 203 AFS/8 FTS. CFS (O-K). Scrap 2.9.57.
WH173 205 AFS (Z-S). 4 FTS. 229 OCU. Scrap 29.2.60.
WH174 To Belgian AF 13.4.53 as ED-12.
WH175 208 AFS. 210 AFS. 211 AFS. RAFFC. 25 Grp Com Flt. RAFFC. soc 24.3.60.
WH176 208 AFS. 211 AFS. Scrap 31.3.58.
WH177 CFS (O-H). To R.Neth AF 21.12.55 as I-325.
WH178 208 AFS. 211 AFS. CFS (O-N). Manby. To Scrap 16.11.62.
WH179 To R.Neth AF 19.11.52 as I-16.
WH180 207 AFS. 2 Sqn. 2 Grp Com Flt. RAFFC. soc 26.7.61, to West Raynham dump, 16.8.61.
WH181 208 AFS. 210 AFS. 118 Sqn. 79 Sqn. Wunstorf Stn Flt. Scrap 30.7.57.
WH182 202 AFS. 207 AFS. 8 FTS. 4 FTS. RAFFC. CFS. Scrap 6.11.62.
WH183 207 AFS. 208 AFS. 207 AFS. 12 FTS. CFS. w/o 8.3.58.
WH184 203 AFS/8 FTS. CFS. 4 FTS. RAFFC. Scrap 2.11.62.
WH185 68 Sqn. Scrap 21.2.58.
WH186 207 AFS. 215 AFS. 203 AFS. 5 FTS. Scrap 30.10.63.
WH187 207 AFS. 210 AFS. 211 AFS. CFS. soc 23.5.57
WH188 207 AFS. 215 AFS. 8 FTS. Driffield. 12 Grp Com Flt (12). Wroughton Stn Flt. RAF Handling Sqn. To Manby dump 24.2.66.
WH189 87 Sqn. w/o 31.8.53.
WH190 207 AFS. 215 AFS. 8 FTS. w/o 27.8.54.
WH191 207 AFS. 12 FTS. 4 FTS. RAFFC. Scrap 6.1.64.
WH192 206 AFS. 211 AFS. CFS. Scrap 16.8.57.
WH193 To R.Neth AF 2.4.52 as I-13.
WH194 207 AFS. 12 FTS (S-19). w/o 15.2.55. Remains dumped at Rufforth.
WH195 206 AFS. 211 AFS. FTU. Scrap 27.3.63.
WH196 To R.Neth AF 2.4.52 as I-14. To MLD 1958.
WH197 206 AFS, 215 AFS. w/o 29.12.53.
WH198 206 AFS. 203 AFS/8 FTS. Linton Stn Flt (V). RAFFC. soc 28.2.63.
WH199 To R.Neth AF 2.4.52 as I-15.
WH200 205 AFS. 207 AFS. CFS. w/o 9.3.55.
WH201 207 AFS. 208 AFS. 210 AFS. 203 AFS/8 FTS. RAFFC. To Lyneham dump 13.10.61.
WH202 To R.Neth AF 19.11.52 as I-17.
WH203 To R.Neth AF 14.2.52 as I-12.
WH204 87 Sqn. Wahn Stn Flt. 83 Grp Com Flt. w/o 21.11.57.
WH205 207 AFS. 211 AFS. Church Fenton Stn Flt. CFE (ITS). BCCS. Scrap 30.10.61.
WH206 219 Sqn. 14 Sqn. 6 Sqn. MECS. Khormaksar Stn Flt. w/o 20.1.59, ditched off Aden.
WH207 To R.Neth AF 20.3.53 as I-301. w/o 17.3.54.
WH208 612 Sqn. 611 Sqn. 612 Sqn. BCCS. 5 FTS. 8 FTS (70). RAFFC. CAW. 229 OCU. w/o 23.6.67 and dumped at Bicester.
WH209 229 OCU (ES-26). Linton Stn Flt (SF later KR). 264 Sqn. 46 Sqn. 60 Sqn. 81 Sqn. soc 12.11.60.
WH215 205 AFS. 4 FTS. RAFFC. 216 Sqn. RAFFC. soc 8.10.63, remains to Staravia, Lasham.

METEOR T.7 *continued*

WH216 207AFS. 87 Sqn. Bruggen Stn Flt. soc 27.4.59.
WH217 CFS. w/o 9.10.52.
WH218 CFS. 12 FTS. RAFFC. Seletar Stn Flt. TTF Seletar. soc 13.1.69.
WH219 203 AFS/8 FTS. CFS. Scrap 2.9.57.
WH220 78 Wing RAAF. w/o 18.1.54 at Takali.
WH221 CFS. 208 AFS. 145 Sqn. 130 Sqn. 68 Sqn. soc 14.1.58.
WH222 To R.Neth AF 20.3.53 as I-322.
WH223 92 Sqn. 264 Sqn. 608 Sqn (P). West Raynham Com Flt. DFCS. 85 Sqn (Z). 5 MU dump 1.6.67.
WH224 Binbrook. JCU Hemswell. Hemswell Stn Flt. 500 Sqn (Z/'Isle of Sheppey'). Duxford Stn Flt. 29 Sqn. 151 Sqn. 25 Sqn. 43 Sqn. 25 Sqn. 23 Sqn (Z). To Strubby dump 11.8.66.
WH225 CFS. 2 TAF. Andover. 607 Sqn (N). w/o 30.10.54.
WH226 207 AFS. 211 AFS/4 FTS. 81 Sqn. 60 Sqn. soc 5.10.67 as 7818M at Seletar.
WH227 205 AFS. w/o 23.6.52.
WH228 205 AFS. 209 AFS (46). 112 Sqn. To France 10.9.55.
WH229 215 AFS. w/o 24.6.52.
WH230 231 OCU. Benson Stn Flt. w/o 9.4.53.
WH231 ETPS (8). w/o 11.3.65.
WH232 Aston Down. w/o 21.2.52.
WH233 To R.Neth AF 23.2.53 as I-19. Preserved at Gilze-Rijen.
WH234 205 AFS. w/o 12.12.52.
WH235 79 Sqn. 207 AFS. 211 AFS. RAFFC. soc 5.6.63.
WH236 145 Sqn. 68 Sqn. w/o 26.9.53.
WH237 To R.Neth AF 20.5.53 as I-308.
WH238 78 Wing RAAF. 32 Sqn. MECS. w/o 10.3.60.
WH239 228 OCU. w/o 18.6.54.
WH240 228 OCU. w/o in ground accident 9.12.52.
WH241 CFS (O-N). APS. Odiham Stn Flt. 54 Sqn. West Raynham Stn Flt. To Gaydon dump 4.8.66.
WH242 228 OCU. 5 FTS. RAFFC. Scrap 30.1.63.
WH243 264 Sqn. w/o 17.7.53.
WH244 209 AFS. w/o 12.2.54.
WH245 CFS (O-M). To R.Neth AF 6.1.55 as I-310 or I-317.
WH246 CFS. 205 AFS. w/o 4.5.53.
WH247 CFS. R.Neth AF 21.10.55 as I-324.
WH248 CFS. 231 OCU. 60 Sqn. Scrap 30.11.61.
WL332 702 Sqn. Ford Stn Flt. Lossiemouth Stn Flt (LM-905). 728 Sqn (571/860). Airwork FRU. To Moston College. Aeroplane Collection Ltd, Croston, Lancs. Loaned to Wales Museum, Swansea.
WL333 702 Sqn.
WL334 702 Sqn.
WL335 702 Sqn (293). Scrapped Brawdy 1965.
WL336 759 Sqn. Lossiemouth Stn Flt. w/o 20.10.55 in Inverness-shire.
WL337 759 Sqn (LM-573). Scrapped Brawdy 1965.
WL338 4 Sqn. 16 Sqn. 83 Grp Com Flt. Bruggen Stn Flt. APS Sylt. JTF. A&AEE. To Linton dump 25.4.68
WL339 208 AFS. 209 AFS/12 FTS. 211 AFS. Scrap 5.7.57.
WL340 229 OCU. ITS. Scrap 12.11.57.
WL341 229 OCU. 233 OCU. 501 Sqn. AFDS. CFE (ITS). AFDS. Scrap 16.11.62.
WL342 OFU. FTU. w/o 10.1.55.
WL343 205 AFS. 4 FTS. w/o 11.9.54.
WL344 205 AFS. 209 AFS/12 FTS. Scrap 30.10.63.
WL345 229 OCU (ES-29). CFE (ITS). CFE Com Flt. ITS. RAFFC. 5 FTS. 8 FTS. Sold to St Leonards Motors for display 1.11.74.
WL346 1 OCU. FTU. Scrap 31.10.62.
WL347 203 AFS. FCCS. Scrap 30.10.63.
WL348 RAFFC. CFE Com Flt. Khormaksar Stn Flt. soc 21.12.61.
WL349 229 OCU. ITS. CFE Com Flt (Y). AFDS. ITS. 2 ANS (Y). 1 ANS (Y). 229 OCU (Z). Painted in 28 Sqn markings 1973. Grounded 1.74. Presented to Gloucester City Council for display at Staverton airport 22.6.76.
WL350 759 Sqn (CW-404). Lossiemouth Stn Flt. 728 Sqn (HF-574). Airwork FRU (044). w/o 13.2.69, at Blandford, Dorset.
WL351 702 Sqn.
WL352 (442). Scrapped Brawdy 1965).
WL353 702 Sqn. Airwork & General Trading Co. 728 Sqn (574/861). Scrapped at Brawdy 1965.
WL354 205 AFS. 211 AFS. w/o 16.3.55.
WL355 79 Sqn. w/o 5.4.55.
WL356 205 AFS. 210 AFS. 211 AFS/4 FTS. RAFFC. To North Coates as instructional airframe 24.8.61.
WL357 206 AFS. 203 AFS. 12 FTS. RAFFC. NEA 5 MU 10.10.63.
WL358 203 AFS/8 FTS. 4 FTS. soc 6.5.58.
WL359 CFS. 4 FTS. w/o 21.4.58.
WL360 215 AFS. 210 AFS. 211 AFS. Wattisham Stn Flt. 1 Sqn. 229 OCU (G). To Locking for display 13.9.66 as 7920M.
WL361 206 AFS. 203 AFS (X-71). 8 FTS. RAFFC. soc 2.5.60.
WL362 206 AFS. 203 AFS. w/o 10.6.53.
WL363 IAM Farnborough. w/o 9.12.54.
WL364 202 AFS. 208 AFS. 210 AFS. CFS. w/o 21.4.55.
WL365 205 AFS. w/o 2.1.53.
WL366 Benson Stn Flt. Wyton Stn Flt. 231 OCU. Scrap 2.9.57.
WL367 2 Sqn. CFS (O-E). RAFFC. 2 ANS (X). 1 ANS (X). 3 CAACU (X). CFS (28). To Kinloss dump 5.9.63.
WL368 CFE (ITS). CFE Com Flt (W). w/o 18.10.57.
WL369 CFS. w/o 16.6.52.
WL370 CFS. RAFFC. 5 FTS. RAFFC. Scrap 30.10.63.
WL371 215 AFS. CFS. 12 FTS (41). RAFFC. Scrap 30.10.61.
WL372 203 AFS. w/o 19.11.52.
WL373 65 Sqn. 206 AFS. 215 AFS. CFS. Scrap 30.7.57.
WL374 CFS. w/o 28.7.54.
WL375 RAE Farnborough. RAE West Freugh. To Dumfries and Galloway Aviation Group.
WL376 207 AFS. 211 AFS. 8 FTS (X-55). Scrap 31.3.58.
WL377 ETPS.
WL378 16 Sqn. 612 Sqn (U). 228 OCU. 25 Sqn. 46 Sqn. 25 Sqn. 64 Sqn. 25 Sqn. 229 OCU. 85 Sqn (W). To Catterick 16.8.72.
WL379 234 Sqn. APS Sylt. Scrap 16.11.62.
WL380 74 Sqn. RAFFC. CAW. RAE Farnborough. NEA 23.2.66.
WL381 CFS. w/o 25.5.53.
WL397 211 AFS. w/o 14.7.53.
WL398 Hemswell Stn Flt. 231 OCU. FTU. 2 TAF Com Sqn. Scrap 14.5.62.
WL399 To Belgian AF 25.7.52 as ED-7.
WL400 14 Sqn. ITF Nicosia. Levant Com Flt. soc 28.5.57.
WL401 205 AFS. 4 FTS. Scrap 21.2.58.
WL402 211 AFS. w/o 4.12.52.
WL403 215 AFS. 8 FTS. CFS. Scrap 2.11.62.
WL404 208 Sqn. w/o 18.12.54.
WL405 Hemswell Stn Flt. JCU. Wittering Stn Flt. 231 OCU. 1 Grp Com Flt. BCCS. RAE Farnborough.
WL406 228 OCU. To Catterick 28.3.60.
WL407 2 Sqn. Wahn Stn Flt. w/o 28.6.56.
WL408 205 AFS. 12 FTS. w/o 2.2.55.
WL409 Wunstorf Meteor Trng Flt. w/o 24.9.52.
WL410 CGS. FWS. soc 12.4.57.
WL411 219 Sqn. 39 Sqn. Scrap 29.1.60.
WL412 203 AFS. RAFFC. To R.Neth AF 14.12.54 as I-312.
WL413 203 AFS/8 FTS (X-68). Bruggen Stn Flt. Laarbruch Stn Flt. RAFFC. RAF Farnborough. NEA 24.2.66.
WL414 205 AFS. 211 AFS/4 FTS. To Valley for ground instruction 29.9.58 as 7576M.
WL415 To Belgian AF 13.4.53 as ED-10.
WL416 205 AFS. 211 AFS. soc 25.11.57.
WL417 211 AFS. Scrap 16.8.57.
WL418 205 AFS. 4 FTS. w/o 26.10.54.
WL419 233 OCU. ITS. 13 Grp Com Flt. 11 Grp Com Flt. 85 Sqn. MOA 8.63, to Martin-Baker as spares aircraft. Made airworthy again in 1979.
WL420 211 AFS. Scrap 16.7.57.
WL421 211 AFS. 8 FTS. 8 FTS (X-57). RAFFC. CAW Scrap 14.12.66.
WL422 211 AFS. 152 Sqn. 34 Sqn. 29 Sqn (X). w/o 7.7.58.
WL423 209 AFS. w/o 12.3.54.
WL424 Manby. APS Sylt. w/o 18.11.59.
WL425 To France 26.6.53.
WL426 To R.Neth AF 29.4.53 as I-306.
WL427 To Belgian AF 25.2.53 as ED-9.
WL428 To Belgian AF 8.4.53 as ED-8.
WL429 211 AFS. RAFFC. Scrap 16.11.62.
WL430 26 Sqn. w/o 16.2.54.
WL431 39 Sqn. w/o 13.5.53.
WL432 209 AFS. w/o 26.1.53.
WL433 209 AFS (45). w/o 7.11.52.
WL434 211 AFS (56). To Israel 29.3.55 as 111.
WL435 211 AFS/4 FTS. soc 19.12.57.
WL436 CFE (ITS). FCCS. Scrap 16.11.62.
WL453 209 AFS/12 FTS. 211 AFS. Scrap 12.7.57.
WL454 20 MU. w/o 17.9.52.
WL455 209 AFS (51). w/o 9.2.53.
WL456 211 AFS/4 FTS. 5 FTS. Scrap 20.12.63.
WL457 211 AFS. CFS. w/o 28.7.54.
WL458 211 AFS. 215 AFS. CFS. w/o 9.11.53.
WL459 226 OCU. Stradishall Stn Flt. 125 Sqn. Stradishall Stn Flt. 152 Sqn. 89 Sqn. Stradishall Stn Flt. 1 Sqn. West Raynham Stn Flt. To Leuchars dump 27.9.72.
WL460 209 AFS/12 FTS (53). 8 FTS. RAFFC. CFS. soc 2.10.59.
WL461 211 AFS. w/o 7.3.55.
WL462 604 Sqn. w/o 3.4.54.
WL463 211 AFS/4 FTS. RAFFC. To Stradishall dump 14.6.65.
WL464 Wunstorf Meteor Trng Flt. 26 Sqn. Oldenburg Stn Flt. Scrap 2.9.57.
WL465 233 OCU. ITS. 5 FTS. w/o 17.1.62.
WL466 211 AFS (68). To Israel 28.10.55 as 112.
WL467 208 AFS. 210 AFS. 209 AFS/12 FTS. w/o 1.12.54.
WL468 233 OCU. 64 Sqn. ITS. AFDS. 81 Grp Com Flt. 56 Sqn. 41 Sqn. RAE Farnborough. NEA 24.2.66 at 5 MU.
WL469 To R.Neth AF 19.11.52 as I-18. To MLD 1958.
WL470 233 OCU. CFE (ITS) (V). 611 Sqn (W). Odiham Stn Flt (V). West Malling Stn Flt. 85 Sqn. w/o 14.3.62
WL471 To France 26.6.53.
WL472 231 OCU. 98 Sqn. 96 Sqn. RAFFC. CAW. Scrap 14.12.66.
WL473 233 OCU. CFE (ITS). Scrap 2.8.57.
WL474 211 AFS (73). w/o 1.4.55.
WL475 504 Sqn. 211 AFS/4 FTS. soc 22.4.58.
WL476 To France 23.6.53.
WL477 To R.Neth AF 15.7.53 as I-309.
WL478 233 OCU. ITS. 4 FTS. RAFFC. w/o 19.2.59.
WL479 209 AFS/12 FTS. 8 FTS. RAFFC. w/o 8.1.57.
WL480 222 Sqn. 602 Sqn (X). 600 Sqn. 41 Sqn. 46 Sqn (W). 12 Grp Com Flt. w/o 15.7.59.
WL481 CFS. RAFFC. w/o 3.6.59.
WL482 To R.Neth AF 23.2.53 as I-20.
WL483 203 AFS/8 FTS. w/o 3.6.53.
WL484 211 AFS. RAFFC. Scrap 21.2.58.
WL485 To France 25.8.53.
WL486 To Belgian AF 1.9.53 as ED-33.
WL487 To R.Neth AF 20.3.53 as I-303.
WL488 ETPS (11). Scrapped at Farnborough late '60s.
WN309 96 Sqn. 112 Sqn. MECS. soc 16.1.60.
WN310 256 Sqn. 11 Sqn. Geilenkirchen Stn Flt. 2 TAF Com Sqn. Geilenkirchen Stn Flt. To Catterick 2.11.72.
WN311 231 OCU. 1 Grp Com Flt. Scrap 16.11.62.
WN312 To France 2.7.53.
WN313 8 Sqn. Aden PCS Sqn. Khormaksar Stn Flt. soc 29.6.58.
WN314 Dev Sqn, Watton. 527 Sqn. Scrap 12.11.62.
WN315 To R.Neth AF 29.4.53 as I-307.
WN316 209 AFS/12 FTS. RAFFC. 4 FTS. w/o 30.6.58.
WN317 211 AFS. Scrap 30.7.57.
WN318 Coningsby Stn Flt. JCU Marham. 231 OCU. 1 Grp Com Flt. BCCS. w/o 11.5.59.
WN319 215 AFS. 209 AFS. 215 AFS. 211 AFS. RAFFC. Scrap 30.10.61.
WN320 To Belgian AF 3.9.53 as ED-34.
WN321 CS (A). To RAAF as A77-4. soc 31.3.59.
WS103 702 Sqn. 703 Sqn (FD-075). LM-709. Airwork FRU. Yeovilton Stn Flt (VL-709). To Wroughton store for FAA museum. soc 6.1.71.
WS104 Lossiemouth Stn Flt (HF-937). Brawdy Stn Flt (BY-902). Scrapped at Brawdy 1969.
WS105 702 Sqn.
WS106 702 Sqn.
WS107 759 Sqn (LM-572). FRU St Davids (BY-005). Lossiemouth Stn Flt. 736 Sqn (LM-405). Scrapped at Brawdy 1965.
WS108 759 Sqn. Scrapped Brawdy 1965.
WS109 759 Sqn. Lossiemouth Stn Flt (938). Scrapped Brawdy 1965.
WS110 702 Sqn.
WS111 Airwork/Sperry trials. 728 Sqn (HF-574). Scrapped at Brawdy 1965.
WS112 759 Sqn (406/LM-736).
WS113 759 Sqn.
WS114 759 Sqn.
WS115 759 Sqn. 728 Sqn (HF-575). Scrapped at Brawdy 1965.
WS116 759 Sqn. 728 Sqn (LM-935/HF-935). Lossiemouth Stn Flt (LM-935). Scrapped at Brawdy in 1965.
WS117 759 Sqn. Brawdy Stn Flt (BY). Scrapped at Brawdy in 1965.
WS140 To Belgian AF 18.9.53 as ED-35.
WS141 To Belgian AF 25.1.54 as ED-36.
WS142 To Brazilian AF as 4300.
WS143 To Brazilian AF as 4301.
WS144 To Brazilian AF as 4302.
WS145 To Brazilian AF as 4303.
WS146 To Brazilian AF as 4304.
WS147 To Brazilian AF as 4305.
WS148 To Brazilian AF as 4306.
WS149 To Brazilian AF as 4307.
WS150 To Brazilian AF as 4308.
WS151 To Brazilian AF as 4309.
XF273 To Belgian AF 25.1.54 as ED-37.
XF274 A&AEE (5). RAE Farnborough. w/o 14.2.75, asymmetric roller at Farnborough.
XF275 To R.Neth AF 6.1.55 as I-310 or I-317.
XF276 To R.Neth AF 3.11.54 as I-311 or I-312.
XF277 To R.Neth AF 3.11.54 as I-311 or I-312.
XF278 To R.Neth AF 9.12.54 as I-314.
XF279 To R.Neth AF 9.12.54 as I-313.

METEOR F.8

G-AMCJ PV/Ground Attack Fighter. Later G-7-1. Converted to T.7 type G-ANSO.
VT150 See under F.4
VZ438 RAE Farnborough. RAE West Freugh. To dump by 1968.
VZ439 CS (A). High altitude and pressurisation trials. Used for U.16 spares.
VZ440 43 Sqn. 66 Sqn (P). Scrap 18.8.59.
VZ441 43 Sqn. 615 Sqn (G). Scrap 13.5.58.
VZ442 Boscombe Down. Remains in Sandhurst scrapyard until at least 1968.
VZ443 CFE (DFLS). 72 Sqn (L). APS. Scrap 24.4.58.
VZ444 257 Sqn. 600 Sqn. RAFFC. soc 11.3.59, to Stradishall dump.
VZ445 54 Sqn. RAFFC. F/R 12.3.59 for conv to U.16. Llanbedr.
VZ446 74 Sqn. w/o 5.5.53.
VZ447 CFE. w/o 28.3.51, undershot at West Raynham
VZ448 222 Sqn. 72 Sqn. 89 Sqn. MOA for U.16 spares 11.10.61.
VZ449 74 Sqn. w/o 5.1.51, lost off the Norfolk coast.
VZ450 To Belgian AF 15.11.50 as EG-201.
VZ451 43 Sqn. ETPS. Scrapped at Warton after accident 31.1.56.
VZ452 74 Sqn. 43 Sqn. 56 Sqn. RAFFC. 5 FTS. RAFFC. soc 24.3.60.
VZ453 92 Sqn. w/o 7.1.52.
VZ454 1 Sqn. To ground instructional use 30.7.53 as 7096M.
VZ455 43 Sqn. 66 Sqn. APS. F/R 20.9.60 for conv to U.21. WRE 1.62.
VZ456 43 Sqn. 609 Sqn (J). Scrap 13.3.58.
VZ457 To Belgian AF 22.11.50 as EG-205.
VZ458 1 Sqn. MOA for U.16 spares 13.10.61.
VZ459 To Belgian AF 24.11.50 as EG-206.
VZ460 RAE Farnborough. Scrap 19.12.57.
VZ461 43 Sqn. w/o 22.10.52, missing.
VZ462 66 Sqn. 92 Sqn (8L-Y/B). 257 Sqn. 54 Sqn. Linton Stn Flt. 615 Sqn. MOA for U.16 spares 18.10.61 Sold to O Haydon-Baillie. To SWWAPS, Lasham, 1980.
VZ463 43 Sqn (SW-H). 66 Sqn (B). 92 Sqn. 66 Sqn. 56 Sqn. soc 17.2.55.
VZ464 Handling Sqn Manby. CSDE Wittering. 63 Sqn (D/H). To 1 STT 4.6.55 as 7214M.
VZ465 245 Sqn (MR-C/C). APS Sylt. Scrap 24.4.59.
VZ466 222 Sqn. 211 AFS. Scrap 4.3.58.
VZ467 A&AEE. 54 Sqn. 500 Sqn. 229 OCU (C/A). 1 TWU (A/01). CFS 22.10.82.

METEOR F.8 *continued*

VZ468 222 Sqn. Leuchars Stn Flt. FCCS. Scrap 9.9.57

VZ469 43 Sqn. w/o 19.1.51, hit sea off Leuchars.

VZ470 1 Sqn. 63 Sqn. 226 OCU. w/o 24.6.54.

VZ471 257 Sqn (A6-M). 615 Sqn. Scrap 21.2.58.

VZ472 500 Sqn (O). 71 MU 14.5.54. To Sutton-on-Hull 3.5.54 as 7149M.

VZ473 A&AEE.

VZ474 222 Sqn. 616 Sqn. Scrap 11.3.59.

VZ475 211 AFS. Scrap 4.3.58.

VZ476 245 Sqn (MR-P/P). Mod for flight-refuelling. APS. soc 20.3.59.

VZ477 245 Sqn. Mod for flight-refuelling. APS. Scrap 22.6.62.

VZ478 CFE (DFLS). 611 Sqn. To 10 STT Kirkham 5.55 as 7209M.

VZ479 92 Sqn. DFLS. w/o 24.3.55.

VZ480 56 Sqn (F). To 10 STT 6.55 as 7213M.

VZ481 257 Sqn. w/o 28.5.53.

VZ482 92 Sqn. 611 Sqn. 610 Sqn (C). Scrap 8.8.59.

VZ483 56 Sqn (T). Scrap 19.5.58.

VZ484 Met Sector, West Malling. 611 Sqn (H). Scrap 28.5.59.

VZ485 92 Sqn. 222 Sqn. F/R 10.3.59 for conv to U.16. Llanbedr.

VZ493 Handling Sqn. CFE (DFLS). 609 Sqn. 5 CAACU. NEA at GAC 24.4.61.

VZ494 222 Sqn (ZD-C). APS (L). 501 Sqn. Scrap 10.4.59.

VZ495 222 Sqn. 609 Sqn. Scrap 11.10.55.

VZ496 1 Sqn. 33 Sqn. 219 Sqn. Scrap 4.3.58.

VZ497 56 Sqn (N/H). w/o 1.11.51, hit by WA940 after landing at Waterbeach.

VZ498 245 Sqn (MR-S/S). w/o 16.2.51 out of fuel at Whittingham, Northumberland.

VZ499 To Belgian AF 22.11.50 as EG-203(?)

VZ500 CFE (AFDS). 600 Sqn (R). Scrap 12.5.58.

VZ501 CS (A). 72 Sqn (E). w/o 17.4.53, missing.

VZ502 92 Sqn. APS. soc 13.8.59.

VZ503 333 Sqn. 1 Sqn. F/R 13.9.60 for conv to U.21. WRE 27.10.61.

VZ504 CS (A). To PEE Shoeburyness 17.1.58.

VZ505 66 Sqn (T). 600 Sqn (W). 226 OCU. 600 Sqn. Scrap 10.4.59.

VZ506 CS (A). APS. F/R 13.4.59 for conv to U.16. Llanbedr.

VZ507 245 Sqn (MR-V). APS. w/o 22.2.56.

VZ508 CFE (AFDS). 43 Sqn. 151 Sqn. Thum Flt. 5 CAACU. F/R 22.2.72 for conv to U.16. Llanbedr.

VZ509 74 Sqn. w/o 19.6.51, spun into water at Barton Broad, Norfolk.

VZ510 263 Sqn (E). w/o 10.9.51, broke-up during a test flight, Westcliffe.

VZ511 92 Sqn. 54 Sqn. 226 OCU. Scrap 21.6.62.

VZ512 74 Sqn (4D-D). Scrap 13.5.58.

VZ513 43 Sqn (SW-Y). 500 Sqn. 25 Sqn (C). MOA for U.16 spares 17.10.61.

VZ514 43 Sqn. 34 Sqn. C (A). 20 MU store. F/R for conv to U.16. Llanbedr. w/o by control failure, Llanbedr.

VZ515 222 Sqn. 74 Sqn. To 10 STT 9.66 as 7283M.

VZ516 222 Sqn. 610 Sqn. Scrap 12.3.58.

VZ517 Rolls-Royce Hucknall. Armstrong Siddeley Bitteswell. To 1 STT 12.4.56 as 7322M.

VZ518 66 Sqn. w/o 12.4.51, cr into hillside at Slidden Moss, Buxton, after mid-air collision with WA791.

VZ519 211 AFS. Scrap 12.3.58.

VZ520 66 Sqn. 19 Sqn (Z). MOA for U.16 spares 2.10.61.

VZ521 74 Sqn. 153 Sqn (X). 85 Sqn (S). 19 Sqn. 5 CAACU. To Catterick 20.10.60.

VZ522 APS (WH-V). 226 OCU. w/o 4.10.54.

VZ523 222 Sqn. 4 FTS. Scrap 13.7.59.

VZ524 74 Sqn (P). Scrap 29.6.59.

VZ525 OFU Chivenor. 72 Sqn (N). 125 Sqn. To Thorney Island 4.2.57 for use in making a film, after which disposed of as Cat.5 (spares).

VZ526 211 AFS. Scrap 12.3.58.

VZ527 66 Sqn. w/o 17.4.51, broke-up during a low run at Linton.

VZ528 245 Sqn (MR-R). Mod for flight-refuelling. APS Sylt. soc 1.4.59.

VZ529 74 Sqn. Scrap 5.8.59.

VZ530 CFE (AFDS). APS. MOA for U.16 spares 18.10.61. Some parts to WE925 at Rhoose museum.

VZ531 92 Sqn. 609 Sqn. Scrap 15.5.58.

VZ532 263 Sqn. 65 Sqn (E). 56 Sqn. Scrap 29.6.59.

VZ540 74 Sqn (4D-I). 56 Sqn. 5 CAACU. B&TT Flt (FEAF). TT Flt, Changi. soc 31.8.66.

VZ541 257 Sqn. Scrap 13.5.58.

VZ542 Tangmere. Tangmere Stn Flt. w/o 9.9.52.

VZ543 245 Sqn (MR-W). APS Sylt. Scrap 14.5.59.

VZ544 74 Sqn (C). To 10 STT 2.56 as 7317M, but painted as 7137M.

VZ545 263 Sqn (A). 500 Sqn (B/'Dartford'). Scrap 11.3.59.

VZ546 263 Sqn. CFE. 263 Sqn. 92 Sqn (C). 63 Sqn (R). 616 Sqn. Scrap 18.8.59.

VZ547 74 Sqn. w/o 21.8.52.

VZ548 1 Sqn. Scrap 16.5.58.

VZ549 1 Sqn (F). w/o 16.8.55.

VZ550 1 Sqn. 263 Sqn. 43 Sqn. 264 Sqn. CGS. RAFFC. Scrap 22.5.58.

VZ551 1 Sqn. 611 Sqn (B). F/R 5.3.59 for conv to U.16. Llanbedr.

VZ552 1 Sqn (JX-L/W). 4 STT 5.9.55 as 7260M (1).

VZ553 To Belgian AF 11.12.50 as EG-211.

VZ554 222 Sqn. 4 FTS. MOA for U.16 spares 24.10.61.

VZ555 222 Sqn. Leuchars Stn Flt. Scottish Sector Leuchars. Leuchars Stn Flt. 66 Sqn. APS. FWS (A). 500 Sqn (A). Scrap 12.5.58.

VZ556 257 Sqn. w/o 8.7.53.

VZ557 74 Sqn (4D-N). Scrap 19.12.57.

VZ558 74 Sqn. w/o 7.12.50.

VZ559 74 Sqn. Horsham St Faith Stn Flt (PB). 245 Sqn (E). 125 Sqn. Scrap 25.4.58.

VZ560 257 Sqn (A6-P). w/o 8.7.53.

VZ561 257 Sqn. 263 Sqn (W/Z). To 4 STT 20.10.55 as 7266M.

VZ562 To Belgian AF 22.11.50 as EG-204(?)

VZ563 63 Sqn (H). w/o 22.10.52.

VZ564 92 Sqn. Scrap 2.6.59.

VZ565 63 Sqn (G). 245 Sqn (Y). 63 Sqn. Scrap 6.7.59.

VZ566 To Belgian AF 17.1.51 as EG-217 (?)

VZ567 263 Sqn. 64 Sqn. 66 Sqn. 245 Sqn. 500 Sqn. 85 Sqn. Met Sector. 85 Sqn. 229 OCU (F). Scrap 15.11.71.

VZ568 63 Sqn (C). To 4 STT 12.10.55 as 7261M.

VZ569 263 Sqn. 65 Sqn. w/o 3.7.51, mid-air collison with WA985, near Strubby.

WA755 To Belgian AF 24.11.50 as EG-220.

WA756 43 Sqn. 211 AFS. F/R 20.3.60 for conv to U.16. Llanbedr.

WA757 263 Sqn (G/M). 152 Sqn. Scrap 1.4.58.

WA758 19 Sqn. w/o 18.8.53.

WA759 92 Sqn. w/o 7.1.52.

WA760 56 Sqn (U). APS. Com Sqn, Colerne. Scrap 12.5.58.

WA761 92 Sqn. 45/33 Sqns. APC. SHQ Butterworth. soc 10.1.58.

WA762 56 Sqn. 63 Sqn. CGS. w/o 14.3.53.

WA763 92 Sqn (8L-G/G). 601 Sqn. 604 Sqn. 4 FTS (18). APS Sylt. Scrap 12.3.63.

WA764 Southern Sector Tangmere. Wattisham Stn Flt. 257 Sqn. To 12 MU for fire practice 13.5.59. Scrap 14.9.59.

WA765 63 Sqn (B). To 4 STT 28.11.55 as 7264M.

WA766 56 Sqn (N). 41 Sqn. 614 Sqn. Scrap 10.4.59.

WA767 56 Sqn (G). 19 Sqn. 92 Sqn. Scrap 4.3.58.

WA768 63 Sqn (U). 54 Sqn. 56 Sqn. To Waddington dump 4.6.59.

WA769 63 Sqn. 56 Sqn (J/C). w/o 16.12.53.

WA770 63 Sqn (T). 211 AFS. Scrap 10.4.59.

WA771 56 Sqn. w/o 24.6.51, stalled on approach to Waterbeach.

WA772 CFE. CFE Com Flt. 74 Sqn (A). Scrap 5.8.59.

WA773 Eastern Sector (JW/KBBC). 245 Sqn (B/SGW). w/o 8.1.54.

WA774 222 Sqn. w/o 5.10.51, overshot at Leuchars.

WA775 A&AEE. RRE Defford. Hunter radar trials. Prototype U.16. F/F as such 22.10.56. Llanbedr. w/o due to control failure.

WA776 63 Sqn (S/E). 610 Sqn (S). Scrap 10.4.59.

WA777 66 Sqn. 12 Grp Com Flt. w/o 20.6.52.

WA778 66 Sqn. w/o 4.9.53.

WA779 263 Sqn. 66 Sqn. w/o 26.11.53.

WA780 66 Sqn (G). Flying accident 28.4.52. Re-cat w/o 15.5.53.

WA781 66 Sqn. 226 OCU. 222 Sqn. 616 Sqn (W). MOA for U.16 spares 23.9.61.

WA782 To RAAF 8.1.51 as A77-730. w/o 7.10.51 due to heavy landing.

WA783 To RAAF 8.1.51 as A77-446. 77 Sqn ('Bobby Toot'). Surplus 28.3.58. Scrap 30.4.59.

WA784 CFE (DFLS). 504 Sqn (T). Scrap 26.5.59.

WA785 66 Sqn. 56 Sqn. 247 Sqn. 56 Sqn. 257 Sqn. 56 Sqn. 63 Sqn. To GAC 14.12.55. To Syrian AF on 26.3.56 as 413.

WA786 To RAAF 8.1.51 as A77-744. 77 Sqn. Surplus 28.3.58. Scrap 30.4.59.

WA787 263 Sqn. w/o 10.10.51, crashed at Westerfield after take-off from Wattisham.

WA788 CFE (AFDS). RAE Farnborough. Flying accident 5.1.55 at Valley. To RAF Med Trng Est, Warton 14.4.55.

WA789 CFE. 63 Sqn (H). 226 OCU. w/o 31.7.52.

WA790 CFE (DFLS). Scrap 19.12.57.

WA791 66 Sqn, w/o 12.4.51, cr into hillside at Slidden Moss, Buxton, after mid-air collision with VZ518.

WA792 66 Sqn. CGS. RAFFC. Scrap 6.5.58.

WA793 92 Sqn. 263 Sqn (U). 63 Sqn (U). Scrap 13.5.58.

WA794 43 Sqn (X). 72 Sqn. 5 CAACU. w/o 11.10.57

WA808 CFE (AFDS). 54 Sqn. 226 OCU. APS Sylt. soc 1.4.59.

WA809 CFE (DFLS). w/o 25.3.53.

WA810 CFE (DFLS). 233 OCU. Scrap 1.4.58.

WA811 CFE (DFLS). 609 Sqn. Scrap 12.8.59.

WA812 CFE. 63 Sqn. Waterbeach Stn Flt. 56 Sqn (Y). 63 Sqn. Scrap 12.5.58.

WA813 92 Sqn. 43 Sqn. RAFFC. Scrap 21.11.63. Remains to Lasham.

WA814 222 Sqn (ZD-N). 74 Sqn. 611 Sqn. Scrap 26.5.59.

WA815 92 Sqn. 500 Sqn. 92 Sqn. 72 Sqn (K/W). 601 Sqn. Scrap 12.8.59.

WA816 66 Sqn. 19 Sqn. 226 OCU. Scrap 4.3.58.

WA817 257 Sqn. 63 Sqn (L). Scrap 22.5.58.

WA818 63 Sqn (V). Scrap 21.2.58.

WA819 257 Sqn (A6-A). 63 Sqn (M). w/o 10.5.55.

WA820 CS (A) Hucclecote. AWA. GAC ASM (Sapphire Meteor). CFE. To 1 STT 31.3.54 as 7141M.

WA821 222 Sqn. w/o 26.7.52.

WA822 66 Sqn (C). w/o 9.9.52.

WA823 245 Sqn (MR-M). Mod for flight-refuelling (M). APS. Scrap 12.8.59.

WA824 74 Sqn. To Valley for ground instruction 6.9.57 as 7462M. To Fire section 24.2.60.

WA825 66 Sqn. 54 Sqn. Handling Sqn. Scrap 19.12.57.

WA826 245 Sqn (MR-F/F). Mod for flight-refuelling. APS Sylt. Scrap 14.9.59.

WA827 245 Sqn (MR-N). Mod for flight-refuelling. w/o 19.5.51, engine cut during roll, near Horsham St Faith

WA828 257 Sqn. Scrap 29.6.59.

WA829 245 Sqn (MR-A/A). Mod for flight refuelling. APS Sylt. soc 15.4.59.

WA830 245 Sqn (MR-X/X). Mod for flight-refuelling. APS Sylt. soc 21.20.59.

WA831 222 Sqn. 72 Sqn (S). 605 Sqn. 611 Sqn. Scrap 10.4.59.

WA832 245 Sqn. Mod for flight-refuelling. RAFFC. Scrap 12.5.58.

WA833 245 Sqn (MR-G). Horsham St Faith. 41 Sqn. 615 Sqn (H). Scrap 17.1.58.

WA834 245 Sqn (MR-H). Mod for flight-refuelling. APS Sylt. Scrap 24.4.59.

WA835 74 Sqn. 226 OCU. w/o 30.11.53.

WA836 245 Sqn (MR-E/E). Mod for flight-refuelling. 74 Sqn. w/o 19.9.53.

WA837 245 Sqn (J). Mod for flight refuelling. APS Sylt. soc 6.10.59.

WA838 74 Sqn. Cat.5 (C) 58 MU 29.8.56.

WA839 43 Sqn. w/o 22.2.53.

WA840 74 Sqn. APS Acklington. RAFFC. Scrap 12.3.58.

WA841 43 Sqn. To 4 STT 4.9.55 as 7262M.

WA842 1 Sqn. NEA 28.5.56. F/R for conv to U.16. Llanbedr.

WA843 92 Sqn. w/o 23.8.51 lost tail recovering from a dive, Beeford, Yorks.

WA844 43 Sqn (SW-N). Western Sector. 604 Sqn. Scrap 11.3.59.

WA845 43 Sqn. 1 Sqn. w/o 28.5.54.

WA846 Rolls-Royce. 63 Sqn (S/E). 253 Sqn (used by Waterbeach Stn Flt as 'T1'). Scrap 14.9.59.

WA847 43 Sqn. FEAF. soc 10.1.58.

WA848 263 Sqn (N); APS. w/o 6.12.55.

WA849 43 Sqn. 222 Sqn. Scrap 5.8.59.

WA850 66 Sqn. 111 Sqn (D). MOA for U.16 spares 6.10.61.

WA851 1 Sqn (JX-C). 500 Sqn (B). Scrap 2.6.59.

WA852 257 Sqn. w/o 15.7.54.

WA853 1 Sqn. APS. Scrap 10.4.59.

WA854 1 Sqn. w/o 17.11.53.

WA855 1 Sqn. 41 Sqn. w/o 13.10.56.

WA856 1 Sqn. w/o 19.8.53.

WA857 GAC. A&AEE rocket trials. 211 AFS. Scrap 12.3.58.

WA867 222 Sqn. w/o 7.10.51.

WA868 1 Sqn. w/o 16.8.53.

WA869 222 Sqn. 610 Sqn. 600 Sqn (X). Scrap 12.3.58.

WA870 To Belgian AF 30.11.50 as EG-208.

WA871 43 Sqn. 222 Sqn. Scrap 26.9.59.

WA872 1 Sqn (R). soc 7.11.57.

WA873 1 Sqn. 74 Sqn. 609 Sqn (H). w/o 19.11.56.

WA874 74 Sqn (4D-K/K). Scrap 6.4.59.

WA875 257 Sqn. Scrap 10.4.59.

WA876 To Belgian AF 30.11.50 as EG-210.

WA877 66 Sqn. w/o 20.6.51 broke-up near Scalby, Yorkshire.

WA878 To Belgian AF 30.11.50 as EG-209.

WA879 74 Sqn (4D-C). w/o 3.1.57.

WA880 257 Sqn (A6-S). 500 Sqn. 43 Sqn. 222 Sqn. Flying College. TT Flt Changi. 1574 Flt. soc 4.11.69, sold to Singapore for ground instruction as SAFTECH-2 To Sentosa museum.

WA881 To Belgian AF 14.11.50 as EG-202(?).

WA882 222 Sqn. w/o 12.2.52.

WA883 To Belgian AF 24.11.50.

WA884 To Belgian AF 11.12.50 as EG-203.

WA885 263 Sqn (H). 245 Sqn. 58MU 3.56. Cockpit only to Thornaby for ground instruction. Allocated 7342M.

WA886 257 Sqn. 226 OCU. Scrap 3.2.58.

WA887 To Belgian AF 12.1.51 as EG-214.

WA888 To Belgian AF 11.12.50 as EG-215.

WA889 To Belgian AF 12.1.51 as EG-216.

WA890 257 Sqn. 263 Sqn (L). Scrap 14.9.59.

WA891 257 Sqn. 63 Sqn. w/o 7.7.55.

WA892 To Belgian AF 12.1.51 as EG-212(?).

WA893 263 Sqn (C). Scrap 3.2.58.

WA894 263 Sqn. w/o 19.8.52.

WA895 To Belgian AF 19.8.52.

WA896 263 Sqn. 64 Sqn (A). 56 Sqn. Scrap 5.8.59.

WA897 63 Sqn (P). To 4 STT 27.10.55 as 7263M, but painted as 7269M.

WA898 To Belgian AF 19.1.51 as EG-219.

WA899 43 Sqn. SHQ Seletar. FECS. SHQ Seletar. FECS. soc 28.11.59.

WA900 To Belgian AF 23.1.51 as EG-221.

WA901 To Belgian AF 9.2.51 as EG-222.

WA902 To Belgian AF 26.1.51 as EG-223.

WA903 63 Sqn (A/H). Cat.5(C) 21.1.57.

WA904 A&AEE Firestreak trials. 33 MU. soc 7.11.57.

WA905 63 Sqn. 56 Sqn (W). 247 Sqn. 56 Sqn. 263 Sqn. 56 Sqn. Scrap 13.1.58.

WA906 66 Sqn. 92 Sqn. 72 Sqn. 608 Sqn. Cat.5(C) 1.11.56.

WA907 56 Sqn. 63 Sqn. 43 Sqn. APS Acklington. Cat.5(C) at 63MU 2.3.56.

WA908 92 Sqn. Hooton Park Stn Flt. 610 Sqn (E). Scrap 2.6.59.

WA909 Yorks Sector. Northern Sector (JG). 226 OCU 141 Sqn. 41 Sqn. 66 Sqn. Scrap 18.8.60.

WA920 263 Sqn (F/B) w/o 28.11.54.

WA921 Yorks Sector. Linton Stn Flt (BD/LM). 92 Sqn. 19 Sqn. 604 Sqn. Scrap 10.4.59.

WA922 56 Sqn (D). w/o 25.11.54.

WA923 56 Sqn (O). 63 Sqn (X). Scrap 14.2.58.

WA924 56 Sqn. 63 Sqn. Scrap 29.6.59.

WA925 CFE. 56 Sqn. 222 Sqn (P). APS Sylt. Scrap 1.4.63.

WA926 263 Sqn (T). Air Attache Paris. APS Sylt (V). Scrap 6.12.62.

WA927 56 Sqn (X). w/o 19.9.53.

WA928 56 Sqn (H). 615 Sqn (S). Scrap 29.6.59.

WA929 56 Sqn. 41 Sqn. 605 Sqn. 611 Sqn. Scrap 14.4.59.

WA930 56 Sqn (C). w/o 16.12.53.

WA931 56 Sqn. 63 Sqn. CFE (AFDS). AWDS. 74 Sqn. 245 Sqn (B). Ouston Stn Flt. Scrap 14.4.59.

WA932 56 Sqn. 63 Sqn. AWDS. APS Acklington. Scrap 4.3.58.

METEOR F.8 *continued*

WA933 Leuchars Stn Flt. Caledonian Sector. 222 Sqn. w/o 22.8.53.
WA934 To RAAF 13.2.51 as A77-354. 77 Sqn. w/o 22.8.51, mid-air collision with A77-128.
WA935 To RAAF 19.2.51 as A77-300. Missing 1.3.51 en route, Persian Gulf.
WA936 To RAAF 8.1.51 as A77-373. 77 Sqn. MIA 15.5.52 in Korea.
WA937 To RAAF 3.1.51 as A77-811. 77 Sqn. w/o 3.11.51 by battle damage.
WA938 To RAAF 8.1.51 as A77-29. 77 Sqn. w/o 1.12.51, out of fuel in Korea.
WA939 To RAAF 19.2.51 as A77-587. 77 Sqn. w/o 11.11.51 in collision with A77-959.
WA940 63 Sqn (R). w/o 1.11.51 hit VZ497 landing at Waterbeach.
WA941 To RAAF 3.1.51 as A77-163. 77 Sqn. MIA 26.3.53 in Korea.
WA942 To RAAF 3.1.51 as A77-735. Ditched 7.5.51 off Japan.
WA943 64 Sqn. 263 Sqn. APS Sylt (U). Scrap 6.12.62.
WA944 To RAAF 19.2.51 as A77-231. 77 Sqn. w/o 14.6.51 Japan, during acceptance check.
WA945 To RAAF 1.3.51 as A77-316. 77 Sqn. MIA 28.8.52 in Korea.
WA946 To RAAF 8.1.51 as A77-911. 77 Sqn. MIA 10.6.52 in Korea.
WA947 To RAAF 3.1.51 as A77-741. w/o 25.1.52 in Korea, crashed in rice field and reduced to spares.
WA948 To RAAF 3.1.51 as A77-740. 77 Sqn. w/o 12.8.51 at Kimpo.
WA993 63 Sqn (O). Cat.5(C) 21.2.57. 7391M ntu.
WA994 41 Sqn. APS Sylt. soc 1.5.59.
WA995 64 Sqn (Y/T). 56 Sqn. 64 Sqn. Scrap 6.7.59.
WA996 64 Sqn. APS Sylt. soc 15.8.55.
WA997 245 Sqn (N). 74 Sqn. Cat.5(C) at 5MU 9.2.56
WA998 To RAAF 19.12.51 as A77-802. 77 Sqn. 23 Sqn. Surplus 17.10.60. Conv to U.21A. Destroyed 16.9.69.
WA999 Waterbeach Stn Flt. 56 Sqn (K). 63 Sqn. Cat.5(C) at 32MU 9.6.55.
WB105 19 Sqn. 604 Sqn. w/o 30.6.56.
WB106 63 Sqn (N). w/o 15.9.51, mid-air collision with WE869.
WB107 19 Sqn. Cat.5(C) at 60MU 23.7.54.
WB108 19 Sqn. 211 AFS. Scrap 21.12.54.
WB109 19 Sqn. 34 Sqn. 229OCU (K). Scrap 14.4.59.
WB110 41 Sqn. w/o 18.6.51, sank back after take-off from Biggin Hill and hit house.
WB111 41 Sqn. Cat.5(C) at 32MU 9.6.55.
WB112 66 Sqn (D). 141 Sqn. CFE Com Flt. 263 Sqn (I). 4 FTS. APS Sylt. Scrap 27.3.63.
WE852 63 Sqn (L). FWS (A). Cat.5(C) at 60MU 14.2.57, dumped at Rufforth.
WE853 41 Sqn. 615 Sqn (A). w/o 26.8.56.
WE854 19 Sqn. w/o 10.1.52.
WE855 19 Sqn. APS. RAE Bedford, barrier trials. 10STT 26.10.56 as 7378M.
WE856 19 Sqn. 609 Sqn. 19 Sqn. w/o 2.10.53.
WE857 19 Sqn. 601 Sqn. Scrap 19.12.57.
WE858 64 Sqn (T). 41 Sqn. 65 Sqn (P). Scrap 5.8.59.
WE859 41 Sqn. 600 Sqn (P). To 1STT 11.5.56 as 7354M.
WE860 64 Sqn (U). w/o 18.2.52.
WE861 226OCU. w/o 26.6.52.
WE862 29MU Flying accident. 616 Sqn. w/o 3.7.53.
WE863 19 Sqn. 34 Sqn (E). Scrap 14.9.59.
WE864 19 Sqn. w/o 20.1.52.
WE865 64 Sqn. 65 Sqn (B). Ouston Stn Flt. Scrap 27.3.58.
WE866 247 Sqn (V). Scrap 12.8.59.
WE867 41 Sqn (S). CFE (AFDS). 604 Sqn (C). F/R for conv to U.16 17.11.61.
WE868 19 Sqn. w/o 20.1.52.
WE869 63 Sqn (X/Q). w/o 15.9.51, mid-air collision with WB106.
WE870 19 Sqn (G). 609 Sqn. 19 Sqn. 609 Sqn. Scrap 12.3.58.
WE871 609 Sqn (E). Scrap 19.5.58.
WE872 226OCU. F/R for conv to U.16 28.10.59.
WE873 247 Sqn. 504 Sqn (R). w/o 1.1.56.
WE874 To RAAF 17.12.51 as A77-953. 77 Sqn. w/o 6.8.52 during take-off in Korea.
WE875 56 Sqn (L). 63 Sqn. Scrap 12.3.58.
WE876 247 Sqn (P). 54 Sqn. 13 Grp Com Flt. Church Fenton Stn Flt. 23 Sqn. APS Sylt. TT Flt Changi. 1574 Flt. Tr to COMFER(RN) 26.7.71;
WE877 To RAAF 12.12.51 as A77-393. 77 Sqn. MIA 10.7.52 in Korea.
WE878 74 Sqn (E). 56 Sqn. 63 Sqn. 56 Sqn. Scrap 27.7.59
WE879 CGS (FJX-B). w/o 18.8.53.
WE880 To RAAF 12.12.51 as A77-120. 77 Sqn. MIA 1.4.52 in Korea.
WE881 609 Sqn. MOA for U.16 spares 2.10.61.
WE882 CGS. w/o 13.11.53.
WE883 56 Sqn. 247 Sqn. 56 Sqn. 257 Sqn. 56 Sqn. 63 Sqn. 610 Sqn (K/R). Scrap 11.3.59.
WE884 63 Sqn (Y). w/o 26.2.55.
WE885 74 Sqn (T). Scrap 6.4.59.
WE886 To RAAF 19.12.51 as A77-643. 77 Sqn. w/o 7.4.53 in Korea. Originally A77-645.
WE887 CGS/FWS. 233OCU. w/o 14.1.57.
WE888 56 Sqn. w/o 4.3.52.
WE889 To RAAF 19.12.51 as A77-157. 38 Sqn Com Flt. Conv to U.21A. Destroyed 16.9.69.
WE890 To RAAF 28.12.51 as A77-570. 77 Sqn. w/o 18.3.54 on take-off.
WE891 610 Sqn. Scrap 2.6.59.
WE895 609 Sqn. w/o 22.4.56.
WE896 To RAAF 12.12.51 as A77-397. 77 Sqn. 78 Wing. Instructional airframe 6.12.55. soc 22.9.58.
WE897 247 Sqn. 43 Sqn. w/o 24.7.54.
WE898 To RAAF 17.12.51 as A77-134. 77 Sqn. w/o 11.6.53 in Korea.
WE899 611 Sqn (J). Scrap 26.5.59.
WE900 To RAAF 17.12.51 as A77-415. 77 Sqn. MIA 22.6.53 in Korea.
WE901 245 Sqn (Z). To Stradishall for ground instruction 17.5.57 as 7430M.
WE902 63 Sqn. RAFFC. F/R for conv to U.21 15.9.60. WRE 7.7.61.
WE903 To RAAF 1.3.51 as A77-31. 77 Sqn. 78 Wing. 22 Sqn. Surplus 21.3.58. Scrap 30.4.59.
WE904 64 Sqn (B). 211 AFS. w/o 12.5.55.
WE905 To RAAF 8.3.51 as A77-207.
WE906 To RAAF 9.2.51 as A77-251. 77 Sqn. MIA 1.12.51 in Korea.
WE907 To RAAF 19.2.51 as A77-734. Scrap 30.4.59.
WE908 To RAAF 13.2.51 as A77-128. 77 Sqn. w/o 22.8.51 mid-air collision with A77-354 over Korea.
WE909 To RAAF 13.2.51 as A77-. . ..
WE910 To RAAF 20.2.51 as A77-559. MIA 27.1.52 in Korea.
WE911 To RAAF 19.2.51 as A77-15. 77 Sqn. MIA 29.1.53 in Korea.
WE912 41 Sqn. 616 Sqn. w/o 27.9.53.
WE913 64 Sqn (F). 141 Sqn. 23 Sqn. Coltishall Stn Flt. 23 Sqn (23). Scrap 14.9.59.
WE914 245 Sqn. w/o 17.11.52.
WE915 263 Sqn (J). Airwork Hurn. C(A). F/R for conv to U.16. Llanbedr.
WE916 65 Sqn. 211 AFS. w/o 26.5.55.
WE917 CGS. 211 AFS. w/o 2.9.53.
WE918 To RAAF 19.2.51 as A77-385. 77 Sqn. w/o 13.5.52 at Kimpo.
WE919 DH Props Hatfield, RATOG trials. RAE Farnborough. MOA for U.16 spares 4.10.61.
WE920 65 Sqn. 64 Sqn (A). 63 Sqn (F). Scrap 5.8.59.
WE921 65 Sqn (C). 54 Sqn. FCCS. APS Sylt. Scrap 17.12.63.
WE922 65 Sqn (D). CGS/FWS. Scrap 10.4.59.
WE923 64 Sqn (G). 65 Sqn (N). 74 Sqn. Scrap 6.7.59
WE924 66 Sqn (B). w/o 10.7.51 landed one wheel up at Linton. U.16 spares.
WE925 64 Sqn. 63 Sqn. 64 Sqn. 92 Sqn. 43 Sqn (H). 34 Sqn. 229OCU. MOA for U.16 spares 10.10.61. To Wales Aircraft Museum, Rhoose 1979.
WE926 64 Sqn (E). 601 Sqn. Scrap 23.5.58.
WE927 64 Sqn (C). Duxford Stn Flt (JR). 65 Sqn. 264 Sqn. 33 Sqn. Scrap 1.12.60.
WE928 To RAAF 12.12.51 as A77-627. 77 Sqn. MIA 19.4.52 in Korea.
WE929 64 Sqn. w/o 5.5.52.
WE930 CSE. Scrap 19.12.57.
WE931 F/R. CGS. 211 AFS. RAFFC. Scrap 29.6.59.
WE932 Biggin Hill Stn Flt. 41 Sqn F/R for conv to U.16 3.11.59. 928B Sqn (656).
WE933 65 Sqn. w/o 6.5.51 near Rawcliffe, Yorks.
WE934 245 Sqn (G). Mod for flight-refuelling. F/R for conv to U.16
WE935 263 Sqn (K). 257 Sqn (K). Scrap 10.4.59.
WE936 CGS. 211 AFS/4 FTS. Cat.5(C) Worksop 12.4.57
WE937 64 Sqn. w/o 29.2.52.
WE938 63 Sqn (K). w/o 18.11.54.
WE939 41 Sqn. MOS (NEA) 7.11.57.
WE942 CGS/FWS. 233OCU. Scrap 27.3.58.
WE943 41 Sqn. 615 Sqn. 41 Sqn. Royal Tournament 21.6.55. To 71MU as instructional airframe. To 10STT as 7218M.
WE944 CFE (DFLS). FWS. 233OCU. Scrap 23.5.58.
WE945 CFE (DFLS). Scrap 12.5.58.
WE946 63 Sqn (G). CGS/FWS. 233OCU. MOA for U.16 spares 20.10.61.
WE947 1 Sqn. w/o 7.8.52.
WE948 211AFS. RAFFC. 211AFS. w/o 7.1.55.
WE949 41 Sqn (E). 615 Sqn (C). To 10STT 2.56 as 7319M, painted as 7139M.
WE950 56 Sqn (A). w/o 8.11.51 belly-landing after engines cut, near Christchurch, Cambs.
WE951 56 Sqn (V/O). w/o 18.8.53.
WE952 64 Sqn. 65 Sqn (E). Scrap 6.7.59.
WE953 CFE (DFLS). Scrap 25.4.58.
WE954 609 Sqn (A). Cat.5(C) at 60MU 29.6.55.
WE955 1 Sqn. w/o 26.6.51 engine cut while on approach to Tangmere.
WE956 41 Sqn. w/o 7.3.53.
WE957 41 Sqn. w/o 5.2.53.
WE958 64 Sqn. 615 Sqn. Scrap 5.8.59.
WE959 66 Sqn. Scrap 18.8.59.
WE960 CFE (AFDS). 74 Sqn. F/R for conv to U.16 25.2.59. WRE. Conv to U.21.
WE961 66 Sqn. 56 Sqn. 63 Sqn (T), used by Waterbeach Stn Flt (T2). Scrap 12.3.58.
WE962 19 Sqn. 211 AFS. F/R for conv to U.16 2.3.61.
WE963 19 Sqn. 34 Sqn. w/o 3.3.55.
WE964 66 Sqn. w/o 18.8.53.
WE965 609 Sqn (C). To Syria 7.5.56 as 418.
WE966 ML Aviation, White Waltham. To 12STT 11.1.56 as 7291M.
WE967 226OCU. Scrap 19.12.57.
WE968 226OCU. Scrap 12.8.59.
WE969 To RAAF 12.12.51 as A77-193. Conv to U.21A. Cat.5 3.4.64.
WE970 611 Sqn (H). TT Flt North Front. Scrap 5.6.59.
WE971 To RAAF 19.12.51 as A77-436. 77 Sqn. Shot down 4.10.52 in Korea.
WE972 CGS. 211AFS. MOS 16.8.57.
WE973 92 Sqn. 500 Sqn (F). 92 Sqn. Scrap 3.1.64.
WE974 65 Sqn (N/S). 74 Sqn. w/o 3.1.57.
WE975 41 Sqn. 600 Sqn. Scrap 10.4.59.
WE976 CGS. RAFFC. Scrap 24.4.58.
WF639 615 Sqn. 600 Sqn. Scrap 24.4.58.
WF640 500 Sqn. w/o 7.11.53.
WF641 257 Sqn (D). 65 Sqn. To Manby for ground instruction 4.55 as 7205M.
WF642 1 Sqn (T). 34 Sqn (P). 1 Sqn. Scrap 14.4.59.
WF643 56 Sqn (P/J). 1 Sqn. 611 Sqn. 29 Sqn (X). soc 29.11.71. To Norfolk and Suffolk Avn Museum.
WF644 500 Sqn. 226OCU. MOS 23.8.57.
WF645 609 Sqn. Scrap 31.3.58.
WF646 92 Sqn. APS. MOA for U.16 spares 16.10.61.
WF647 74 Sqn. 615 Sqn. Scrap 10.4.59.
WF648 56 Sqn. 257 Sqn. w/o 4.9.53.
WF649 92 Sqn. 611 Sqn. 610 Sqn (C). Scrap 9.5.58.
WF650 63 Sqn (M/W). Scrap 12.5.58.
WF651 74 Sqn (T). Scrap 12.5.58.
WF652 74 Sqn. Cat.5(C) 20.7.55.
WF653 To RAAF 17.12.51 as A77-920. 77 Sqn. MIA 15.2.52 in Korea.
WF654 56 Sqn. 64 Sqn (R). 29 Sqn (W). 85 Sqn (Z). To Cottesmore dump 22.6.72.
WF655 64 Sqn. 66 Sqn (E/T). 74 Sqn (L). Cat.5(C) 11.10.55.
WF656 74 Sqn. Scrap 29.6.59.
WF657 65 Sqn. DFLS. To ground instructional airframe at Biggin Hill as 7463M as 8.8.57.
WF658 609 Sqn. Scrap 15.5.58.
WF659 65 Sqn (M). F/R for conv to U.21 9.9.60. WRE.
WF660 65 Sqn (H). To Biggin Hill for ground instruction 23.8.57.
WF661 609 Sqn (G). Scrap 19.5.58.
WF662 65 Sqn. 66 Sqn. 111 Sqn (B). 4 FTS. RAFFC To Waddington dump 3.3.60.
WF677 Church Fenton Stn Flt (MS/PFS/RWO). Scrap 5.2.59.
WF678 615 Sqn (D). Scrap 14.4.59.
WF679 245 Sqn (O/D). Scrap 8.4.58.
WF680 66 Sqn. 220OCU. SHQ Seletar. soc 7.7.58.
WF681 615 Sqn. 41 Sqn. MOA for U.16 spares, 15.11.61.
WF682 504 Sqn (C). Scrap 26.5.59.
WF683 FCCS. APS. 600 Sqn. Scrap 6.3.58.
WF684 615 Sqn. 600 Sqn. Scrap 12.5.58.
WF685 615 Sqn (B). MOA for U.16 spares 6.10.61.
WF686 600 Sqn (Q). 615 Sqn. 226OCU. Scrap 27.1.58
WF687 226OCU. w/o 4.11.52.
WF688 CFE (DFLS). 504 Sqn. Scrap 4.3.58.
WF689 56 Sqn. 501 Sqn. 219 Sqn. Scrap 12.5.58.
WF690 CGS. RAFFC. Scrap 4.3.58.
WF691 To Fokker 1.10.51. To Belgian AF as EG-148
WF692 To Fokker 11.7.51. To Belgian AF as EG-146
WF693 To Fokker 11.7.51. To Belgian AF as EG-147
WF694 To R.Neth AF 11.7.51 as I-93. w/o 12.4.57.
WF695 245 Sqn. Horsham St Faith Stn Flt (RDY). w/o 11.9.53.
WF696 To R.Neth AF 11.7.51 as I-94.
WF697 To R.Neth AF 19.7.51 as I-90.
WF698 To R.Neth AF 19.7.51 as I-91.
WF699 To R.Neth AF 19.7.51 as I-92. w/o 3.4.54.
WF700 41 Sqn (H). w/o 12.4.52.
WF701 To Fokker 9.10.51. To Belgian AF as EG-149
WF702 41 Sqn. 615 Sqn. Cat.5(C) 10.6.55.
WF703 65 Sqn (J). 92 Sqn. Scrap 27.7.59.
WF704 65 Sqn (B). 64 Sqn. w/o 9.9.54.
WF705 63 Sqn (J). Scrap 12.5.58.
WF706 63 Sqn. CFE (DFLS). 19 Sqn. 600 Sqn. F/R for conv to U.16 22.11.61.
WF707 12 Grp Com Flt (RA). 264 Sqn. 66 Sqn. F/R for conv to U.16 12.11.59. Llanbedr.
WF708 74 Sqn. Scrap 29.6.59.
WF709 74 Sqn. 56 Sqn (Y). 604 Sqn. Scrap 12.5.58.
WF710 74 Sqn (J). 245 Sqn (J). Scrap 29.4.58.
WF711 92 Sqn (J). 19 Sqn. 5CAACU. RAFFC. 5CAACU. F/R for conv to U.16 18.2.72.
WF712 245 Sqn. 74 Sqn. Cat.5(C) 21.11.56.
WF713 65 Sqn; 64 Sqn (U). 600 Sqn. w/o 18.6.56 in Malta.
WF714 56 Sqn. 66 Sqn. 500 Sqn (K). w/o 8.9.54.
WF715 66 Sqn (H). APS Sylt. Scrap 24.4.59.
WF716 GAC. F/R for conv to U.16. 728B Sqn. Llanbedr.
WF736 64 Sqn. SHQ Seletar. SHQ Kai Tak. soc 28.11.59.
WF737 65 Sqn. 56 Sqn. 63 Sqn (V). Scrap 6.4.59.
WF738 65 Sqn (A). 64 Sqn. 601 Sqn. Scrap 29.6.59.
WF739 12 Grp Com Flt. CFE Com Flt. 41 Sqn. 34 Sqn (N). Scrap 6.5.58.
WF740 245 Sqn (K). 63 Sqn (K). Cat.5(C) at 71MU 7.1.57.
WF741 610 Sqn. Hooton Park Stn Flt. 611 Sqn (E). MOA for U.16 spares 13.11.59.
WF742 247 Sqn. 34 Sqn (F). To 1STT 8.5.56 as 7320M.
WF743 72 Sqn (V). 609 Sqn (B). F/R for conv to U.16 16.11.61.
WF744 226OCU. Scrap 21.2.58.
WF745 CGS. w/o 21.5.52, missing.
WF746 To RAAF 18.12.51 as A77-46. 77 Sqn. MIA 11.2.53 Korea.
WF747 600 Sqn. w/o 25.4.53.
WF748 CGS. 500 Sqn (H/'Chatham and Gillingham'). Scrap 26.5.59.
WF749 63 Sqn. 222 Sqn. APS Sylt. soc 3.3.58.
WF750 To RAAF 18.12.51 as A77-422.
WF751 226OCU. F/R for conv to U.16 25.4.60. Llanbedr.
WF752 DH Props. AWA. To RNAS Bramcote as A2430 7.5.57. Scrap 2.59.
WF753 600 Sqn. 92 Sqn. 54 Sqn. 56 Sqn. 63 Sqn (Y) soc 14.11.57.
WF754 600 Sqn. w/o 13.2.54.
WF755 263 Sqn (B). F/R for conv to U.16 5.9.60.
WF756 41 Sqn. 247 Sqn (N). F/R for conv to U.16 6.5.60. Llanbedr.
WF757 615 Sqn. 600 Sqn (J). Scrap 12.5.58.
WF758 500 Sqn (E). 611 Sqn. Scrap 23.5.58.
WF759 615 Sqn (W). 600 Sqn (U). To 1STT 10.11.55 as 7294M.
WF760 615 Sqn (K). w/o 22.3.53.
WH249 19 Sqn. CFE (DFLS) (L). 19 Sqn. Cat.5(S) 29.8.55.

METEOR F.8 *continued*

WH250 226OCU. APS Sylt. w/o 1.10.57.
WH251 To RAAF 18.12.51 as A77-510.
WH252 To RAAF 18.12.51 as A77-793. 77 Sqn. Surplus 28.3.58. Scrap 30.4.59.
WH253 615 Sqn (F). 600 Sqn. w/o 19.11.55.
WH254 To RAAF 18.12.51 as A77-258. 77 Sqn. 23 Sqn. Surplus 2.3.58. Scrap 30.4.59.
WH255 504 Sqn (E). Scrap 6.5.58.
WH256 226OCU. MC & TTS Luqa and Takali. soc 2.7.59.
WH257 504 Sqn (D). Scrap 6.8.59.
WH258 615 Sqn. 257 Sqn. 600 Sqn (P). F/R for conv to U.16. Llanbedr.
WH259 To RAAF 17.12.51 as A77-11. 77 Sqn. dbr 26.5.53 in Korea.
WH260 616 Sqn (P). To Syria 7.5.56 as 419.
WH261 600 Sqn (Z). 85 Sqn. Scrap 5.8.59.
WH262 500 Sqn. West Malling Stn Flt. 504 Sqn (FJ). 616 Sqn. Scrap 18.8.59.
WH263 616 Sqn (N). Scrap 14.8.59.
WH272 66 Sqn. AWDS. AW/Night Wg. CFE(DFLS). 600 Sqn. Scrap 4.3.58.
WH273 610 Sqn (A). 43 Sqn. FCCS. 245 Sqn. 125 Sqn. Scrap 11.3.59.
WH274 To RAAF 17.12.51 as A77-343. 77 Sqn. MIA 8.3.53 in Korea.
WH275 19 Sqn (T). 66 Sqn (T/S). To Sutton-on-Hull dump 9.2.59.
WH276 616 Sqn. Flying accident 18.9.52. To 60MU as 7665M.
WH277 616 Sqn. Scrap 4.3.58.
WH278 616 Sqn. w/o 22.5.54.
WH279 FCCS. 1 Sqn. APS. 615 Sqn. Scrap 17.5.58.
WH280 600 Sqn. 615 Sqn. soc 26.8.56.
WH281 600 Sqn (V). MOA for U.16 spares 12.10.61.
WH282 504 Sqn (K). Scrap 6.8.59.
WH283 56 Sqn (A). w/o 16.12.53.
WH284 TRE Defford. Airwork Hurn. RRE. Folland. F/R for conv to U.16. Llanbedr (E). Destroyed by missile 9.11.60.
WH285 600 Sqn. 25 Sqn. 500 Sqn (D). Scrap 4.3.58.
WH286 1 Sqn. 34 Sqn. 229OCU (T/A). F/R for conv to U.16 16.5.72, (final conversion).
WH287 263 Sqn (S). w/o 13.9.54.
WH288 226OCU. w/o 19.1.54.
WH289 FCCS. 19 Sqn. FWS. Scrap 6.5.58.
WH290 226OCU. Scrap 6.5.58.
WH291 257 Sqn. RAFFC. CAW (E). 85 Sqn (T). 229 OCU/79 Sqn. NEA 20.8.74 at 5MU. To O.Haydon-Baillie 10.2.76. To SWWAPS, Lasham, 1980.
WH292 54 Sqn. w/o 3.6.52.
WH293 610 Sqn (B). 43 Sqn (Y). Scrap 21.11.63.
WH294 226OCU. Missing 9.9.52.
WH295 226OCU. MOS 23.8.57.
WH296 263 Sqn (W). 2 Sqn. 79 Sqn. soc 11.6.56.
WH297 257 Sqn. 34 Sqn (S). APS. FWS. To 10STT 19.11.56 as 7389M.
WH298 257 Sqn. w/o 24.1.54.
WH299 263 Sqn (L). 257 Sqn. w/o 21.12.54.
WH300 257 Sqn. APS Sylt. soc 1.5.59.
WH301 CFE (DFLS). 609 Sqn. RAFFC (F). 85 Sqn (T). NEA 30.11.65 at 5MU. To RAF Museum store 17.2.67, allocated 7930M but not worn. To Hendon 1979.
WH302 610 Sqn. w/o 18.9.54.
WH303 610 Sqn. 5CAACU. Scrap 27.3.63.
WH304 72 Sqn. 19 Sqn (L). To 10STT 9.56 as 7367M.
WH305 500 Sqn. 72 Sqn. 245 Sqn. Stradishall Stn Flt 85 Sqn (V). FCCS. West Ravnham. 85 Sqn. soc 15.11.71 to Honington dump.
WH306 65 Sqn (C/R). Scrap 5.8.59.
WH307 504 Sqn (G). 616 Sqn (M). Scrap 24.4.58.
WH308 226OCU. w/o 3.6.54.
WH309 604 Sqn. F/R for conv to U.16 26.10.61.
WH310 504 Sqn (J). Scrap 6.8.59.
WH311 226OCU. w/o 25.2.53.
WH312 ETPS. w/o 31.3.54.
WH313 64 Sqn (U). 19 Sqn. 610 Sqn. Scrap 29.4.58.
WH314 64 Sqn. w/o 6.10.54.
WH315 226OCU. APS. F/R for U.16 conv 3.3.60 (A)
WH316 41 Sqn. 111 Sqn (V). Scrap 10.4.59.
WH317 226OCU. APS. Scrap 10.4.59.
WH318 504 Sqn. Scrap 24.8.59.
WH319 226OCU. Scrap 29.6.59.
WH320 CS (A). CFE. AWDS. F/R for conv to U.16 7.4.59. Llanbedr (N).
WH342 66 Sqn. w/o 29.2.52.
WH343 54 Sqn (M). 63 Sqn (W). Scrap 5.8.59.
WH344 504 Sqn (B). F/R for conv to U.16 13.4.60. Llanbedr (O).
WH345 54 Sqn. Scrap 29.6.59.
WH346 64 Sqn. APS Sylt. soc 11.10.57.
WH347 CGS. w/o 13.4.53.
WH348 19 Sqn. w/o 19.7.55.
WH349 601 Sqn (C). F/R for conv to U.16 17.3.60. Llanbedr.
WH350 19 Sqn. 1 Sqn. To GAC 31.3.55. To Egypt 18.4.55 as 1415.
WH351 19 Sqn. w/o 18.3.53.
WH352 226OCU. Scrap 29.6.59.
WH353 CGS. FWS. Scrap 6.7.59.
WH354 226OCU. 111 Sqn. 233OCU. Scrap 1.4.58.
WH355 CFE (DFLS). FWS. w/o 28.6.56.
WH356 CFE (DFLS). 500 Sqn (F). Scrap 8.4.58.
WH357 74 Sqn. 245 Sqn (V). To 1STT 31.5.55 as 7254M.
WH358 CFE (DFLS). w/o 24.3.54.
WH359 611 Sqn (K). F/R for conv to U.16 10.3.60. Llanbedr.
WH360 226OCU. 229OCU. Scrap 12.3.58.
WH361 41 Sqn. 211AFS. RAFFC. Cat.5(C) 8.2.57
WH362 226OCU. w/o 4.11.52.
WH363 APS. FWS. Scrap 12.5.58.
WH364 601 Sqn. Takali. Safi. Idris. MC&TT. 85 Sqn (U). NEA 3.9.71 at 5MU. To Kemble gate 9.2.72 in 601 Sqn colours.
WH365 611 Sqn (D). 600 Sqn. 615 Sqn. To F/R for conv to U.16 14.3.60. Llanbedr.
WH366 64 Sqn (V). To 10 STT 2.56, allocated 7318M but painted as 7138M.
WH367 226 OCU. 229 OCU. Scrap 27.7.59.
WH368 611 Sqn. 41 Sqn (Y). Scrap 29.6.59.
WH369 92 Sqn. 222 Sqn. F/R for conv to U.16 19.11.59.
WH370 54 Sqn (N). 85 Sqn. 500 Sqn (D/'City of Canterbury'). Scrap 13.5.58.
WH371 F/R. RAE Farnborough (brake-chute trials). To GAC 14.3.55. To Egypt 19.5.55 as 1420.
WH372 226OCU. F/R for conv to U.16 17.3.59. Llanbedr.
WH373 226 OCU. F/R for conv to U.16 9.2.61.
WH374 63 Sqn (A). w/o 23.8.56.
WH375 1 Sqn (H). APS Sylt. w/o 14.9.55.
WH376 226 OCU. 19 Sqn (T). 604 Sqn. F/R for conv to U.16 24.3.61.
WH377 63 Sqn (T). APS Sylt. w/o 11.11.55.
WH378 54 Sqn. 56 Sqn. w/o 19.4.55.
WH379 CFE (DFLS). 45/33 Sqn. w/o 8.8.55.
WH380 CFE (DFLS). CFE Com Flt. Metropolitan Sector. 85 Sqn. Scrap 28.5.59.
WH381 CFE (DFLS). 611 Sqn. F/R for conv to U.16 11.11.59.
WH382 263 Sqn (V). To 4 STT 20.10.55 as 7265M.
WH383 610 Sqn. w/o 14.11.53.
WH384 610 Sqn. w/o 14.11.53.
WH385 CGS. FWS. Scrap 4.3.58.
WH386 610 Sqn. Scrap 24.8.59.
WH395 CGS. w/o 14.8.55.
WH396 54 Sqn. Scrap 9.9.57.
WH397 54 Sqn (K). 500 Sqn (E/'Ashford'). Scrap 11.3.59.
WH398 611 Sqn. SHQ Seletar. soc 12.1.62.
WH399 500 Sqn. Cat.5(C). 13.2.53.
WH400 226OCU. w/o 4.10.54.
WH401 66 Sqn. Linton Stn Flt (BD/LM). MC & TT Luqa/Takali. Scrap 30.10.63.
WH402 245 Sqn (L). 23 Sqn. 141 Sqn. 23 Sqn. MC & TT. Scrap 8.1.64.
WH403 92 Sqn (Q). 66 Sqn. 43 Sqn. 12 Grp Com Flt. Scrap 6.7.59.
WH404 54 Sqn. 56 Sqn. 253 Sqn (used by Waterbeach Stn Cdr as 'RGD'). 153 Sqn. 25 Sqn (JGT). Scrap 1.4.63
WH405 To RAAF 16.7.53 as A77-865. 77 Sqn. 22 Sqn. Surplus 28.3.58. Scrap 30.4.59.
WH406 604 Sqn. Scrap 27.1.58.
WH407 226 OCU. w/o 28.9.53.
WH408 604 Sqn (D). w/o 5.12.54, lost control in a dive and crashed in the Thames estuary.
WH409 226 OCU. Scrap 19.12.57.
WH410 226 OCU. FETS. APC. 45/33 Sqn. APC. SHQ Butterworth. B & TT Flt. 1574 Flt. soc 27.1.69 to Singapore Def Cmnd as SAFTECH-3.
WH411 CGS. 229OCU. Waterbeach Stn Flt (T3). 46 Sqn. Scrap 30.12.63.
WH412 CGS. FWS. Scrap 6.7.59.
WH413 CGS. FWS. Cat.5(C) 16.1.57.
WH414 To RAAF 17.7.52 as A77-866. 77 Sqn. w/o 31.5.54, mid air collision with A77-862 in Korea.
WH415 56 Sqn. Waterbeach Stn Flt. 63 Sqn. w/o 14.5.56.
WH416 245 Sqn (F). Scrap 1.4.58.
WH417 To RAAF 16.7.52 as A77-862. 77 Sqn. w/o 31.5.54 (see WH414).
WH418 To RAAF 16.7.52 as A77-861. Instructional airframe 4.6.58.
WH419 604 Sqn (E). MOA for U.16 spares 20.12.61.
WH420 247 Sqn (H/Y). F/R for conv to U.16 20.11.59
WH421 226OCU. 611 Sqn. w/o 26.7.56 in Malta.
WH422 226OCU (HX-S). w/o 27.5.54.
WH423 12 Grp Com Flt. 25 Sqn. Scrap 12.8.59.
WH424 247 Sqn. w/o 18.12.52.
WH425 CGS. w/o 12.12.52.
WH426 247 Sqn. 500 Sqn (T/'Gravesend'). Scrap 11.3.59.
WH442 247 Sqn (G). w/o 18.12.52.
WH443 247 Sqn (W). 54 Sqn. 25 Sqn (A). w/o 10.1.56. To Falfield CD, later Hucknall dump.
WH444 247 Sqn. Odiham Stn Flt. w/o 28.10.54.
WH445 615 Sqn (S/B). Scrap 20.5.58.
WH446 56 Sqn (S). APS Sylt. soc 20.3.59.
WH447 Handling Sqn Manby. 610 Sqn (H). A & AEE Scrap 19.12.57.
WH448 To Fokker 1.10.51. To Belgian AF as EG-150
WH449 63 Sqn (R). To 10 STT 3.9.56 as 7366M, later to Halton.
WH450 500 Sqn (B). 153 Sqn (A/R). Eastern Sector. 23 Sqn. Scrap 7.3.63.
WH451 500 Sqn (G). 504 Sqn. Scrap 7.5.58.
WH452 616 Sqn. APS. soc 2.4.57.
WH453 222 Sqn. 72 Sqn. 5 CAACU (L). F/R for conv to U.16 13.10.71.
WH454 504 Sqn. 601 Sqn. Scrap 12.3.58.
WH455 616 Sqn. w/o 11.12.52.
WH456 616 Sqn (L). Scrap 6.5.58.
WH457 CGS. FWS. 233OCU. Scrap 10.4.59.
WH458 CGS. RAFFC. w/o 27.8.54.
WH459 65 Sqn (Q). w/o 12.3.58.
WH460 64 Sqn. 65 Sqn. 64 Sqn. 65 Sqn. F/R for conv to U.21 1.9.60.
WH461 64 Sqn. 63 Sqn (B). Scrap 6.7.59.
WH462 66 Sqn (D). 56 Sqn (G). RAFFC. Scrap 7.9.59.
WH463 72 Sqn (F). 604 Sqn. Scrap 14.4.59.
WH464 504 Sqn (F). 616 Sqn (K). Scrap 29.5.58.
WH465 600 Sqn (Y). Scrap 3.2.58.
WH466 222 Sqn. 43 Sqn (R). w/o 9.4.56.
WH467 263 Sqn. w/o 26.10.53.
WH468 247 Sqn (S/C). Scrap 19.5.58.
WH469 226 OCU. 141 Sqn. MOA. soc 7.5.65.
WH470 600 Sqn. Scrap 24.4.58.
WH471 54 Sqn (Z). 601 Sqn (L). Scrap 12.5.58.
WH472 263 Sqn. w/o 29.9.52.
WH473 616 Sqn. w/o 11.12.52, missing.
WH474 616 Sqn (K). 600 Sqn (P). Scrap 29.5.58.
WH475 To RAAF 29.11.51 as A77-65. 77 Sqn. w/o 12.2.53 while landing in Korea.
WH476 263 Sqn (E). 226 OCU. Stradishall Stn Flt. 245 Sqn (V). 89 Sqn. Scrap 24.4.59.
WH477 257 Sqn. w/o 27.2.53.
WH478 63 Sqn. 56 Sqn. w/o 11.3.54.
WH479 Handling Sqn Manby. To RAAF 16.7.52 as A77-852. 77 Sqn. MIA 26.12.52 in Korea.
WH480 41 Sqn. Biggin Hill Stn Flt. Scrap 17.1.58.
WH481 CGS. FWS. Scrap 6.7.59.
WH482 CFE (DFLS). APS Sylt (J). soc for fire practice 17.9.62.
WH483 RAE Farnborough. 211 AFS. Scrap 11.3.59.
WH484 64 Sqn (Z). 247 Sqn. Cat.5(C) 24.6.57 at Odiham.
WH498 ETPS (6). soc 12.4.57.
WH499 CGS. F/R for conv to U.16 2.3.59. Llanbedr.
WH500 CGS. 72 Sqn (H). 504 Sqn (FJ). Wymeswold Stn Flt. F/R for conv to U.16 6.11.59. Llanbedr.
WH501 226OCU. Scrap 29.6.59.
WH502 226 OCU. 500 Sqn (C/'Rochester'). Scrap 10.4.59.
WH503 611 Sqn (F). To Syria 13.6.56 as 417.
WH504 611 Sqn. Hooton Park Stn Flt. 504 Sqn (U). Scrap 19.5.58.
WH505 61 Sqn (A). 611 Sqn. 600 Sqn. 615 Sqn. F/R for conv to U.16 22.3.60. Destroyed 27.9.61.
WH506 610 Sqn (JAS). F/R for conv to U.16 18.11.59.
WH507 1 Sqn. SHQ Seletar. soc 31.5.57.
WH508 66 Sqn. 111 Sqn (F). Scrap 4.3.58.
WH509 CFE (DFLS). 63 Sqn. 610 Sqn. F/R for conv to U.16 9.3.61.
WH510 56 Sqn (E). w/o 16.12.53.
WH511 CFE (DFLS). 504 Sqn. 264 Sqn. Scrap 4.3.58
WH512 CFE (DFLS). 72 Sqn. 66 Sqn. 264 Sqn. 33 Sqn. Scrap 28.4.59.
WH513 500 Sqn. w/o 7.2.53.
WK647 611 Sqn. Odiham Stn Flt. w/o 28.7.52.
WK648 A & AEE. 615 Sqn. 41 Sqn. 615 Sqn. F/R for conv to U.16 15.11.61.
WK649 APS. 45/33 Sqn. SHQ Seletar. soc 20.3.60.
WK650 To RAAF 16.7.52 as A77-854. 77 Sqn. Surplus 28.3.58. Scrap 30.4.59.
WK651 54 Sqn. w/o 22.12.52.
WK652 APS. w/o 6.12.55. Allocated 7351M.
WK653 226 OCU. MOS 23.8.57.
WK654 247 Sqn (E). 46 Sqn (X). AWFCS. CFE. 85 Sqn (X). NEA 23.12.69. To Neatishead for display 9.4.76.
WK655 500 Sqn (M). 151 Sqn (R). RAFFC. CAW (B) NEA 3.9.71. To Henlow dump 19.7.72. Scrap 11.78.
WK656 72 Sqn (A). 66 Sqn (S). Scrap 5.8.59.
WK657 92 Sqn (A). w/o 14.8.52.
WK658 63 Sqn (G).
WK659 Duxford Stn Flt. 64 Sqn. Scrap 5.8.59.
WK660 RAE Farnborough. ETPS (9). GAC. soc 28.7.59 wings to WA982.
WK661 APS. 211 AFS. Scrap 4.3.58.
WK662 226 OCU. Scrap 5.8.59.
WK663 226 OCU (HX-O). FWS. Scrap 6.7.59.
WK664 226 OCU. FWS. Scrap 6.7.59.
WK665 CFE (DFLS). 72 Sqn. 19 Sqn. 608 Sqn. Scrap 26.5.59.
WK666 226 OCU. 245 Sqn. FWS. Scrap 5.8.59.
WK667 226 OCU. Tangmere Stn Flt. 79 Sqn. Scrap 10.4.59.
WK668 247 Sqn (A). MOS 31.8.57.
WK669 54 Sqn (X). 56 Sqn. 63 Sqn. Scrap 6.7.59.
WK670 To RAAF 16.7.52 as A77-860. 77 Sqn. w/o 16.7.53 during take-off.
WK671 247 Sqn (Z). 600 Sqn (L). Cat.5(C) 21.1.57.
WK672 247 Sqn (X). FCCS (AKG). 111 Sqn. 41 Sqn. Malta. Scrap 12.3.63.
WK673 54 Sqn (Y). Scrap 28.5.59.
WK674 To RAAF 16.7.52 as A77-868. 77 Sqn. 22 Sqn. Surplus 28.3.58. To Camden Museum of Aviation.
WK675 CGS. FWS. MOA for U.16 spares 8.11.61.
WK676 226 OCU (HX-O). 81 Grp Com Sqn. To 14 STT 21.9.56 as 7376M.
WK677 72 Sqn (R). APS Sylt. Scrap 6.12.62.
WK678 CGS. FWS. Scrap 29.6.59.
WK679 72 Sqn (B/D). w/o 15.10.54.
WK680 66 Sqn. 12 Grp Com Flt (RA). 616 Sqn. Scrap 19.12.57.
WK681 65 Sqn (R/H). w/o 4.1.57.
WK682 To RAAF 16.7.52 as A77-858. 77 Sqn. w/o 20.8.52. To stores depot, Regents Park.
WK683 To RAAF 16.7.52 as A77-851. 77 Sqn. Surplus 17.10.60. Conv to U.21A. Edinburgh Field. Scrap 10.65.
WK684 To RAAF 16.7.52 as A77-857. 77 Sqn. w/o 8.9.53.
WK685 To RAAF 14.7.52 as A77-867. 77 Sqn. 22 Sqn. Instructional airframe 8.5.58. To Moorabin Air Museum, Victoria.
WK686 To RAAF 16.7.52 as A77-856. 77 Sqn. w/o 18.5.53.
WK687 226 OCU. Scrap 5.8.59.
WK688 To RAAF 16.7.52 as A77-859. 77 Sqn. w/o 4.8.53.
WK689 72 Sqn. North Weald Stn Flt (NW). Southern Com Flt. Scrap 5.8.59.
WK690 72 Sqn. w/o 17.10.52.
WK691 72 Sqn (X). 19 Sqn. Scrap 29.6.59.
WK692 604 Sqn (F). w/o 20.2.54.
WK693 604 Sqn. 111 Sqn (T). F/R for conv to U.16 7.9.60.
WK694 APS. FWS. FCCS. soc 22.3.63.
WK695 CGS. FWS. Scrap 4.3.58.

METEOR F.8 *continued*

WK696 604 Sqn. w/o 20.2.54.
WK707 54 Sqn. 247 Sqn. 1 Sqn. Scrap 23.8.57.
WK708 54 Sqn. w/o 6.6.52.
WK709 54 Sqn. F/R for conv to U.16 29.3.61.
WK710 54 Sqn. F/R for conv to U.16 13.9.60. Later conv to U.21.
WK711 54 Sqn (C). CGS. RAFFC. Scrap 4.3.58.
WK712 54 Sqn. RAFFC. soc 10.12.62, allocated 7795M.
WK713 226 OCU. 65 Sqn (L). 222 Sqn. Scrap 28.5.59
WK714 72 Sqn (G). 19 Sqn. 616 Sqn. Scrap 10.4.59.
WK715 To RAAF 17.7.52 as A77-853. w/o 28.12.53 during landing.
WK716 226 OCU. 229 OCU. MOA for U.16 spares, 7.12.61.
WK717 226 OCU. F/R for conv to U.16 29.10.59. Llanbedr.
WK718 66 Sqn. 111 Sqn (Q). Scrap 4.3.58.
WK719 66 Sqn. 111 Sqn (C). Scrap 12.8.59.
WK720 66 Sqn. AWDS. AW/Night Wing. 63 Sqn (D). Scrap 6.7.59.
WK721 Flying accident. AWA Baginton. 211 AFS. 34 Sqn. 226 OCU. 229 OCU. 601 Sqn (K). MOA for U.16 spares 27.10.61.
WK722 601 Sqn (Y/A). w/o 14.6.54 in Malta.
WK723 CGS. w/o 21.12.54.
WK724 Northern Sector (HH). w/o 20.7.53.
WK725 247 Sqn (B). 500 Sqn (P/'Dover'). Scrap 11.3.59.
WK726 56 Sqn (P). w/o 19.4.55.
WK727 To RAAF 10.10.52 as A77-869. 77 Sqn. 22 Sqn. w/o 2.12.59 at Holsworthy.
WK728 To RAAF 16.7.52 as A77-855. 77 Sqn. 22 Sqn. Surplus 17.10.60. Conv to U.21A. w/o 19.2.63.
WK729 CGS. FWS. F/R for conv to U.16 28.4.60. Llanbedr.
WK730 To RAAF 16.7.52 as A77-863. Conv to U.21A. w/o 14.2.69.
WK731 Tangmere Stn Flt (JAK). 34 Sqn (HP/MP). MOA for U.16 spares 14.12.61.
WK732 CGS. FWS (F). w/o 18.8.55. Remains to Rufforth.
WK733 211 AFS. Scrap 19.11.57.
WK734 19 Sqn. Caledonian Sector. Scrap 10.4.59.
WK735 To RAAF 16.7.52 as A77-864. 77 Sqn. w/o 13.2.54, overshot landing in Korea.
WK736 72 Sqn (P). 19 Sqn. Scrap 16.7.59.
WK737 604 Sqn (K). MOA for U.16 spares 8.1.62.
WK738 66 Sqn (M). 111 Sqn (M). F/R for conv to U.16 13.10.61, although not conv until 2.70. Llanbedr.
WK739 601 Sqn. Scrap 12.3.58.
WK740 601 Sqn. APS Sylt. To Little Rissington dump 19.8.62.
WK741 66 Sqn. 111 Sqn (U). 4 FTS. RAFFC. To Topcliffe dump 23.11.59.
WK742 601 Sqn (F). 41 Sqn. 601 Sqn. Scrap 7.5.58.
WK743 604 Sqn (L). F/R for conv to U.16 11.2.61.
WK744 601 Sqn. North Weald Stn Flt. 601 Sqn. MOA for U.16 spares 15.11.61.
WK745 601 Sqn (H). MOA for U.16 programme 23.11.61.
WK746 APS. CGS. FWS. MOA for U.16 programme 11.12.61.
WK747 APS. FWS. MOA for U.16 programme 30.11.61
WK748 To RAAF 10.10.52 as A77-870. 77 Sqn. To Instructional airframe 4.6.58. To RAAF Museum at Point Cook.
WK749 72 Sqn. w/o 7.10.52.
WK750 72 Sqn (C). 19 Sqn. 608 Sqn. Scrap 19.5.58.
WK751 72 Sqn (D). 92 Sqn. 264 Sqn. Scrap 6.5.58.
WK752 APS. RAFFC. w/o 4.6.56.
WK753 APS. FWS. Scrap 4.3.58.
WK754 APS (WH-S). FWS. FCS Trng (E). Loaned to 46 Sqn (E). To Chivenor dump 11.7.62.
WK755 FCCS. w/o 13.4.55.
WK756 211 AFS. RAFFC. Scrap 12.3.58.
WK783 601 Sqn (J). F/R for conv to U.16 5.12.61.
WK784 604 Sqn. F/R for conv to U.16 17.3.61.
WK785 247 Sqn (H). 46 Sqn (H). soc 10.3.58 and dumped at Odiham.
WK786 72 Sqn (T). APS Sylt (P). To Coltishall dump 3.8.62.
WK787 222 Sqn. Caledonian Sector (CGL/MWSR). w/o 11.9.56.
WK788 APS. Scrap 19.12.57.
WK789 601 Sqn (K). F/R for conv to U.16 6.12.61.
WK790 226 OCU. F/R for conv to U.16 23.2.61.
WK791 To RAAF 5.11.52 as A77-871. 77 Sqn. Instructional airframe 4.6.58. To Wagga-Wagga gate.
WK792 To RAAF 12.12.52 as A77-872. 77 Sqn. 78 Wing. 23 Sqn. Surplus 17.10.60. Conv to U.21A. Destroyed 28.5.68.
WK793 APS. FWS. F/R for conv to U.16 29.3.61.
WK794 43 Sqn, crashed in transit on delivery 7.10.52. Repaired. APS. w/o 11.3.55.
WK795 Eastern Sector (SCW/JW/JE). F/R for conv to U.16 24.11.61.
WK796 To RAAF 12.12.52 as A77-873. 77 Sqn. 78 Wing 23 Sqn. Surplus 21.12.60. Conv to U.21A.
WK797 GAC. F/R for conv to U.16. To Australia 5.4.60. Conv to U.21.
WK798 To RAAF 28.1.53 as A77-875. 77 Sqn. Preserved at Williamtown, NSW.
WK799 92 Sqn (A). 257 Sqn. F/R for conv to U.16 9.3.61.
WK800 To Andover for Battle of Britain display 17.9.52, then to RAAF 21.2.53 as A77-876. 77 Sqn. 78 Wing. 23 Sqn. Surplus 17.10.60. Conv to U.21A. Returned to Llanbedr as D.16 1971 (Z).
WK801 65 Sqn (F). w/o 9.10.56 near Duxford.
WK802 263 Sqn (D). 257 Sqn. 152 Sqn. Scrap 24.4.59.
WK803 56 Sqn (P/V). RAFFC. 229 OCU. Geilenkirchen Stn Flt. NEA 28.11.72. To Manston fire school 21.2.73.
WK804 74 Sqn. Cat.5(C) at 58MU 7.6.56.
WK805 500 Sqn. w/o 7.11.53.
WK806 CFE (DFLS). 604 Sqn. Scrap 27.1.58.
WK807 600 Sqn (W). Western Sector. F/R for conv to U.16 21.2.61.
WK808 4 STT. 257 Sqn. 1 Sqn. w/o 17.3.56.
WK809 4 STT. APS. Cat.5(C) 16.1.58.
WK810 247 Sqn. 615 Sqn (E). Scrap 10.4.59.
WK811 211 AFS. Scrap 12.3.58.
WK812 4 STT. 111 Sqn (K). F/R for conv to U.16 24.3.60. Llanbedr.
WK813 Handling Sqn Manby. 211 AFS. Scrap 19.12.57
WK814 43 Sqn. Leuchars Stn Flt. Coltishall Stn Flt. 23 Sqn 41 Sqn. Nicosia Stn Flt. 41 Sqn. 5 CAACU. RAFFC. Scrap 21.11.63
WK815 CFE. AWDS. Air Attache Paris. APS Sylt. Scrap 10.5.62.
WK816 74 Sqn (M). Scrap 6.7.59.
WK817 CFE. AWDS. 19 Sqn. 72 Sqn (K, later Z). Scrap 10.1.64.
WK818 211 AFS/4 FTS. Used by AVM Atcherley (RLRA). RAFFC. Scrap 6.12.62, although allocated 7756M.
WK819 211 AFS. RAFFC. Scrap 12.5.58.
WK820 245 Sqn (N). w/o 15.9.55.
WK821 To RAAF 27.1.53 as A77-879. 77 Sqn. 78 Wing. Surplus 19.9.57. Scrap 8.5.58.
WK822 211 AFS. TTF North Front. Scrap 24.4.59.
WK823 211 AFS. w/o 9.6.53.
WK824 CFE. AWDS. APS Sylt (S). soc for fire practice 7.9.62.
WK825 247 Sqn. Scrap 12.8.59.
WK826 211 AFS (43). Cat.5(C) at 32 MU 9.6.55.
WK827 65 Sqn (T). Scrap 5.8.59.
WK849 211 AFS. Scrap 4.3.58.
WK850 211 AFS. Scrap 19.12.57.
WK851 211 AFS. Scrap 19.12.57.
WK852 611 Sqn (C). F/R for conv to U.16 9.3.60.
WK853 604 Sqn (H). Scrap 29.6.59.
WK854 211 AFS (43). 4 FTS (20). Scrap 27.3.58.
WK855 226 OCU. 500 Sqn. F/R for conv to U.16 7.11.61.
WK856 43 Sqn. 616 Sqn. APS Sylt. Scrap 12.3.63.
WK857 211 AFS. RAFFC. w/o 5.10.55.
WK858 19 Sqn. w/o 18.3.53.
WK859 43 Sqn. 19 Sqn. 610 Sqn (G). F/R for conv to U.16 27.10.61.
WK860 211 AFS/4 FTS (18). Scrap 13.5.58.
WK861 222 Sqn. Scrap 28.5.59.
WK862 600 Sqn. Scrap 7.9.59.
WK863 245 Sqn (S). w/o 5.3.54.
WK864 616 Sqn (G). APS Sylt. Scrap 21.11.63 remains to Lasham.
WK865 Wing Leader Metropolitan Sector. Scrap 4.3.58
WK866 211 AFS. Scrap 17.5.58.
WK867 211 AFS. F/R for conv to U.16 14.4.59. Llanbedr.
WK868 257 Sqn. 615 Sqn. To Syria 13.6.56 as 415.
WK869 222 Sqn. 610 Sqn (D). Scrap 7.8.59.
WK870 211 AFS. F/R for conv to U.16 10.3.59. 728B Sqn.
WK871 43 Sqn. 72 Sqn. 19 Sqn. 500 Sqn. Scrap 11.3.59.
WK872 211 AFS/4 FTS. Scrap 27.3.58.
WK873 43 Sqn. APS. soc 8.5.58.
WK874 247 Sqn (L). w/o 4.10.56.
WK875 211 AFS. Scrap 17.1.58.
WK876 247 Sqn (F). 4 FTS. RAFFC. CAW (A). NEA 3.9.71. To Manston dump 31.7.72.
WK877 54 Sqn. 56 Sqn. F/R for U.16 conv 20.10.61.
WK878 MOS. soc 31.12.57.
WK879 54 Sqn. F/R for conv to U.21 15.9.60. WRE.
WK880 245 Sqn (Q). Scrap 24.4.58.
WK881 245 Sqn (V). APS Sylt. Scrap 30.10.63.
WK882 245 Sqn (X). Scrap 4.3.58.
WK883 616 Sqn (J). F/R for conv to U.16 9.1.62.
WK884 616 Sqn. 5 CAACU. Scrap 17.12.63.
WK885 CGS. RAFFC. 211 AFS. RAFFC. F/R for conv to U.16 14.3.61.
WK886 245 Sqn. w/o 4.11.53.
WK887 64 Sqn. Duxford Stn Flt (JH/PW). 65 Sqn. 229 OCU. Geilenkirchen Stn Flt. 85 Sqn (S/Y). NEA 3.9.71. To Manston dump 31.7.72.
WK888 41 Sqn. 71 MU 21.6.55 after display at Royal Tournament. To 10 STT as 7217M.
WK889 CGS. FWS. Scrap 12.3.58.
WK890 245 Sqn (A). Scrap 2.6.59.
WK891 245 Sqn. w/o 5.3.54.
WK892 41 Sqn. 34 Sqn. 245 Sqn (R). Scrap 2.6.59.
WK893 245 Sqn (G). Scrap 4.3.58.
WK906 211 AFS. w/o 8.6.54.
WK907 To RAAF 28.1.53 as A77-878. 77 Sqn. 78 Wing. Instructional airframe 4.6.58. To RAAF Villawood, Sydney, for display.
WK908 1 Sqn. Scrap 2.6.59.
WK909 To RAAF 19.12.52 as A77-874. 77 Sqn. 78 Wing. Instructional airframe 4.6.58. To Wagga-Wagga gate.
WK910 To RAAF 10.3.53 as A77-880. 77 Sqn. Scrap 14.1.59.
WK911 263 Sqn. 34 Sqn (M). APS. FWS. F/R for conv to U.16 9.11.61.
WK912 To RAAF 31.3.53 as A77-883. 77 Sqn. 78 Wing 22 Sqn. Scrap 14.10.59.
WK913 To RAAF 21.3.53 as A77-877. 77 Sqn. 78 Wing. 22 Sqn. w/o 23.6.59.
WK914 19 Sqn (B). 5 CAACU. RAFFC. CAW (H). 85 Sqn (Y). NEA 28.11.72. To Manston dump 2.3.73. To RAes Medway Branch for restoration 1981.
WK915 CGS. FWS. Cat.5(C) 14.7.55.
WK916 1 Sqn. 34 Sqn. 219 Sqn (X). w/o 26.7.57.
WK917 1 Sqn. w/o 27.7.53.
WK918 222 Sqn. 56 Sqn. 253 Sqn. 153 Sqn. 25 Sqn. Scrap 27.3.59.
WK919 4 STT. Wattisham. 263 Sqn (Q). Scrap 12.8.59.
WK920 211 AFS. Cat.5(C) 2.55.
WK921 222 Sqn. 29 Sqn (K). Scrap 1.4.63.
WK922 211 AFS. Scrap 17.1.58.
WK923 226 OCU. FWS. Scrap 4.3.58.
WK924 211 AFS. w/o 4.2.53.
WK925 211 AFS. F/R for conv to U.16 19.3.59. Llanbedr.
WK926 TRE. Conv to U.16 1960.
WK927 616 Sqn. 12 Grp Com Flt. Scrap 27.7.59.
WK928 245 Sqn (C). Stradishall Stn Flt. Scrap 5.8.59.
WK929 211 AFS. w/o 19.5.53.
WK930 CGS. APS Sylt. To Wattisham dump 18.7.62.
WK931 To RAAF 24.4.53 as A77-884. Conv to U.21A Destroyed 3.11.68.
WK932 245 Sqn (GMS). F/R for conv to U.16 9.1.62.
WK933 TTF. Nicosia. w/o 10.6.55.
WK934 19 Sqn. 245 Sqn (G/T). Scrap 10.4.59.
WK935 IAM. Conv to prone-pilot Meteor. AHB 12.1.65 as 7869M at Colerne. To St Athan museum. To Cosford Aerospace museum.
WK936 245 Sqn (H). w/o 9.8.54.
WK937 To RAAF 27.3.53 as A77-882. 77 Sqn. 78 Wing 23 Sqn. Surplus 17.10.60. Conv to U.21A. Destroyed 13.10.68.
WK938 To RAAF 18.5.53 as A77-886. 77 Sqn. 78 Wing. Instructional airframe 4.6.58.
WK939 222 Sqn. w/o 5.10.53.
WK940 Levant Com Flt. soc 8.4.59.
WK941 245 Sqn. 222 Sqn. 609 Sqn. 33 Sqn. 229 OCU (E). F/R for conv to U.16 16.5.72. Llanbedr (T).
WK942 CFE (AWDS) (ET). 63 Sqn (N). F/R for conv to U.16 4.5.60. Llanbedr.
WK943 257 Sqn (N). 34 Sqn. 46 Sqn. Odiham Stn Flt 11 Grp Com Flt (VSB) flown by AVM V.S.Bowling. Scrap 29.3.63.
WK944 To RAAF 10.3.53 as A77-881. 77 Sqn. Surplus 19.9.57. Fire practice airframe 26.10.61.
WK945 TTF Nicosia. Scrap 11.2.58.
WK946 TTF Nicosia. Habbaniya Stn Flt. soc 25.2.58.
WK947 245 Sqn (W). Scrap 26.5.59.
WK948 TTF Nicosia (E). Scrap 12.5.58.
WK949 TTF Nicosia. Command reserve Nicosia. Levant Com Flt. 208 Sqn. F/R for U.16 conv 14.2.61
WK950 245 Sqn (P). Scrap 14.4.59.
WK951 41 Sqn (S). 600 Sqn (Y). Scrap 10.4.59.
WK952 TTF Nicosia. Command reserve Nicosia. Levant Com Flt. soc 27.7.60.
WK953 TTF Nicosia. Command reserve Nicosia. Levant Com Flt. 208 Sqn. soc 11.9.57.
WK954 TTF Nicosia. Levant Com Flt. soc 11.6.59.
WK955 TTF Nicosia. 208 Sqn. Scrap 19.12.57.
WK966 64 Sqn. w/o 23.8.53.
WK967 CGS. FWS. Scrap 4.3.58.
WK968 64 Sqn (F). 63 Sqn (N). 56 Sqn. 46 Sqn. RAFFC. CAW (A/C). NEA 10.7.69. To Odiham gate 1.1.70.
WK969 12 Grp Com Flt (RGD). Scrap 12.8.59.
WK970 64 Sqn. 65 Sqn. Scrap 29.6.59.
WK971 TTF Nicosia. Levant Com Flt. 208 Sqn. F/R for conv to U.16 29.11.61.
WK972 CGS. FWS (S). Scrap 4.3.58.
WK973 To RAAF 1.5.53 as A77-885. 77 Sqn. 78 Wing. 23 Sqn. Surplus 17.10.60. Conv to U.21A. Burnt at Elizabeth Field 10.65.
WK974 72 Sqn (E). 19 Sqn (A). 609 Sqn. Scrap 26.5.59
WK975 TTF Nicosia. 208 Sqn. Scrap 19.12.57.
WK976 TTF Nicosia. Scrap 12.5.58.
WK977 72 Sqn (Y). 19 Sqn. 601 Sqn. Scrap 10.4.59.
WK978 64 Sqn. w/o 22.7.53.
WK979 74 Sqn. FCCS, flown by C-in-C Fighter Command, Dermot Boyle (DB) 1953. Scrap 29.3.63.
WK980 CGS. 79 Sqn. F/R for conv to U.16 20.4.60. Llanbedr.
WK981 FCCS. w/o 14.6.57.
WK982 CGS. FWS. w/o 14.8.55.
WK983 CGS. FWS. Cat.5(C) 7.3.57.
WK984 257 Sqn. 615 Sqn (B). To Syria 13.6.56 as 416.
WK985 1 Sqn (C). APS. 608 Sqn. Missing 27.8.56.
WK986 64 Sqn (P). Metropolitan Sector. North Weald Stn Flt. 11 Grp Com Flt. FCCS. Scrap 12.3.63.
WK987 65 Sqn (D). Scrap 29.6.58.
WK988 610 Sqn (JAS). APS Sylt (K). To Ternhill dump 19.8.62.
WK989 1 Sqn. F/R for conv to U.16 13.12.61.
WK990 19 Sqn. 601 Sqn. Scrap 10.4.59.
WK991 Northern Sector (VSB/ES). 13 Grp Com Flt. 46 Sqn (V). 56 Sqn. NEA 15.4.61. To IWM 10.12.63. To Duxford. Allocated 7825M.
WK992 211 AFS/4 FTS. Scrap 14.4.59.
WK993 247 Sqn. 1 Sqn. 34 Sqn. F/R for conv to U.16 6.4.60.
WK994 66 Sqn. Linton Stn Flt. 222 Sqn. 43 Sqn (X). F/R for conv to U.16 11.4.60.
WL104 19 Sqn (N). 85 Sqn. 229 OCU. Scrap 29.6.59.
WL105 41 Sqn. 34 Sqn. 2 Sqn. soc 31.8.55.
WL106 41 Sqn (J). 600 Sqn. 615 Sqn. 41 Sqn. Waterbeach Stn Flt (T4). 25 Sqn. CFE (DFCS). FBS. 85 Sqn (Y). soc 21.6.66 to Binbrook dump.
WL107 19 Sqn (P). 609 Sqn. Scrap 10.4.59.
WL108 257 Sqn. Wattisham Stn Flt. 263 Sqn. 152 Sqn. 89 Sqn. 1 Sqn. Scrap 23.12.63.
WL109 19 Sqn. 600 Sqn. APS Sylt (H). soc for fire practice 17.9.62.
WL110 610 Sqn. Hooton Park Stn Flt. F/R for conv to U.16 1.3.61.
WL111 41 Sqn (B). MOA for U.16 spares 20.12.61.
WL112 41 Sqn. To 1 STT 1.8.55 as 7259M.
WL113 263 Sqn (N). Colerne Com Sqn. 66 Sqn. 29 Sqn (L). 43 Sqn. Scrap 7.3.63.
WL114 43 Sqn. w/o 24.7.54.
WL115 263 Sqn (R). 1 Sqn. 111 Sqn. Scrap 20.3.63.
WL116 65 Sqn (O). Turnhouse Com Sqn (RCH). To Scrap 29.6.59.

METEOR F.8 *continued*

WL117 19 Sqn. 72 Sqn (J). 19 Sqn. Used by Church Fenton TT Flt (1). soc 28.9.62 for display, but then scrapped at 5 MU.
WL118 111 Sqn (L). 604 Sqn. Scrap 12.5.58.
WL119 263 Sqn. w/o 14.12.53.
WL120 43 Sqn. 72 Sqn. 19 Sqn. 600 Sqn. APS Sylt. soc for fire practice 31.8.62.
WL121 111Sqn (E). 604 Sqn (S). APS Sylt. To Tangmere dump 27.7.62.
WL122 111 Sqn (G). 601 Sqn. APS Sylt. To Catterick 3.8.62.
WL123 111 Sqn (H). Scrap 27.7.59.
WL124 111 Sqn (L). 604 Sqn. F/R for conv to U.16 13.4.60. Llanbedr.
WL125 72 Sqn. 226 OCU. To 1 STT 5.55 as 7210M.
WL126 72 Sqn. 19 Sqn. 615 Sqn. Scrap 10.4.59.
WL127 111 Sqn (J). 604 Sqn (B). F/R for conv to U.16 4.5.60. 728B Sqn.
WL128 111 Sqn. w/o 3.4.54.
WL129 111 Sqn (P). 601 Sqn. Scrap 13.5.58.
WL130 111 Sqn (R). 601 Sqn. 33 Sqn. Scrap 2.1.64.
WL131 111 Sqn (S). 601 Sqn. APS Sylt. Scrap 16.11.62, allocated 7751M, nose section to Ternhill.
WL132 604 Sqn (F). w/o 18.7.54.
WL133 19 Sqn. w/o 21.11.55.
WL134 41 Sqn. Biggin Hill Stn Flt (PT). 615 Sqn (A). MOA for U.16 spares 28.11.61.
WL135 245 Sqn. Scrap 26.5.59.
WL136 257 Sqn. 64 Sqn (C). 229 OCU. F/R for conv to U.21 20.9.60. WRE.
WL137 19 Sqn. w/o 5.10.56.
WL138 72 Sqn. 19 Sqn. w/o 4.6.56.
WL139 257 Sqn. 64 Sqn. w/o 19.10.54. Front fuselage to 71 MU for ground instruction.
WL140 263 Sqn (G). 1 Sqn. Scrap 14.9.59.
WL141 257 Sqn (HNT). 64 Sqn. 65 Sqn (H). w/o 29.11.55.
WL142 1 Sqn. APS Sylt. w/o 4.8.59.
WL143 257 Sqn. 54 Sqn (Z). Scrap 1.1.64.
WL158 54 Sqn. w/o 9.8.55.
WL159 263 Sqn (A). 1 Sqn. 85 Sqn. To Cottesmore dump 8.11.62.
WL160 111 Sqn (W). 601 Sqn. F/R for conv to U.16 21.3.60. Llanbedr.
WL161 604 Sqn. RAFFC. CAW (D). To Catterick 16.8.72, most of the airframe later to Brunel College, Bristol.
WL162 41 Sqn. 615 Sqn (J). 600 Sqn. F/R for conv to U.16 25.4.60. Llanbedr.
WL163 74 Sqn (J). F/R for conv to U.16 21.3.61.
WL164 74 Sqn (X). Scrap 7.3.63.
WL165 500 Sqn. 1 Sqn. 64 Sqn. 65 Sqn (A). Scrap 14.9.59.
WL166 616 Sqn (B/KB). RAFFC. CAW. To Catterick 2.11.72.
WL167 111 Sqn (N). 601 Sqn. Scrap 1.5.58.
WL168 111 Sqn (X). 604 Sqn. APS Sylt. To 35 MU for display 10.5.62, allocated 7750M. To Finningley museum painted as WH456 (L). To Swinderby 1977. St Athan 1979, repainted as WL168. 111 Sqn (A).
WL169 41 Sqn. Biggin Hill Stn Flt (DGS). 34 Sqn (C). 500 Sqn (V/'Dover/Maidstone'). Scrap 17.8.59.
WL170 1 Sqn (N). 64 Sqn (Y). Scrap 7.3.63.
WL171 FETS. Kai Tak. 45/33 Sqn. APC. SHQ Seletar. soc 31.1.61.
WL172 19 Sqn. Cat.5(S) 28.11.55.
WL173 245 Sqn. Horsham St Faith Flt (JH). Scrap 14.9.59.
WL174 Tangmere Stn Flt. 34 Sqn. To GAC 14.12.55. To Syria 26.3.56 as 414.
WL175 Tangmere Stn Flt. 34 Sqn (B). 500 Sqn (M/ 'Bexley'). Scrap 14.8.59.
WL176 1 Sqn. 34 Sqn (RIKE). 1 Sqn. FCCS. Scrap 24.4.59.
WL177 1 Sqn. 64 Sqn (H). 65 Sqn (F). w/o 17.4.57 at Duxford.
WL178 72 Sqn (K). w/o 7.7.55.
WL179 41 Sqn. Scrap 29.6.59.
WL180 FEAF Trng Sqn. APC. 45/33 Sqn. APC. SHQ Butterworth. FECS. B & TT Seletar. 1574 Flt. Transferred to COMFEF RN 26.7.71.
WL181 Tangmere Stn Flt. 34 Sqn. RAFFC CAW (G). Acklington dump 2.72.To NEVVAS museum 18.3.75.
WL182 601 Sqn. Scrap 14.8.59.
WL183 To GAC 28.2.55. To Egypt 19.5.55 as 1423.
WL184 601 Sqn. Scrap 14.8.59.
WL185 To GAC 9.3.55. To Egypt 6.6.55 as 1424.
WL186 To GAC 18.2.55. To Egypt 19.5.55 as 1421.
WL187 To GAC 28.2.55. To Egypt 6.6.55 as 1425.
WL188 To GAC 28.2.55. To Egypt 18.4.55 as 1419.
WL189 APS Sylt. Scrap 30.10.63.
WL190 34 Sqn. 219 Sqn. RAFFC. soc 9.8.63.
WL191 To GAC 4.3.55. To Egypt 6.6.55 as 1426.

METEOR FR.9

VW360 GAC. A & AEE. Ferranti. To PEE 2.9.57.
VW361 208 Sqn. Scrap 11.2.58.
VW362 CS (A).
VW363 208 Sqn (O). Scrap 3.1.58.
VW364 CSDE. 2 Sqn (D). To 4 STT 30.11.56 as 7383M. To South Cerney dump 25.10.65.
VW365 2 Sqn. w/o 18.12.52.
VW366 CFE. To Ecuador 16.8.54 as 703.
VW367 208 Sqn. AHQ Malta. Scrap 31.10.57.
VW368 208 Sqn (S). w/o 5.2.53.
VW369 Fayid Stn Flt. 208 Sqn. Scrap 5.9.57.
VW370 208 Sqn (A). w/o 24.3.57.
VW371 2 Sqn. 79 Sqn. Scrap 8.6.56.
VZ577 2 Sqn. 208 Sqn. Scrap 17.4.57.
VZ578 208 Sqn (R). Scrap 11.2.58.
VZ579 Fayid. 208 Sqn (M). Scrap 5.9.57.
VZ580 2 Sqn. w/o 29.1.53.
VZ581 208 Sqn. w/o 17.9.51.
VZ582 208 Sqn. Scrap 5.5.54.
VZ583 208 Sqn (N). w/o 17.6.52.
VZ584 208 Sqn. Scrap 21.2.58.
VZ585 2 Sqn. w/o 15.2.51.
VZ586 2 Sqn. 79 Sqn. 208 Sqn. Scrap 20.2.58.
VZ587 2 Sqn. w/o 4.12.51.
VZ588 208 Sqn. Scrap 21.2.55 following flying accident.
VZ589 208 Sqn. w/o 24.10.51.
VZ590 2 Sqn. 79 Sqn. Scrap 7.2.58.
VZ591 208 Sqn. w/o 21.2.52.
VZ592 208 Sqn (B). Scrap 14.12.56.
VZ593 208 Sqn. Scrap 7.2.58.
VZ594 208 Sqn. w/o 30.11.53.
VZ595 Fayid. 208 Sqn. Scrap 5.9.57.
VZ596 2 Sqn. Scrap 22.6.56.
VZ597 To Ecuador 9.7.54 as 701.
VZ598 208 Sqn. Scrap 21.2.58.
VZ599 2 Sqn. 208 Sqn. soc 11.9.57.
VZ600 79 Sqn. w/o 24.2.54.
VZ601 2 Sqn. 208 Sqn. 8 Sqn. FR Flt (Z). Scrap 31.3.60.
VZ602 226 OCU 208 Sqn. AHQ Malta. Scrap 31.10.57
VZ603 2 Sqn (B-A). 79 Sqn. 208 Sqn. 8 Sqn. Khormaksar Stn Flt. FR Flt (W). Scrap 9.5.60.
VZ604 208 Sqn. Eastleigh Stn Flt. Khormaksar Stn Flt. FR Flt (V). Scrap 9.5.60.
VZ605 2 Sqn (B-S). Scrap 30.12.57.
VZ606 208 Sqn (Z). Scrap 21.2.58.
VZ607 2 Sqn. 79 Sqn (T-S). Scrap 5.9.57.
VZ608 Rolls-Royce. soc 29.9.65. To Newark Air Museum.
VZ609 79 Sqn. 2 Sqn. Scrap 13.4.56.
VZ610 To Ecuador 13.9.54 as 705
VZ611 2 Sqn (B-Z). w/o 17.11.54.
WB113 2 Sqn. 79 Sqn. w/o 24.7.53.
WB114 2 Sqn. w/o 9.8.51.
WB115 79 Sqn. 2 Grp Com Flt. 2 Sqn. 79 Sqn. To CD training 13.11.58 as 7593M.
WB116 79 Sqn. 2 Sqn (B-G), later G). To 10STT 6.12.56 as 7384M.
WB117 208 Sqn. w/o 4.4.53.
WB118 2 Sqn. 79 Sqn. w/o 31.10.53.
WB119 79 Sqn. w/o 5.5.52.
WB120 208 Sqn. w/o 4.6.52.
WB121 79 Sqn. 208 Sqn. To Malta for ground instruction. Scrap 25.2.58.
WB122 79 Sqn (D). w/o 7.9.55.
WB123 79 Sqn. 2 Sqn. To Israel 15.3.55 as 213.
WB124 79 Sqn. 2 Sqn (B-V). w/o 11.5.56.
WB125 226 OCU. 208 Sqn. w/o 18.8.56.
WB133 79 Sqn. 2 Sqn. To Syria 17.7.56 as 480.
WB134 RAE Farnborough. To PEE 31.10.57.
WB135 79 Sqn. Scrap 14.8.57.
WB136 79 Sqn. To Ecuador 23.8.54 as 704.
WB137 226 OCU. 2 Sqn. Scrap 14.8.57.
WB138 226 OCU. 79 Sqn. 208 Sqn. Scrap 17.4.57.
WB139 79 Sqn. w/o 22.7.52.
WB140 79 Sqn. To Israel 15.3.55 as 214.
WB141 79 Sqn. 208 Sqn. soc 25.2.58.
WB142 79 Sqn. w/o 17.2.53.
WB143 2 Sqn (B-U). w/o 8.4.54.
WH533 79 Sqn. Scrap 5.9.57.
WH534 79 Sqn. Scrap 7.2.58.
WH535 CS (A). Scrap 6.9.57.
WH536 226 OCU. 79 Sqn. Scrap 4.8.57.
WH537 Wg Ldr Gutersloh. 79 Sqn. Scrap 5.9.57.
WH538 208 Sqn. w/o 8.4.54.
WH539 79 Sqn. 2 Sqn. 79 Sqn. 208 Sqn. 8 Sqn (Y). Khormaksar Stn Flt (R). w/o 1.10.58.
WH540 To Ecuador 15.9.54 as 706.
WH541 2 Sqn. 208 Sqn. Scrap 21.10.57.
WH542 2 Sqn (B-K). w/o 15.3.56.
WH543 To Ecuador 29.9.54 as 707.
WH544 79 Sqn. 208 Sqn. Scrap 4.11.57.
WH545 79 Sqn. FR Flt. Scrap 9.5.60.
WH546 79 Sqn. FR Flt. Display a/c at Khormaksar 1.9.61. Inst.63.
WH547 To Ecuador 14.7.54 as 702.
WH548 2 Sqn. Scrap 30.12.57.
WH549 To Ecuador 23.9.54 as 708.
WH550 To Ecuador 7.10.54 as 709.
WH551 208 Sqn. 8 Sqn. Khormaksar Stn Flt (X). Scrap 30.8.59.
WH552 79 Sqn. 2 Sqn (B-E). Scrap 16.9.57.
WH553 To Ecuador 20.10.54 as 710.
WH554 To Ecuador 29.10.54 as 711.
WH555 To Ecuador 19.11.54 as 712.
WH556 208 Sqn (X). Scrap 5.9.57.
WH557 79 Sqn. Scrap 14.8.57.
WL255 79 Sqn. 2 Sqn. 79 Sqn. Scrap 7.2.58.
WL256 79 Sqn. To Maintenance Command S of TT, Aston Down 29.10.57 as 7477M. Scrap 31.8.59.
WL257 79 Sqn. Scrap 30.12.57.
WL258 208 Sqn. Scrap 31.10.57.
WL259 To Israel 4.5.55 as 212.
WL260 79 Sqn. Scrap 30.12.57.
WL261 79 Sqn. 208 Sqn. Scrap 15.10.57.
WL262 79 Sqn. w/o 23.9.55.
WL263 79 Sqn. 208 Sqn (O). Eastleigh Stn Flt. FR Flt. Scrap 9.5.60.
WL264 79 Sqn. Scrap 1.3.61.
WL265 79 Sqn. w/o 24.6.55.
WX962 208 Sqn (Q). Scrap 7.2.58.
WX963 To Israel 17.12.54 as 216.
WX964 CFE (AFDS). Scrap 7.2.58.
WX965 2 Sqn (B-Z). 79 Sqn. Scrap 7.2.58.
WX966 208 Sqn. Khormaksar Stn Flt. Scrap 15.3.60.
WX967 187 Sqn. To Israel 4.5.55 as 211.
WX968 2 Sqn. Scrap 30.12.57.
WX969 208 Sqn. Scrap 7.2.58.
WX970 208 Sqn. Scrap 14.12.56.
WX971 2 Sqn. 79 Sqn. Scrap 14.8.57.
WX972 79 Sqn. To Syria 17.7.56 as 481.
WX973 2 Sqn. 79 Sqn. w/o 16.7.53.
WX974 2 Sqn. w/o 3.12.54.
WX975 187 Sqn. To Israel 9.12.54 as 215.
WX976 208 Sqn. Scrap 17.4.57.
WX977 79 Sqn. Scrap 11.2.58.
WX978 2 Sqn (B-E). 79 Sqn. 208 Sqn (Z). 8 Sqn (Z). Khormaksar Stn Flt. Scrap 24.2.59.
WX979 CS (A). soc 27.8.58.
WX980 To Israel 22.12.54 as 217.
WX981 187 Sqn. 226 OCU. 2 Sqn. 79 Sqn. Scrap 5.9.57

METEOR PR.10

VS968 A & AEE. GAC. 541 Sqn (A-W). Scrap 7.7.58
VS969 GAC. 81 Sqn. w/o 13.10.54.
VS970 541 Sqn. 81 Sqn. Scrap 1.6.60.
VS971 Handling Sqn Manby. CSDE. 81 Sqn. w/o 2.12.58 after aborted take-off.
VS972 541 Sqn. w/o 10.6.54, mid-air collision with VS973.
VS973 541 Sqn. w/o 10.6.54.
VS974 2 Sqn. 541 Sqn. Scrap 12.9.57.
VS975 541 Sqn (WY-N, later A-N). To Kenley 19.8.58. Scrap 10.58.
VS976 541 Sqn. Scrap 12.9.57.
VS977 541 Sqn (WY-P, later A-P). Scrap 10.9.57.
VS978 541 Sqn (A-R). Scrap 10.9.57.
VS979 541 Sqn. Scrap 10.9.57.
VS980 541 Sqn. 81 Sqn. w/o 29.4.58.
VS981 541 Sqn (WY-E, later A-E). To PEE 4.11.57.
VS982 541 Sqn (WY-S, later A-S). w/o 30.11.56.
VS983 541 Sqn (WY-G, later A-G). w/o 11.2.53 while on delivery to 33 MU.
VS984 541 Sqn. Scrap 10.9.57.
VS985 541 Sqn (WY-B, later A-T). Scrap 12.9.57.
VS986 2 Sqn. 81 Sqn. w/o 5.8.55.
VS987 2 Sqn. 81 Sqn. Scrap 10.4.61.
VW376 541 Sqn (WY-C, later A-D). Scrap 10.9.57.
VW377 2 Sqn. 81 Sqn. Scrap 30.11.61.
VW378 541 Sqn (WY-D, later A-A). Scrap 7.11.58.
VW379 2 Sqn. 541 Sqn (A-O). To Kenley 27.8.58. Scrap 10.58.
VZ620 237 OCU/231 OCU. MOS 5.12.57.
WB153 237 OCU/231 OCU. 81 Sqn. Scrap 15.8.60.
WB154 2 Sqn. 541 Sqn. Scrap 10.9.57.
WB155 2 Sqn. Scrap 7.12.60.
WB156 2 Sqn. 541 Sqn (A-B). To PEE 6.60.
WB157 GAC. 231 OCU. MOS 3.1.58.
WB158 237 OCU/231 OCU. w/o 28.5.52.
WB159 81 Sqn. Scrap 7.8.61.
WB160 237 OCU/231 OCU. MOS 14.1.58.
WB161 13 Sqn. w/o 7.6.52, missing.
WB162 13 Sqn (H). To PEE 8.11.57.
WB163 RAE Farnborough. 81 Sqn. Scrap 17.9.59.
WB164 GAC. NGTE. A & AEE. GAC. Scrap 19.2.58.
WB165 13 Sqn. 81 Sqn. To ground instructional use 6.8.60. Sold to R.Malaysian AF 11.63.
WB166 13 Sqn. 81 Sqn. Scrap 30.11.61.
WB167 Allocated to FEAF but saw no sqn service. Scrap 9.3.60.
WB168 13 Sqn (G). MOS 3.1.58.
WB169 81 Sqn. w/o 21.9.55.
WB170 231 OCU. MOS 14.1.58.
WB171 Allocated to MEAF but saw no sqn service. Scrap 7.11.58.
WB172 13 Sqn (F). MOS 14.1.58.
WB173 541 Sqn. w/o 22.12.52.
WB174 13 Sqn (N). To PEE 8.11.57.
WB175 13 Sqn (L). MOS 5.12.57.
WB176 13 Sqn (J). w/o 3.4.56.
WB177 13 Sqn (C). MOS 5.12.57.
WB178 13 Sqn (D). Scrap 23.8.56.
WB179 13 Sqn. 231 OCU. To PEE 1.11.57.
WB180 13 Sqn. w/o 1.8.56.
WB181 A & AEE. 541 Sqn (A-X). To PEE 4.11.57.
WH569 13 Sqn (A). w/o 3.4.56.
WH570 541 Sqn. 2 TAF Com Flt. Scrap 31.1.62.
WH571 541 Sqn (A-Y). Scrap 7.11.58.
WH572 13 Sqn. MOS 14.1.58.
WH573 541 Sqn (A-G). Scrap 7.11.58.

METEOR NF.11

VW413 see T.7.
WA546 RAE Farnborough. A & AEE.
WA547 A & AEE.
WB543 TRE. RAE Farnborough.
WD585 CFE. 256 Sqn (B). To RN as TT.20. FRU Hurn. Scrap 7.11.66.
WD586 TRE. soc 5.9.57.
WD587 TRE. A & AEE.
WD588 CFE. MOS 15.3.54.
WD589 RAE. AWA. 256 Sqn. soc 31.3.58.
WD590 RAFFC. 1551 Sqn. To Belgium 23.2.56 as EN-19. To OO-ARZ.
WD591 CFE. 68 Sqn (M). Conv to TT.20. 1574 Flt. Scrap 12.1.71.
WD592 CSDE. 264 Sqn. 141 Sqn. 125 Sqn (D). 46 Sqn. To RN as TT.20. 728 Sqn (HF-579/HF-864). Sold to Letcher and Associates as N94749 18.6.75.
WD593 A & AEE. 151 Sqn (A). w/o 21.9.54, mid-air collision with WD643 near Leuchars.
WD594 CFE. 96 Sqn. To Belgium 23.2.56 as EN-16.
WD595 CFE. 87 Sqn (D). Scrap 5.6.56.
WD596 AWA. A & AEE. To Belgium 6.3.56 as EN-20.
WD597 29 Sqn (B). Scrap 21.5.58.
WD598 29 Sqn (T). 228 OCU. Scrap 9.6.58.
WD599 29 Sqn (P, later O). Scrap 5.6.58.
WD600 29 Sqn (S). Scrap 6.11.58.
WD601 29 Sqn. 96 Sqn (L-X, later X). Scrap 31.5.58.
WD602 29 Sqn (A). To Belgium 23.2.56 as EN-13.
WD603 29 Sqn (C). w/o 20.10.53 out of fuel nr Ford

METEOR NF.11 *continued*

WD604 A & AEE. DH.

WD605 29 Sqn (D). w/o nr Selsey Bill 20.5.55.

WD606 141 Sqn (P). Conv to TT.20. Seletar. 1574 Flt To RN. Scrap 3.5.63

WD607 141 Sqn. w/o 20.5.52, mid-air collision with WD613 near Great Yarmouth.

WD608 141 Sqn. w/o 24.7.52 near Great Yarmouth.

WD609 141 Sqn. 264 Sqn. 228 OCU. Scrap 5.6.58.

WD610 141 Sqn (T). To RN as TT.20. FRU Hurn. Scrap 7.11.66.

WD611 141 Sqn. Scrap 13.3.59.

WD612 141 Sqn (U). To RN as TT.20. 728 Sqn (HF-578/HF-865). Scrap 20.7.67.

WD613 141 Sqn (X). 85 Sqn. 29 Sqn (K). Scrap 6.5.58

WD614 85 Sqn. 228 OCU. 125 Sqn (F). 46 Sqn. Scrap 14.2.58

WD615 85 Sqn (A). 29 Sqn (Z). 228 OCU (B). Scrap 5.6.58.

WD616 85 Sqn. 29 Sqn (H). Scrap 21.5.58.

WD617 85 Sqn. 29 Sqn (M). Scrap 6.3.58.

WD618 85 Sqn. 228 OCU. Scrap 21.5.58.

WD619 85 Sqn. To France 18.1.55.

WD620 85 Sqn. 151 Sqn. Coltishall. Scrap 6.11.58.

WD621 256 Sqn. w/o 8.9.53 at Nordhorn..

WD622 96 Sqn (L-W). To Belgium 19.1.56 as EN-15.

WD623 151 Sqn (S). 68 Sqn. 5 Sqn (S). Conv to TT.20. Changi. 1574 Flt. Scrap 24.10.68.

WD624 96 Sqn. 256 Sqn. Scrap 30.1.59.

WD625 85 Sqn (R). 29 Sqn (R). Scrap 21.3.58.

WD626 CFE. 228 OCU. Scrap 12.2.59.

WD627 96 Sqn (L-E). Scrap 8.7.59.

WD628 96 Sqn. To France 15.11.54.

WD629 151 Sqn (C). 125 Sqn (V). 5 Sqn (G). Conv to TT.20. Handling Sqn. 1574 Slt. Scrap 12.1.71.

WD630 151 Sqn (D). 125 Sqn (W). 5 Sqn. Conv to TT.20. 3/4 CAACU (Q). Scrap 24.3.75.

WD631 256 Sqn. To France 11.8.54.

WD632 256 Sqn (T-Y). w/o 16.8.55, engine cut on take-off at Sylt.

WD633 96 Sqn (L-S, later S). Scrap 31.3.58.

WD634 87 Sqn. RAE. Scrap 20.3.59.

WD640 151 Sqn (C/O). Scrap 13.3.59.

WD641 29 Sqn (C). 256 Sqn. 11 Sqn. Conv to TT.20. MoA. 1574 Flt. Scrap 12.1.71.

WD642 256 Sqn (A). Scrap 30.10.58.

WD643 151 Sqn (L). To RN as TT.20. 728 Sqn (HF-585). Scrap 11.66.

WD644 141 Sqn (W). Scrap 5.6.58.

WD645 Odiham. 256 Sqn (T-H/T-M). Conv to TT.20 for RN, but loaned to RAF. Seletar. 1574 Flt. Scrap 7.8.63.

WD646 CSE. Conv to TT.20. Lossiemouth Handling Sqn. 8 CAACU. 5 CAACU (R). To Sheldon ATC as 8189M (not carried) 12.71.

WD647 141 Sqn (Q). 264 Sqn (S). 141 Sqn. Conv to TT.20. 3/4 CAACU (S). Woomera 12.71. To Queensland Museum 15.7.75.

WD648 264 Sqn. CFE (FDH). w/o 10.10.52 at West Raynham during take-off.

WD649 264 Sqn (C). 226 OCU. 125 Sqn (A). 46 Sqn. To RN as TT.20. FRU Hurn (043/843). To France 11.12.74 as F-ZABD.

WD650 264 Sqn. 228 OCU. w/o 23.3.55 while on approach near Leeming.

WD651 68 Sqn (T). Scrap 31.10.57.

WD652 264 Sqn (E). To RN as TT.20. FRU Hurn (042/840). To France 3.12.74 as F-ZABD.

WD653 264 Sqn. w/o 7.1.52, out of fuel nr Leeming.

WD654 264 Sqn. w/o 21.1.53, out of fuel nr Shipton.

WD655 264 Sqn (A). To France 4.9.54. (rejected by RN as poss TT.20).

WD656 68 Sqn (S). Scrap 6.5.58.

WD657 264 Sqn (D). 226 OCU. 125 Sqn (B). 46 Sqn. To RN as TT.20. FRU Hurn (041). 700 Sqn (041). FRU (041/042). Scrap 11.66.

WD658 87 Sqn (A). Scrap 12.5.58.

WD659 68 Sqn. w/o 21.8.53 on take-off from Wahn.

WD660 264 Sqn (L). 228 OCU. Scrap 6.5.58.

WD661 264 Sqn (M). To Belgium 6.3.56 as EN-18.

WD662 87 Sqn (B). Scrap 31.10.57.

WD663 68 Sqn. 96 Sqn. 5 Sqn (C). Scrap 24.1.62.

WD664 68 Sqn (H). 5 Sqn. Scrap 30.9.59.

WD665 264 Sqn. 87 Sqn (X). Scrap 6.5.58.

WD666 87 Sqn. w/o 21.9.52, overshot at Fassberg.

WD667 68 Sqn (E). Scrap 12.2.59.

WD668 68 Sqn (G). 5 Sqn (G). Scrap 31.1.62.

WD669 87 Sqn. To France 12.5.54.

WD670 MoS. AFEE. Ferranti.

WD671 96 Sqn. 256 Sqn. Scrap 4.1.57.

WD672 96 Sqn (L-C/C/U). Scrap 13.4.59.

WD673 87 Sqn (F). Scrap 30.10.58.

WD674 87 Sqn. To France 11.8.54.

WD675 87 Sqn. soc 20.1.53.

WD676 87 Sqn. 68 Sqn. w/o 19.3.53, spun in, Polder, Holland.

WD677 68 Sqn (O/G). Scrap 12.3.58. (rejected by RN as poss TT.20).

WD678 68 Sqn. To RN as TT.20. Loan to RAF. Seletar Stn Flt. Seletar Stn and TT Flt. Scrap 7.8.63.

WD679 87 Sqn. Conv to TT.20. 3/4 CAACU (T). w/o 16.7.68 at Exeter on overshoot.

WD680 68 Sqn (B). Scrap 6.11.58.

WD681 87 Sqn. soc 6.3.53.

WD682 87 Sqn. 68 Sqn. w/o 26.9.55, mid-air collision with WH236 near Bonn.

WD683 256 Sqn. To France 21.7.54.

WD684 68 Sqn. 87 Sqn (W). Scrap 3.7.57.

WD685 87 Sqn. w/o 21.9.52, while on approach to Fassberg.

WD686 TRE. RAE Bedford. To IWM, Duxford 1.74.

WD687 MOS. A & AEE. Conv to NF.12 standard. Scrapped at Stansted

WD688 87 Sqn (T). Scrap 6.3.58.

WD689 256 Sqn. Scrap 12.2.59.

WD696 96 Sqn (L-B, later B). Scrap 5.6.58.

WD697 96 Sqn (L-Y/Y). Scrap 16.4.59.

WD698 96 Sqn. To France 7.7.54.

WD699 96 Sqn. (L-Z/Z). Scrap 7.9.59.

WD700 68 Sqn (C). Scrap 21.3.59.

WD701 256 Sqn. To France 4.9.59

WD702 228 OCU. 256 Sqn. 11 Sqn. 5 Sqn (E). Conv to TT.20. 3/4 CAACU (U). To Valley as 8149M 10.71 To Conway scrapyard.

WD703 228 OCU. 29 Sqn (K). Scrap 12.2.59.

WD704 256 Sqn. Scrap 31.8.58.

WD705 228 OCU. To MoS 27.6.58.

WD706 228 OCU (B). To RN as TT.20. A & AEE. Returned to RAF. 3/4 CAACU (T). Scrap 1975.

WD707 96 Sqn. 256 Sqn. To 7599M 2.59.

WD708 228 OCU. Scrap 5.6.58.

WD709 228 OCU. 29 Sqn. Scrap 12.2.59.

WD710 264 Sqn (O/P/Q). 228 OCU. 29 Sqn (G). Scrap 5.6.58.

WD711 228 OCU. 125 Sqn (G). To RN as TT.20. 728 Sqn (HF-579). w/o 14.10.60, off Linosa, Malta.

WD712 29 Sqn. w/o 24.4.52 after fire following a bird strike.

WD713 228 OCU. w/o Leeming 30.3.53 after belly-landing.

WD714 228 OCU. w/o 19.8.52 after mid-air collision with WD772.

WD715 29 Sqn (V/W). Scrap 12.2.59.

WD716 228 OCU. w/o 19.7.52 after engine failure and crashed off Whitby.

WD717 228 OCU. Scrap 5.6.58.

WD718 228 OCU (K). Scrap 7.8.58.

WD719 228 OCU. Scrap 12.2.59.

WD720 228 OCU. Scrap 12.5.58.

WD721 MoS. A & AEE. 96 Sqn (W). 68 Sqn. Scrap 6.11.58.

WD722 29 Sqn (E). Scrap 5.6.58.

WD723 228 OCU. w/o 17.11.52, blew up off Sunderland

WD724 264 Sqn (F). To Belgium 9.2.56 as EN-14.

WD725 29 Sqn (F). w/o 15.4.57 on during take-off at Acklington.

WD726 To Belgium 25.7.52 as EN-1.

WD727 To Belgium 26.8.52 as EN-7. w/o 27.4.53.

WD728 To Belgium 22.8.52 as EN-4. w/o 12.7.54.

WD729 To Belgium 22.8.52 as EN-5. To OO-ARW.

WD730 To Belgium 22.8.52 as EN-6. To OO-ARO.

WD731 To Belgium 26.8.52 as EN-8. w/o 12.4.56.

WD732 To Belgium 26.8.52 as EN-9. w/o 25.11.54.

WD733 To Belgium 17.9.52 as EN-10. w/o 1.8.57.

WD734 87 Sqn. 68 Sqn. w/o 28.5.52 during take-off from Wahn.

WD735 To Belgium 22.9.52 as EN-11. To OO-ARX.

WD736 To Belgium 24.2.53 as EN-12.

WD737 256 Sqn. 68 Sqn (N). Scrap 13.4.59.

WD738 151 Sqn (W). 228 OCU. 151 Sqn. 125 Sqn (E). 46 Sqn. Scrap 7.8.58.

WD739 228 OCU. 29 Sqn. Scrap 21.3.58.

WD740 228 OCU. 141 Sqn. 68 Sqn. 5 Sqn. Laarbruch Stn Flt. Scrap 16.10.61.

WD741 228 OCU. To Belgium 22.2.56 as EN-21.

WD742 228 OCU. 29 Sqn (L). Scrap 5.6.58.

WD743 Fairey Aviation.

WD744 RRE. Fairey Aviation.

WD745 Fairey Aviation.

WD751 228 OCU (I). Scrap 6.5.58.

WD752 228 OCU. 5 Sqn (H). Scrap 24.1.62.

WD753 228 OCU. Scrap 31.3.58.

WD754 228 OCU. 256 Sqn. w/o 21.4.55 on take-off from Oldenburg.

WD755 228 OCU. w/o 1.9.52 during take-off from Leeming.

WD756 228 OCU. To France 11.8.54.

WD757 228 OCU. 81 Grp Com Sqn. 228 OCU. w/o 9.12.52 belly-landing at Linton-on-Ouse

WD758 228 OCU. Scrap 12.2.55.

WD759 228 OCU. 68 Sqn (A). 5 Sqn (A). Scrap 31.1.62.

WD760 228 OCU (K). To Belgium 5.3.56 as EN-17.

WD761 228 OCU. w/o 2.12.52 near Boroughbridge after engine failure.

WD762 29 Sqn (X). Scrap 6.5.57.

WD763 85 Sqn (F/H). 151 Sqn (Y). To Belgium 20.1.56 as EN-22. w/o 13.3.56.

WD764 228 OCU. Scrap 6.5.58.

WD765 228 OCU. ETPS (5/6). w/o 20.10.58 Basingstoke

WD766 228 OCU (G). Scrap 5.6.58.

WD767 Conv to TT.20. A & AEE. RAE Llanbedr. To Woomera 1970. To Mildura museum 10.7.75.

WD768 228 OCU. 29 Sqn (C). Scrap 21.5.58.

WD769 ETPS (1). Scrap 1959.

WD770 141 Sqn (S). w/o 11.3.53, belly-landed at Wyton

WD771 228 OCU. 96 Sqn. 256 Sqn. 5 Sqn. Scrap 24.1.62.

WD772 228 OCU. w/o 19.8.52, mid-air collision with WD714, near Stanhope.

WD773 96 Sqn. 256 Sqn (T-D). Scrap 12.2.59.

WD774 87 Sqn (C). Scrap 31.10.57.

WD775 To Belgium 30.7.52 as EN-2. To OO-ARR.

WD776 96 Sqn. 256 Sqn. 68 Sqn (D). 5 Sqn (D). Scrap 31.1.62.

WD777 To Belgium 30.7.52 as EN-3. w/o 1.12.53.

WD778 96 Sqn. 228 OCU. w/o 24.3.54 while on approach to Leeming.

WD779 96 Sqn. 256 Sqn (E). Scrap 13.4.59.

WD780 228 OCU. Coltishall Stn Flt. 151 Sqn (R). To RN as TT.20. FRU Hurn (044). To France 3.12.74 as F-ZABD.

WD781 96 Sqn. 256 Sqn. Scrap 23.2.59.

WD782 Fairey Aviation. Ferranti.

WD783 264 Sqn. To France 2.6.54.

WD784 96 Sqn (L-F). Scrap 12.2.59.

WD785 527 Sqn (Z). To RN as TT.20. 728 Sqn (HF-582/HF-866). FRU Hurn (846). To Bicester dump 7.70.

WD786 228 OCU. 29 Sqn (A). Scrap 5.6.58.

WD787 151 Sqn (T). 29 Sqn (Z). Scrap 6.5.58.

WD788 96 Sqn. w/o 11.9.53 hit tress while on approach to Ahlhorn.

WD789 87 Sqn. w/o 26.3.53, hit vehicle while landing at Wahn.

WD790 TRE. Ferranti. Mod to NF.12 standard. RRE. RAE Llanbedr. Scrap at Leeming 1982.

WD791 TRE. Ferranti. Scrapped (in Sandhurst yard by 1965).

WD792 29 Sqn (U). Scrap 6.5.58.

WD793 87 Sqn (S). 83 Grp Com Flt. 68 Sqn. Scrap 23.2.59.

WD794 96 Sqn (L-H/H). Scrap 30.1.59.

WD795 87 Sqn (E). 68 Sqn. Scrap 30.10.58.

WD796 87 Sqn (U). Scrap 30.10.58.

WD797 A & AEE. Scrap 5.6.58.

WD798 CFE. A & AEE. Scrap 5.6.58.

WD799 CFE. 228 OCU. Scrap 12.2.59.

WD800 256 Sqn (T-T). Scrap 31.3.58.

WM143 219 Sqn. 264 Sqn (X). 151 Sqn (P). 29 Sqn (V/Y). Scrap 6.5.58.

WM144 219 Sqn. 96 Sqn (L-A/A). Scrap 11.3.59.

WM145 219 Sqn. 151 Sqn (F). 29 Sqn (A). 5 Sqn (D/J). Scrap 30.10.63.

WM146 256 Sqn. w/o 29.7.53 near Bruggen, following a mid-air collision with an F-86.

WM147 219 Sqn. 256 Sqn (T-R). To RN as TT.20. A & AEE. 728 Sqn (HF-580/HF-862). Scrap 6.67.

WM148 151 Sqn (K). To RN as TT.20. Milltown Handling Sqn. To RAF. 3/4 CAACU (V). Scrapped.

WM149 96 Sqn. w/o 28.1.53, out of fuel near Zwolle, Holland.

WM150 96 Sqn (L-G/G). Scrap 6.11.58.

WM151 228 OCU (L). 125 Sqn (C). To RN as TT.20. 728 Sqn (HF-583). FRU Hurn. HS Dunsfold, A & AEE To Kemble dump 10.70.

WM152 228 OCU (G/A). Scrap 30.10.63.

WM153 219 Sqn. 527 Sqn. To France 4.9.54.

WM154 West Malling Stn Flt. 29 Sqn (V). 12 JSTU. 256 Sq, 11 Sqn. Scrap 16.10.61.

WM155 151 Sqn (H). 29 Sqn (T). Scrap 6.11.58.

WM156 219 Sqn. 87 Sqn (D). 68 Sqn (WL). 5 Sqn (E/L). Scrap 31.1.62.

WM157 141 Sqn (N). 29 Sqn (S). Scrap 12.2.59.

WM158 96 Sqn (L-T/T). Scrap 11.3.59.

WM159 264 Sqn. 141 Sqn. To RN as TT.20. Hurn FRU (040/840). Scrap 20.7.70.

WM160 141 Sqn (R/M). To RN as TT.20. 728 Sqn (HF-584). Scrap 11.66.

WM161 87 Sqn (Y). Scrap 21.5.58.

WM162 141 Sqn (X). Scrap 4.3.58.

WM163 219 Sqn. 68 Sqn (D/U). Rejected by RN as possible TT.20. Scrap 6.5.58.

WM164 141 Sqn (Y). To France 4.9.54.

WM165 141 Sqn (Z). 87 Sqn (G). Scrap 3.7.57.

WM166 228 OCU. w/o 17.7.53, undershot at Leeming

WM167 228 OCU. Conv to TT.20. F/R. RAE Llanbedr To Blackbushe museum. Re-conv to NF.11. To Hurn as G-LOSM

WM168 219 Sqn. 87 Sqn (R). Scrap 30.10.58.

WM169 87 Sqn (H). w/o 22.2.55, stalled while on approach to Wahn.

WM170 Ahlhorn Wing Leader. 96 Sqn. Scrap 23.2.59.

WM171 228 OCU. 125 Sqn (O). 228 OCU. Scrap 12.2.59

WM172 256 Sqn. 68 Sqn (F). Rejected bt RN as a possible TT.20. Scrap 6.5.58.

WM173 228 OCU. Scrap 15.1.58.

WM174 85 Sqn. 29 Sqn (L). Scrap 6.5.58.

WM175 85 Sqn. w/o 21.2.54, out of fuel nr Whitstable.

WM176 85 Sqn. 29 Sqn (Y). Scrap 6.5.58.

WM177 85 Sqn. w/o 19.8.53 near Oakington.

WM178 228 OCU. 29 Sqn. Scrap 21.5.58.

WM179 Wahn Wing Leader. w/o 21.10.54 while on approach to Wahn.

WM180 TRE. Scrap 16.6.58.

WM181 264 Sqn (M). 141 Sqn. To RN as TT.20. Stored. Scrap 11.66.

WM182 96 Sqn. 68 Sqn. 256 Sqn. 11 Sqn (A). Scrap 24.1.62.

WM183 256 Sqn. 87 Sqn. w/o 1.9.53.

WM184 527 Sqn. w/o 27.7.54, out of fuel and crashed Gardelegen, East Germany.

WM185 To ground instructional use as 7359M 18.6.56

WM186 264 Sqn (HMT). 151 Sqn (A). Scrap 6.11.58.

WM187 151 Sqn (G). 29 Sqn (B). Scrap 12.2.59.

WM188 264 Sqn. 141 Sqn. w/o 1.11.54 while on approach to Ahlhorn.

WM189 RAFFC. 256 Sqn. 11 Sqn. Scrap 16.10.61.

WM190 264 Sqn. 141 Sqn. 87 Sqn (H). Scrap 30.10.58

WM191 264 Sqn. 141 Sqn. 87 Sqn. Scrap 30.10.55.

WM192 To ground instructional use as 7360M 18.6.56.

WM221 527 Sqn. To Belgium 19.1.56 as EN-23.

WM222 256 Sqn. 68 Sqn. w/o 28.7.53, hit trees near Soulme, Belgium.

WL223 Odiham. 151 Sqn (U). To RN as TT.20. Returned to RAF. 3/4 CAACU (W). Scrap 21.2.75.

WL224 228 OCU (E). 29 Sqn (V). Conv to TT.20. 3/4 CAACU (X). 5 CAACU (X). Allocated 8177M 15.10.71 and preserved at North Weald.

WM225 141 Sqn. 68 Sqn (P). Scrap 19.2.59.

WM226 CFE. w/o 15.8.53 during take-off from West Raynham.

WM227 228 OCU (R/E). Scrap 30.10.63.

WM228 228 OCU (N). Scrap 5.6.58.

WM229 264 Sqn. 151 Sqn (M). Scrap 6.11.58.

WM230 228 OCU. To RN as TT.20. Returned to RAF. Seletar TT Flt. Kai Tak TT Flt. w/o 29.10.62.

WM231 256 Sqn. Scrap 11.3.59.

WM232 DH Props. Scrap 4.11.58.

WM233 68 Sqn. w/o 27.5.54, out of fuel near Wahn.

WM234 264 Sqn. 68 Sqn (Q). Conv to TT.20. F/R. A & AEE. F/R. Scrap 7.7.70. Parts to various museums.

WM235 68 Sqn. To France 19.10.54.

WM236 151 Sqn (V). 29 Sqn (N). Scrap 12.2.59.

METEOR NF.11 *continued*

WM237 228 OCU (S). 125 Sqn (R). Scrap 23.6.58.
WM238 256 Sqn (R). 11 Sqn. To MoA 24.7.60.
WM239 256 Sqn. 96 Sqn (L-U/L-Z). Scrap 21.5.58.
WM240 87 Sqn. w/o 27.5.54 on take-off at Wahn.
WM241 228 OCU. 141 Sqn. 256 Sqn. 11 Sqn. Scrap 16.10.61.
WM242 264 Sqn (C). 85 Sqn. 264 Sqn. 141 Sqn. To RN as TT.20. 700 Sqn (511). Yeovilton Stn Flt (VL-942). FRU Hurn (042/842). To France 28.11.74 as F-ZABD.
WM243 151 Sqn. To France 6.7.54.
WM244 96 Sqn (L-D/E). Scrap 13.4.59.
WM245 87 Sqn. 151 Sqn (Q). 5 Sqn (M). Conv to TT.20. Changi TT Flt. 1574 Flt. Scrap 24.10.68.
WM246 151 Sqn (B/C). 256 Sqn. 11 Sqn. Wildenrath Stn Flt. 2 TAF Com Sqn. Conv to TT.20. Changi TT Flt. 1574 Flt. Scrap 12.6.67.
WM247 141 Sqn (L). Scrap 7.8.58.
WM248 87 Sqn. w/o 18.3.54, Kampen, West Germany.
WM249 228 OCU. 125 Sqn (T). 228 OCU. Scrap 23.2.59.
WM250 228 OCU. Scrap 31.1.62.
WM251 151 Sqn. w/o 8.2.54 on take-off at Leuchars.
WM252 Westland. To MoS as Short SC.1 chase aircraft.
WM253 Wahn Wing Leader. 256 Sqn. 11 Sqn (C). Scrap 26.7.60.
WM254 228 OCU. 264 Sqn. 141 Sqn. 256 Sqn. 11 Sqn (A). Scrapped.
WM255 141 Sqn. To RN as TT.20. 728 Sqn (HF-581). FRU Hurn (845). To France 28.11.74 as F-ZABD.
WM256 228 OCU. Scrap 23.2.59.
WM257 29 Sqn (G). 228 OCU (G). Scrap 30.10.63.
WM258 264 Sqn. w/o 13.6.53, Easton.
WM259 87 Sqn (V). Scrap 31.10.57.
WM260 151 Sqn (E). 125 Sqn (H). 46 Sqn. To RN as TT.20. 728 Sqn (HF-863). FRU Hurn (026). Scrap 5.68.
WM261 AWA. EEC. Conv to NF.14 prototype.
WM262 AWA. To RAAF as A77-3 at Woomera. Scrap 22.2.56.
WM263 527 Sqn. To Belgium 22.2.56 as EN-24.
WM264 96 Sqn (L-V/V/F). Scrap 13.4.59.
WM265 228 OCU. To France 21.9.54.
WM266 29 Sqn (Q). Scrap 5.6.58.
WM267 151 Sqn (X). 256 Sqn. 11 Sqn. Scrap 30.10.63
WM268 264 Sqn. 141 Sqn. w/o 9.5.55, off Cromer.
WM269 228 OCU (P). 125 Sqn (S). 228 OCU (M). AWDS. Scrap 30.10.63.
WM270 151 Sqn (J). 5 Sqn. Conv to TT.20 3/4 CAACU (Y). Scrap 15.9.75.
WM292 527 Sqn. To RN as TT.20. FRU Hurn (041/841). FAA museum Yeovilton 4.6.69. Loaned to the Rhoose museum 1984.
WM293 228 OCU. 141 Sqn. 68 Sqn (B). 5 Sqn (B). Conv to TT.20. 3/4 CAACU (Z). To France 11.12.74 as F-ZABD.
WM294 CFE. 29 Sqn. 125 Sqn (P). 46 Sqn. Scrap 7.8.58
WM295 Vickers.
WM296 to WM307 all delivered direct to France.
WM368 to WM371 all delivered direct to France.
WM372 Fairey Aviation. A & AEE. To Woomera 29.11.54.
WM373 Fairey Aviation. RRE. To Woomera 13.4.55.
WM374 AWA. RRE. Scrap 22.8.58.
WM375 to WM383 all delivered direct to France.
WM384 to WM404 all delivered direct to Denmark as 501 to 520.

METEOR NF.12

WD687 see NF.11.
WS590 AWOCU/238 OCU. 64 Sqn (G). Scrap 5.2.59.
WS591 A & AEE. 72 Sqn (F). To 7603M 5.59.
WS592 228 OCU (A). AWOCU. 152 Sqn. Scrap 30.1.59
WS593 228 OCU (B). AWOCU. 29 Sqn. 85 Sqn (X). Scrap 24.3.59.
WS594 264 Sqn. 238 OCU (C). Scrap 5.2.59.
WS595 Never issued from 15 MU. Scrap 16.3.59.
WS596 AWOCU. 264 Sqn (D). Scrap 11.3.59.
WS597 CSE (Q). Scrap 30.1.59.
WS598 228 OCU. AWOCU. 64 Sqn (A). Scrap 11.3.59
WS599 228 OCU. AWOCU. 64 Sqn (B). Scrap 24.3.59.
WS600 85 Sqn. w/o 29.6.54, Berwick, Sussex.
WS601 85 Sqn (A). Scrap 31.3.59.
WS602 85 Sqn (B/Y). Scrap 24.4.59.
WS603 152 Sqn (A). To 7567M 7.58.
WS604 228 OCU. AWOCU. 264 Sqn (U). 33 Sqn (U). Scrap 30.1.59.
WS605 228 OCU. AWOCU. 64 Sqn (D/O). Scrap 12.1.59.
WS606 CFE. 152 Sqn (E). Scrap 30.1.59.
WS607 46 Sqn (A). 72 Sqn (A). Scrap 31.12.59.
WS608 85 Sqn (C/Z). Scrap 24.4.59.
WS609 46 Sqn (B). 72 Sqn (B). Scrap 31.12.59.
WS610 228 OCU. AWOCU (D). Scrap 11.3.59.
WS611 46 Sqn (N). 72 Sqn (N). w/o 11.7.58 during take-off from Church Fenton.
WS612 25 Sqn (E/H). 153 Sqn (H). 25 Sqn. Scrap 16.4.59.
WS613 25 Sqn (J/A). 153 Sqn (J). 25 Sqn. Scrap 6.8.58.
WS614 CFE (M). 64 Sqn (J). Scrap 24.3.59.
WS615 AWOCU (E/F). Scrap 11.3.59.
WS616 FWS (T). Scrap 5.2.59.
WS617 AWOCU. 64 Sqn (A). Scrap 24.3.59.
WS618 Never issued from 15 MU. Scrap 16.3.59.
WS619 AWOCU. w/o 11.1.56, hit trees while on approach to North Luffenham.
WS620 FWS (P). 85 Sqn (D). Scrap 24.4.59.
WS621 228 OCU. AWOCU. w/o 21.9.55, mid-air collision with WS683 over Church Broughton.
WS622 25 Sqn (K/R). 153 Sqn (K). 25 Sqn. Scrap 16.4.59.
WS623 FWS. 72 Sqn (Q). Scrap 31.12.59.
WS624 FWS. 72 Sqn. Scrap 31.12.59.
WS625 228 OCU. AWOCU (F). 238 OCU (F). Scrap 31.3.59.
WS626 FWS. Scrap 5.2.59.
WS627 228 OCU. AWOCU (G). Scrap 12.1.59.
WS628 FWS. 72 Sqn. Scrap 31.12.59.
WS629 228 OCU. AWOCU (H). 29 Sqn. Scrap 30.1.59
WS630 AWOCU (I). Scrap 11.3.59.
WS631 Never issued from 15 MU. Scrap 16.3.59.
WS632 AWOCU (E). Scrap 12.1.59.
WS633 CFE. 152 Sqn (J). Scrap 11.3.59.
WS634 FWS (Q). Scrap 12.1.59.
WS635 AWA. CSE. CFE. DH.
WS636 228 OCU. AWOCU. 64 Sqn (F). Scrap 24.3.59.
WS637 25 Sqn (L). Scrap 31.1.59.
WS638 46 Sqn. 72 Sqn (O). w/o 25.11.57. mid-air collision with F-84F near Newmarket.
WS639 228 OCU. AWOCU. 64 Sqn (C). Scrap 24.3.59.
WS658 Never issued from 15 MU. Scrap 16.3.59.
WS659 Never issued from 15 MU. Scrap 16.3.59.
WS660 FWS. 85 Sqn (Q). Scrap 24.4.59.
WS661 228 OCU. AWOCU. w/o 20.1.56, hit house near Wadhurst.
WS662 153 Sqn. w/o 30.6.55 during take-off from West Malling.
WS663 Never issued from 38 MU. Scrap 11.3.59.
WS664 Never issued from 15 MU. Scrap 16.3.59.
WS665 153 Sqn (L). 25 Sqn (L). Scrap 16.4.59.
WS666 AWOCU (J). To 7568M 8.58.
WS667 228 OCU. AWOCU. To 7635M, Catterick 6.60.
WS668 228 OCU. AWOCU. 64 Sqn (E). Scrap 24.3.59.
WS669 Never issued from 15 MU. Scrap 16.3.59.
WS670 46 Sqn (P). w/o 25.1.66 following a heavy landing at Odiham.
WS671 Never issued from 33 MU. Scrap 16.3.59.
WS672 AWOCU (K). Scrap 5.2.59.
WS673 228 OCU. AWOCU (L). Scrap 11.3.59.
WS674 152 Sqn (V). Scrap 30.1.59.
WS675 264 Sqn (S). Scrap 16.3.59.
WS676 46 Sqn (F). 72 Sqn (F). Scrap 12.1.59.
WS677 Never issued from MU. Scrap 16.3.59.
WS678 85 Sqn (E). Scrap 24.4.59.
WS679 228 OCU. AWOCU (M). 29 Sqn. 228 OCU. Scrap 31.5.59.
WS680 25 Sqn (T). Scrap 31.3.59.
WS681 228 OCU. AWOCU. 64 Sqn (K). Scrap 24.3.59.
WS682 AWOCU. 64 Sqn (H). Scrap 24.3.59.
WS683 228 OCU. AWOCU. w/o 21.9.55, mid-air collision with WS621, Great Gubley.
WS684 AWOCU (N). Scrap 11.3.59.
WS685 153 Sqn (D). 25 Sqn (D). Scrap 16.4.59.
WS686 153 Sqn (E). 25 Sqn (E). Scrap 13.8.58.
WS687 228 OCU (O). To Henlow as 7566M 6.58. Scrapped.
WS688 153 Sqn (M). Scrap 24.6.58.
WS689 228 OCU. 46 Sqn. CFE. Scrap 31.3.59.
WS690 Handling Sqn. 152 Sqn (V). 264 Sqn. 85 Sqn (E). Scrap 31.3.59.
WS691 152 Sqn w/o 4.10.54, collided with F-86 on approach to Wattisham.
WS692 46 Sqn (C). 72 Sqn (C). To Henlow as 7605M 5.59 (incorrectly painted as 7065M). To Cranwell and then Newark Air Museum.
WS693 25 Sqn (S/M). 153 Sqn (M). 25 Sqn. soc 10.4.59 and sent to Booker dump.
WS694 25 Sqn (O). 153 Sqn. w/o 16.4.56 on take-off from West Malling.
WS695 25 Sqn (Q). 85 Sqn (U). Scrap 24.4.59.
WS696 25 Sqn (F). Scrap 31.3.59.
WS697 25 Sqn (N). 72 Sqn (T). Scrap 31.12.59.
WS698 CFE. Scrap 31.3.59.
WS699 25 Sqn (C/N). 153 Sqn (N). 25 Sqn. Scrap 17.9.58.
WS700 46 Sqn. 72 Sqn (D/P). w/o 4.3.58, mid-air with WS782, Kelfield.
WS715 Never issued from MU. Scrap 16.3.59.
WS716 25 Sqn (B/M). Scrap 31.3.59.
WS717 25 Sqn (F). 153 Sqn (F). 25 Sqn. Scrap 17.7.59.
WS718 85 Sqn (F). Scrap 31.3.59.
WS719 25 Sqn (D). Scrap 31.3.59.
WS720 153 Sqn (G). 25 Sqn (G). Scrap 17.7.59.
WS721 25 Sqn. 228 OCU. AWOCU (P). Scrap 11.3.59.

METEOR NF.13

WM308 39 Sqn. soc 22.7.58.
WM309 219 Sqn. To Israel 10.5.56 as 4X-FND.
WM310 39 Sqn. w/o 1.3.57, landing at Nicosia.
WM311 39 Sqn. Scrap 29.12.58.
WM312 219 Sqn. To Israel 10.5.56 as 4X-FNC.
WM313 39 Sqn (D). Scrap 29.12.56.
WM314 39 Sqn (E). w/o 6.12.56, on approach, Nicosia
WM315 39 Sqn (H/F). Scrap 29.12.58.
WM316 219 Sqn. Scrap 14.11.58.
WM317 39 Sqn (J). Scrap 20.2.59.
WM318 RAFFC. 39 Sqn. Scrap 20.2.59.
WM319 219 Sqn. Scrap 14.11.58.
WM320 219 Sqn. To Israel 25.4.56 as 4X-FNE.
WM321 219 Sqn. w/o 30.4.54 after mid-air fire.
WM322 39 Sqn (A/H). Scrap 29.12.58.
WM323 39 Sqn. 219 Sqn. 39 Sqn. Scrap 20.2.59.
WM324 219 Sqn. w/o 21.9.53 on take-off, Kabrit.
WM325 To Egypt 21.6.55 as 1427.
WM326 To Egypt 21.6.55 as 1428.
WM327 Kabrit Wing Leader. 29 Sqn (E/S). 39 Sqn (S). Scrap 29.12.58.
WM328 To Egypt 22.6.55 as 1429.
WM329 39 Sqn (C).
WM330 To Syria 11.5.54 as 473.
WM331 219 Sqn. Scrap 22.7.58.
WM332 To Syria 6.5.54 as 471.
WM333 To Syria 26.5.54 as 476.
WM334 To Israel 24.4.56 as 4X-FNB.
WM335 219 Sqn. To Israel 25.4.56 as 4X-FNF.
WM336 To Syria 10.5.54 as 472.
WM337 To Syria 21.5.54 as 474.
WM338 To Egypt 12.8.55 as 1430.
WM339 39 Sqn. 219 Sqn. 39 Sqn. Scrap 18.7.58.
WM340 To Egypt 15.8.55 as 1431.
WM341 To Syria 25.5.54 as 475.
WM362 To Egypt 12.8.55 as 1432.
WM363 CSE. A & AEE. 39 Sqn (H). Scrap 20.2.59.
WM364 To France 28.3.56 as NF-F364.
WM365 To France 9.4.56 as NF-F365.
WM366 RRE. A & AEE. To Israel 20.4.56 as 4X-FNA. To Lasham museum 1982.
WM367 AWA. A & AEE. Non-airworthy by 1970. Sold to Visionair 1981, but possibly retained at Boscombe Down.

The 'export' dates quoted for the Syrian, Egyptian and Israeli NF.13s are now thought to be those when the aircraft were transferred from RAF stocks to AWA, ie prior to overhaul and res-spray etc. The departure dates (ex-Bitteswell) are in the Overseas Operators appendix.

METEOR NF.14

WM261 Conv from NF.11. To Ferranti as G-ARCX. East Fortune museum.
WS722 AWA. CFE. 228 OCU. Scrap 31.1.62.
WS723 85 Sqn. 153 Sqn (T). 25 Sqn (T). 228 OCU (K). Scrap 9.4.62.
WS724 RAFFC. A & AEE. 46 Sqn (P). 72 Sqn (P). Scrap 18.4.62.
WS725 25 Sqn (G). Scrap 18.4.62.
WS726 25 Sqn (H). Conv to NF(T).14. 2 ANS (G). 1 ANS (G). To Royton ATC as 7960M 6.67.
WS727 85 Sqn. 153 Sqn. w/o 9.1.56, Hunton Hill.
WS728 25 Sqn (P). 72 Sqn. Scrap 25.9.61.
WS729 85 Sqn. 153 Sqn (A). 25 Sqn (A). Scrap 30.1.61.
WS730 85 Sqn (G/P). Scrap 25.9.61.
WS731 TRE. 228 OCU. 238 OCU (Q). 64 Sqn (N). Scrap 6.12.63.
WS732 25 Sqn (L). w/o 30.12.55, on take-off from West Malling.
WS733 25 Sqn (S). 64 Sqn (Z). Scrap 6.12.63.
WS734 85 Sqn (H). Scrap 25.9.61.
WS735 152 Sqn (X). Scrap 6.12.63.
WS736 85 Sqn. 153 Sqn (P). 25 Sqn (P). 228 OCU (C/M). Scrap 30.11.61.
WS737 85 Sqn (J). Conv to NF(T). 14. 2 ANS (H). 1 ANS (H). soc 17.5.66, to Manston fire school.
WS738 85 Sqn. 153 Sqn (B). 25 Sqn (B). Scrap 30.11.61.
WS739 25 Sqn (X). Conv to NF(T).14. 2 ANS (F). 1 ANS (F). To Church Fenton 10.67 as 7961M. To L. Jackson at Misson. Nostell Aviation Museum.
WS740 85 Sqn (K). Scrap 18.4.62.
WS741 85 Sqn (L). Scrap 30.11.61.
WS742 64 Sqn (Z). Scrap 6.12.63.
WS743 85 Sqn (M). Scrap 18.4.62.
WS744 85 Sqn. Conv to NF(T).14. 2 ANS (A). 1 ANS (A). To Leeming as 7962M.
WS745 CFE (EC-J). Scrap 6.12.63.
WS746 85 Sqn. w/o 26.4.54, out of fuel nr Eastbourne.
WS747 264 Sqn. To France 28.8.55 as 747. CEV.
WS748 25 Sqn (V). 85 Sqn (W). Scrap 25.9.61.
WS749 142 Sqn (N). Scrap 30.11.61.
WS750 25 Sqn (W). Scrap 30.11.61.
WS751 CFE (K). To Finningley 5.3.68 as 7963M. Scrapped.
WS752 85 Sqn. 153 Sqn (Q). 25 Sqn (Q). 228 OCU (L). Scrap 31.1.62.
WS753 25 Sqn (J). w/o 4.2.57, near Oxford.
WS754 152 Sqn (D). 60 Sqn.
WS755 152 Sqn (B). 60 Sqn (C). Scrap 7.8.61.
WS756 264 Sqn (G). 33 Sqn (G). 60 Sqn (D). Scrap 27.7.61.
WS757 153 Sqn (C). 25 Sqn (C). 228 OCU (L). Scrap 31.1.62.
WS758 152 Sqn (W). Scrap 6.12.63.
WS759 264 Sqn (Y). 33 Sqn (Y). 60 Sqn (B). Scrap 7.8.61.
WS760 AWOCU. 64 Sqn (U). Conv to NF(T).14. 1 ANS (P). To Upwood 6.67 as 7964M. To Brampton gate and then Duxford 8.8.76. Bushey 1983.
WS774 AWOCU (S). Conv to NF(T).14 2 ANS (D). 1 ANS (D). To Upwood 6.67 as 7959M, then Ely gate. Repainted in 264 Sqn markings.
WS775 85 Sqn (N). 33 Sqn. 228 OCU (V). 13 Grp Com Flt (V). RAE Llanbedr (V). Scrapped.
WS776 25 Sqn (K). 85 Sqn (J). 72 Sqn. 228 OCU. To 7716M 5.61. North Luffenham gate.
WS777 85 Sqn (O). 12 Grp Com Flt. To Buchan 31.7.63 as 7813M. Dumped at Leuchars.
WS778 CFE (L). To Manston fire school 3.5.66.
WS779 CFE. 46 Sqn (T). 72 Sqn (T). 228 OCU. Scrap 9.4.62.
WS780 85 Sqn (P). 72 Sqn. Scrap 25.9.61.
WS781 West Malling Stn Flt. 25 Sqn (J). 85 Sqn (L). 13 Grp Com Flt. Scrap 14.7.60.
WS782 85 Sqn (Q). w/o 4.3.58, mid-air collision with WS700, Cawood. Dumped at Rufforth.
WS783 152 Sqn (T). Scrap 6.12.63.
WS784 CFE. w/o 24.1.56, out of fuel nr Gayton.
WS785 152 Sqn (C). 60 Sqn (L). Scrap 12.10.61.
WS786 152 Sqn (F). Scrap 6.12.63.
WS787 152 Sqn (G). 60 Sqn (G). Last operational Meteor flt 17.8.61. soc 1.9.61, to Tengah gate. To scrap
WS788 152 Sqn (Z). Conv to NF(T).14. 2 ANS (C). 1 ANS (C). To Patrington 6.67 as 7967M. To Leeming gate and later painted WS844.
WS789 152 Sqn (R). Scrap 6.12.63.
WS790 46 Sqn (D). 264 Sqn (H). 33 Sqn (H). 60 Sqn (E). Scrap 12.3.62.

WS791 46 Sqn (O). 264 Sqn (B). 33 Sqn (B). 25 Sqn (J). 60 Sqn (H). Scrap 12.3.62.
WS792 Conv to NF(T).14 2 ANS (K). 1 ANS (K). To Cosford 6.67 as 7965M. To Carlisle gate;
WS793 72 Sqn (H). ETPS (5). Scrapped.
WS794 264 Sqn (E/S). 33 Sqn (E). 60 Sqn (K). Scrap 12.10.61.
WS795 264 Sqn (Z). 33 Sqn (Z). Scrap 30.11.61.
WS796 To France 20.10.55 as 796.
WS797 527 Sqn. 64 Sqn (V). 228 OCU. Conv to NF(T).14 1 ANS (O). To Binbrook 6.67 as 7966M.
WS798 264 Sqn (A/C). 33 Sqn (A). 228 OCU (R). Scrap 9.4.62.
WS799 152 Sqn (H). 60 Sqn. Scrap 23.12.60.
WS800 152 Sqn (Y). 60 Sqn (A). Scrap 7.8.61.
WS801 AWOCU (T). 64 Sqn (M). Scrap 6.12.63.
WS802 46 Sqn (E). 72 Sqn (E). Conv to NF(T).14. 2 ANS (K). 1 ANS (L). To Machrihanish 6.67 as 7968M.
WS803 527 Sqn. 64 Sqn (P). Scrap 12.63.
WS804 228 OCU (W). RAE Bedford ('Epner'). To Target Towing Aircraft Co 28.8.69 as G-AXNE. Last heard of in Senegal 23.9.69.
WS805 152 Sqn (P). 60 Sqn (M). Scrap 7.8.61.
WS806 264 Sqn (D). 33 Sqn (D). 228 OCU (O). Scrap 31.1.62.
WS807 46 Sqn (N). Conv to NF(T).14. 2 ANS (J). 1 ANS (J). To Watton 6.67 as 7973M. Painted as N of 46 Sqn.
WS808 46 Sqn (U). 72 Sqn (U). 2 TAF Com Sqn. Scrap 28.6.61.
WS809 264 Sqn (E). 64 Sqn (T). Scrap 6.12.62.
WS810 264 Sqn (B/V). 33 Sqn (V). 60 Sqn (F). To Tengah fire dump. Scrap 8.9.61.
WS811 AWOCU (U). 64 Sqn (O). Scrap 6.12.63.
WS812 264 Sqn (F). 152 Sqn (O). Scrap 6.12.63.
WS827 264 Sqn (F). 33 Sqn (F). Scrap 12.3.62.
WS828 264 Sqn (C/O). 33 Sqn (C). 60 Sqn (J). Scrap 7.8.61.
WS829 AWOCU. 228 OCU. To Rolls-Royce as G-ASLW 16.9.63. To Target Towing Aircraft 1969. Last heard of in Africa 9.69.
WS830 46 Sqn (H). 72 Sqn (H). 64 Sqn (X). w/o 20.11.57 Wicken Fen.
WS831 264 Sqn (X). Hit building at Linton after brake failure 17.5.56. Became 7353M.
WS832 AWOCU (W). RAE Llanbedr (W). RRE. To Solway Aviation Group, Carlisle, 15.1.77.
WS833 46 Sqn (G). 72 Sqn (MS/G). Scrap 18.4.62.
WS834 264 Sqn (W). 33 Sqn (W). 228 OCU (J). Scrap 18.4.62.
WS835 46 Sqn. w/o 25.1.55, out of fuel near Kingsley Green.
WS836 264 Sqn (P). 33 Sqn (P). 228 OCU (F/T). Scrap 25.9.61.
WS837 46 Sqn (S). 72 Sqn (S). 228 OCU (N). Scrap 18.4.62.
WS838 AWOCU (X). 64 Sqn (P). RRE. To Colerne museum, later Shawbury, Cosford and Manchester. Returned to Cosford 1983.
WS839 AWOCU (Y). Scrap 6.12.63.
WS840 264 Sqn (H). 64 Sqn (S). 2 TAF Com Flt. Conv to NF(T).14. 1 ANS (N). To Bishopscourt 6.67 as 7969M. To Aldergrove dump.
WS841 264 Sqn (HMT/JCF). 33 Sqn. Scrap 12.3.62.
WS842 AWOCU (Z). Conv to NF(T).14. 2 ANS (B). 1 ANS (B). soc 22.11.67 to Ouston dump.
WS843 228 OCU. Conv to NF(T).14. 1 ANS (M). To Henlow 3.67 as 7937M. To St Athan museum, painted as Y of 64 Sqn.
WS844 A & AEE. 264 Sqn (HMT). 33 Sqn. (NP). 228 OCU (P). Scrap 31.1.62.
WS845 Rolls-Royce Hucknall. 64 Sqn (W). 72 Sqn. ETPS (6). To Stansted fire school 1963.
WS846 46 Sqn (R). 72 Sqn (R). Scrap 31.1.62.
WS847 AWOCU (HMT). Scrap 31.1.62.
WS848 AWA. CFE (F). FCCS. Scrap 6.12.63.

SUMMARY OF PRODUCTION FOR OVERSEAS CUSTOMERS

Model	Quantity/Source	Customer
F.4	50 (GAC)	Argentina
	48 (GAC)	Belgium
	20 (GAC)	Denmark
	12 (GAC)	Egypt
	38 (GAC)	Netherlands
T.7	3 (GAC)	Belgium
	9 (GAC)	Denmark
	3 (GAC)	Egypt
	42 (GAC)	Netherlands
	2 (GAC)	Syria (diverted to France)
	2 (F/AF)	Israel
	4 (GAC)	Israel
	8 (GAC)	Brazil
F.8	217 (F/AF)	Belgium
	55 (GAC)	Brazil
	20 (GAC)	Denmark
	11 (GAC)	Israel
	155 (F/AF)	Netherlands

Total number of Meteors built, 3,922.

Note: GAC = Gloster Aircraft Company
AWA = Armstrong Whitworth Aircraft
F/AF = Fokker/Avions Fairey

Many additional ex-RAF Meteors ultimately found their way overseas, and are detailed in the production listing.

Abbreviations

A & AEE Aeroplane & Armament Experimental Establishment
ACFE Air Command Far East
AFDS Air Fighting Development Squadron
AFDU Air Fighting Development Unit
AFS Advanced Flying School
AHB Air Historical Branch
AHQ Air Headquarters
AHU Aircraft Holding Unit
AIEU Armament and Instrument Experimental Unit
ANS Air Navigation School
APC Armament Practice Camp
APS Armament Practice Station
ATC Air Training Corps
ATF Armament Training Flight
AWA Armstrong-Whitworth Aircraft
AWDS All Weather Development Squadron
AWFCS All Weather Fighter Combat School
AWOCU All Weather Operation Conversion Unit
BAFO British Air Forces of Occupation
BCCF Bomber Command Communications Flight
BCCS Bomber Command Communications Squadron
BFAP British Forces Aden Protectorate
BLEU Blind Landing Experimental Unit
B & TT Flt Banner and Target Towing Flight
Cat 5(C) Category 5 (components), ie an airframe used for spares
Cat 5(S) Category 5 (scrap)
CAACU Civilian Anti-Aircraft Co-operation Unit
CAW College of Air Warfare
CBE Central Bomber Establishment
CD Civil Defence
CFE Central Fighter Establishment
CFS Central Flying School
CGS Central Gunnery School
CNS Central Navigation School
COMFER Commander Far East Reserve
CRD Controller of Research and Development
CS(A) Controller of Supplies (Aircraft)
CSDE Centralised Servicing Development Establishment
CSE Central Signals Establishment
CU Conversion Unit
D Drone (unmanned aircraft)
DFLS Day Fighter Leaders School
EAAS Empire Air Armament School
EANS Empire Air Navigation School
ECFS Empire Central Flying School
EFS Empire Flying School
ETPS Empire Test Pilots School
F Fighter
FBS Fighter-Bomber Squadron
FCCS Fighter Command Communications Squadron
FCIRS Fighter Command Instrument Rating Squadron
FE Far East
FEAF Far East Air Force
FECS Far East Communications Squadron
FETS Far East Training Squadron
F/F First Flight
Flt Ref Flight Refuelling Ltd
FR Fighter Reconnaissance
F/R Flight Refuelling Ltd
FRS Flying Refresher School
FRU Fleet Requirements Unit
FSS Ferry Support Squadron
FTS Flying Training Squadron
F(TT) Fighter (Target Tug)
FTU Ferry Training Unit
FWS Fighter Weapons School
GAC Gloster Aircraft Company
GWDS Guided Weapons Development Squadron
GCF Group Communications Flight
HSF Horsham St Faith
IAM Institute of Aviation Medicine
ITF Instrument Training Flight
ITS Instrument Training Squadron
JCU Jet Conversion Unit
JSTU Joint Services Trials Unit
JTF Jet Training Flight
MC & TTS Malta Communications and Target Towing Squadron
MEAF Middle East Air Force
MIA Missing in Action
MOA Ministry of Aviation
MOS Ministry of Supply
MU Maintenance Unit
NEA Non Effective Airframe
NEVVS North East Veteran and Vintage (Aircraft) Society
NF Night Fighter
NGTE National Gas Turbine Establishment
OCU Operational Conversion Unit
OFU Overseas Ferry Unit
OTU Operational Training Unit
PC & S Sqn Protectorate Communications and Standards Squadron
PEE Proof and Experimental Establishement
PR Photo Reconnaissance
PRDU Photo Reconnaissance Development Unit
(P)RFU (Pilot) Reserve Flying Unit
RAAF Royal Australian Air Force
RAE Royal Aircraft Establishment
RAFC Royal Air Force College
RAFFC Royal Air Force Flying College
RAFM Royal Air Force Museum
RATOG Rocket Assisted Take-Off Gear
RN Royal Navy
RNAY Royal Naval Air Yard
RRE Royal Radar Establishment
SAF Singapore Air Force
SHQ Station Headquarters
SOC Struck Off Charge
SRF School of Refresher Flying
Stn Flt Station Flight
STT School of Technical Training
SWWAPS Second World War Aircraft Preservation Society
TAF Tactical Air Force
TFU Telecommunications Flying Unit
THUM Flt Temperature and Humidity Measuring Flight
T/O Take-off
TRE Telecommunications Research Establishment
TT Target Tug
TTF Target Towing Flight
TWU Tactical Weapons Unit
WEE Weapons Experimental Establishment
WFU Withdrawn from use
W/O Written off
WRE Weapons Research Establishment

Select Technical Data

	F.9/40	Meteor F.4	Meteor T.7	Meteor F.8	Meteor NF.14
Powerplant	W.2B/23	Derwent 5	Derwent 8	Derwent 8	Derwent 8
Static Thrust	1,600 lb	3,500 lb	3,500 lb	3,500 lb	3,700 lb
Wing Span	43ft 0in	37ft 2in	37ft 2in	37ft 2in	43ft 0in
Length	41ft 5in	41ft 0in	43ft 6in	44ft 7in	51ft 4in
Height	13ft 8in	13ft 0in	13ft 0in	13ft 0in	13ft 11in
Weight Empty	9,654 lb	11,217 lb	10,645 lb	10,684 lb	12,620 lb
Weight Loaded	11,775 lb	14,545 lb	14,230 lb	15,700 lb	21,200 lb
Maximum Speed	420 mph	580 mph	590 mph	598 mph	578 mph
Time to 30,000ft	17 minutes	6 minutes	5.6 minutes	6.5 minutes	13.2 minutes
Service Ceiling	37,000ft	44,500ft	45,000ft	43,000ft	40,000ft
Maximum Range	550 miles	980 miles	1,000 miles	1,200 miles	950 miles
Maximum fuel	300 gallons	505 gallons	700 gallons	795 gallons	750 gallons

Meteor Bibliography

Aerobatic Teams 1950-1971, Volumes 1 and 2; Richard Ward, Aircam srs, Osprey Publishing

Aircraft Camouflage and Markings 1907-1954; Bruce Robertson, Harleyford: 1965/1967.

Aircraft in Profile No. 12: Gloster Meteor F.8; C.F. Andrews, Profile Publications Ltd: 1971.

Aircraft in Profile No. 78: Gloster Meteor F.4; J.J.Partridge, Profile Publications Ltd: 1966.

Aircraft Markings of the World, 1912-1967; by Bruce Robertson, Harleyford: 1967.

Aircraft of the RAF: A Pictorial Record 1918-1978; J.W.R.Taylor, Mac. & Janes: 1978.

Aircraft of the Royal Air Force since 1918 (7th edition); Owen G. Thetford, Putnam: 1979.

Airfields of Lincolnshire since 1912, The; Ron Blake, Mike Hodgson and Bill Taylor, Midland Counties Publications: 1984.

Aviation Photo Album, Vols 1 & 2; Michael J.F. Bowyer, Patrick Stephens Ltd: 1978, 1980.

Belgian Military Aviation 1945-1977; Paul Jackson, Midland Counties Publications, 1977.

British Aircraft of World War II; David Monday, Hamlyn: 1982.

British Civil Aircraft since 1919, volume 2; by A.J. Jackson, Putnam: 1973.

British Fighter since 1912, The; Peter Lewis, Putnam, 1979.

British Fighters of World War II; Bill Gunston, Hamlyn/Aerospace, 1982.

British Military Aircraft Serials, 1911-1979; by Bruce Robertson, Patrick Stephens Ltd: 1979.

British Museum Aircraft; Ken Ellis and Phil H. Butler, Merseyside Aviation Society, 1977.

British Naval Aircraft since 1912 (5th edition); Owen G. Thetford, Putnam, 1982.

Camera Above the Clouds; Anthony Harold and Charles E. Brown, Airlife, 1983.

Camouflage and Markings, RAF Fighter Command 1936-45; James Goulding and Robert Jones. Ducimus Books, 1971.

Coastal, Support and Special Squadrons of the RAF, John D.R. Rawlings, Janes, 1982.

Dutch Military Aviation 1945-1978; Paul Jackson, Midland Counties Publications, 1978.

Encyclopedia of British Military Aircraft; Chaz Bowyer, Arms & Armour Press, 1982.

Famous Fighter Squadrons of the RAF, Vol 1; James J. Halley, Hylton Lacy, 1971.

Fighters of the Fifties; Bill Gunston, Patrick Stephens Limited: 1981.

Fighter Squadrons of the RAF and their Aircraft; J.D.R. Rawlings, MacDonald & Janes, 1969.

Fighting Colours, RAF Fighter Camouflage and Markings 1937-75; Michael J.F. Bowyer, Patrick Stephens Limited, 1975.

Flying Colours; William Green and Gordon Swanborough, Salamander 1981.

Flying Navy, The; Richard E. Gardner, Almark Publications, 1971.

French Military Aviation (2nd edn); Paul Jackson, Midland Counties Publications, 1979.

Gloster Aircraft since 1917; Derek N. James, Putnam, 1971.

Gloster Meteor, The; Edward Shacklady, MacDonald and Company, 1962.

History of 208 Squadron; D. S. B. Marr, Official Squadron Publication, 1966.

History of the RAF; C. Bowyer, Hamlyn, 1977.

Latin American Military Aviation; J.M.Andrade, Midland Counties Publications, 1982.

Pictorial History of the RAF, Volume 3; J.W.R. Taylor and P.J.R. Moyes, Ian Allan, 1970.

Pilots Notes: Meteor III; Air Data Publications.

RAF, a Pictorial History, The; Bruce Robertson, Robert Hale Limited: 1978.

Royal Air Force Unit Histories, Two volumes; James J. Halley. Air Britain, 1969 and 1973.

Squadron Codes 1937-56; Michael J.F. Bowyer & John D.R. Rawlings, Patrick Stephens, 1979

Squadron Histories, RFC, RNAS and RAF, since 1912; Peter Lewis, Putnam, 1968.

Squadrons of the Fleet Air Arm; Ray Sturtivant, Air Britain, 1984.

Squadrons of the Royal Air Force, J. J. Halley, Air Britain, 1980.

Treble One: the Story of 111 Squadron, RAF: Flying Officer R.P.D. Sands, 1957.

Twenty-One Squadrons: History of R.Aux.A.F. 1925-57; Leslie Hunt, Garnstone Press, 1972.

Veteran & Vintage Aircraft; Leslie Hunt. Garnstone Press, 1974.

Wrecks & Relics, 9th edition; Ken Ellis. Merseyside Aviation Society & M.C.P.: 1984.

Yesterday's RAF Fighters; Philip J.R. Moyes, Vintage Aviation Publications; 1976.

PERIODICALS

Aeroplane Monthly; July 1975, November 1975 July 1977, August 1979, October 1983.

Aeroplane Spotter; Temple Press, 1941-1948.

Air Classics Quarterly; Summer 1974.

Air Enthusiast, No.25; Finescroll Limited.

Air Extra, No.20; Ian Allan Limited 1978.

Aviation News, 11-24 September 1981 issue.

Illustrated Encyclopedia of Aircraft, 45; Orbis.

Modelaid Quarterly, issue No.1.

PAM News, Vol.5 issues 1 and 2.

Roundel; British Aviation Research Group, 1977.

Scale Aircraft Modelling; Alan Hall Publications March 79 and October 84 issues.

Wings Magazine; In the Cockpit srs pp 253-257, Vintage Aviation Publications